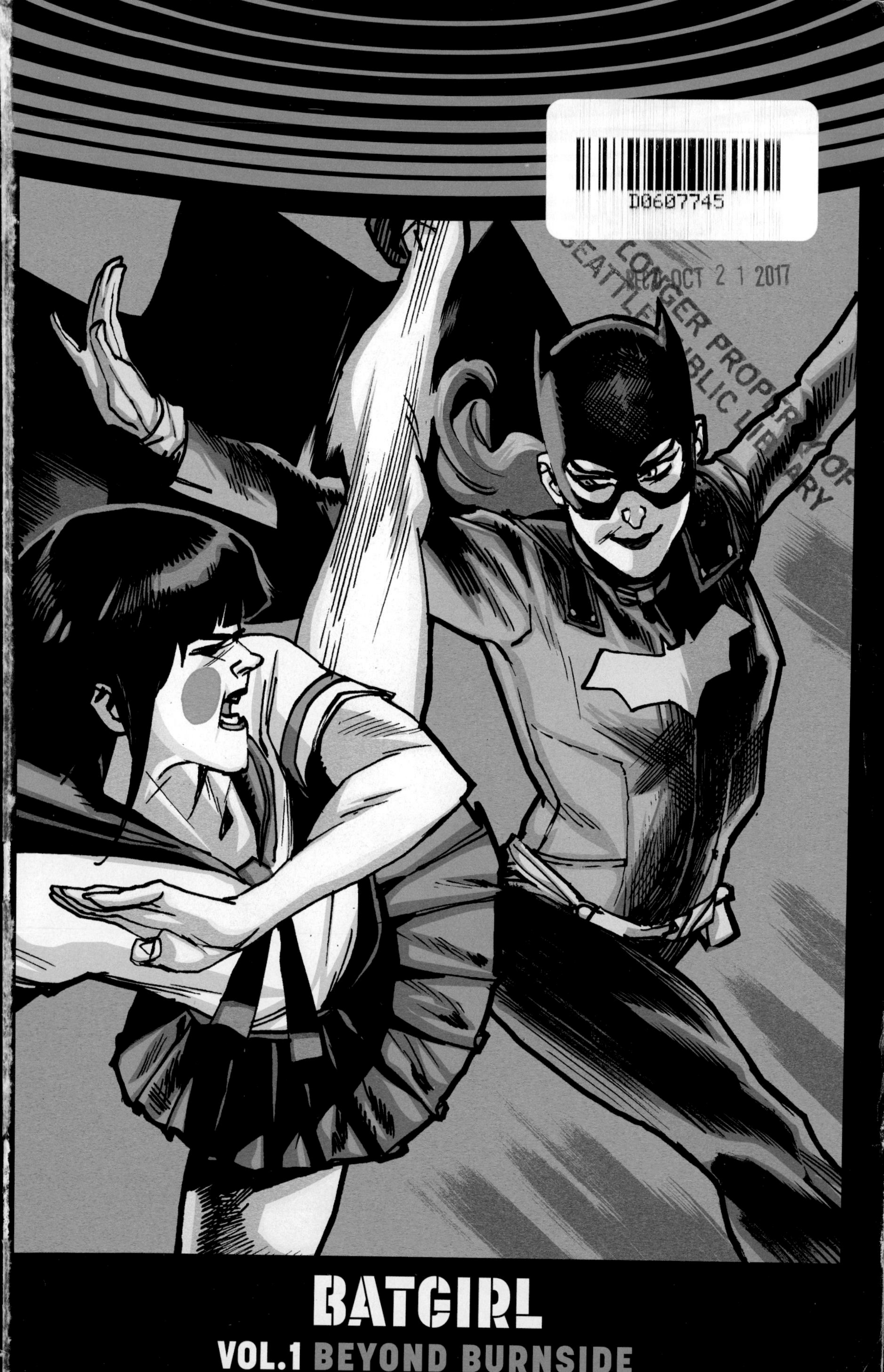



# BATGIRL

## VOL.1 BEYOND BURNSIDE

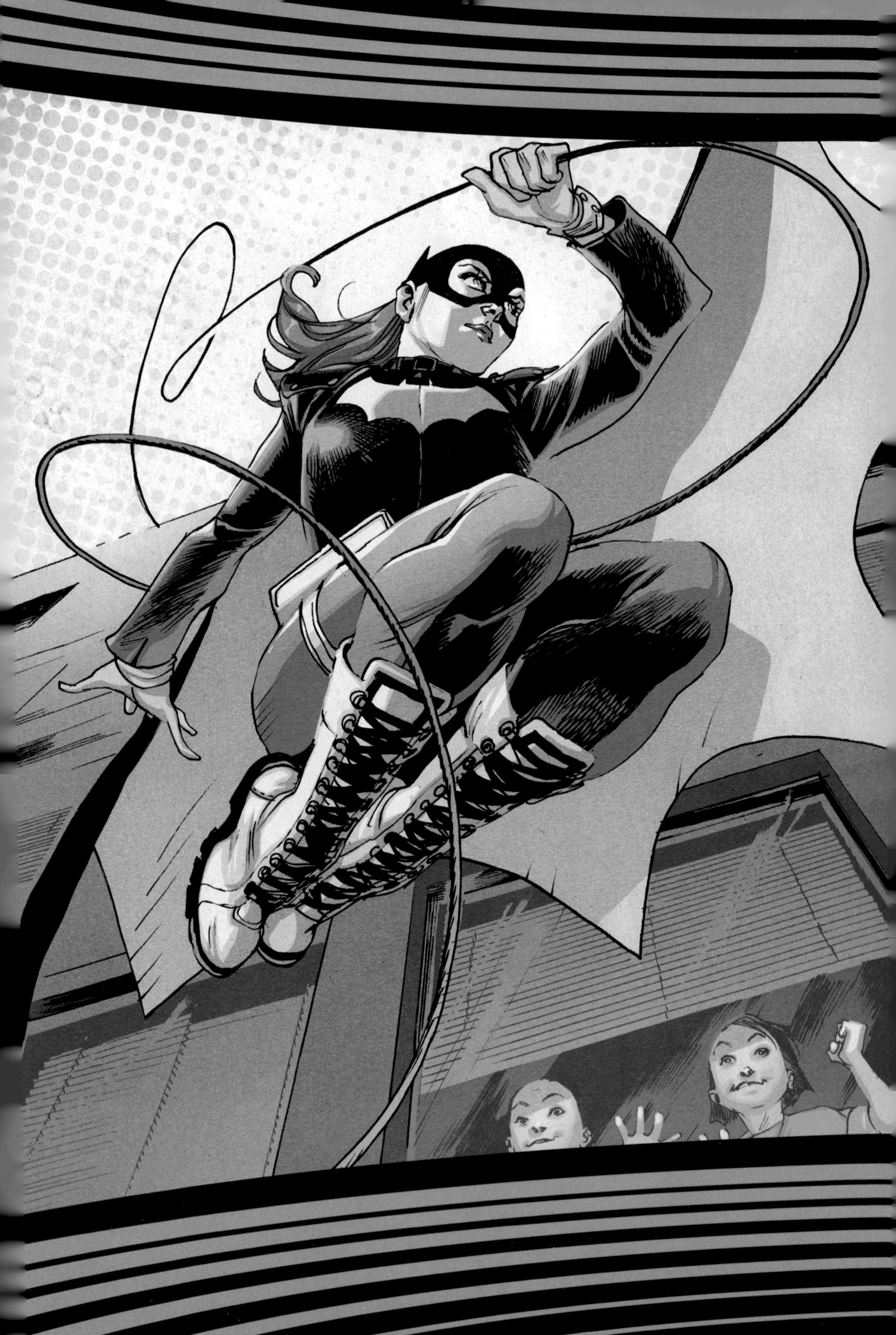

# BATGIRL

## VOL.1 BEYOND BURNSIDE

**HOPE LARSON**
writer

**RAFAEL ALBUQUERQUE**
artist

**DAVE McCAIG**
colorist

**DERON BENNETT**
letterer

**RAFAEL ALBUQUERQUE**
collection and original series cover artist

BATMAN created by **BOB KANE** with **BILL FINGER**

**MARK DOYLE** Editor - Original Series ✷ **REBECCA TAYLOR** Associate Editor - Original Series ✷ **JEB WOODARD** Group Editor - Collected Editions
**ROBIN WILDMAN** Editor - Collected Edition ✷ **STEVE COOK** Design Director - Books ✷ **MONIQUE GRUSPE** Publication Design

**BOB HARRAS** Senior VP - Editor-in-Chief, DC Comics

**DIANE NELSON** President ✷ **DAN DiDIO** Publisher ✷ **JIM LEE** Publisher ✷ **GEOFF JOHNS** President & Chief Creative Officer
**AMIT DESAI** Executive VP - Business & Marketing Strategy, Direct to Consumer & Global Franchise Management ✷ **SAM ADES** Senior VP - Direct to Consumer
**BOBBIE CHASE** VP - Talent Development ✷ **MARK CHIARELLO** Senior VP - Art, Design & Collected Editions
**JOHN CUNNINGHAM** Senior VP - Sales & Trade Marketing ✷ **ANNE DePIES** Senior VP - Business Strategy, Finance & Administration
**DON FALLETTI** VP - Manufacturing Operations ✷ **LAWRENCE GANEM** VP - Editorial Administration & Talent Relations
**ALISON GILL** Senior VP - Manufacturing & Operations ✷ **HANK KANALZ** Senior VP - Editorial Strategy & Administration
**JAY KOGAN** VP - Legal Affairs ✷ **THOMAS LOFTUS** VP - Business Affairs
**JACK MAHAN** VP - Business Affairs ✷ **NICK J. NAPOLITANO** VP - Manufacturing Administration
**EDDIE SCANNELL** VP - Consumer Marketing ✷ **COURTNEY SIMMONS** Senior VP - Publicity & Communications
**JIM (SKI) SOKOLOWSKI** VP - Comic Book Specialty Sales & Trade Marketing ✷ **NANCY SPEARS** VP - Mass, Book, Digital Sales & Trade Marketing

**BATGIRL VOLUME 1: BEYOND BURNSIDE**

Published by DC Comics. Compilation, cover and all new material Copyright © 2017 DC Comics. All Rights Reserved.
Originally published in single magazine form in BATGIRL 1-6. Copyright © 2016 DC Comics.
All Rights Reserved. All characters, their distinctive likenesses and related elements featured in this publication are trademarks of DC Comics.
The stories, characters and incidents featured in this publication are entirely fictional.
DC Comics does not read or accept unsolicited submissions of ideas, stories or artwork.

DC Comics, 2900 West Alameda Ave., Burbank, CA 91505. Printed by LSC Communications, Salem, VA, USA. 2/17/17.
First Printing. ISBN: 978-1-4012-6840-4
Barnes & Noble Exclusive Edition ISBN: 978-1-4012-7637-9

Library of Congress Cataloging-in-Publication Data is available.

**PEFC Certified**

Printed on paper from
sustainably managed
forests, controlled
sources

**PEFC**

PEFC/29-31-337

www.pefc.org

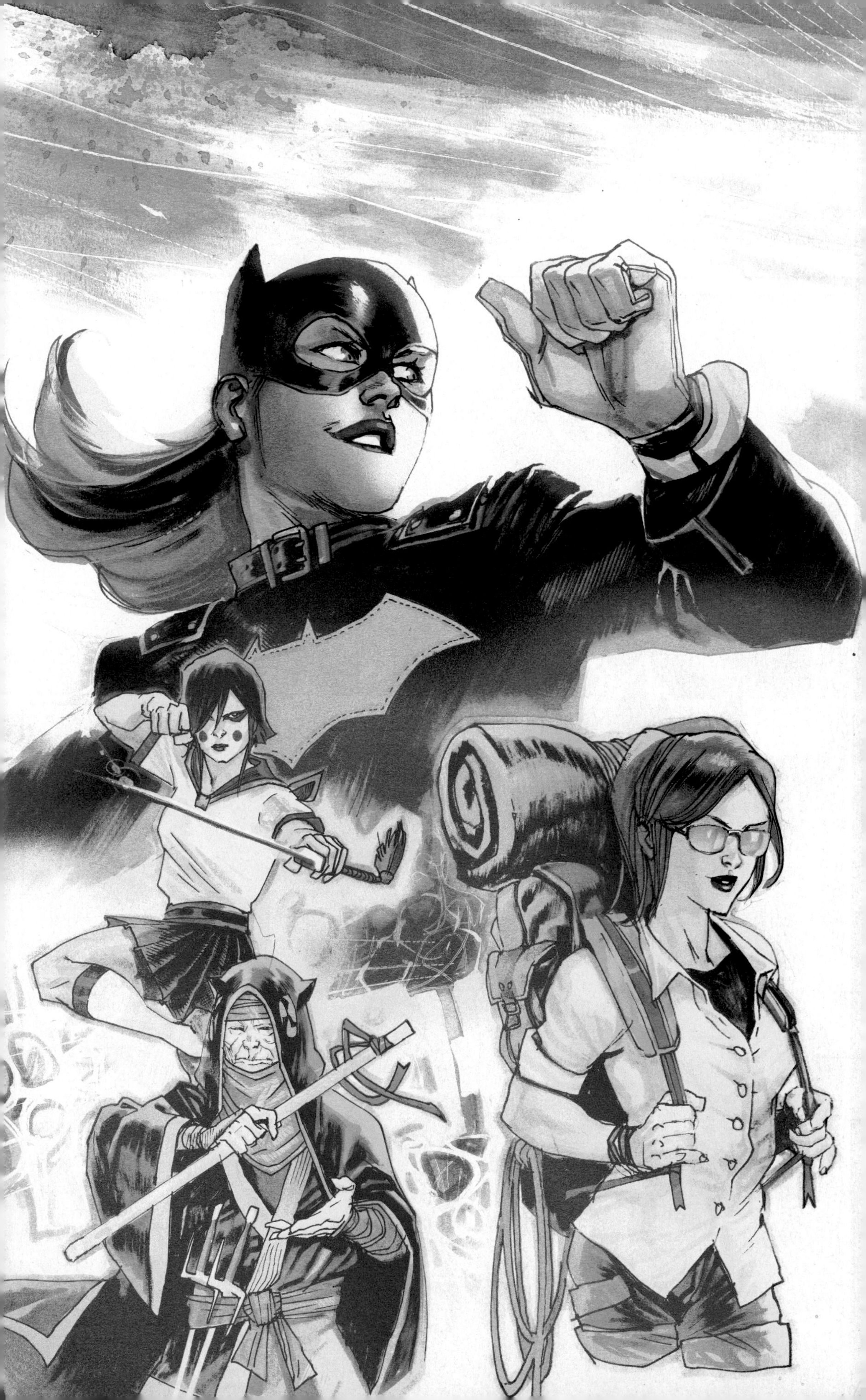

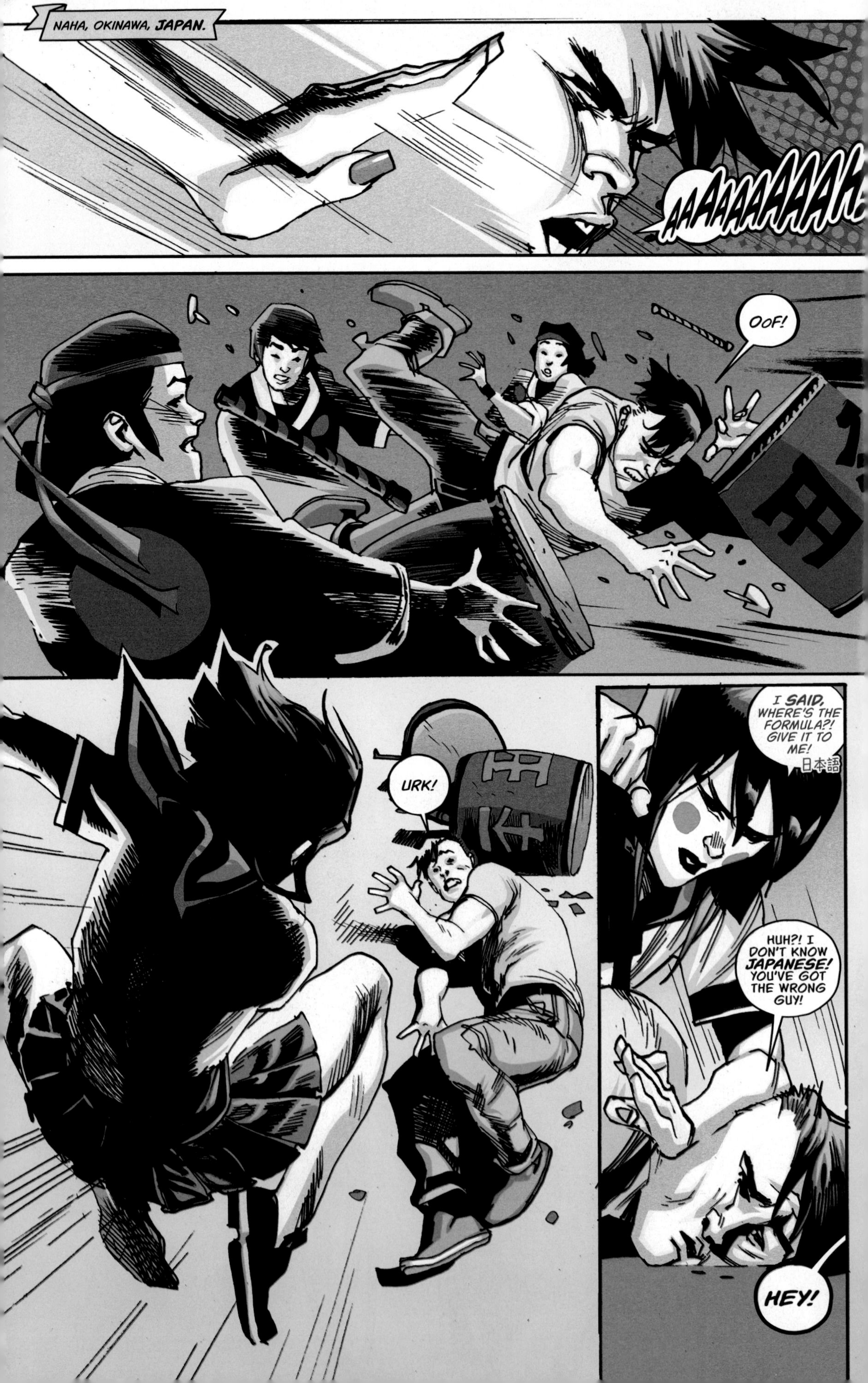
NAHA, OKINAWA, JAPAN.
AAAAAAAAAAH
OOF!
URK!
I SAID, WHERE'S THE FORMULA?! GIVE IT TO ME!
日本語
HUH?! I DON'T KNOW JAPANESE! YOU'VE GOT THE WRONG GUY!
HEY!

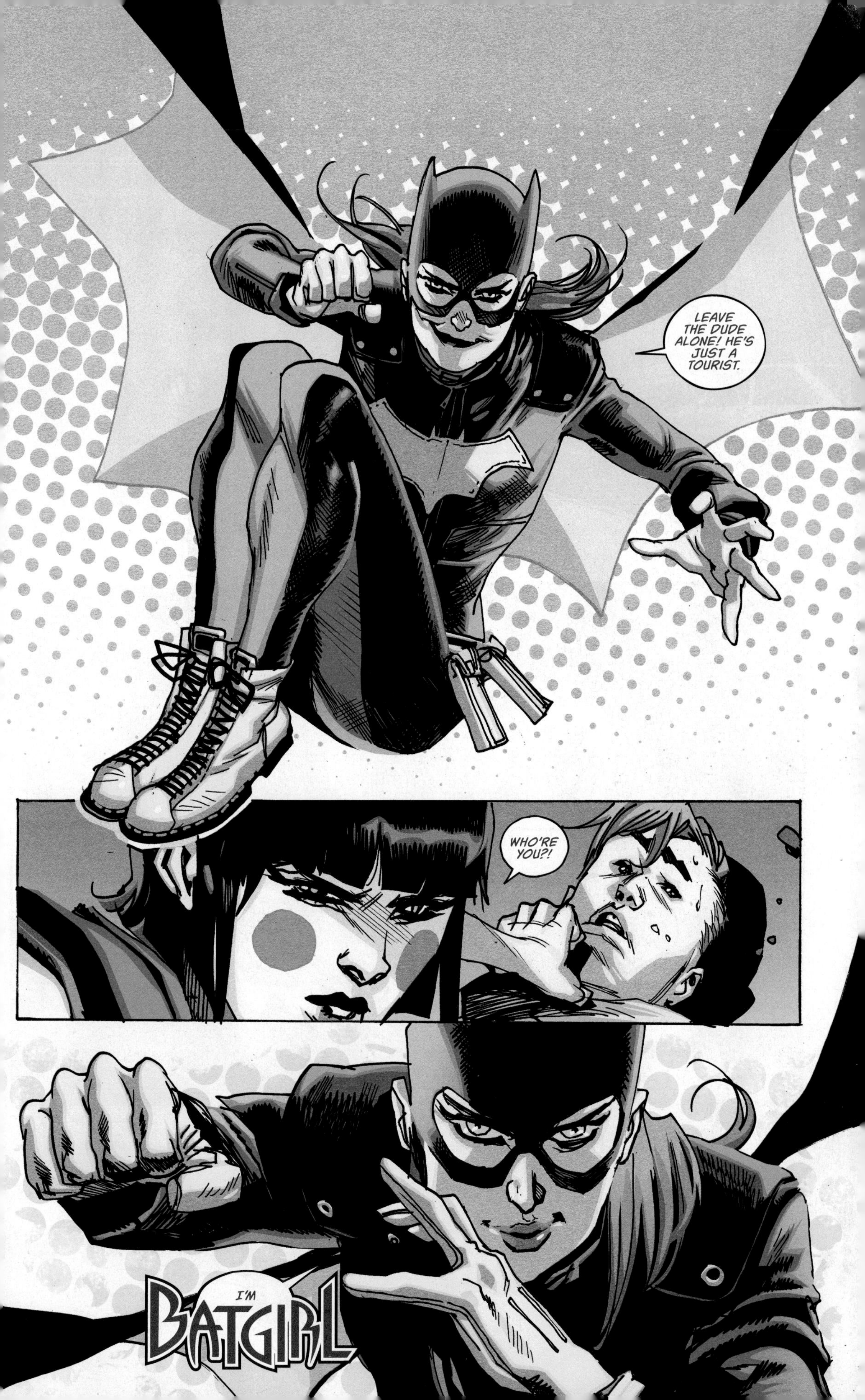
LEAVE THE DUDE ALONE! HE'S JUST A TOURIST.
WHO'RE YOU?!
I'M
BATGIRL

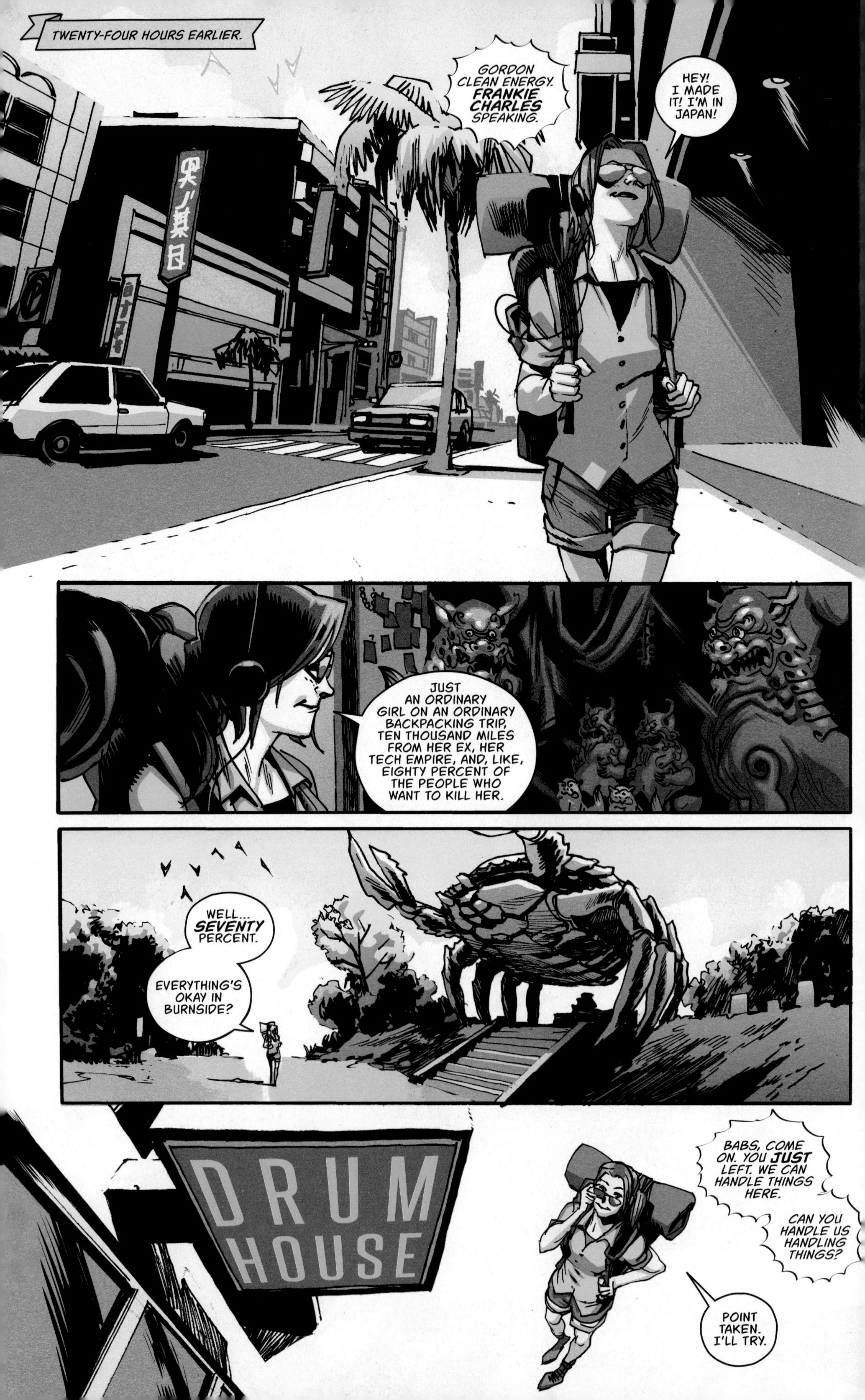
TWENTY-FOUR HOURS EARLIER.
GORDON CLEAN ENERGY. FRANKIE CHARLES SPEAKING.
HEY! I MADE IT! I'M IN JAPAN!
JUST AN ORDINARY GIRL ON AN ORDINARY BACKPACKING TRIP, TEN THOUSAND MILES FROM HER EX, HER TECH EMPIRE, AND, LIKE, EIGHTY PERCENT OF THE PEOPLE WHO WANT TO KILL HER.
WELL... SEVENTY PERCENT.
EVERYTHING'S OKAY IN BURNSIDE?
DRUM HOUSE
BABS, COME ON. YOU JUST LEFT. WE CAN HANDLE THINGS HERE.
CAN YOU HANDLE US HANDLING THINGS?
POINT TAKEN. I'LL TRY.

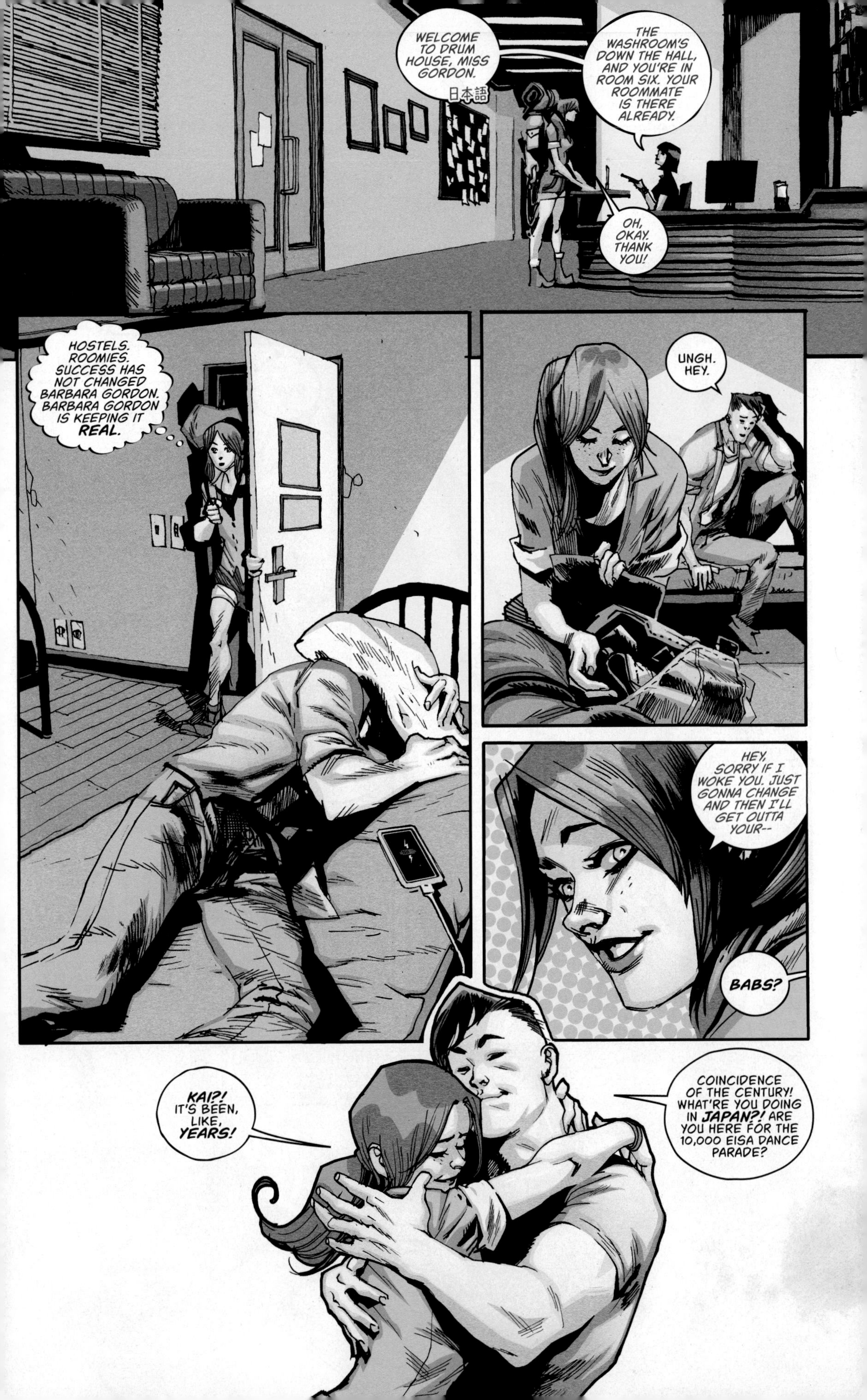
WELCOME TO DRUM HOUSE, MISS GORDON.
日本語
THE WASHROOM'S DOWN THE HALL, AND YOU'RE IN ROOM SIX. YOUR ROOMMATE IS THERE ALREADY.
OH, OKAY. THANK YOU!
HOSTELS. ROOMIES. SUCCESS HAS NOT CHANGED BARBARA GORDON. BARBARA GORDON IS KEEPING IT REAL.
UNGH. HEY.
HEY, SORRY IF I WOKE YOU. JUST GONNA CHANGE AND THEN I'LL GET OUTTA YOUR--
BABS?
KAI?! IT'S BEEN, LIKE, YEARS!
COINCIDENCE OF THE CENTURY! WHAT'RE YOU DOING IN JAPAN?! ARE YOU HERE FOR THE 10,000 EISA DANCE PARADE?

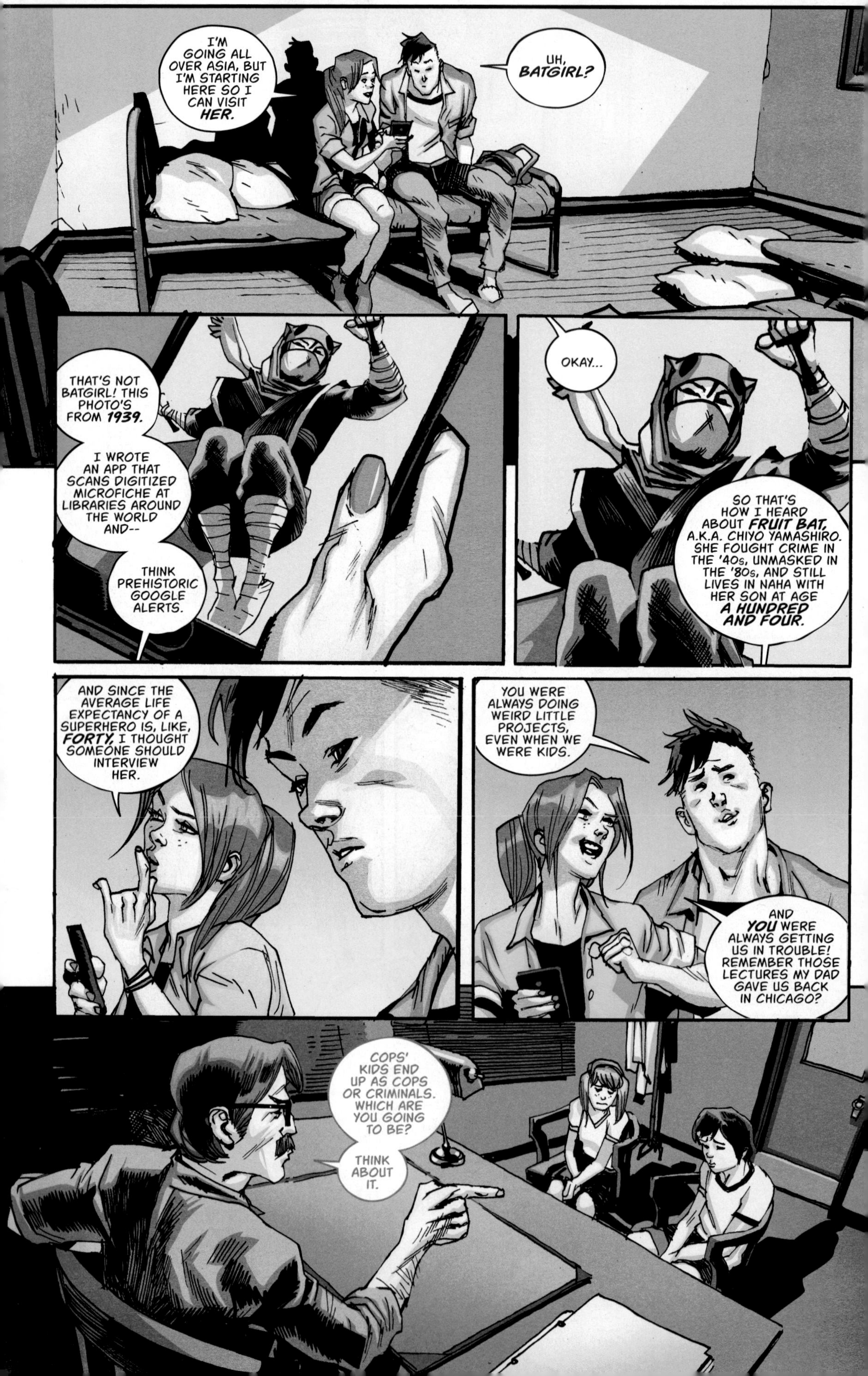
I'M GOING ALL OVER ASIA, BUT I'M STARTING HERE SO I CAN VISIT HER.
UH, BATGIRL?
THAT'S NOT BATGIRL! THIS PHOTO'S FROM 1939.
I WROTE AN APP THAT SCANS DIGITIZED MICROFICHE AT LIBRARIES AROUND THE WORLD AND--
THINK PREHISTORIC GOOGLE ALERTS.
OKAY...
SO THAT'S HOW I HEARD ABOUT FRUIT BAT, A.K.A. CHIYO YAMASHIRO. SHE FOUGHT CRIME IN THE '40s, UNMASKED IN THE '80s, AND STILL LIVES IN NAHA WITH HER SON AT AGE A HUNDRED AND FOUR.
AND SINCE THE AVERAGE LIFE EXPECTANCY OF A SUPERHERO IS, LIKE, FORTY, I THOUGHT SOMEONE SHOULD INTERVIEW HER.
YOU WERE ALWAYS DOING WEIRD LITTLE PROJECTS, EVEN WHEN WE WERE KIDS.
AND YOU WERE ALWAYS GETTING US IN TROUBLE! REMEMBER THOSE LECTURES MY DAD GAVE US BACK IN CHICAGO?
COPS' KIDS END UP AS COPS OR CRIMINALS. WHICH ARE YOU GOING TO BE?
THINK ABOUT IT.

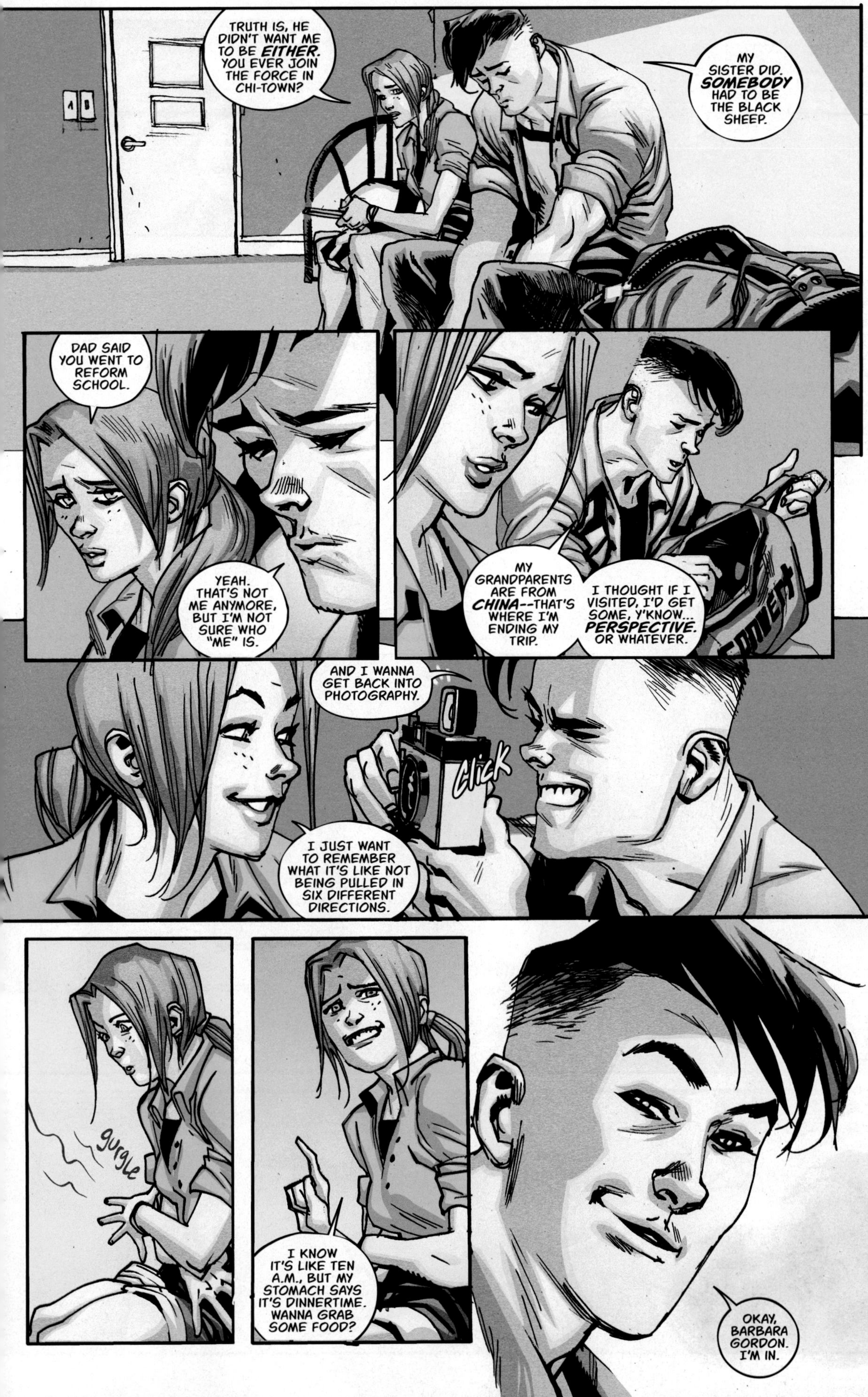
TRUTH IS, HE DIDN'T WANT ME TO BE EITHER. YOU EVER JOIN THE FORCE IN CHI-TOWN?
MY SISTER DID. SOMEBODY HAD TO BE THE BLACK SHEEP.
DAD SAID YOU WENT TO REFORM SCHOOL.
YEAH. THAT'S NOT ME ANYMORE, BUT I'M NOT SURE WHO "ME" IS.
MY GRANDPARENTS ARE FROM CHINA--THAT'S WHERE I'M ENDING MY TRIP.
I THOUGHT IF I VISITED, I'D GET SOME, Y'KNOW... PERSPECTIVE. OR WHATEVER.
AND I WANNA GET BACK INTO PHOTOGRAPHY.
CLICK
I JUST WANT TO REMEMBER WHAT IT'S LIKE NOT BEING PULLED IN SIX DIFFERENT DIRECTIONS.
gurgle
I KNOW IT'S LIKE TEN A.M., BUT MY STOMACH SAYS IT'S DINNERTIME. WANNA GRAB SOME FOOD?
OKAY, BARBARA GORDON. I'M IN.

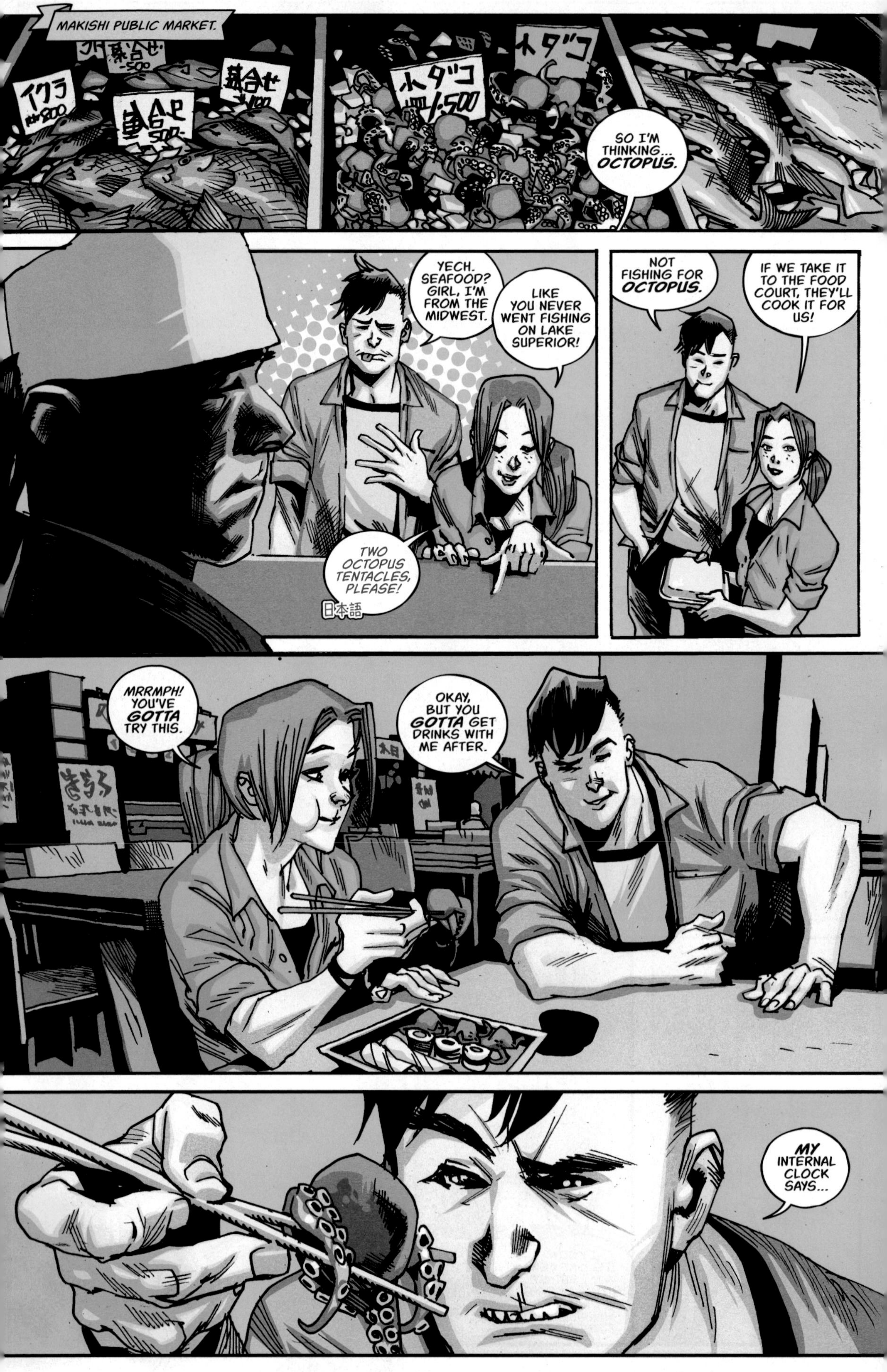

MAKISHI PUBLIC MARKET.
イクラ
小ダコ
小ダコ
SO I'M THINKING... OCTOPUS.
YECH. SEAFOOD? GIRL, I'M FROM THE MIDWEST.
LIKE YOU NEVER WENT FISHING ON LAKE SUPERIOR!
TWO OCTOPUS TENTACLES, PLEASE!
日本語
NOT FISHING FOR OCTOPUS.
IF WE TAKE IT TO THE FOOD COURT, THEY'LL COOK IT FOR US!
MRRMPH! YOU'VE GOTTA TRY THIS.
OKAY, BUT YOU GOTTA GET DRINKS WITH ME AFTER.
MY INTERNAL CLOCK SAYS...

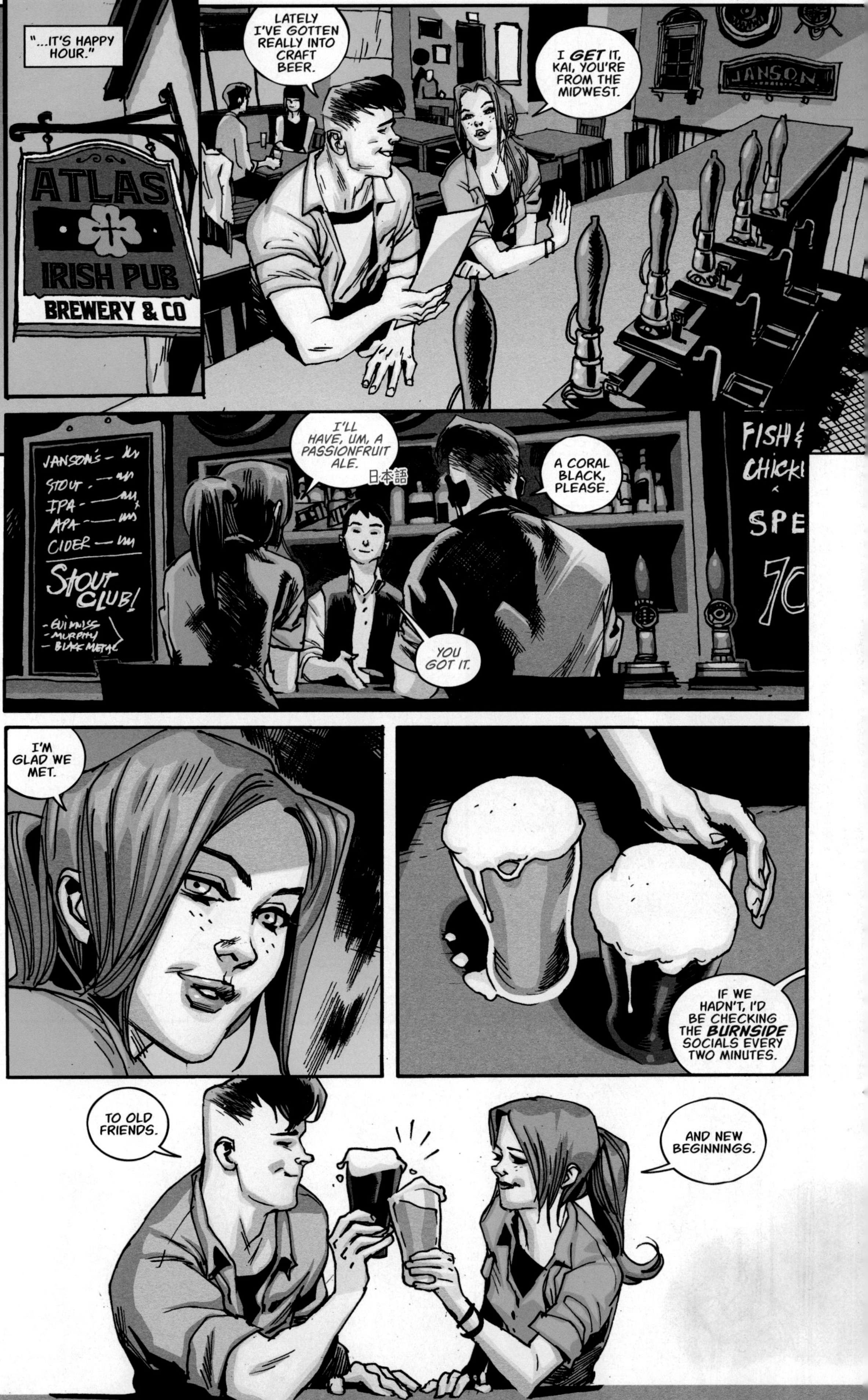
"...IT'S HAPPY HOUR."
ATLAS
IRISH PUB
BREWERY & CO
LATELY I'VE GOTTEN REALLY INTO CRAFT BEER.
I GET IT, KAI, YOU'RE FROM THE MIDWEST.
JANSON
JANSON'S
STOUT
IPA
APA
CIDER
STOUT CLUB!
FISH &
CHICK
SPE
I'LL HAVE, UM, A PASSIONFRUIT ALE.
日本語
A CORAL BLACK, PLEASE.
YOU GOT IT.
I'M GLAD WE MET.
IF WE HADN'T, I'D BE CHECKING THE BURNSIDE SOCIALS EVERY TWO MINUTES.
TO OLD FRIENDS.
AND NEW BEGINNINGS.

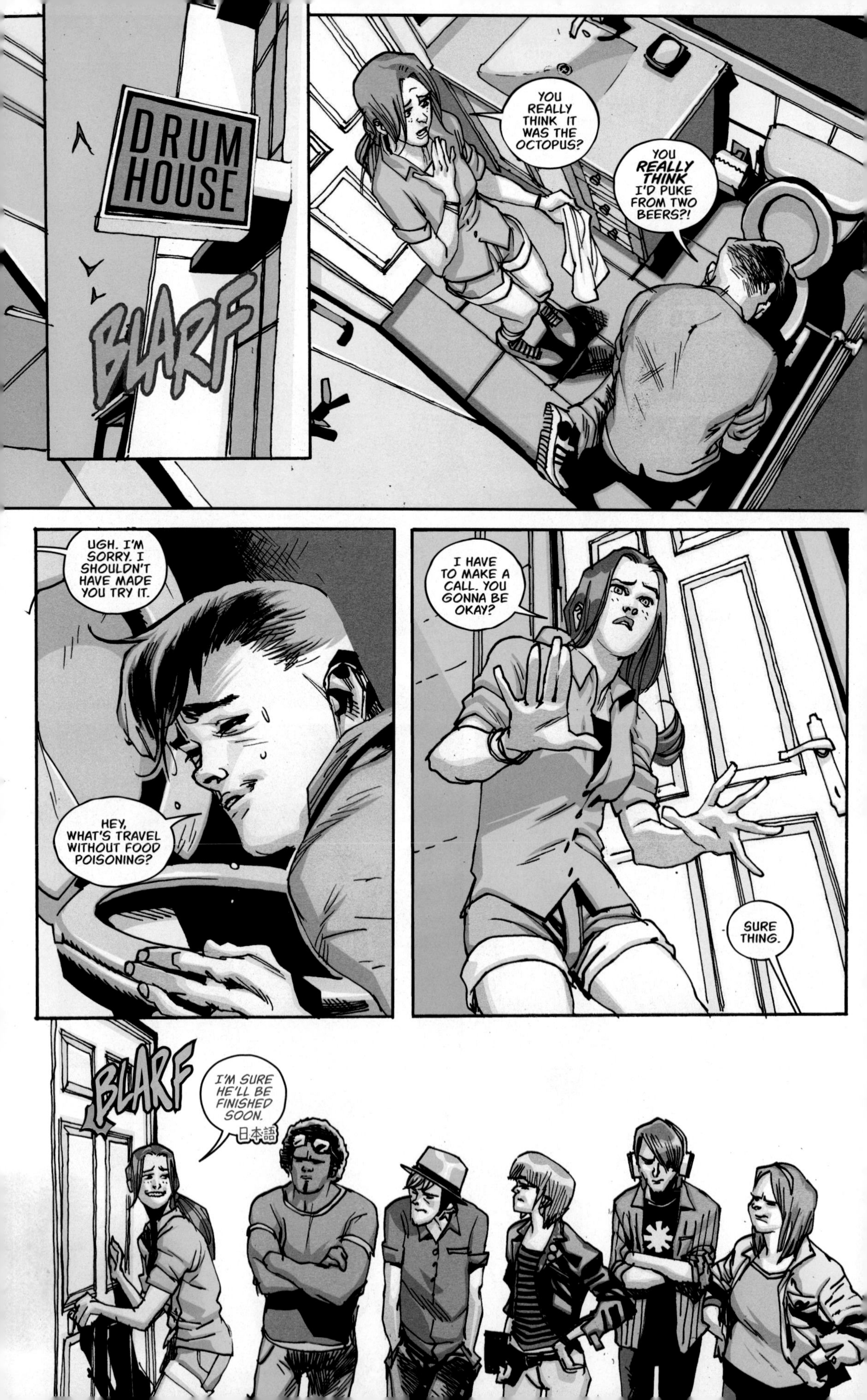
DRUM HOUSE
BLARF
YOU REALLY THINK IT WAS THE OCTOPUS?
YOU REALLY THINK I'D PUKE FROM TWO BEERS?!
UGH. I'M SORRY. I SHOULDN'T HAVE MADE YOU TRY IT.
HEY, WHAT'S TRAVEL WITHOUT FOOD POISONING?
I HAVE TO MAKE A CALL. YOU GONNA BE OKAY?
SURE THING.
BLARF
I'M SURE HE'LL BE FINISHED SOON.
日本語

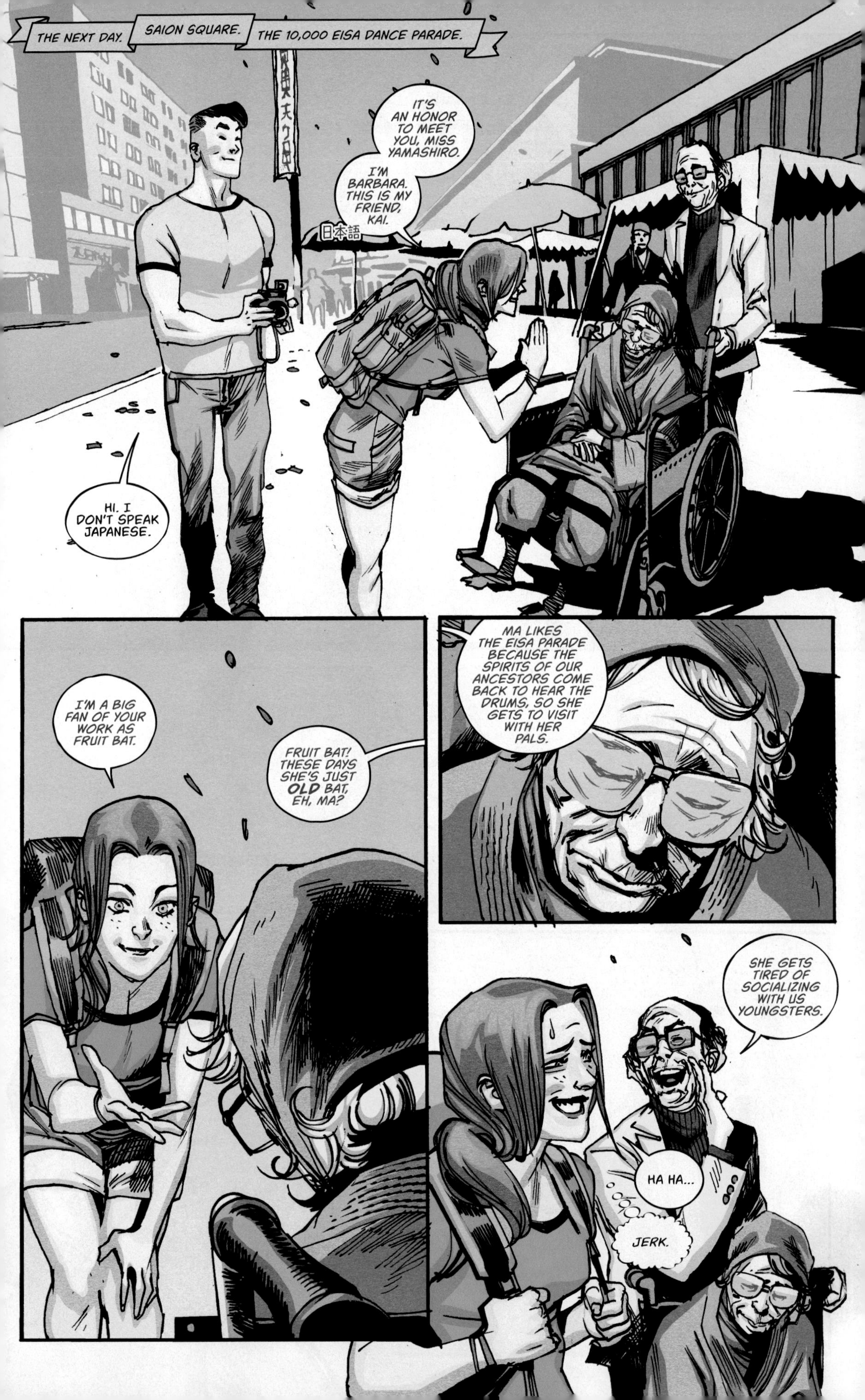

THE NEXT DAY.
SAION SQUARE.
THE 10,000 EISA DANCE PARADE.
IT'S AN HONOR TO MEET YOU, MISS YAMASHIRO.
I'M BARBARA. THIS IS MY FRIEND, KAI.
日本語
HI. I DON'T SPEAK JAPANESE.
I'M A BIG FAN OF YOUR WORK AS FRUIT BAT.
FRUIT BAT! THESE DAYS SHE'S JUST OLD BAT, EH, MA?
MA LIKES THE EISA PARADE BECAUSE THE SPIRITS OF OUR ANCESTORS COME BACK TO HEAR THE DRUMS, SO SHE GETS TO VISIT WITH HER PALS.
SHE GETS TIRED OF SOCIALIZING WITH US YOUNGSTERS.
HA HA...
JERK.

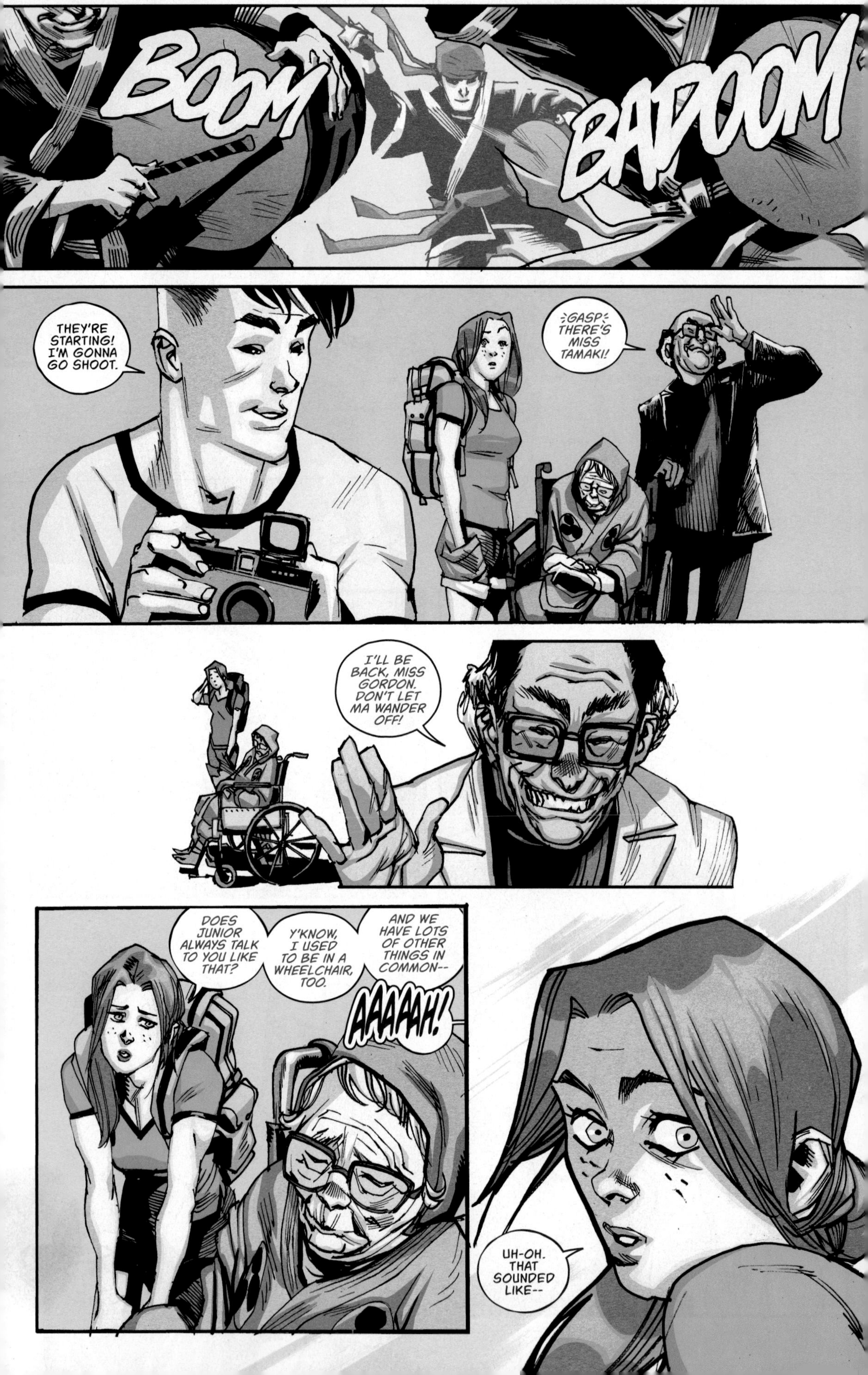
BOOM
BADOOM
THEY'RE STARTING! I'M GONNA GO SHOOT.
GASP THERE'S MISS TAMAKI!
I'LL BE BACK, MISS GORDON. DON'T LET MA WANDER OFF!
DOES JUNIOR ALWAYS TALK TO YOU LIKE THAT?
Y'KNOW, I USED TO BE IN A WHEELCHAIR, TOO.
AND WE HAVE LOTS OF OTHER THINGS IN COMMON--
AAAAAH!
UH-OH. THAT SOUNDED LIKE--

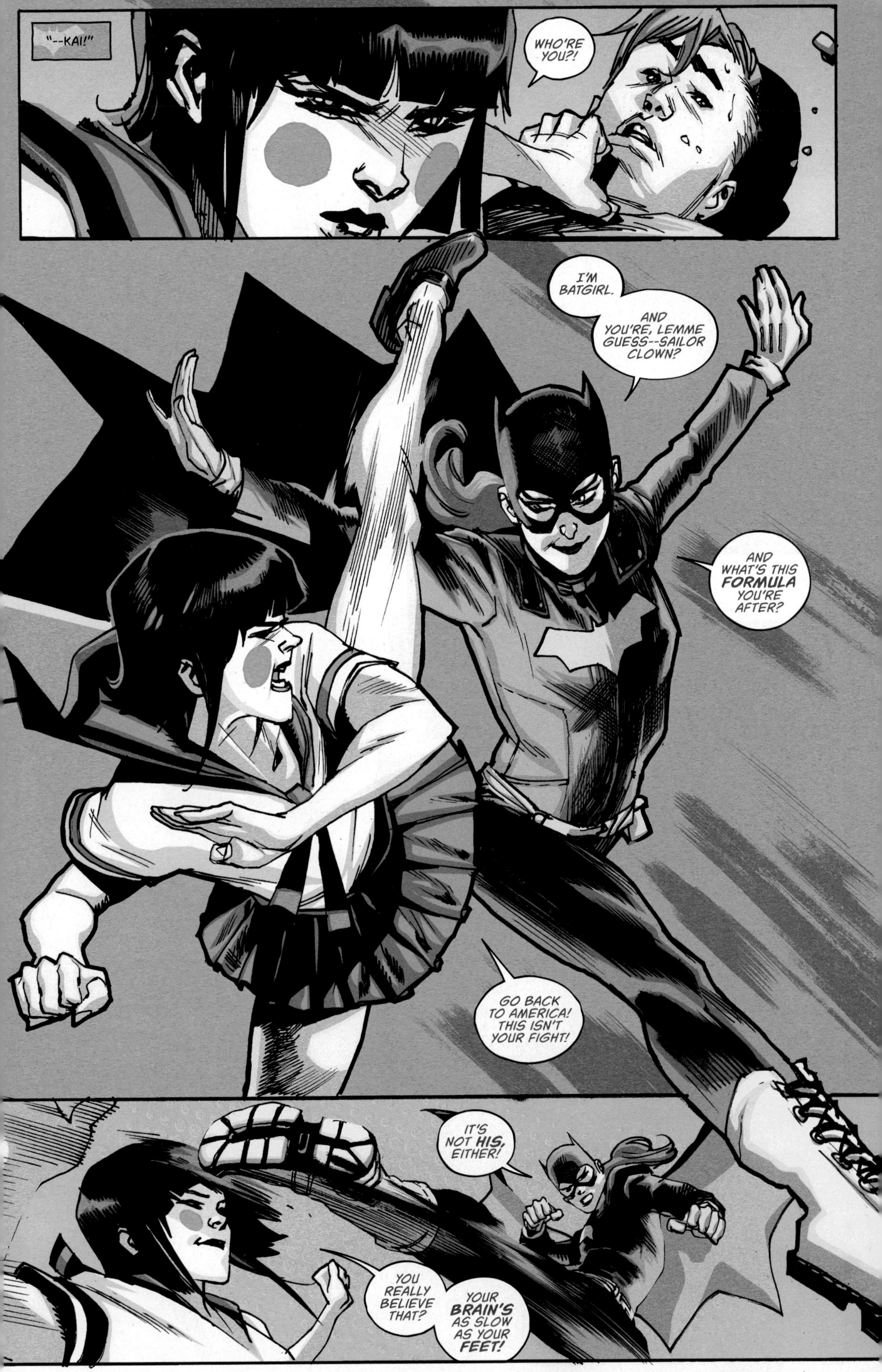
"--KAI!"
WHO'RE YOU?!
I'M BATGIRL.
AND YOU'RE, LEMME GUESS--SAILOR CLOWN?
AND WHAT'S THIS FORMULA YOU'RE AFTER?
GO BACK TO AMERICA! THIS ISN'T YOUR FIGHT!
IT'S NOT HIS, EITHER!
YOU REALLY BELIEVE THAT?
YOUR BRAIN'S AS SLOW AS YOUR FEET!

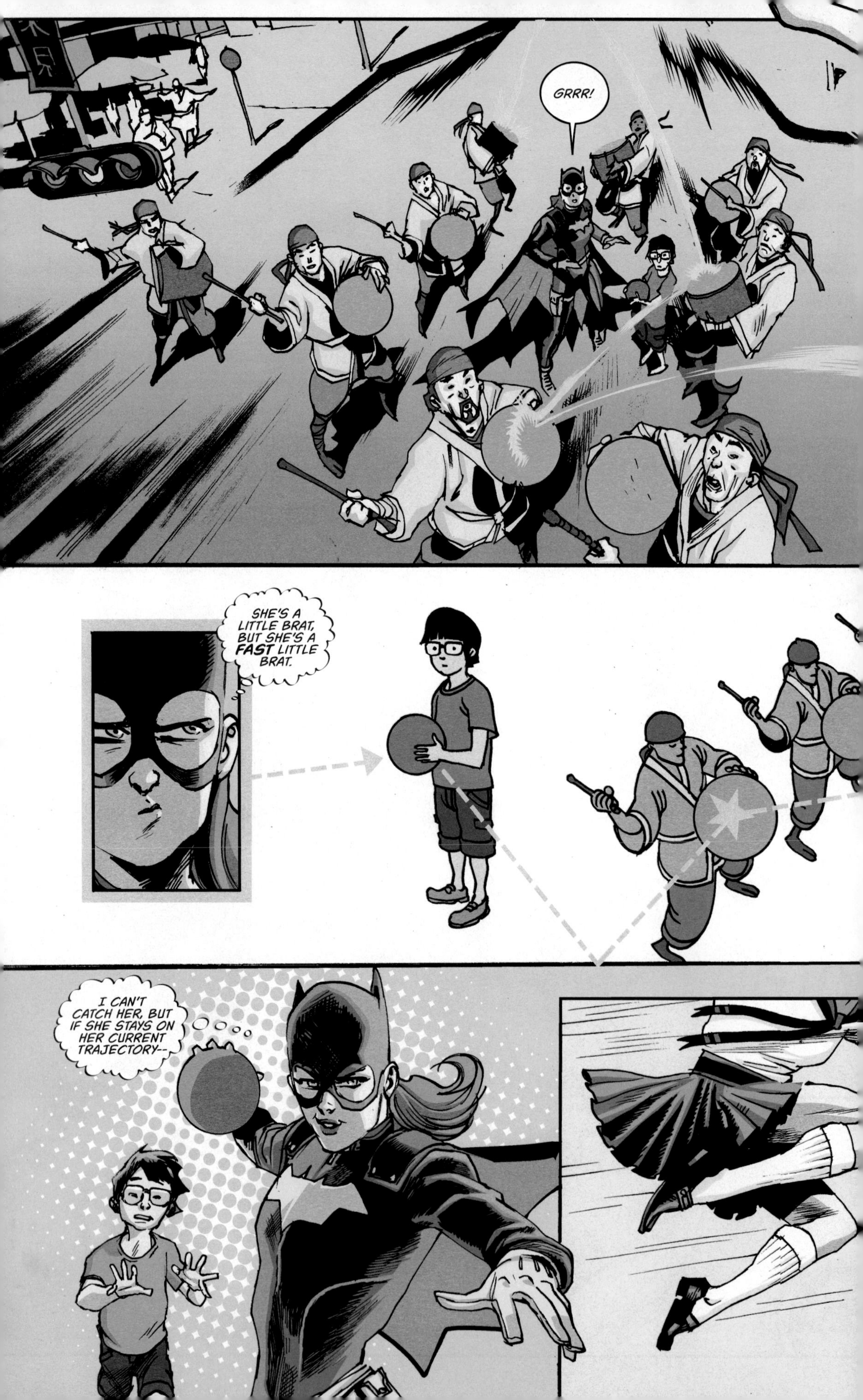
GRRR!
SHE'S A LITTLE BRAT, BUT SHE'S A FAST LITTLE BRAT.
I CAN'T CATCH HER, BUT IF SHE STAYS ON HER CURRENT TRAJECTORY--

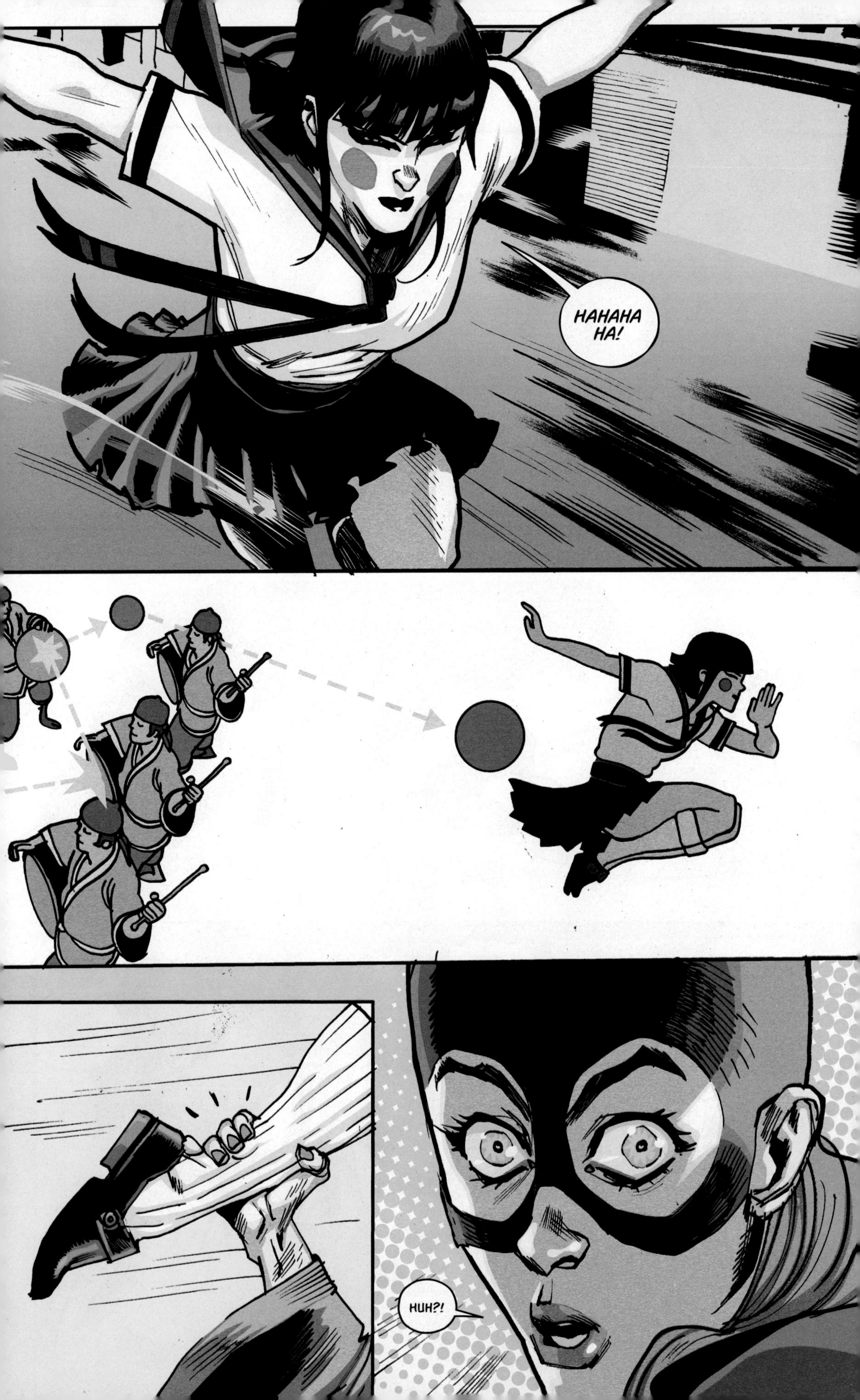
HAHAHA HA!
HUH?!

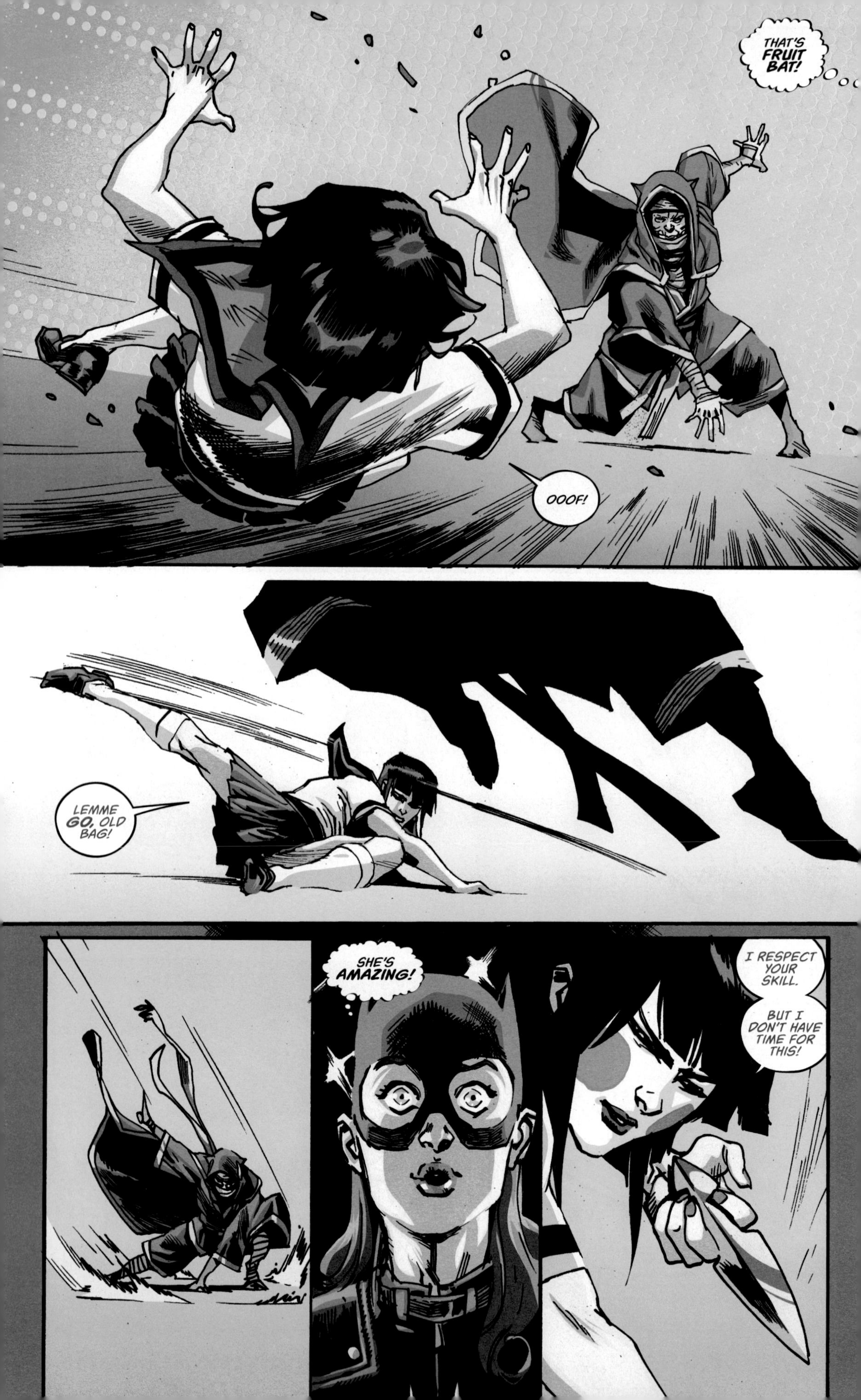
THAT'S FRUIT BAT!
OOOF!
LEMME GO, OLD BAG!
SHE'S AMAZING!
I RESPECT YOUR SKILL.
BUT I DON'T HAVE TIME FOR THIS!

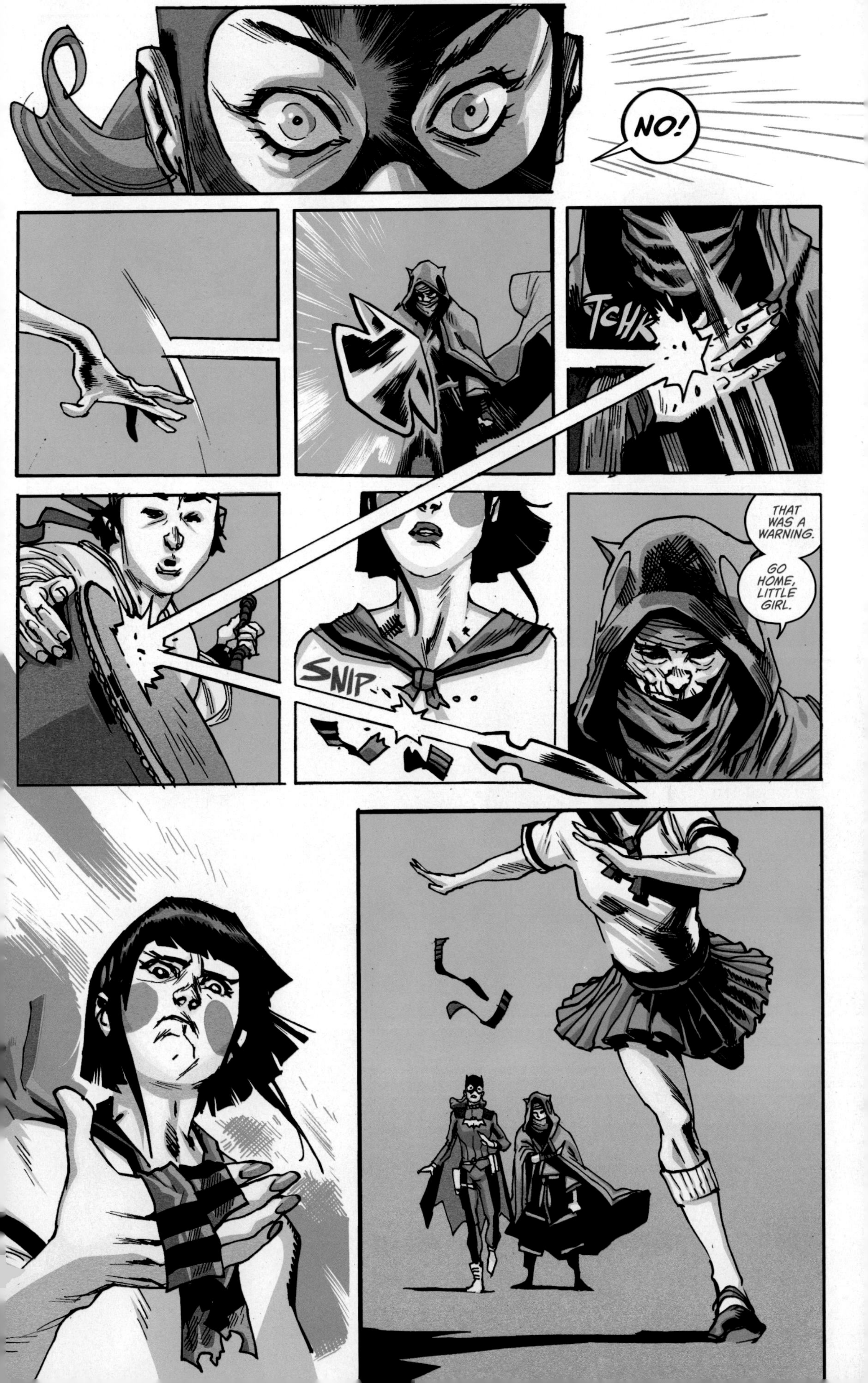
NO!
TCHK
SNIP
THAT WAS A WARNING.
GO HOME, LITTLE GIRL.

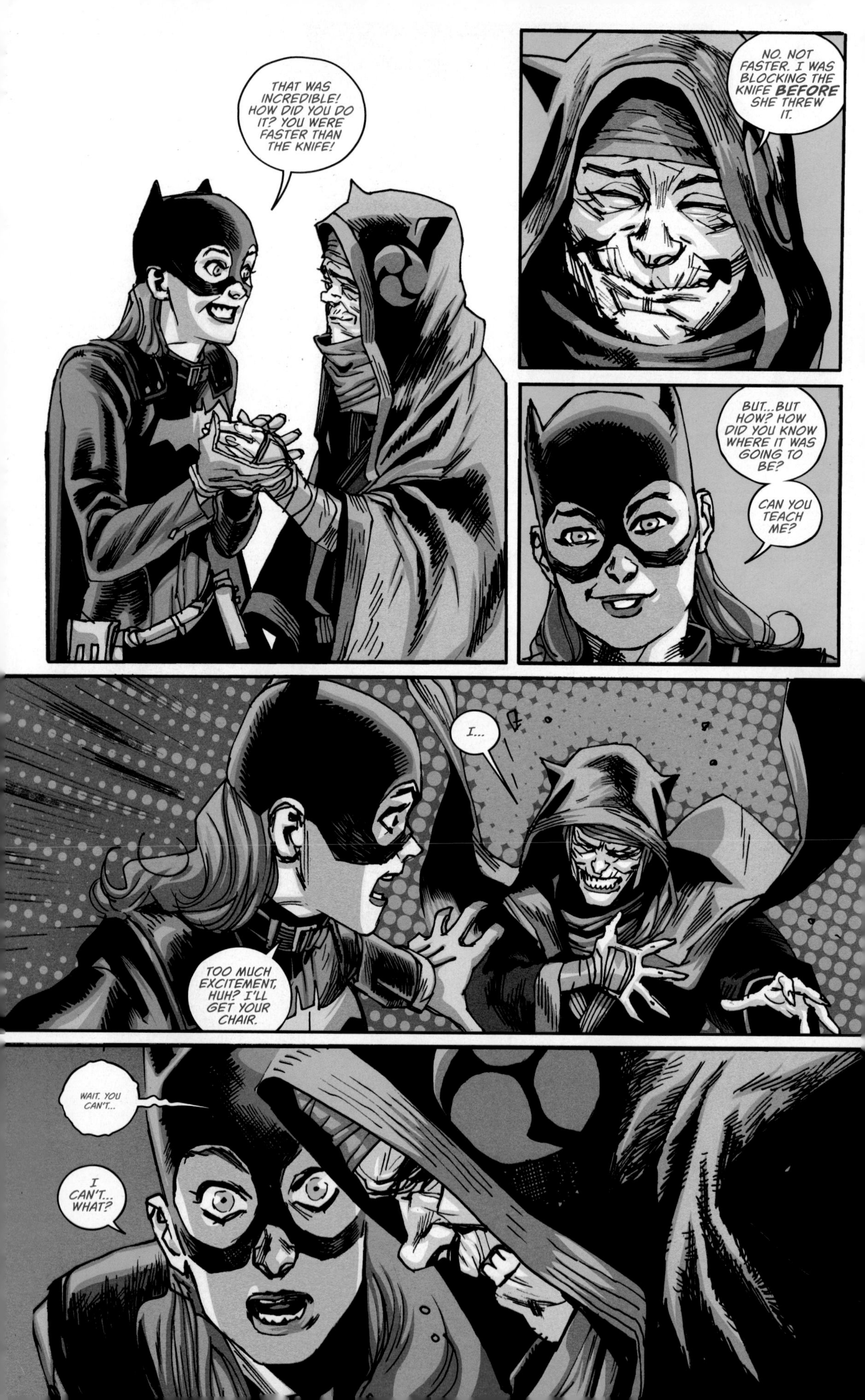
THAT WAS INCREDIBLE! HOW DID YOU DO IT? YOU WERE FASTER THAN THE KNIFE!
NO. NOT FASTER. I WAS BLOCKING THE KNIFE **BEFORE** SHE THREW IT.
BUT...BUT HOW? HOW DID YOU KNOW WHERE IT WAS GOING TO BE?
CAN YOU TEACH ME?
I...
TOO MUCH EXCITEMENT, HUH? I'LL GET YOUR CHAIR.
WAIT. YOU CAN'T...
I CAN'T... WHAT?

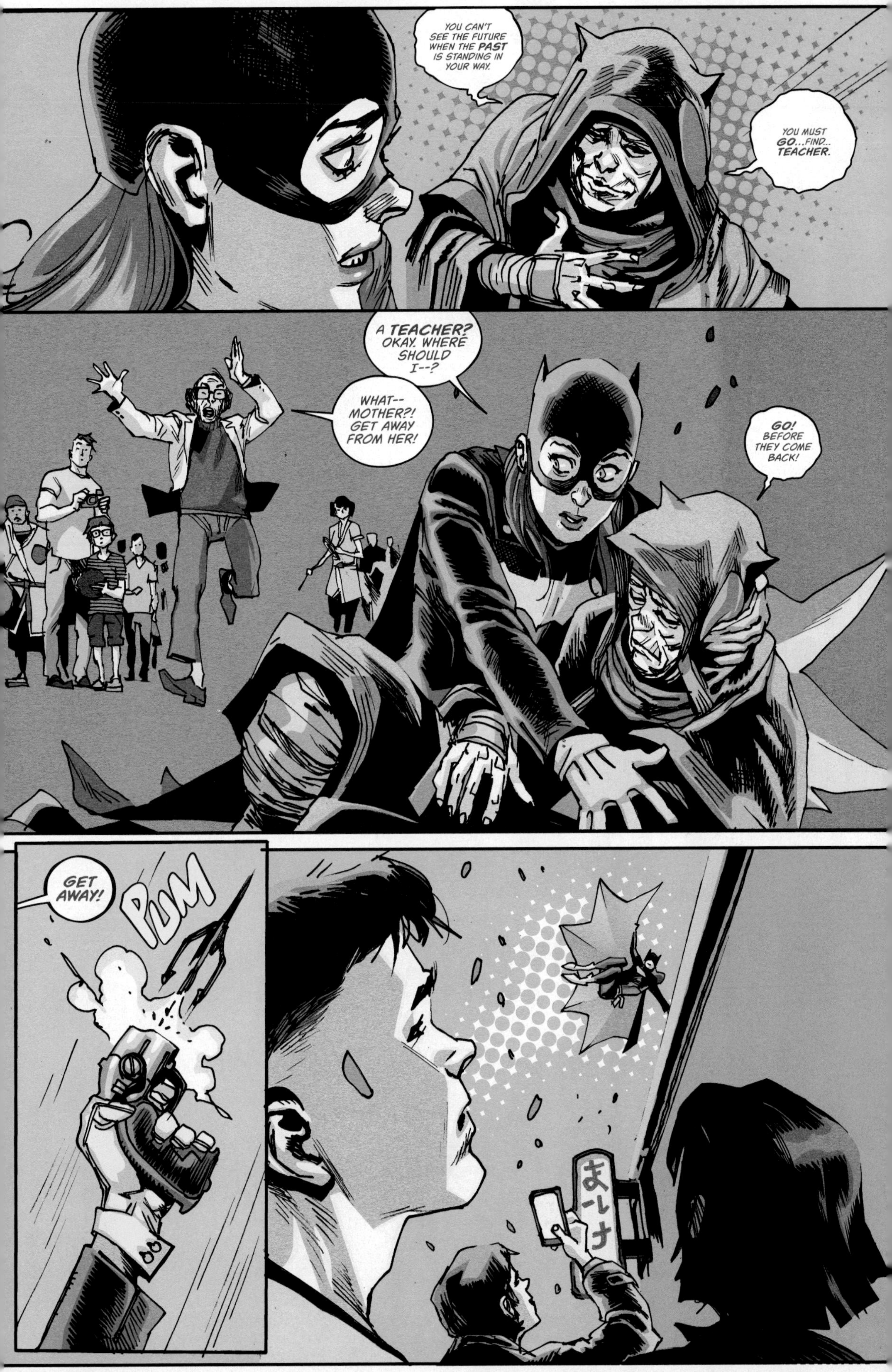
YOU CAN'T SEE THE FUTURE WHEN THE PAST IS STANDING IN YOUR WAY.
YOU MUST GO...FIND... TEACHER.
A TEACHER? OKAY. WHERE SHOULD I--?
WHAT-- MOTHER?! GET AWAY FROM HER!
GO! BEFORE THEY COME BACK!
GET AWAY!
PUM

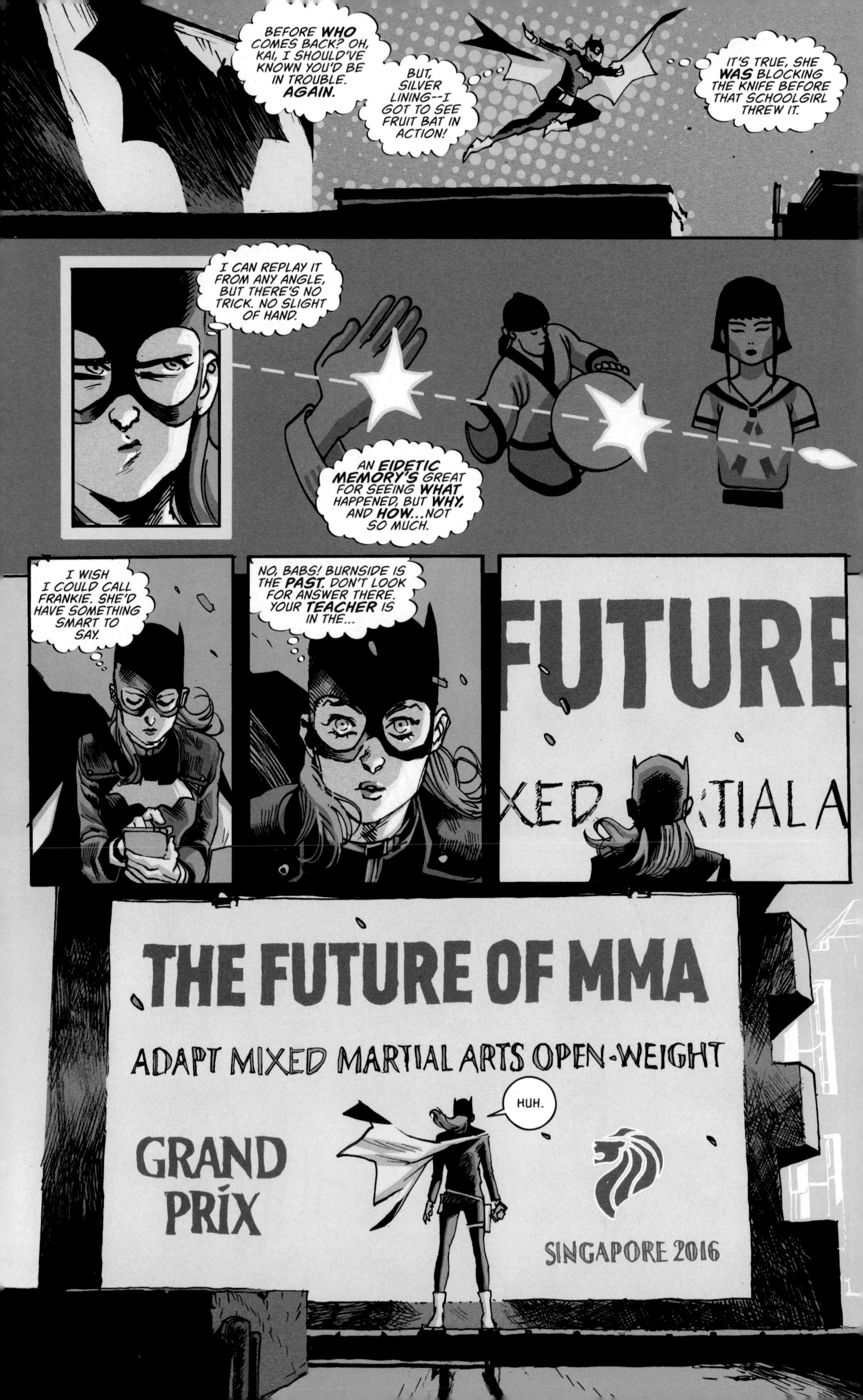
BEFORE WHO COMES BACK? OH, KAI, I SHOULD'VE KNOWN YOU'D BE IN TROUBLE. AGAIN.
BUT, SILVER LINING--I GOT TO SEE FRUIT BAT IN ACTION!
IT'S TRUE, SHE WAS BLOCKING THE KNIFE BEFORE THAT SCHOOLGIRL THREW IT.
I CAN REPLAY IT FROM ANY ANGLE, BUT THERE'S NO TRICK. NO SLIGHT OF HAND.
AN EIDETIC MEMORY'S GREAT FOR SEEING WHAT HAPPENED, BUT WHY, AND HOW...NOT SO MUCH.
I WISH I COULD CALL FRANKIE. SHE'D HAVE SOMETHING SMART TO SAY.
NO, BABS! BURNSIDE IS THE PAST. DON'T LOOK FOR ANSWER THERE. YOUR TEACHER IS IN THE...
FUTURE
XED TIAL A
THE FUTURE OF MMA
ADAPT MIXED MARTIAL ARTS OPEN-WEIGHT
GRAND PRIX
HUH.
SINGAPORE 2016

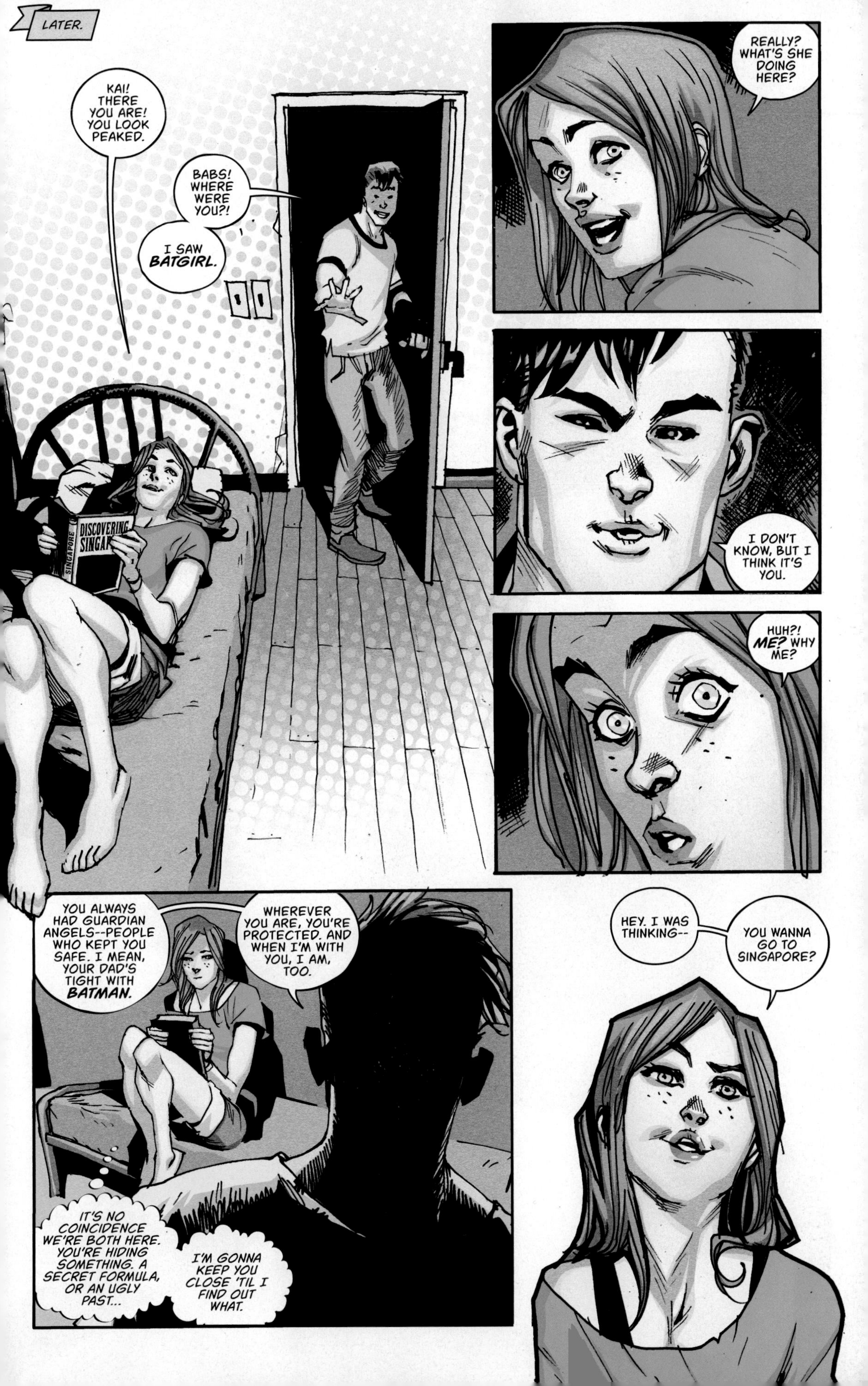
LATER.
KAI! THERE YOU ARE! YOU LOOK PEAKED.
BABS! WHERE WERE YOU?!
I SAW BATGIRL.
DISCOVERING SINGA
SINGAPORE
REALLY? WHAT'S SHE DOING HERE?
I DON'T KNOW, BUT I THINK IT'S YOU.
HUH?! ME? WHY ME?
YOU ALWAYS HAD GUARDIAN ANGELS--PEOPLE WHO KEPT YOU SAFE. I MEAN, YOUR DAD'S TIGHT WITH BATMAN.
WHEREVER YOU ARE, YOU'RE PROTECTED. AND WHEN I'M WITH YOU, I AM, TOO.
IT'S NO COINCIDENCE WE'RE BOTH HERE. YOU'RE HIDING SOMETHING. A SECRET FORMULA, OR AN UGLY PAST...
I'M GONNA KEEP YOU CLOSE 'TIL I FIND OUT WHAT.
HEY. I WAS THINKING--
YOU WANNA GO TO SINGAPORE?

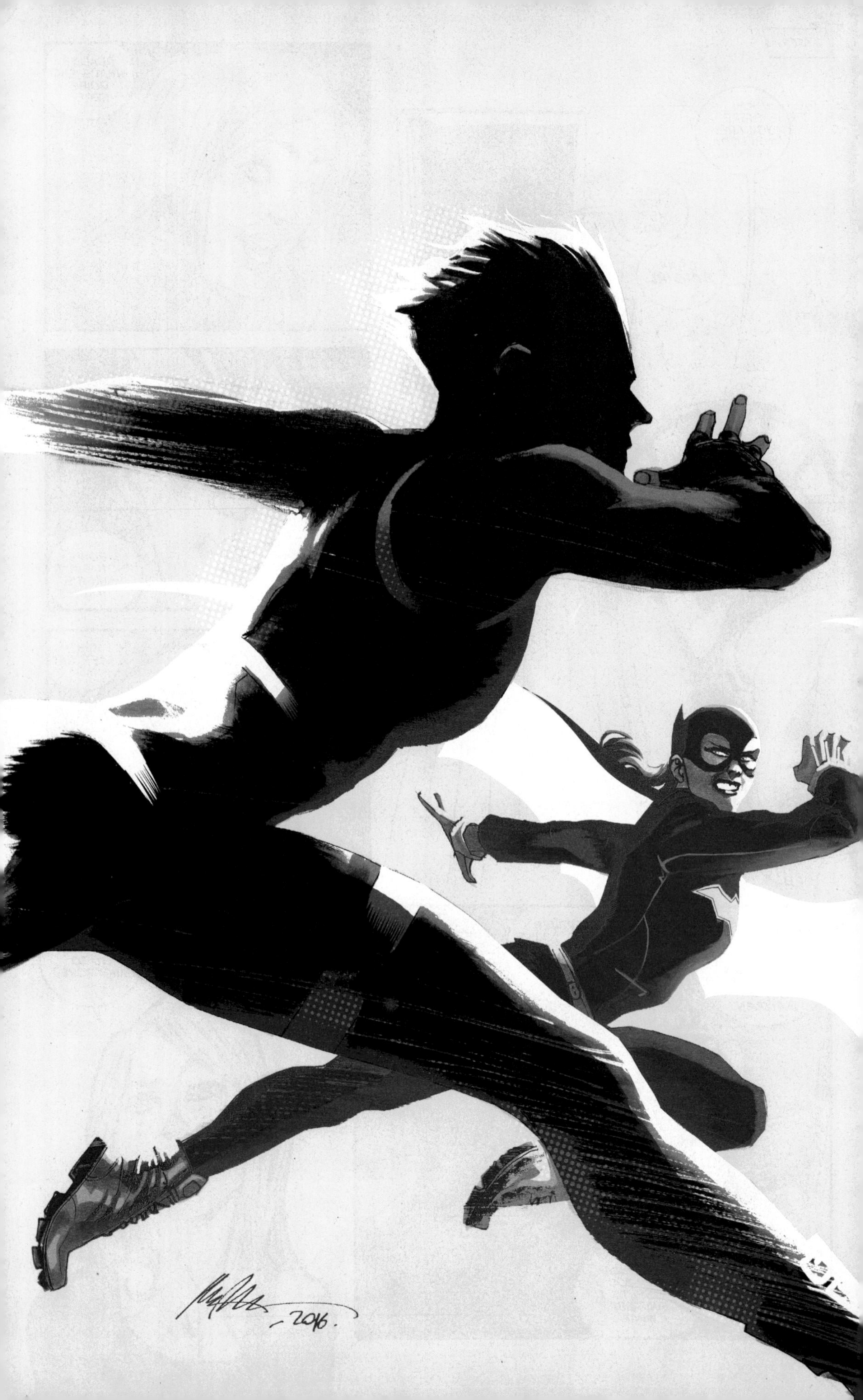
2016.

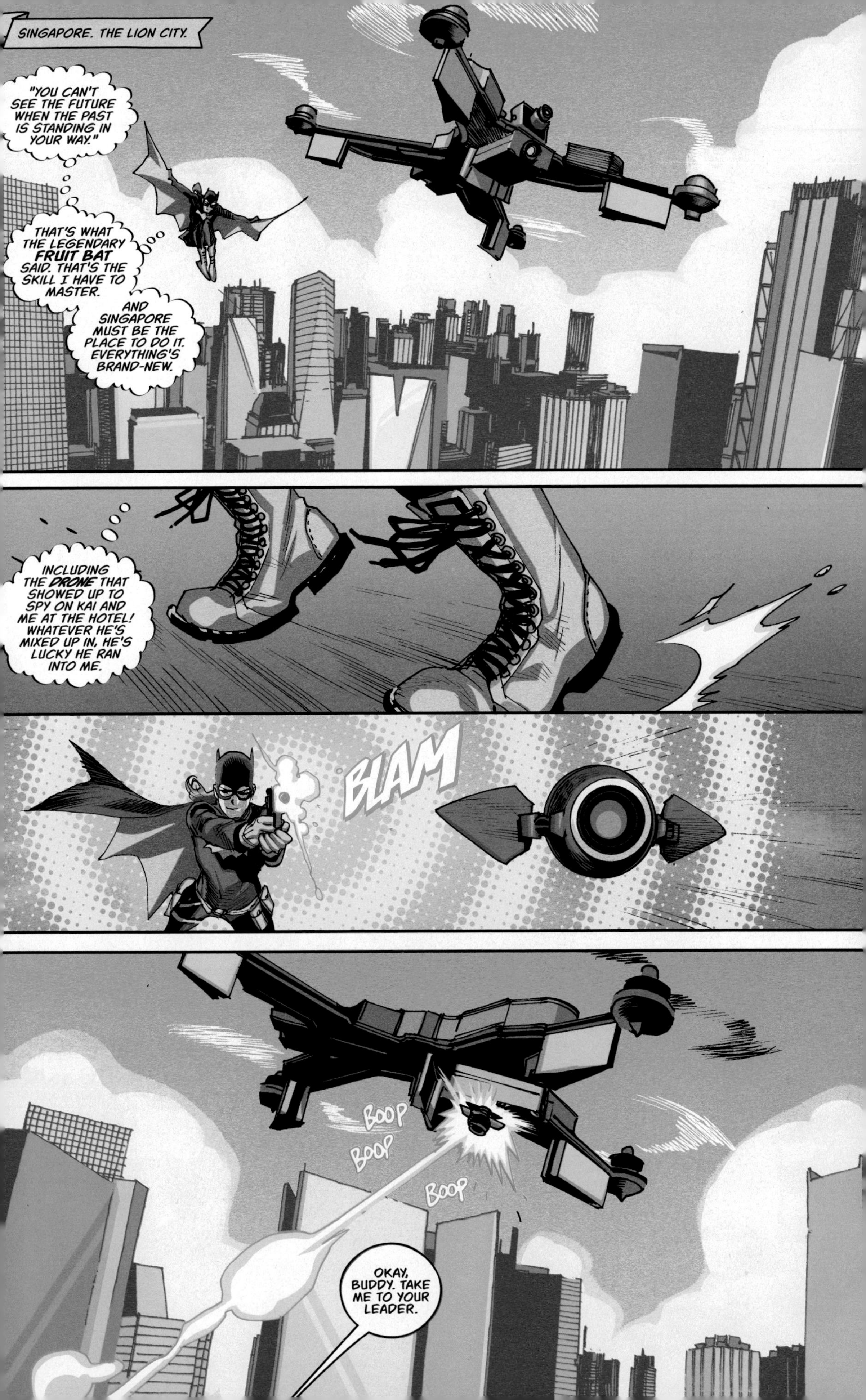

SINGAPORE. THE LION CITY.
"YOU CAN'T SEE THE FUTURE WHEN THE PAST IS STANDING IN YOUR WAY."
THAT'S WHAT THE LEGENDARY FRUIT BAT SAID. THAT'S THE SKILL I HAVE TO MASTER.
AND SINGAPORE MUST BE THE PLACE TO DO IT. EVERYTHING'S BRAND-NEW.
INCLUDING THE DRONE THAT SHOWED UP TO SPY ON KAI AND ME AT THE HOTEL! WHATEVER HE'S MIXED UP IN, HE'S LUCKY HE RAN INTO ME.
BLAM
BOOP
BOOP
BOOP
OKAY, BUDDY. TAKE ME TO YOUR LEADER.

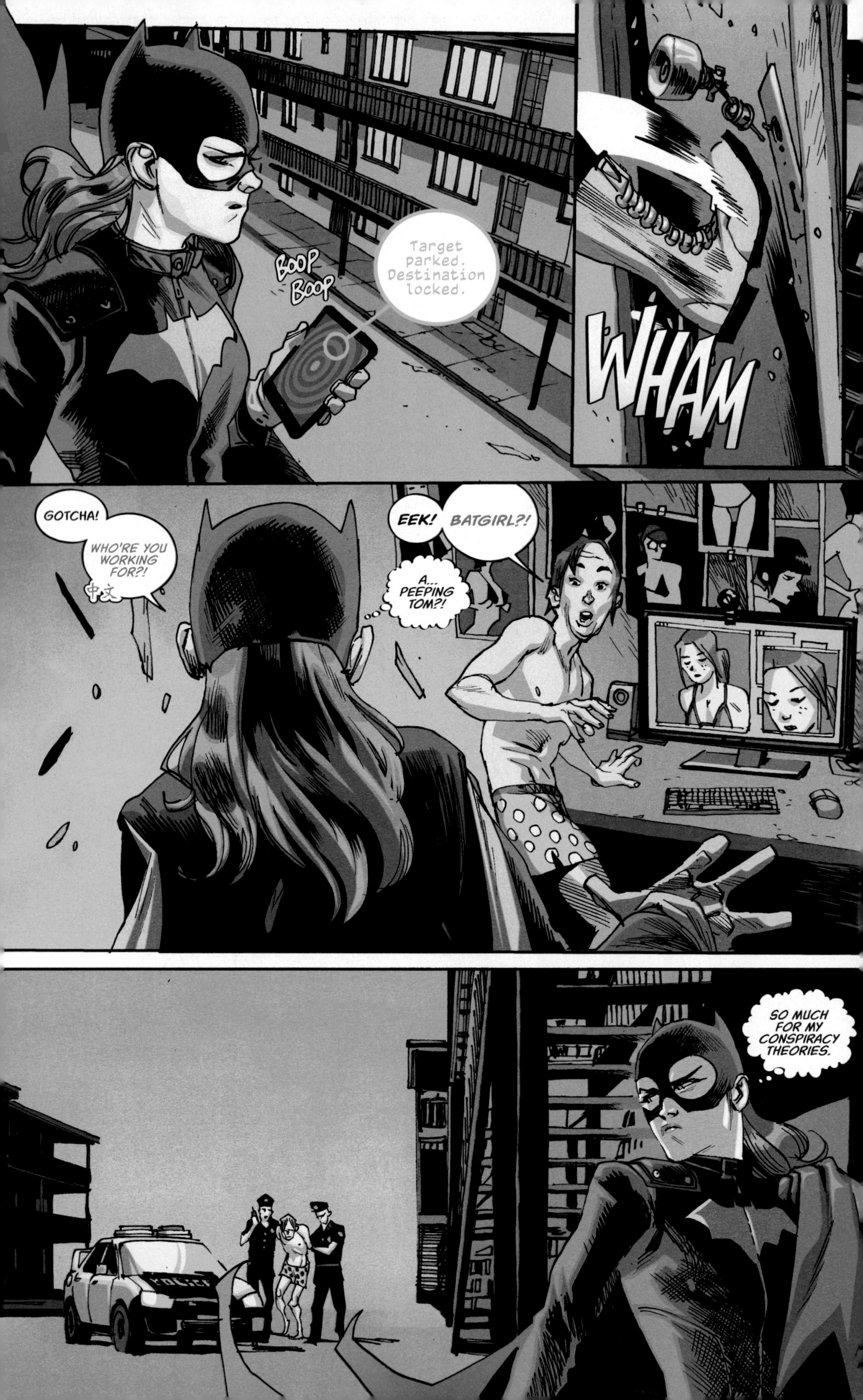
BOOP BOOP
Target parked. Destination locked.
WHAM
GOTCHA!
WHO'RE YOU WORKING FOR?!
中文
EEK!
BATGIRL?!
A... PEEPING TOM?!
SO MUCH FOR MY CONSPIRACY THEORIES.

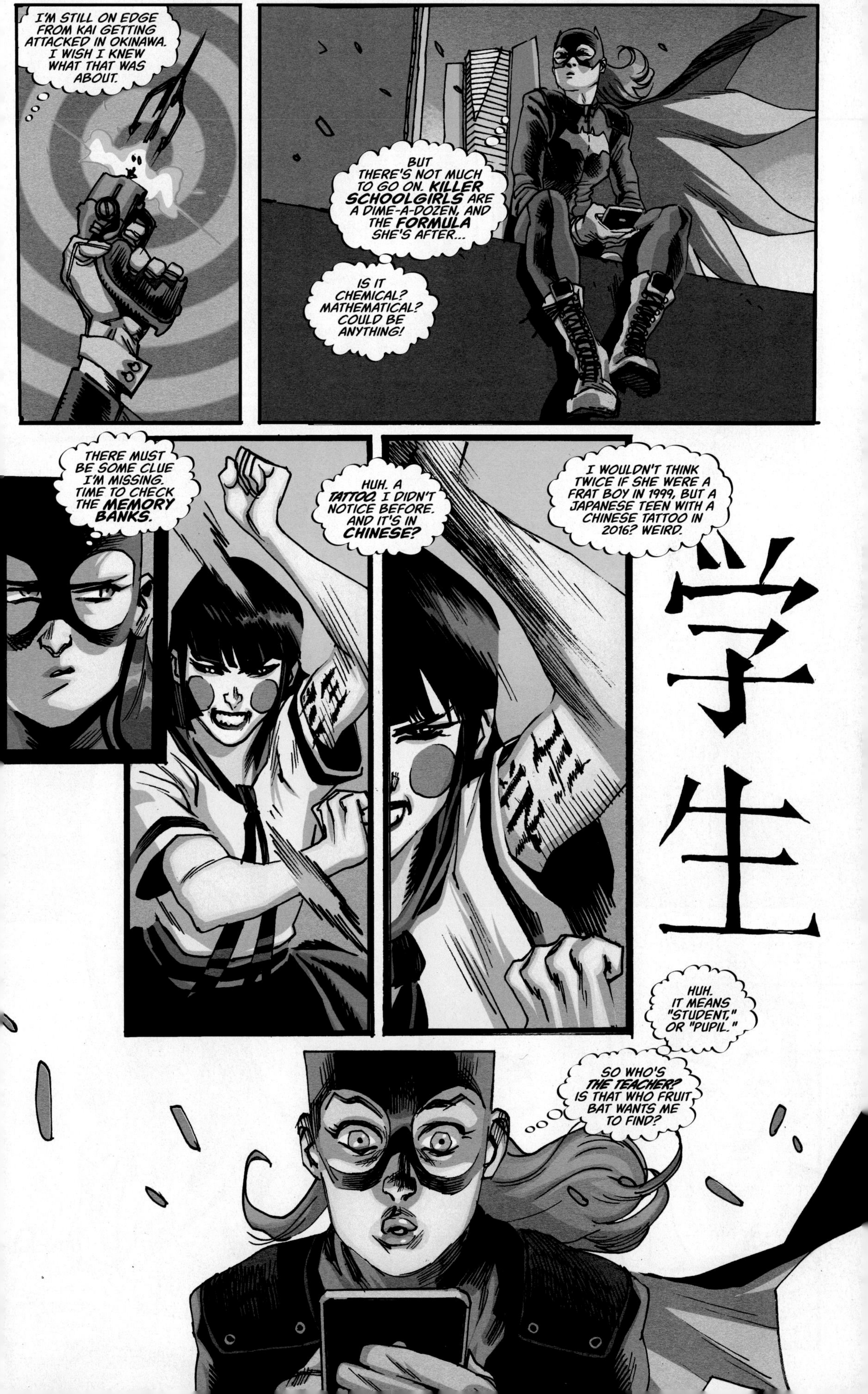
I'M STILL ON EDGE FROM KAI GETTING ATTACKED IN OKINAWA. I WISH I KNEW WHAT THAT WAS ABOUT.
BUT THERE'S NOT MUCH TO GO ON. KILLER SCHOOLGIRLS ARE A DIME-A-DOZEN, AND THE FORMULA SHE'S AFTER...
IS IT CHEMICAL? MATHEMATICAL? COULD BE ANYTHING!
THERE MUST BE SOME CLUE I'M MISSING. TIME TO CHECK THE MEMORY BANKS.
HUH. A TATTOO. I DIDN'T NOTICE BEFORE. AND IT'S IN CHINESE?
I WOULDN'T THINK TWICE IF SHE WERE A FRAT BOY IN 1999, BUT A JAPANESE TEEN WITH A CHINESE TATTOO IN 2016? WEIRD.
学生
HUH. IT MEANS "STUDENT," OR "PUPIL."
SO WHO'S THE TEACHER? IS THAT WHO FRUIT BAT WANTS ME TO FIND?

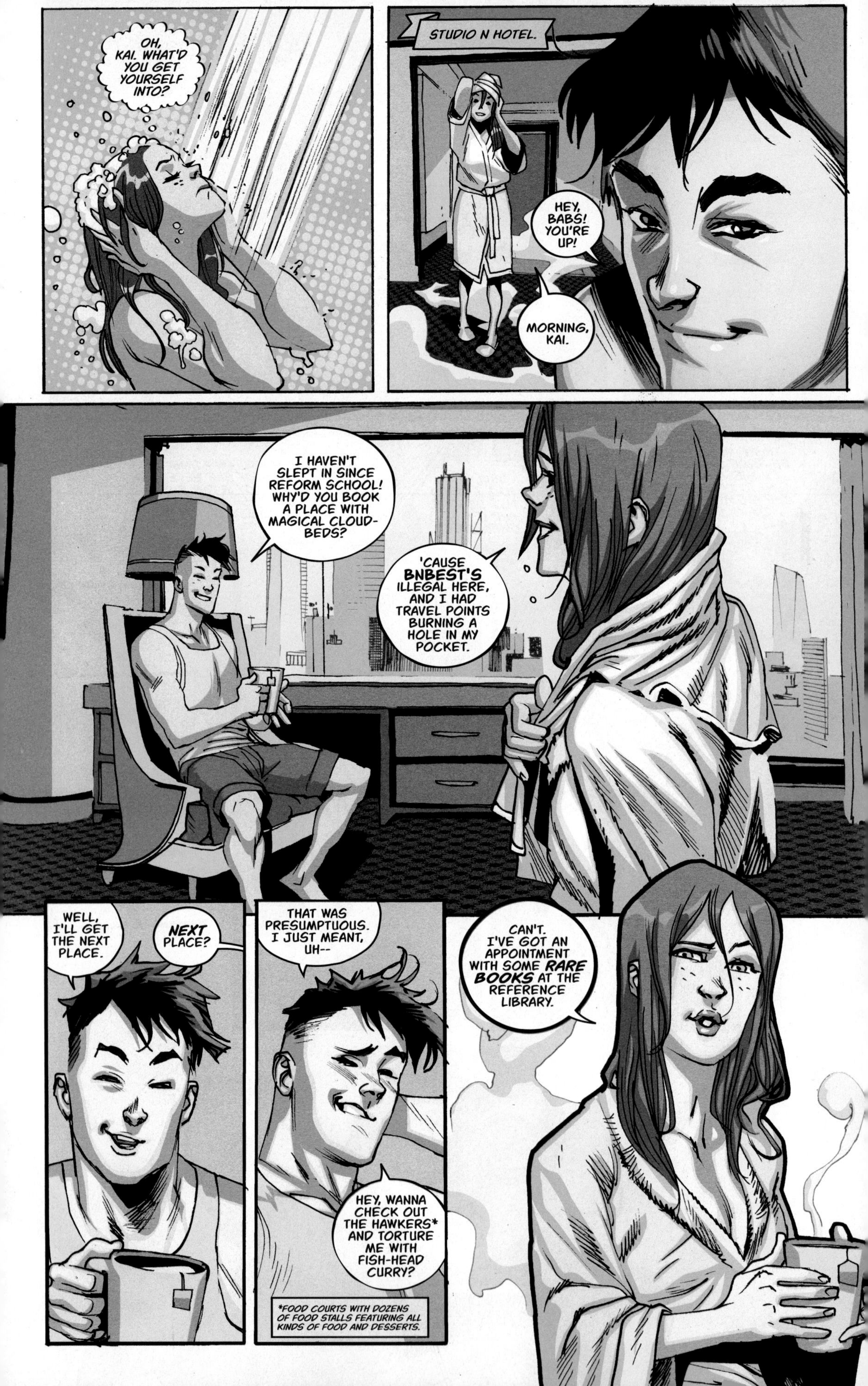
OH, KAI. WHAT'D YOU GET YOURSELF INTO?
STUDIO N HOTEL.
HEY, BABS! YOU'RE UP!
MORNING, KAI.
I HAVEN'T SLEPT IN SINCE REFORM SCHOOL! WHY'D YOU BOOK A PLACE WITH MAGICAL CLOUD-BEDS?
'CAUSE BNBEST'S ILLEGAL HERE, AND I HAD TRAVEL POINTS BURNING A HOLE IN MY POCKET.
WELL, I'LL GET THE NEXT PLACE.
NEXT PLACE?
THAT WAS PRESUMPTUOUS. I JUST MEANT, UH--
HEY, WANNA CHECK OUT THE HAWKERS* AND TORTURE ME WITH FISH-HEAD CURRY?
*FOOD COURTS WITH DOZENS OF FOOD STALLS FEATURING ALL KINDS OF FOOD AND DESSERTS.
CAN'T. I'VE GOT AN APPOINTMENT WITH SOME RARE BOOKS AT THE REFERENCE LIBRARY.

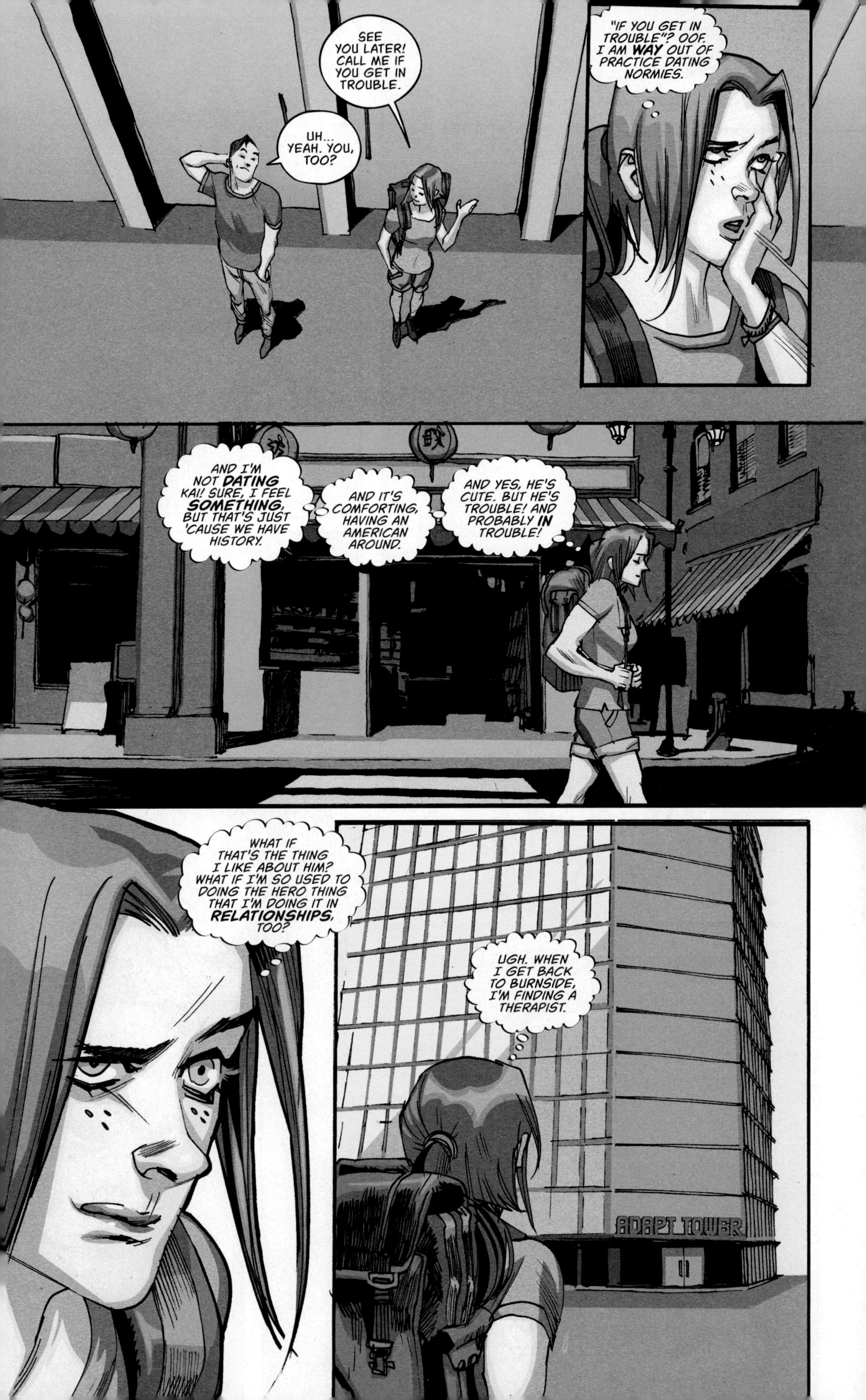
SEE YOU LATER! CALL ME IF YOU GET IN TROUBLE.
UH... YEAH. YOU, TOO?
"IF YOU GET IN TROUBLE"? OOF. I AM WAY OUT OF PRACTICE DATING NORMIES.
AND I'M NOT DATING KAI! SURE, I FEEL SOMETHING, BUT THAT'S JUST 'CAUSE WE HAVE HISTORY.
AND IT'S COMFORTING, HAVING AN AMERICAN AROUND.
AND YES, HE'S CUTE. BUT HE'S TROUBLE! AND PROBABLY IN TROUBLE!
WHAT IF THAT'S THE THING I LIKE ABOUT HIM? WHAT IF I'M SO USED TO DOING THE HERO THING THAT I'M DOING IT IN RELATIONSHIPS, TOO?
UGH. WHEN I GET BACK TO BURNSIDE, I'M FINDING A THERAPIST.
ADAPT TOWER

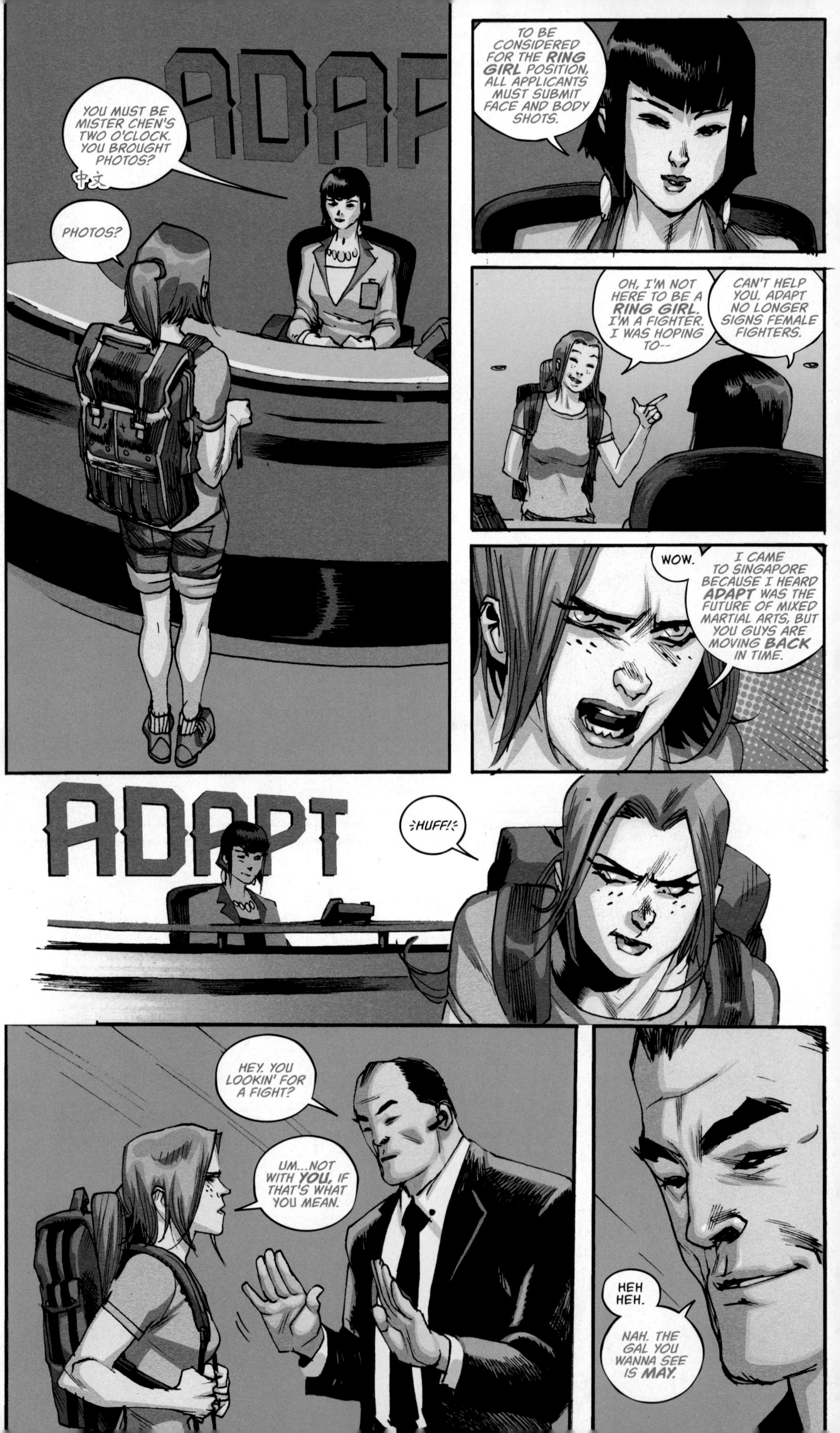
ADAPT
YOU MUST BE MISTER CHEN'S TWO O'CLOCK. YOU BROUGHT PHOTOS?
中文
PHOTOS?
TO BE CONSIDERED FOR THE RING GIRL POSITION, ALL APPLICANTS MUST SUBMIT FACE AND BODY SHOTS.
OH, I'M NOT HERE TO BE A RING GIRL. I'M A FIGHTER. I WAS HOPING TO--
CAN'T HELP YOU. ADAPT NO LONGER SIGNS FEMALE FIGHTERS.
WOW.
I CAME TO SINGAPORE BECAUSE I HEARD ADAPT WAS THE FUTURE OF MIXED MARTIAL ARTS, BUT YOU GUYS ARE MOVING BACK IN TIME.
ADAPT
HUFF!
HEY. YOU LOOKIN' FOR A FIGHT?
UM...NOT WITH YOU, IF THAT'S WHAT YOU MEAN.
HEH HEH.
NAH. THE GAL YOU WANNA SEE IS MAY.

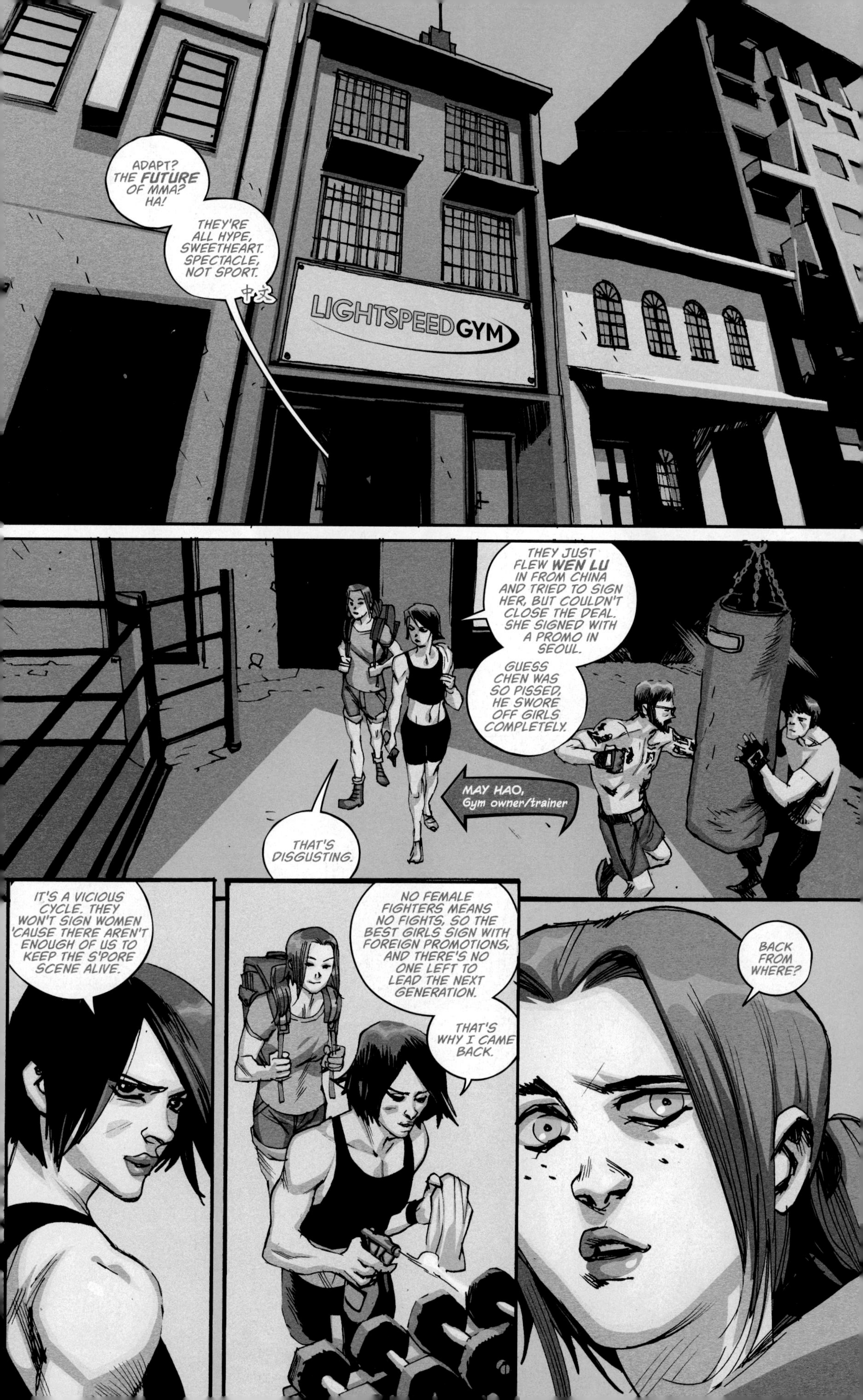
ADAPT? THE FUTURE OF MMA? HA!
THEY'RE ALL HYPE, SWEETHEART. SPECTACLE, NOT SPORT.
中文
LIGHTSPEED GYM
THEY JUST FLEW WEN LU IN FROM CHINA AND TRIED TO SIGN HER, BUT COULDN'T CLOSE THE DEAL. SHE SIGNED WITH A PROMO IN SEOUL.
GUESS CHEN WAS SO PISSED, HE SWORE OFF GIRLS COMPLETELY.
THAT'S DISGUSTING.
MAY HAO, Gym owner/trainer
IT'S A VICIOUS CYCLE. THEY WON'T SIGN WOMEN 'CAUSE THERE AREN'T ENOUGH OF US TO KEEP THE S'PORE SCENE ALIVE.
NO FEMALE FIGHTERS MEANS NO FIGHTS, SO THE BEST GIRLS SIGN WITH FOREIGN PROMOTIONS, AND THERE'S NO ONE LEFT TO LEAD THE NEXT GENERATION.
THAT'S WHY I CAME BACK.
BACK FROM WHERE?

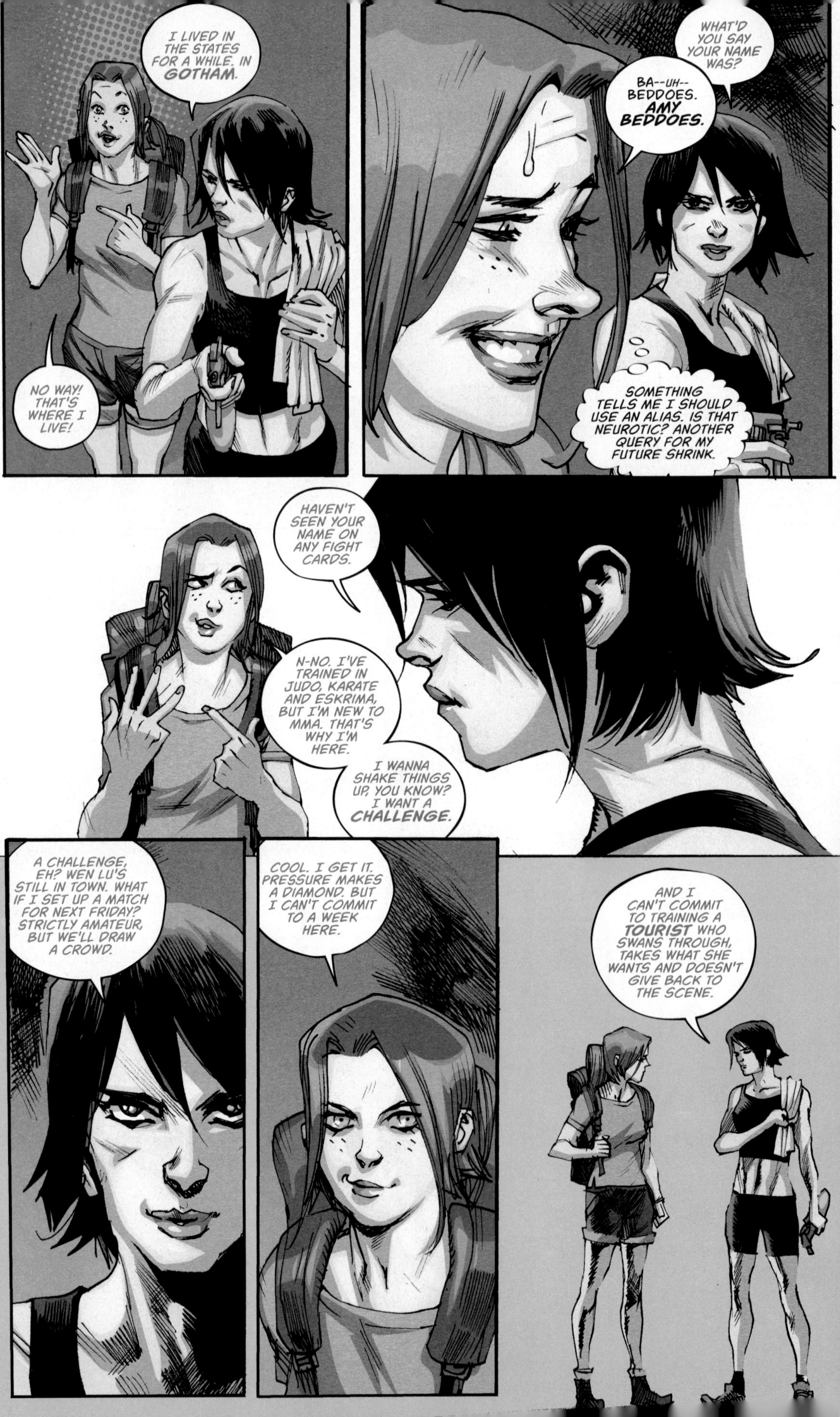
I LIVED IN THE STATES FOR A WHILE. IN GOTHAM.
NO WAY! THAT'S WHERE I LIVE!
WHAT'D YOU SAY YOUR NAME WAS?
BA--UH-- BEDDOES. AMY BEDDOES.
SOMETHING TELLS ME I SHOULD USE AN ALIAS. IS THAT NEUROTIC? ANOTHER QUERY FOR MY FUTURE SHRINK.
HAVEN'T SEEN YOUR NAME ON ANY FIGHT CARDS.
N-NO. I'VE TRAINED IN JUDO, KARATE AND ESKRIMA, BUT I'M NEW TO MMA. THAT'S WHY I'M HERE.
I WANNA SHAKE THINGS UP, YOU KNOW? I WANT A CHALLENGE.
A CHALLENGE, EH? WEN LU'S STILL IN TOWN. WHAT IF I SET UP A MATCH FOR NEXT FRIDAY? STRICTLY AMATEUR, BUT WE'LL DRAW A CROWD.
COOL. I GET IT. PRESSURE MAKES A DIAMOND. BUT I CAN'T COMMIT TO A WEEK HERE.
AND I CAN'T COMMIT TO TRAINING A TOURIST WHO SWANS THROUGH, TAKES WHAT SHE WANTS AND DOESN'T GIVE BACK TO THE SCENE.

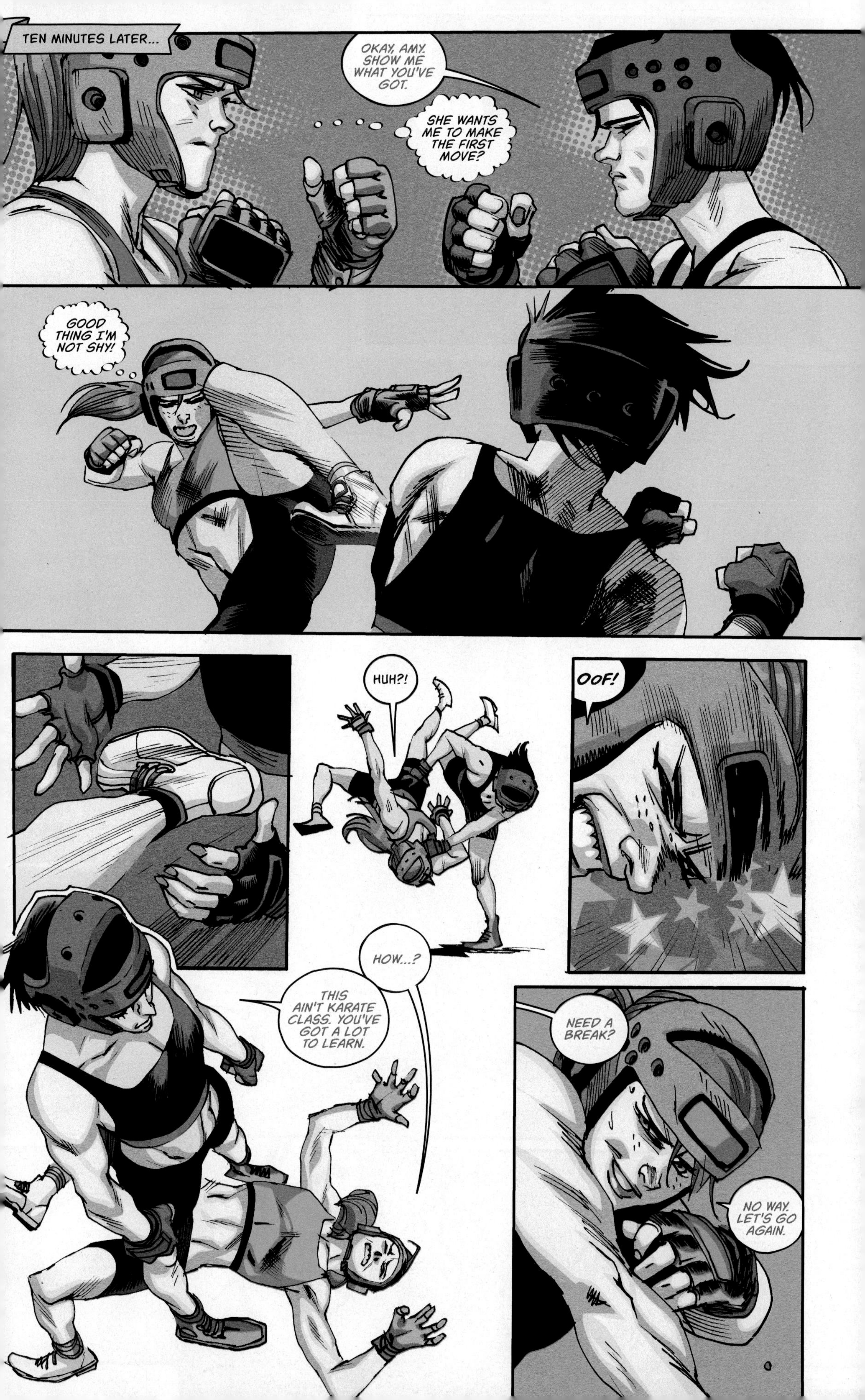

TEN MINUTES LATER...
OKAY, AMY. SHOW ME WHAT YOU'VE GOT.
SHE WANTS ME TO MAKE THE FIRST MOVE?
GOOD THING I'M NOT SHY!
HUH?!
OOF!
HOW...?
THIS AIN'T KARATE CLASS. YOU'VE GOT A LOT TO LEARN.
NEED A BREAK?
NO WAY. LET'S GO AGAIN.

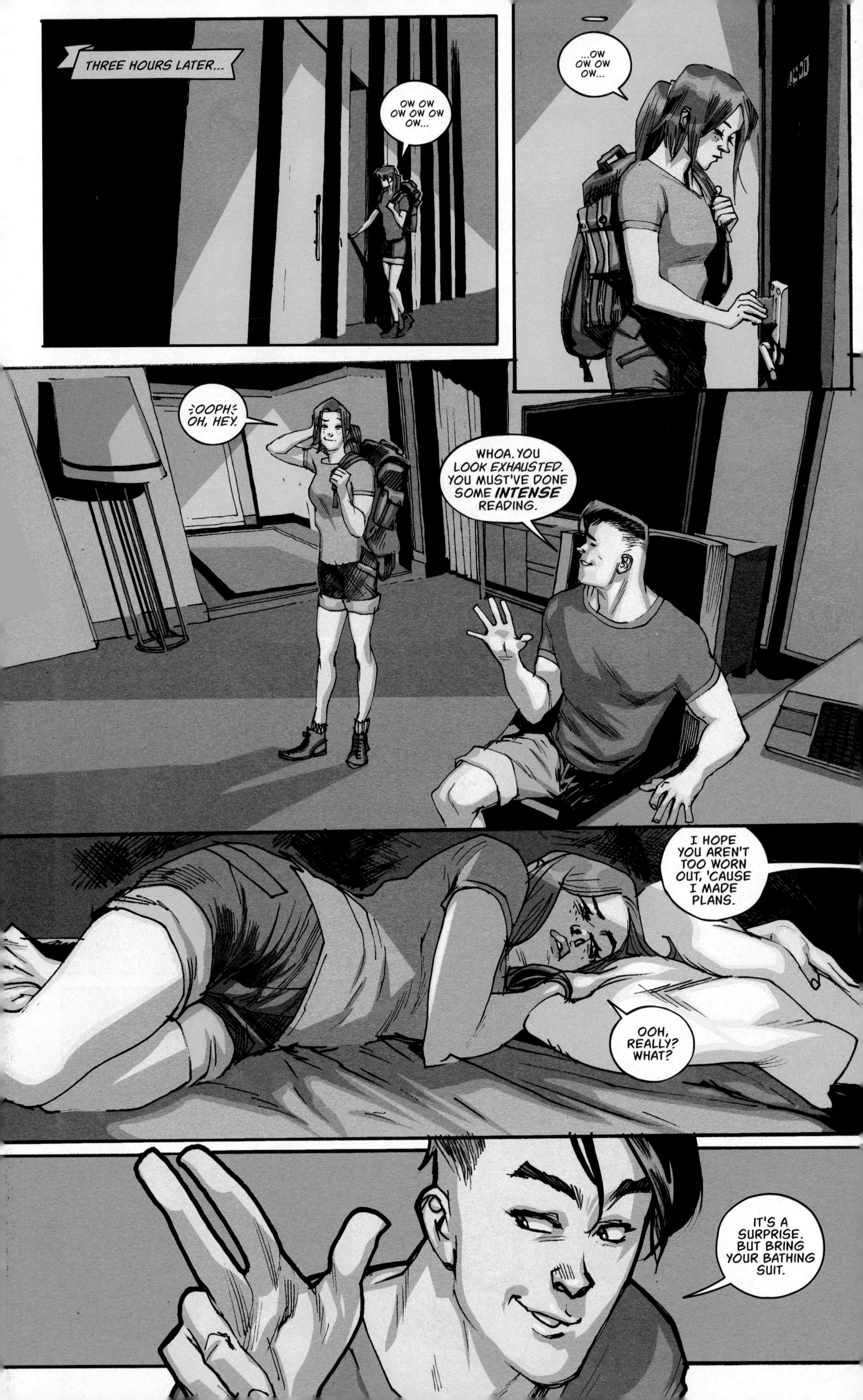
THREE HOURS LATER...
OW OW OW OW OW OW...
...OW OW OW OW...
OOPH OH, HEY.
WHOA. YOU LOOK EXHAUSTED. YOU MUST'VE DONE SOME **INTENSE** READING.
I HOPE YOU AREN'T TOO WORN OUT, 'CAUSE I MADE PLANS.
OOH, REALLY? WHAT?
IT'S A SURPRISE. BUT BRING YOUR BATHING SUIT.

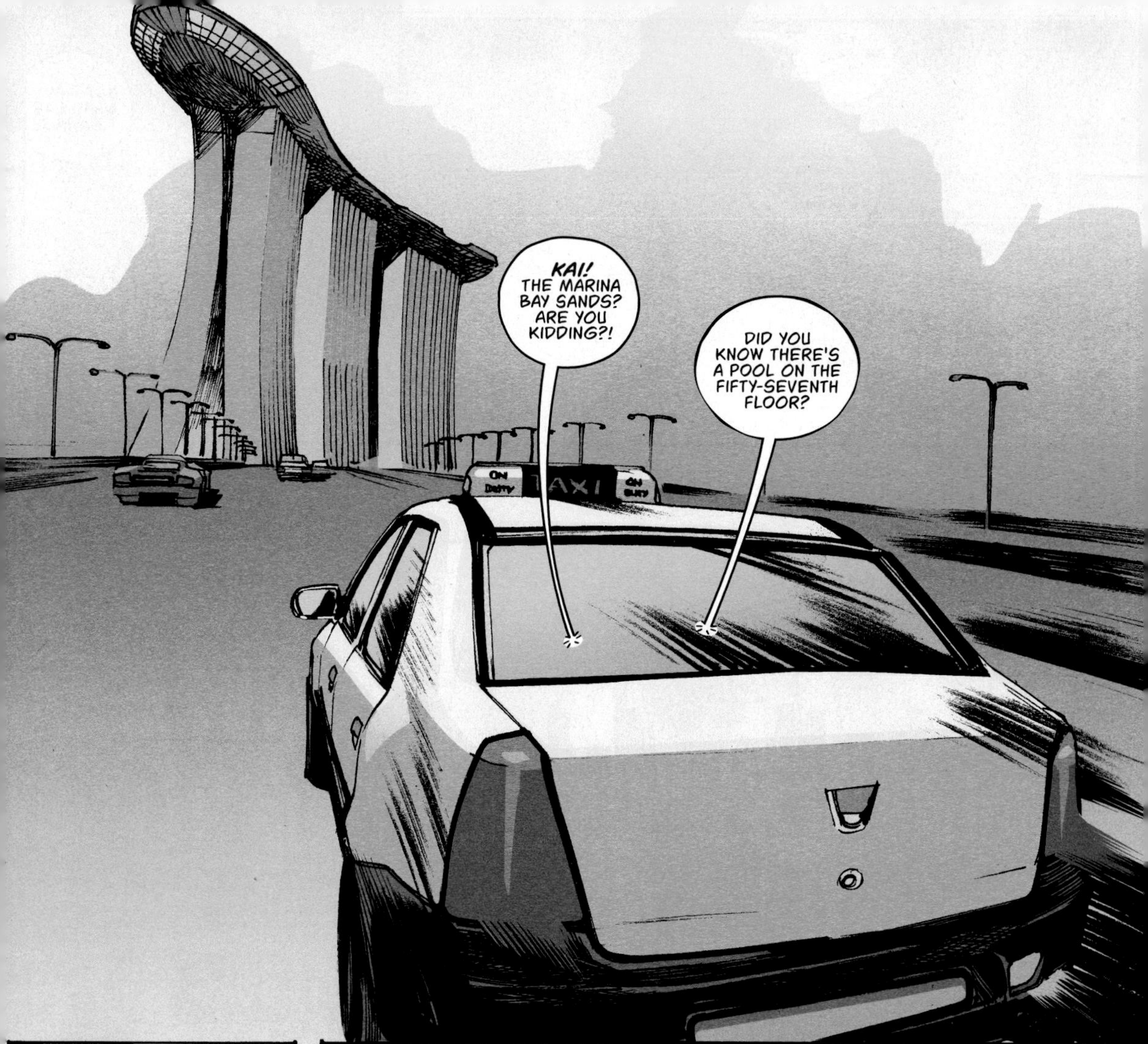
ON DUTY
TAXI
ON DUTY
KAI! THE MARINA BAY SANDS? ARE YOU KIDDING?!
DID YOU KNOW THERE'S A POOL ON THE FIFTY-SEVENTH FLOOR?

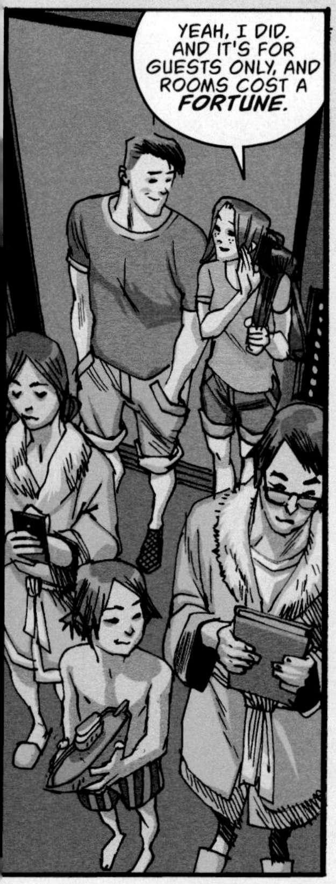
YEAH, I DID. AND IT'S FOR GUESTS ONLY, AND ROOMS COST A **FORTUNE.**

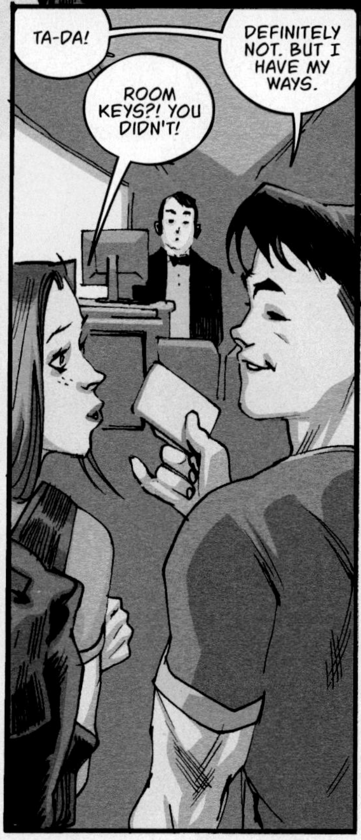
TA-DA!
ROOM KEYS?! YOU DIDN'T!
DEFINITELY NOT. BUT I HAVE MY WAYS.

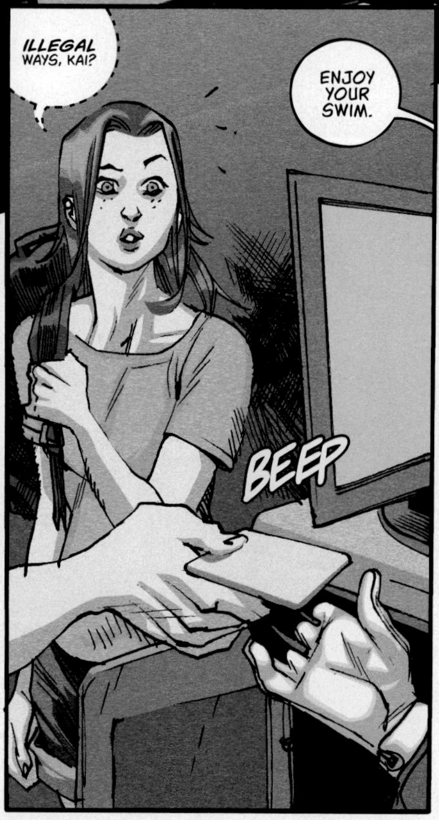
*ILLEGAL* WAYS, KAI?
ENJOY YOUR SWIM.
BEEP

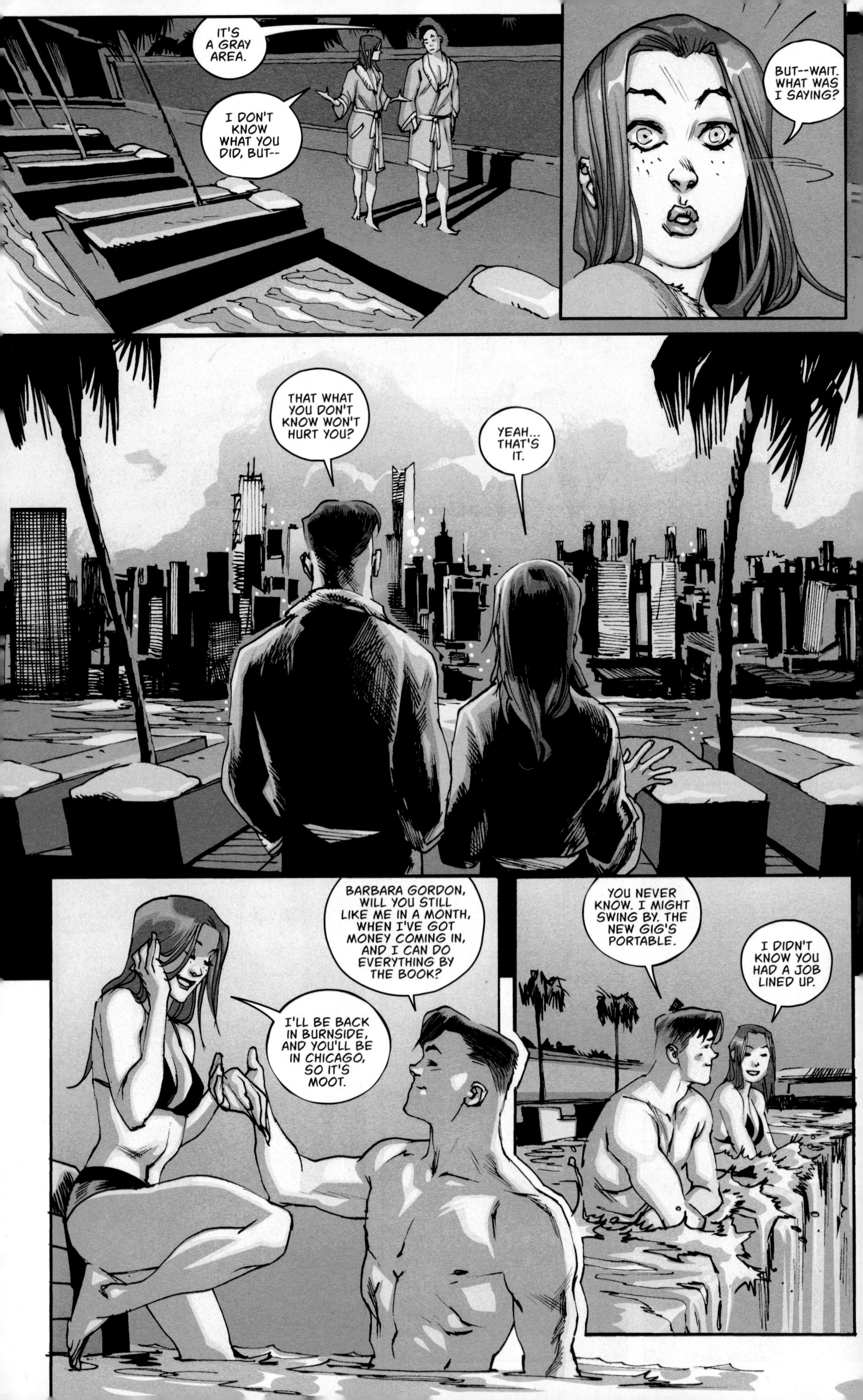
IT'S A GRAY AREA.
I DON'T KNOW WHAT YOU DID, BUT--
BUT--WAIT. WHAT WAS I SAYING?
THAT WHAT YOU DON'T KNOW WON'T HURT YOU?
YEAH... THAT'S IT.
BARBARA GORDON, WILL YOU STILL LIKE ME IN A MONTH, WHEN I'VE GOT MONEY COMING IN, AND I CAN DO EVERYTHING BY THE BOOK?
I'LL BE BACK IN BURNSIDE, AND YOU'LL BE IN CHICAGO, SO IT'S MOOT.
YOU NEVER KNOW. I MIGHT SWING BY. THE NEW GIG'S PORTABLE.
I DIDN'T KNOW YOU HAD A JOB LINED UP.

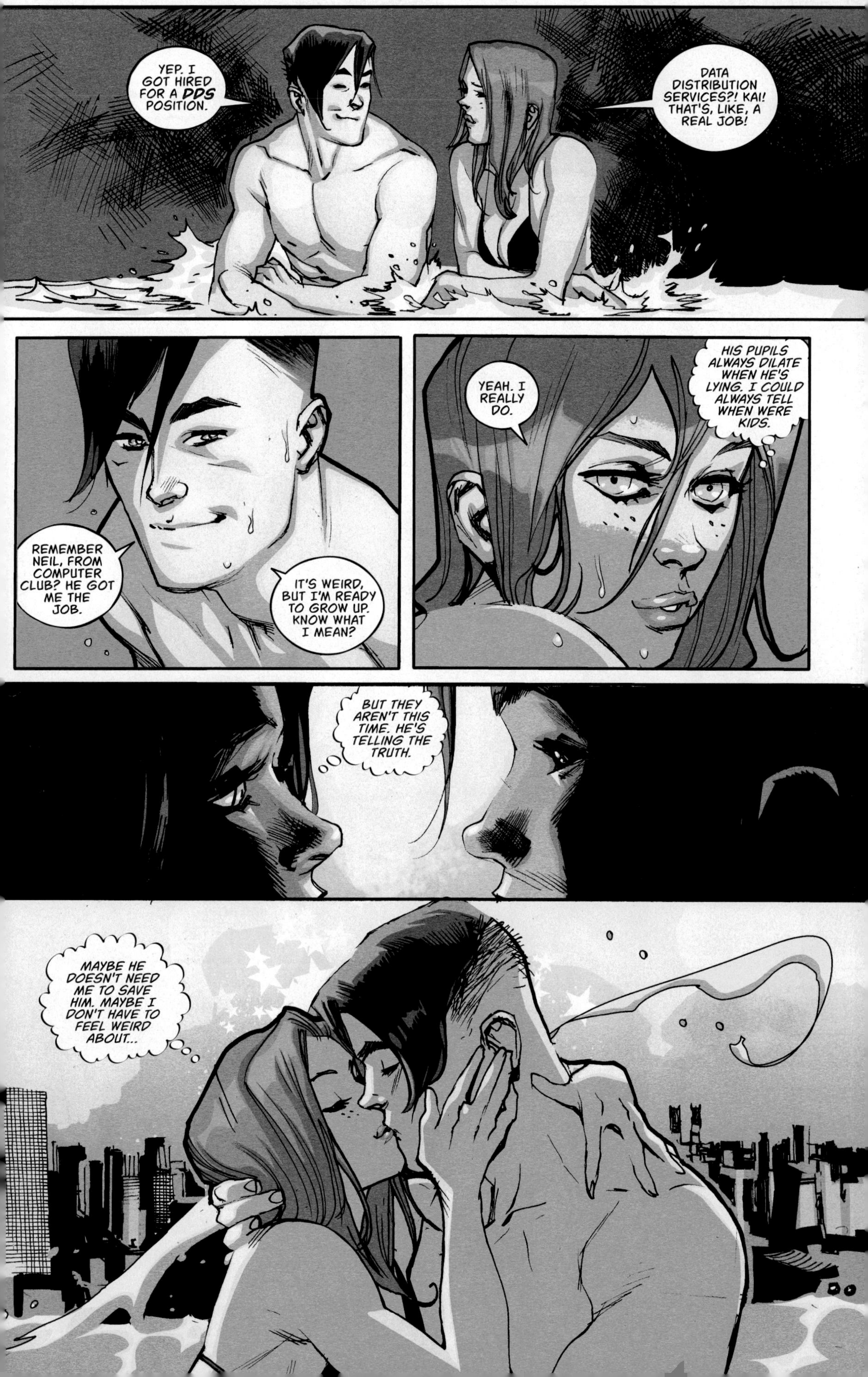
YEP. I GOT HIRED FOR A DDS POSITION.
DATA DISTRIBUTION SERVICES?! KAI! THAT'S, LIKE, A REAL JOB!
REMEMBER NEIL, FROM COMPUTER CLUB? HE GOT ME THE JOB.
IT'S WEIRD, BUT I'M READY TO GROW UP. KNOW WHAT I MEAN?
YEAH. I REALLY DO.
HIS PUPILS ALWAYS DILATE WHEN HE'S LYING. I COULD ALWAYS TELL WHEN WERE KIDS.
BUT THEY AREN'T THIS TIME. HE'S TELLING THE TRUTH.
MAYBE HE DOESN'T NEED ME TO SAVE HIM. MAYBE I DON'T HAVE TO FEEL WEIRD ABOUT...

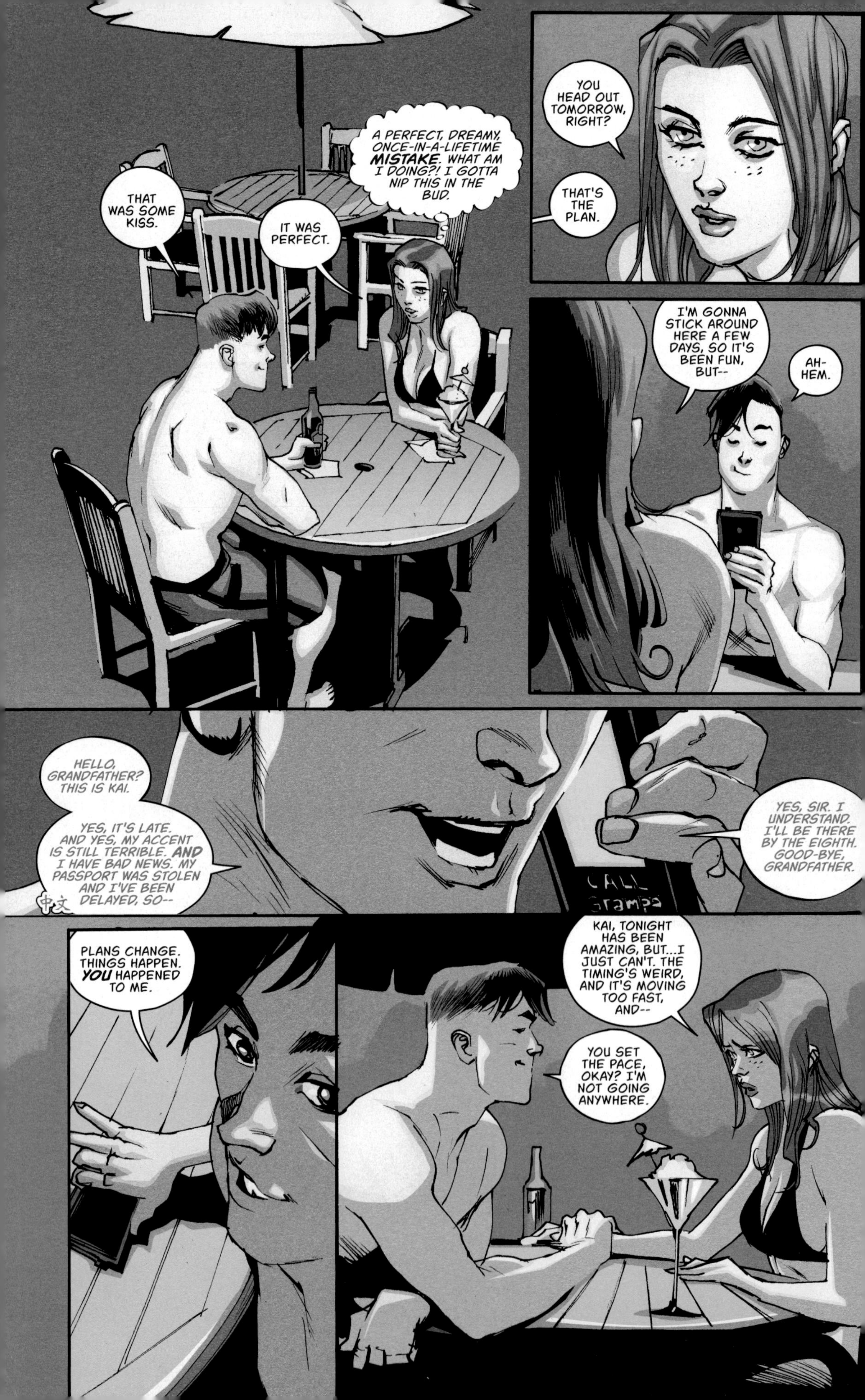
THAT WAS SOME KISS.
IT WAS PERFECT.
A PERFECT, DREAMY, ONCE-IN-A-LIFETIME MISTAKE. WHAT AM I DOING?! I GOTTA NIP THIS IN THE BUD.
YOU HEAD OUT TOMORROW, RIGHT?
THAT'S THE PLAN.
I'M GONNA STICK AROUND HERE A FEW DAYS, SO IT'S BEEN FUN, BUT--
AH-HEM.
HELLO, GRANDFATHER? THIS IS KAI.
YES, IT'S LATE. AND YES, MY ACCENT IS STILL TERRIBLE. AND I HAVE BAD NEWS. MY PASSPORT WAS STOLEN AND I'VE BEEN DELAYED, SO--
中文
CALL Gramps
YES, SIR. I UNDERSTAND. I'LL BE THERE BY THE EIGHTH. GOOD-BYE, GRANDFATHER.
PLANS CHANGE. THINGS HAPPEN. YOU HAPPENED TO ME.
KAI, TONIGHT HAS BEEN AMAZING, BUT...I JUST CAN'T. THE TIMING'S WEIRD, AND IT'S MOVING TOO FAST, AND--
YOU SET THE PACE, OKAY? I'M NOT GOING ANYWHERE.

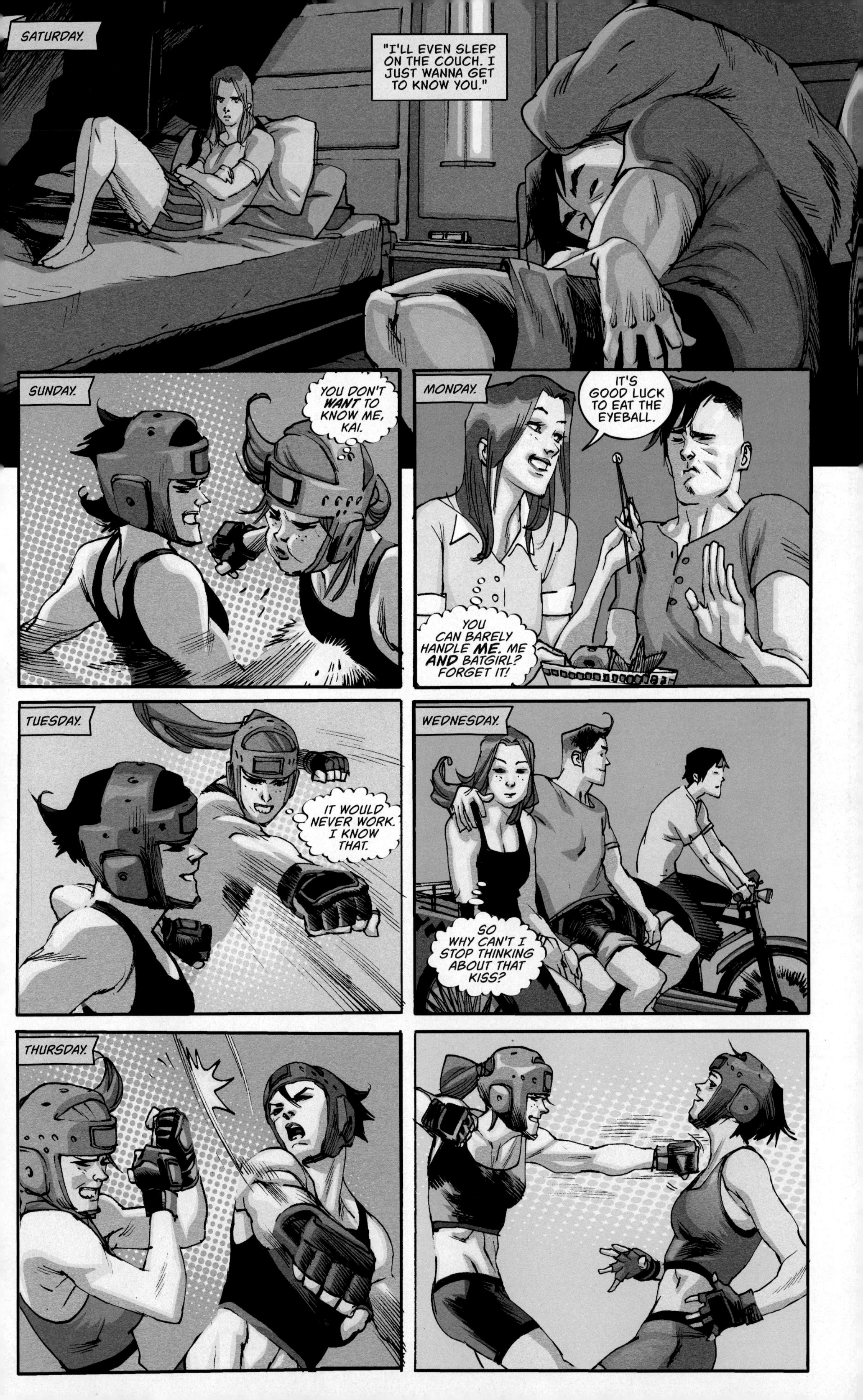
SATURDAY.
"I'LL EVEN SLEEP ON THE COUCH. I JUST WANNA GET TO KNOW YOU."
SUNDAY.
YOU DON'T WANT TO KNOW ME, KAI.
MONDAY.
IT'S GOOD LUCK TO EAT THE EYEBALL.
YOU CAN BARELY HANDLE ME. ME AND BATGIRL? FORGET IT!
TUESDAY.
IT WOULD NEVER WORK. I KNOW THAT.
WEDNESDAY.
SO WHY CAN'T I STOP THINKING ABOUT THAT KISS?
THURSDAY.

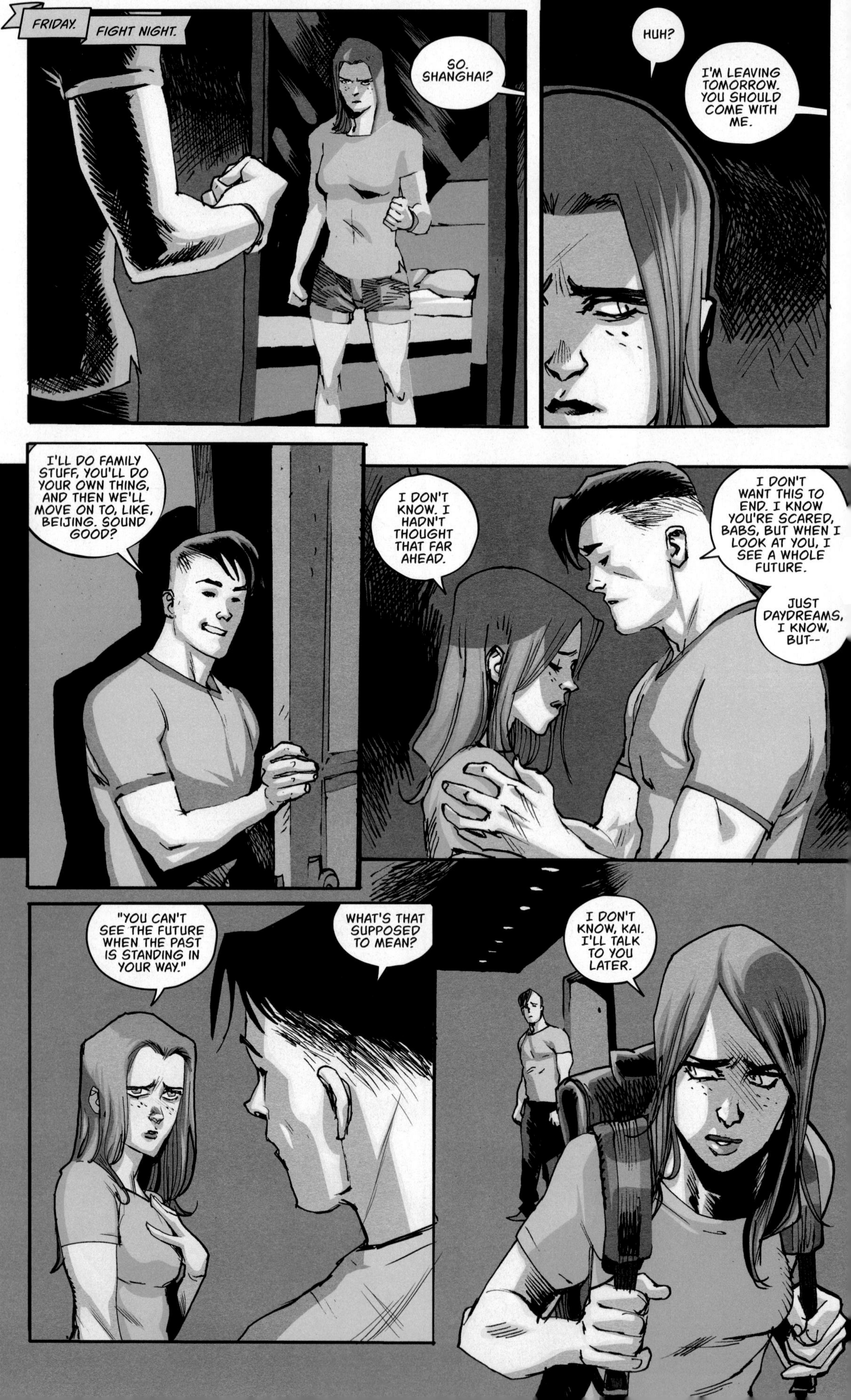

FRIDAY.
FIGHT NIGHT.
SO. SHANGHAI?
HUH?
I'M LEAVING TOMORROW. YOU SHOULD COME WITH ME.
I'LL DO FAMILY STUFF, YOU'LL DO YOUR OWN THING, AND THEN WE'LL MOVE ON TO, LIKE, BEIJING. SOUND GOOD?
I DON'T KNOW. I HADN'T THOUGHT THAT FAR AHEAD.
I DON'T WANT THIS TO END. I KNOW YOU'RE SCARED, BABS, BUT WHEN I LOOK AT YOU, I SEE A WHOLE FUTURE.
JUST DAYDREAMS, I KNOW, BUT--
"YOU CAN'T SEE THE FUTURE WHEN THE PAST IS STANDING IN YOUR WAY."
WHAT'S THAT SUPPOSED TO MEAN?
I DON'T KNOW, KAI. I'LL TALK TO YOU LATER.

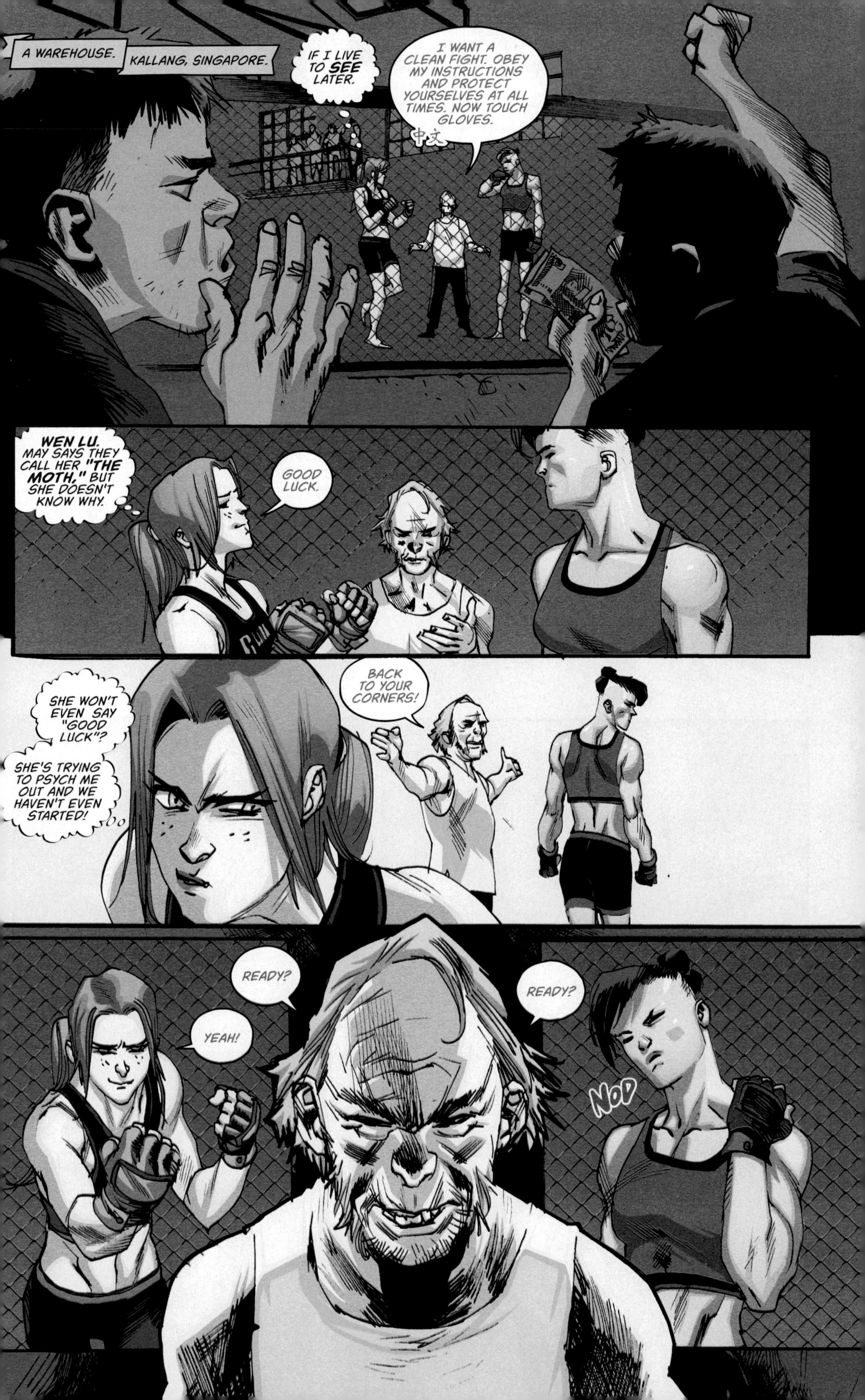
A WAREHOUSE.
KALLANG, SINGAPORE.
IF I LIVE TO SEE LATER.
I WANT A CLEAN FIGHT. OBEY MY INSTRUCTIONS AND PROTECT YOURSELVES AT ALL TIMES. NOW TOUCH GLOVES.
WEN LU. MAY SAYS THEY CALL HER "THE MOTH," BUT SHE DOESN'T KNOW WHY.
GOOD LUCK.
SHE WON'T EVEN SAY "GOOD LUCK"?
SHE'S TRYING TO PSYCH ME OUT AND WE HAVEN'T EVEN STARTED!
BACK TO YOUR CORNERS!
READY?
YEAH!
READY?
NOD

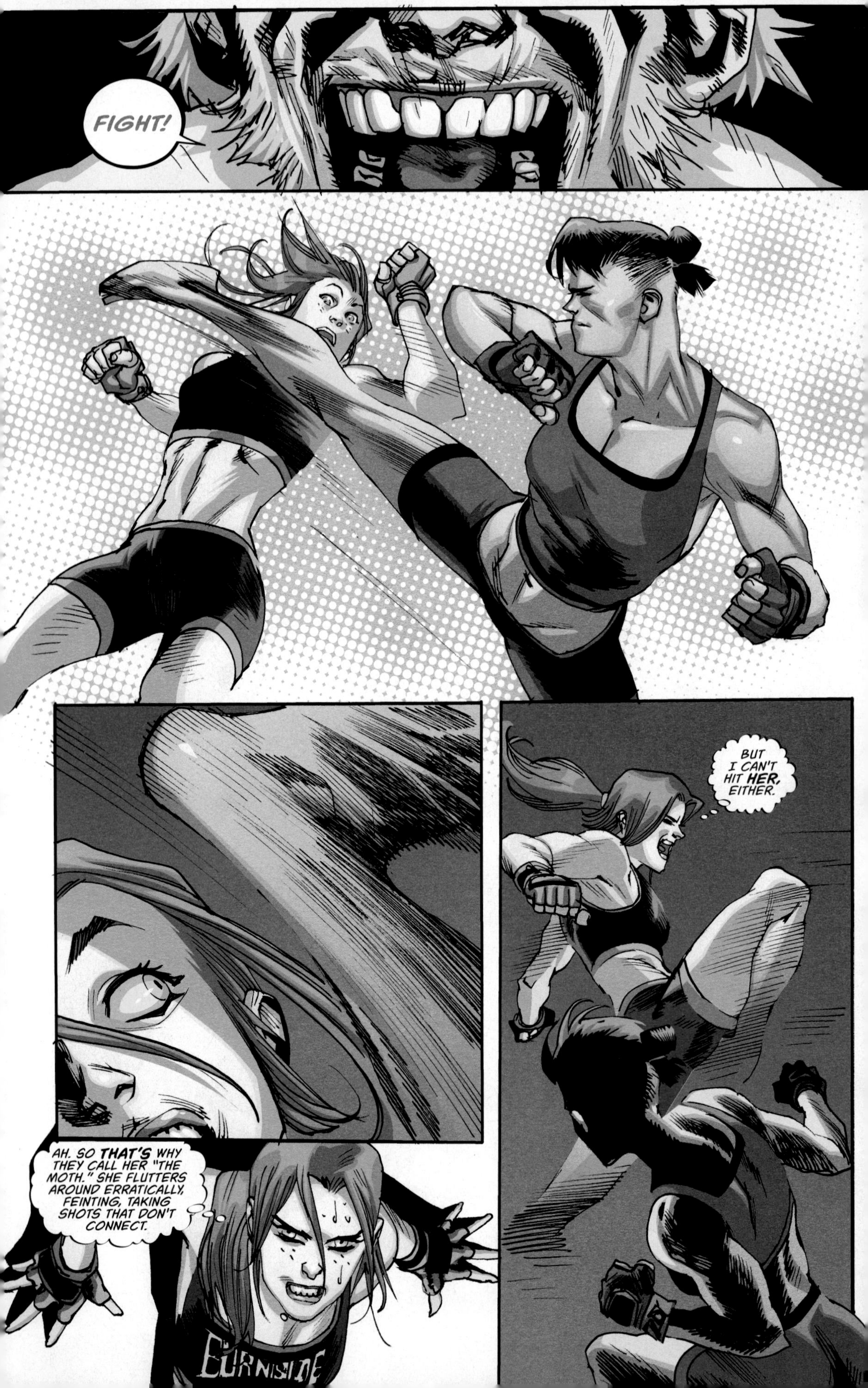
FIGHT!
BUT I CAN'T HIT HER, EITHER.
AH. SO THAT'S WHY THEY CALL HER "THE MOTH." SHE FLUTTERS AROUND ERRATICALLY, FEINTING, TAKING SHOTS THAT DON'T CONNECT.
BURNSIDE

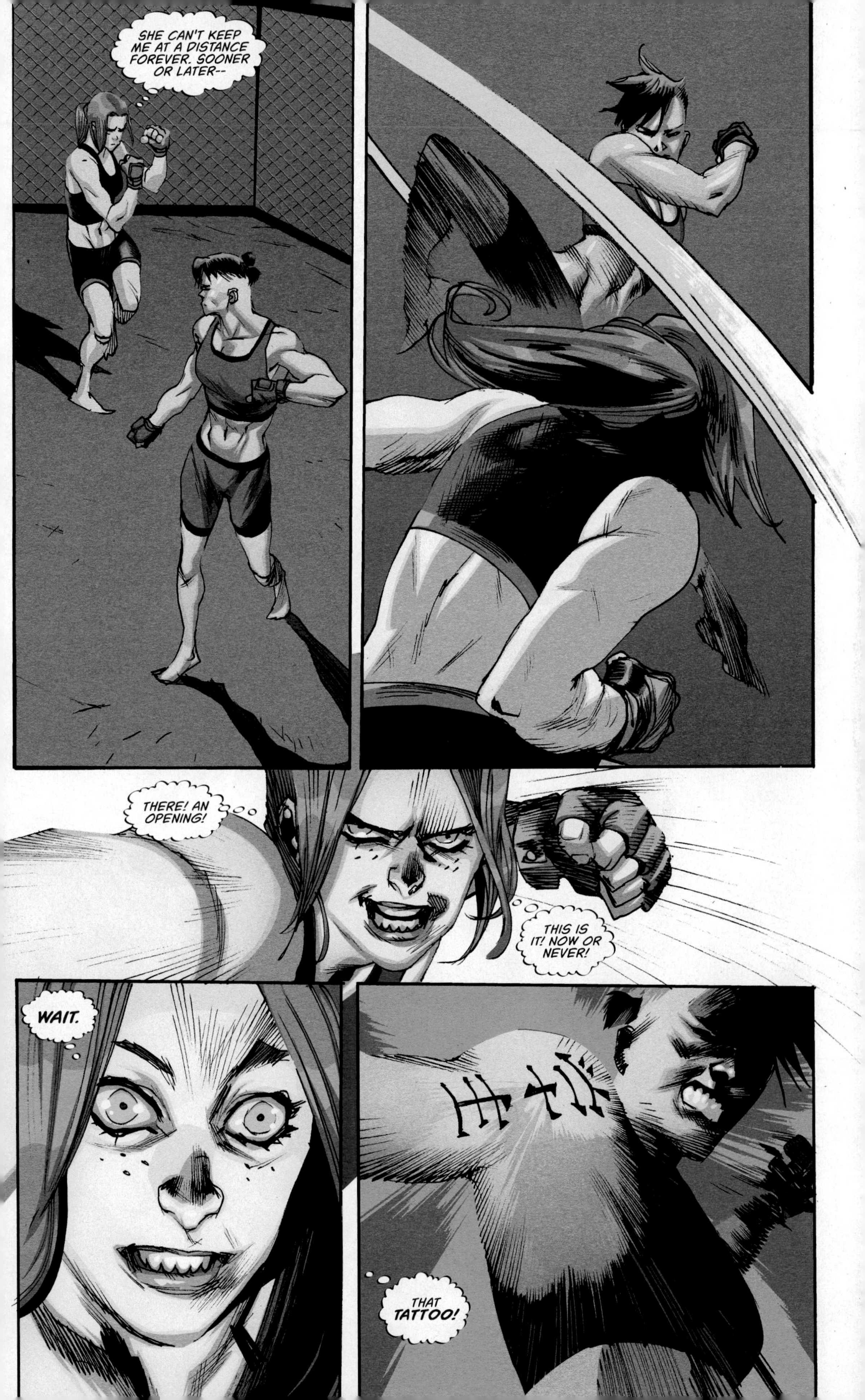
SHE CAN'T KEEP ME AT A DISTANCE FOREVER. SOONER OR LATER--
THERE! AN OPENING!
THIS IS IT! NOW OR NEVER!
WAIT.
THAT TATTOO!

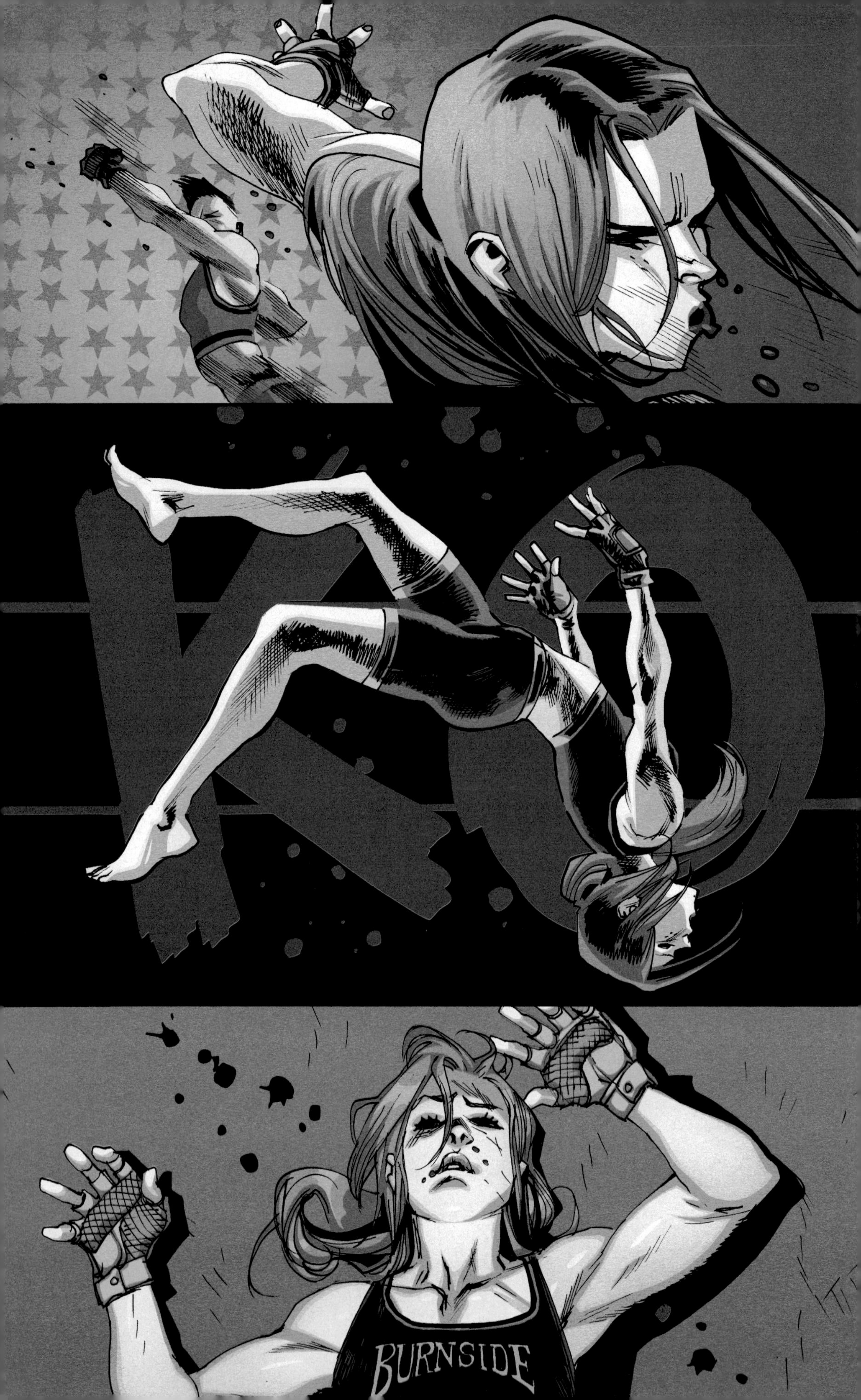
KO
BURNSIDE

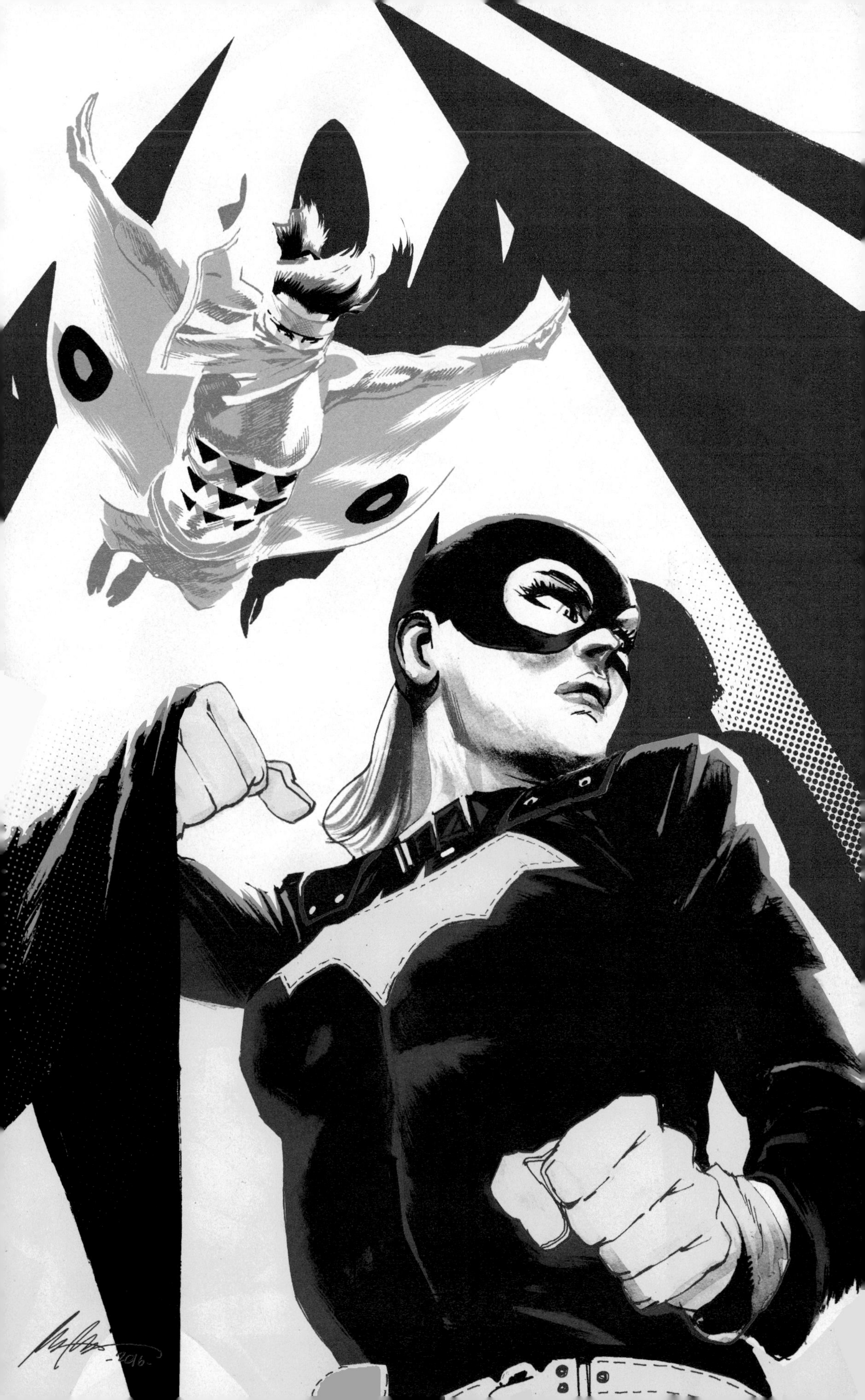

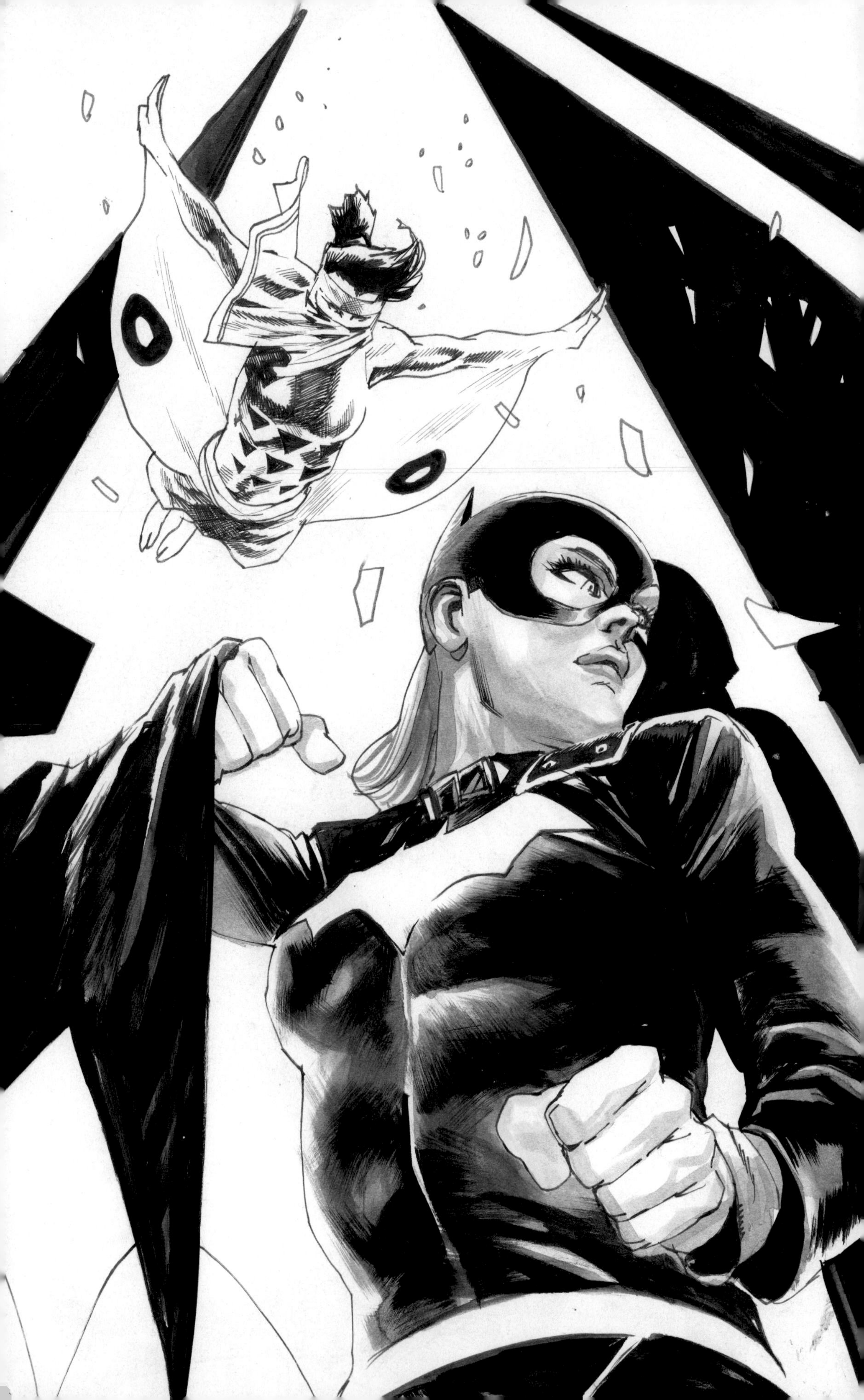

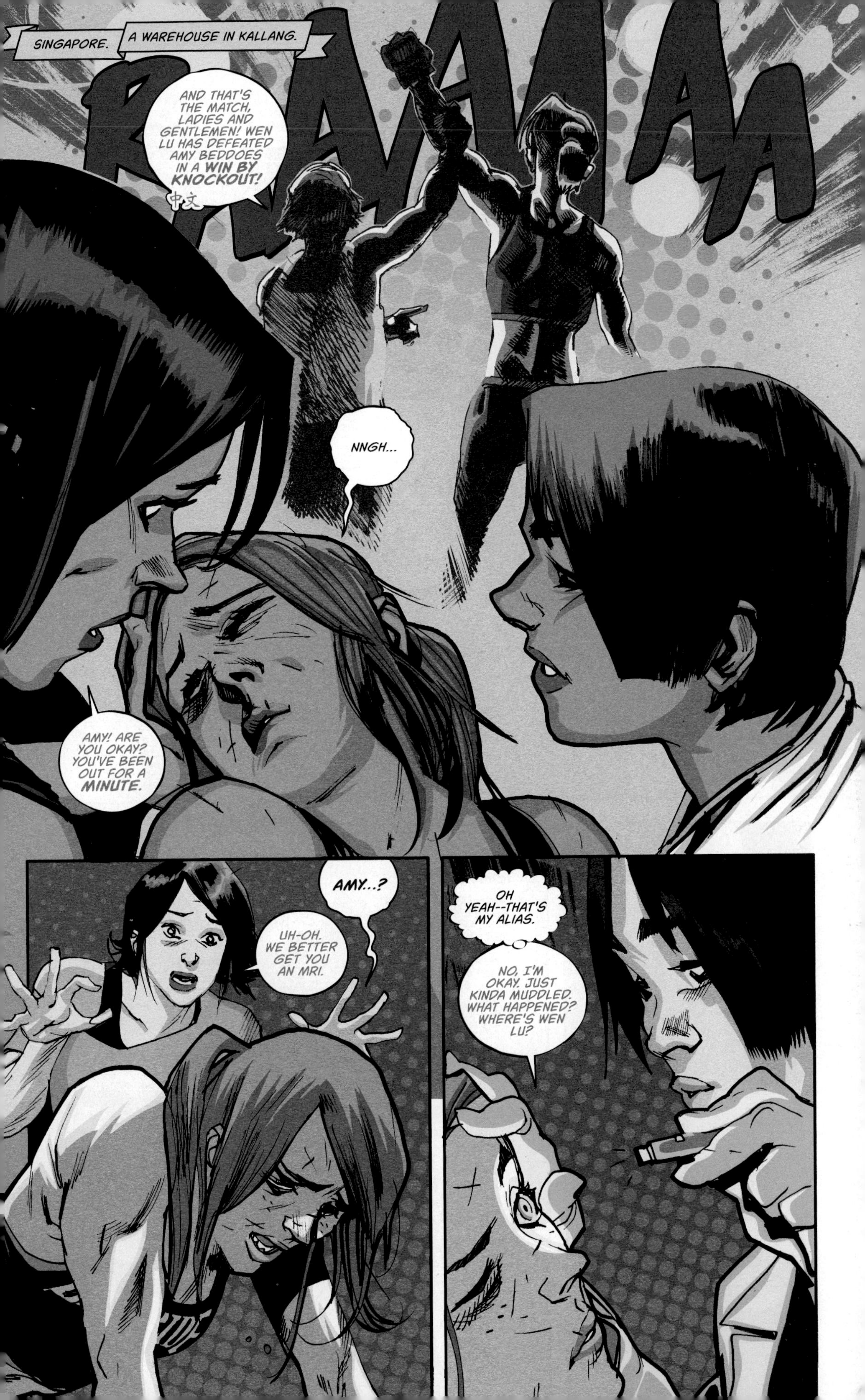
SINGAPORE.
A WAREHOUSE IN KALLANG.
AND THAT'S THE MATCH, LADIES AND GENTLEMEN! WEN LU HAS DEFEATED AMY BEDDOES IN A **WIN BY KNOCKOUT!**
中文
NNGH...
AMY! ARE YOU OKAY? YOU'VE BEEN OUT FOR A **MINUTE**.
AMY...?
UH-OH. WE BETTER GET YOU AN MRI.
OH YEAH--THAT'S MY ALIAS.
NO, I'M OKAY. JUST KINDA MUDDLED. WHAT HAPPENED? WHERE'S WEN LU?

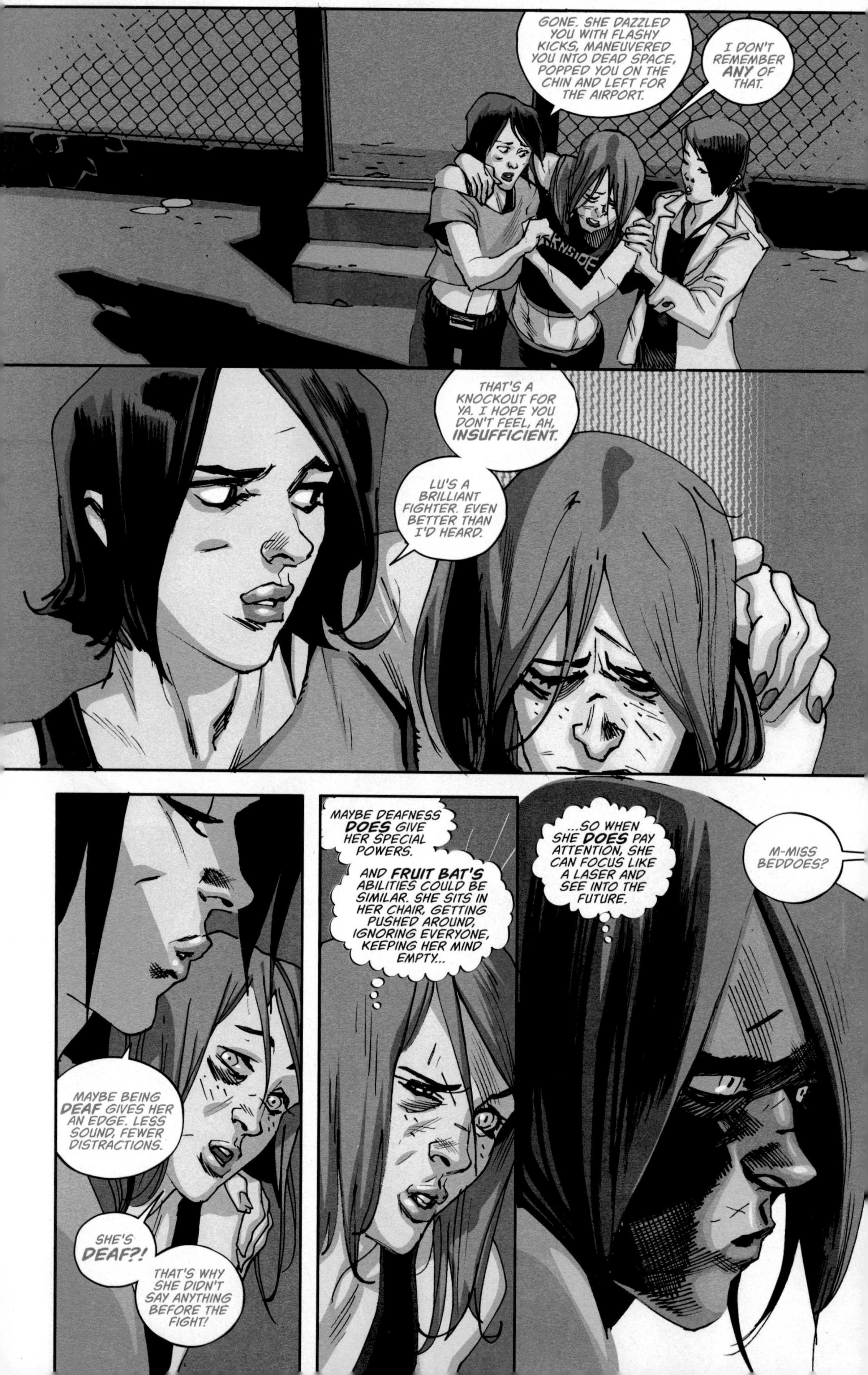
GONE. SHE DAZZLED YOU WITH FLASHY KICKS, MANEUVERED YOU INTO DEAD SPACE, POPPED YOU ON THE CHIN AND LEFT FOR THE AIRPORT.
I DON'T REMEMBER ANY OF THAT.
THAT'S A KNOCKOUT FOR YA. I HOPE YOU DON'T FEEL, AH, INSUFFICIENT.
LU'S A BRILLIANT FIGHTER. EVEN BETTER THAN I'D HEARD.
MAYBE BEING DEAF GIVES HER AN EDGE. LESS SOUND, FEWER DISTRACTIONS.
SHE'S DEAF?!
THAT'S WHY SHE DIDN'T SAY ANYTHING BEFORE THE FIGHT!
MAYBE DEAFNESS DOES GIVE HER SPECIAL POWERS.
AND FRUIT BAT'S ABILITIES COULD BE SIMILAR. SHE SITS IN HER CHAIR, GETTING PUSHED AROUND, IGNORING EVERYONE, KEEPING HER MIND EMPTY...
...SO WHEN SHE DOES PAY ATTENTION, SHE CAN FOCUS LIKE A LASER AND SEE INTO THE FUTURE.
M-MISS BEDDOES?

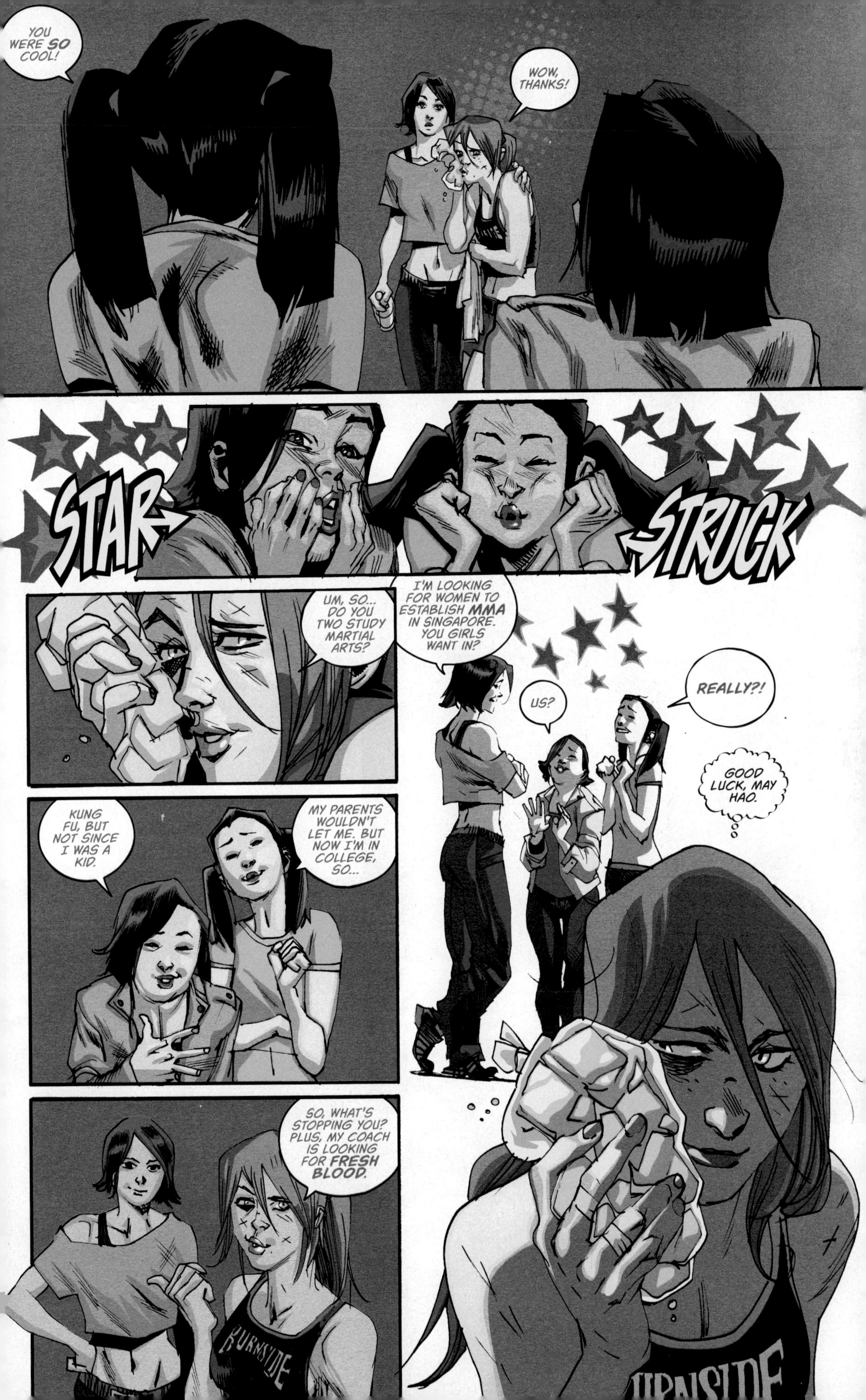
YOU WERE SO COOL!
WOW, THANKS!
STAR
STRUCK
UM, SO... DO YOU TWO STUDY MARTIAL ARTS?
KUNG FU, BUT NOT SINCE I WAS A KID.
MY PARENTS WOULDN'T LET ME. BUT NOW I'M IN COLLEGE, SO...
SO, WHAT'S STOPPING YOU? PLUS, MY COACH IS LOOKING FOR FRESH BLOOD.
I'M LOOKING FOR WOMEN TO ESTABLISH MMA IN SINGAPORE. YOU GIRLS WANT IN?
US?
REALLY?!
GOOD LUCK, MAY HAO.

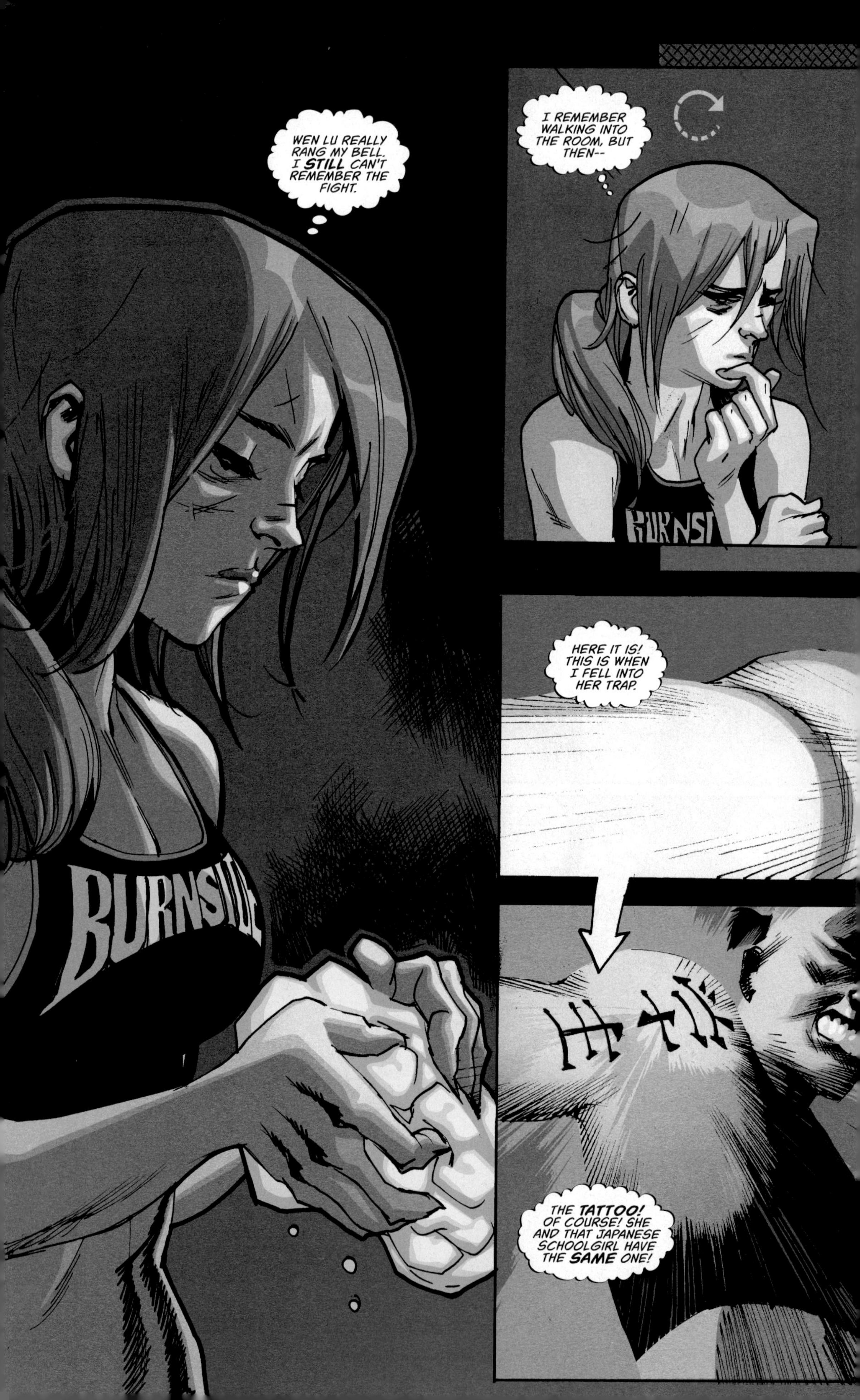
WEN LU REALLY RANG MY BELL. I STILL CAN'T REMEMBER THE FIGHT.
I REMEMBER WALKING INTO THE ROOM, BUT THEN--
BURNSI
HERE IT IS! THIS IS WHEN I FELL INTO HER TRAP.
THE TATTOO! OF COURSE! SHE AND THAT JAPANESE SCHOOLGIRL HAVE THE SAME ONE!
BURNSIDE

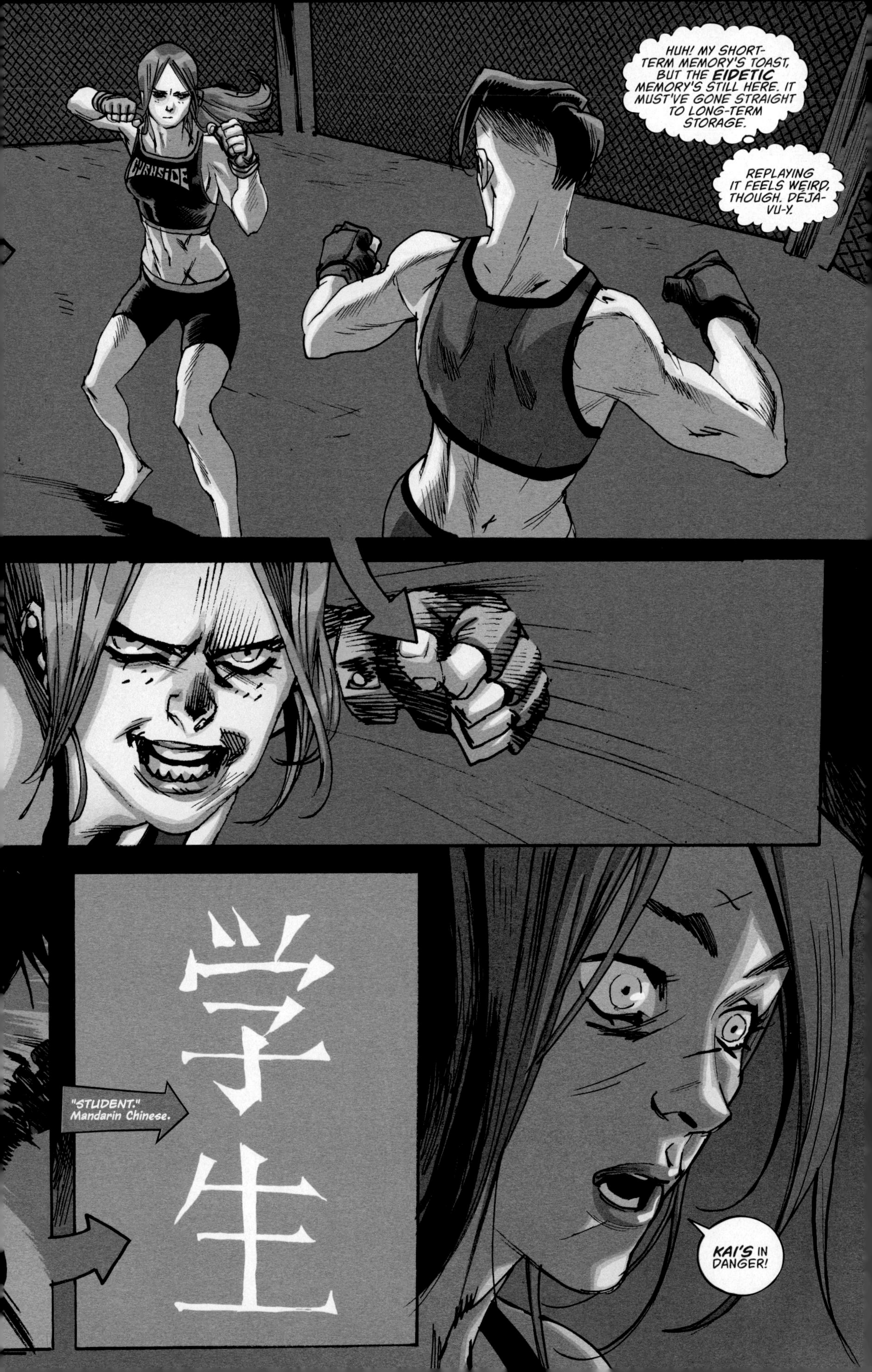

HUH! MY SHORT-TERM MEMORY'S TOAST, BUT THE EIDETIC MEMORY'S STILL HERE. IT MUST'VE GONE STRAIGHT TO LONG-TERM STORAGE.
REPLAYING IT FEELS WEIRD, THOUGH. DÉJA-VU-Y.
CURBSIDE
学生
"STUDENT." Mandarin Chinese.
KAI'S IN DANGER!

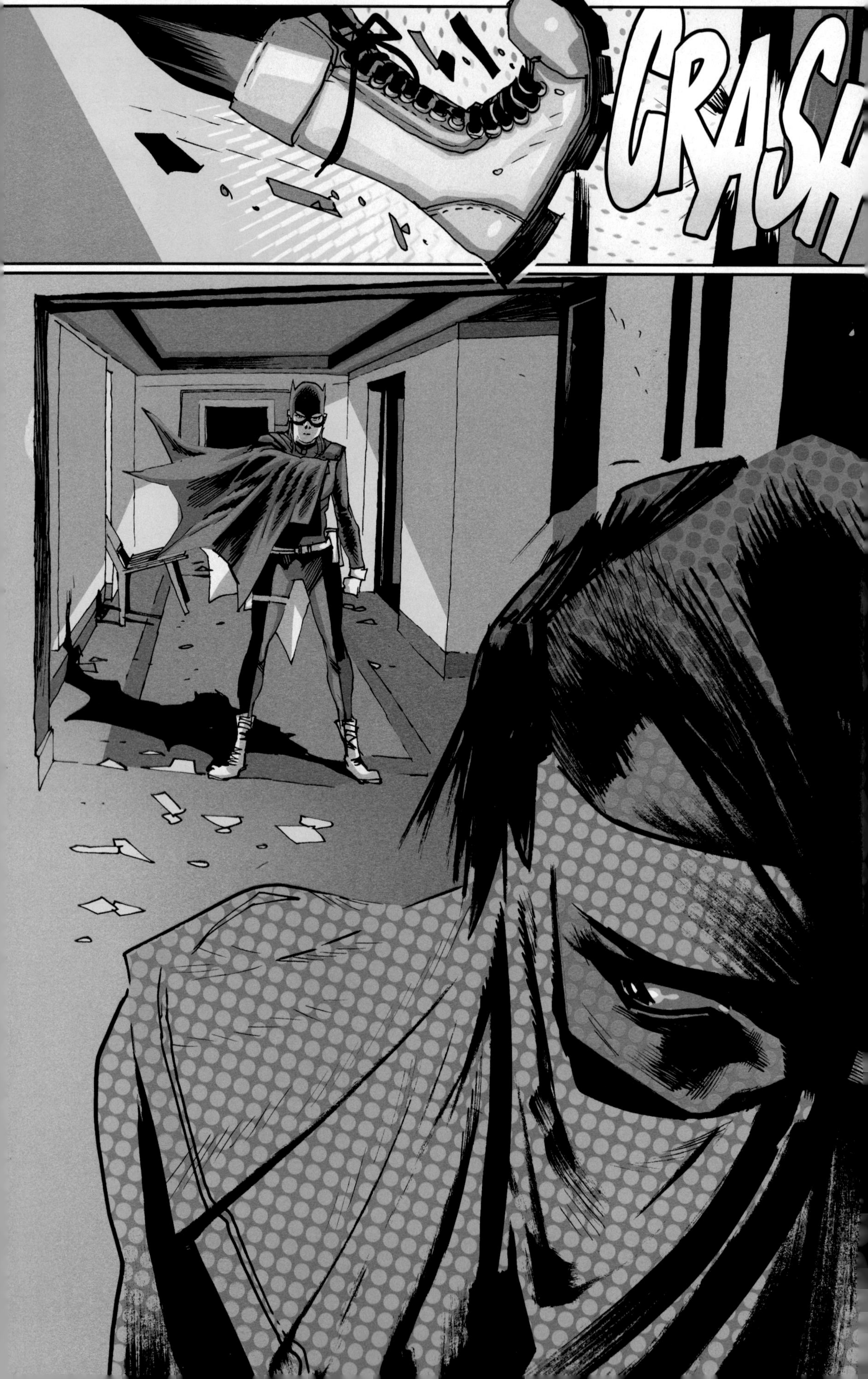
CRASH

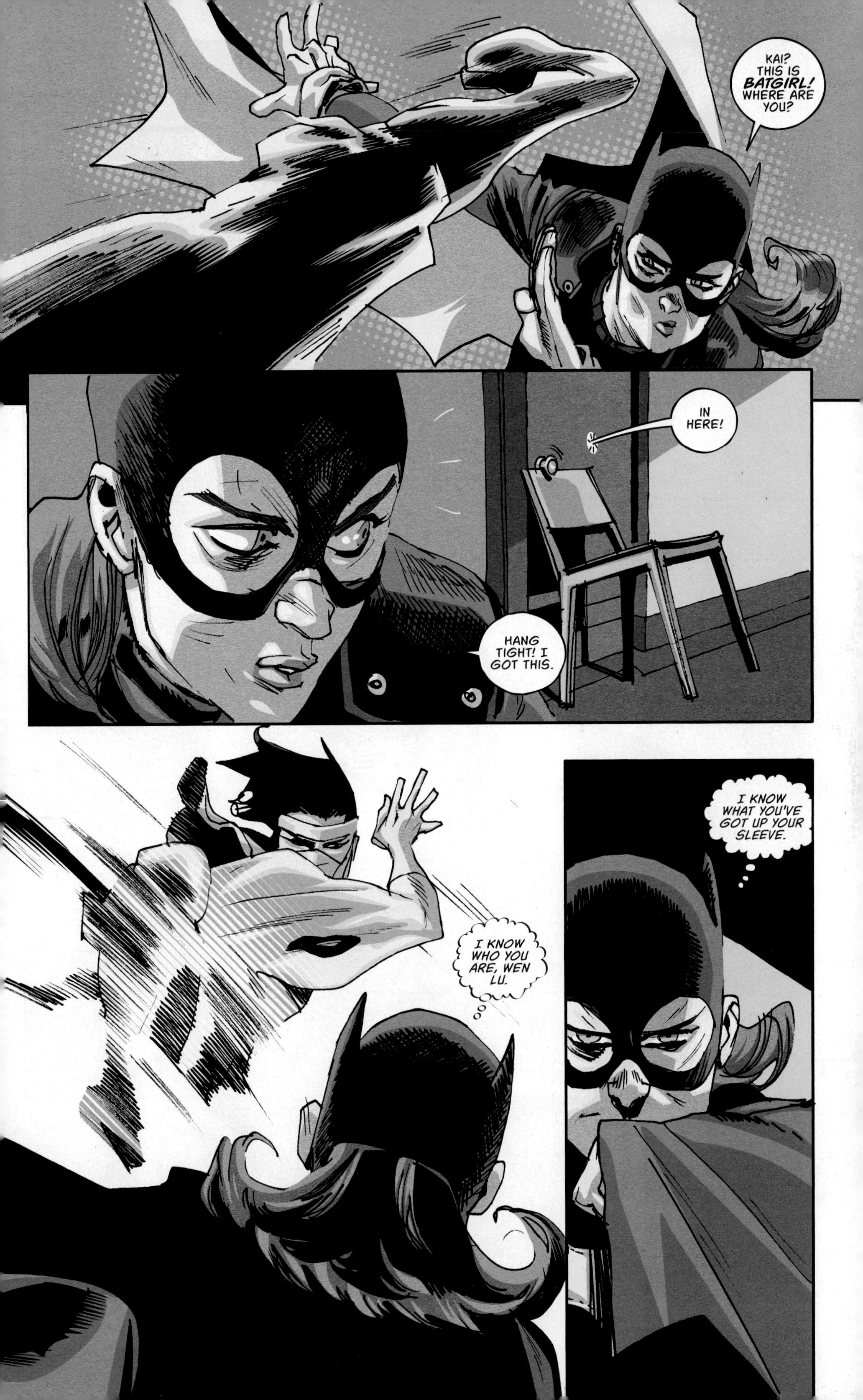
KAI? THIS IS BATGIRL! WHERE ARE YOU?
IN HERE!
HANG TIGHT! I GOT THIS.
I KNOW WHO YOU ARE, WEN LU.
I KNOW WHAT YOU'VE GOT UP YOUR SLEEVE.

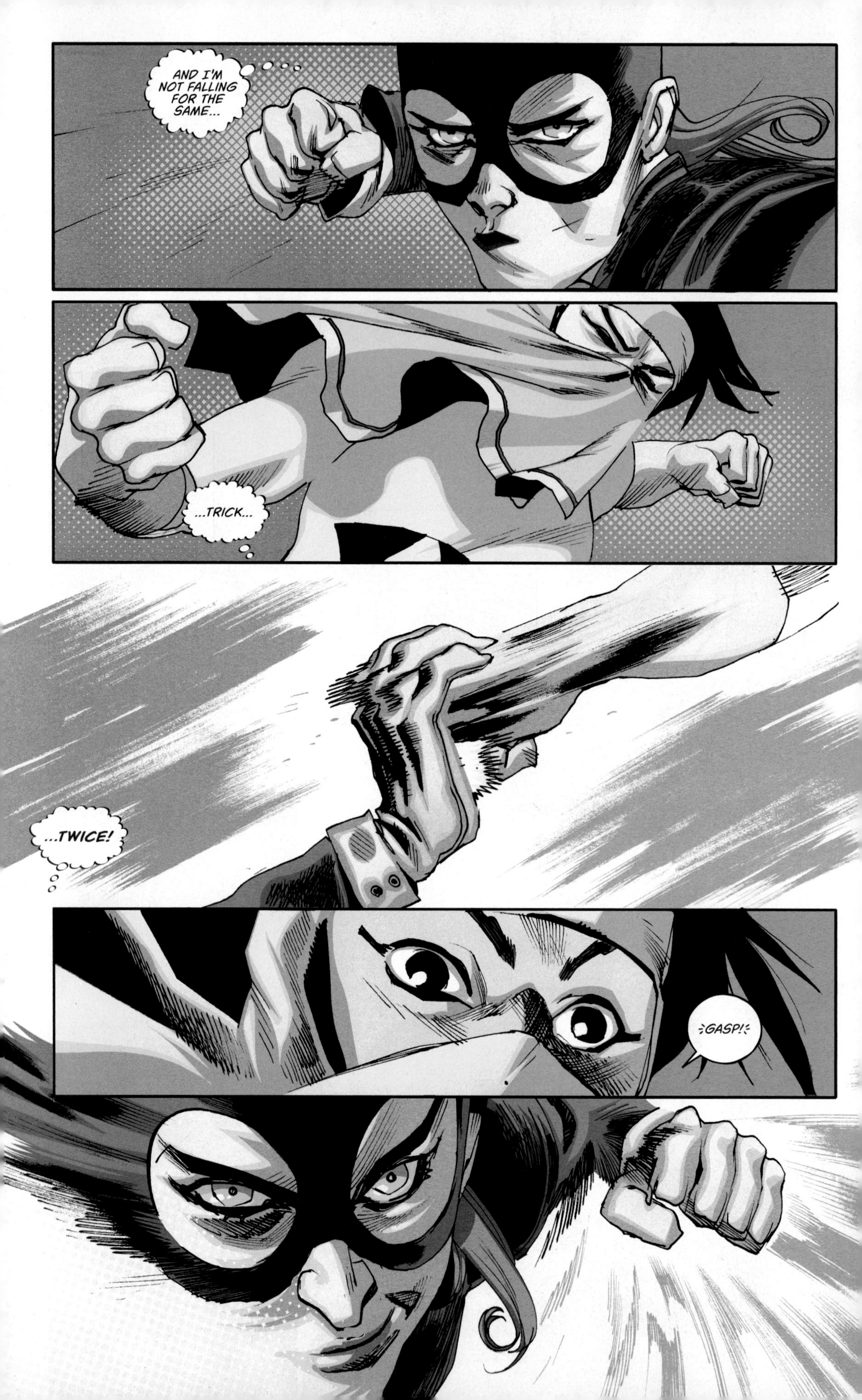
AND I'M NOT FALLING FOR THE SAME...
...TRICK...
...TWICE!
GASP!

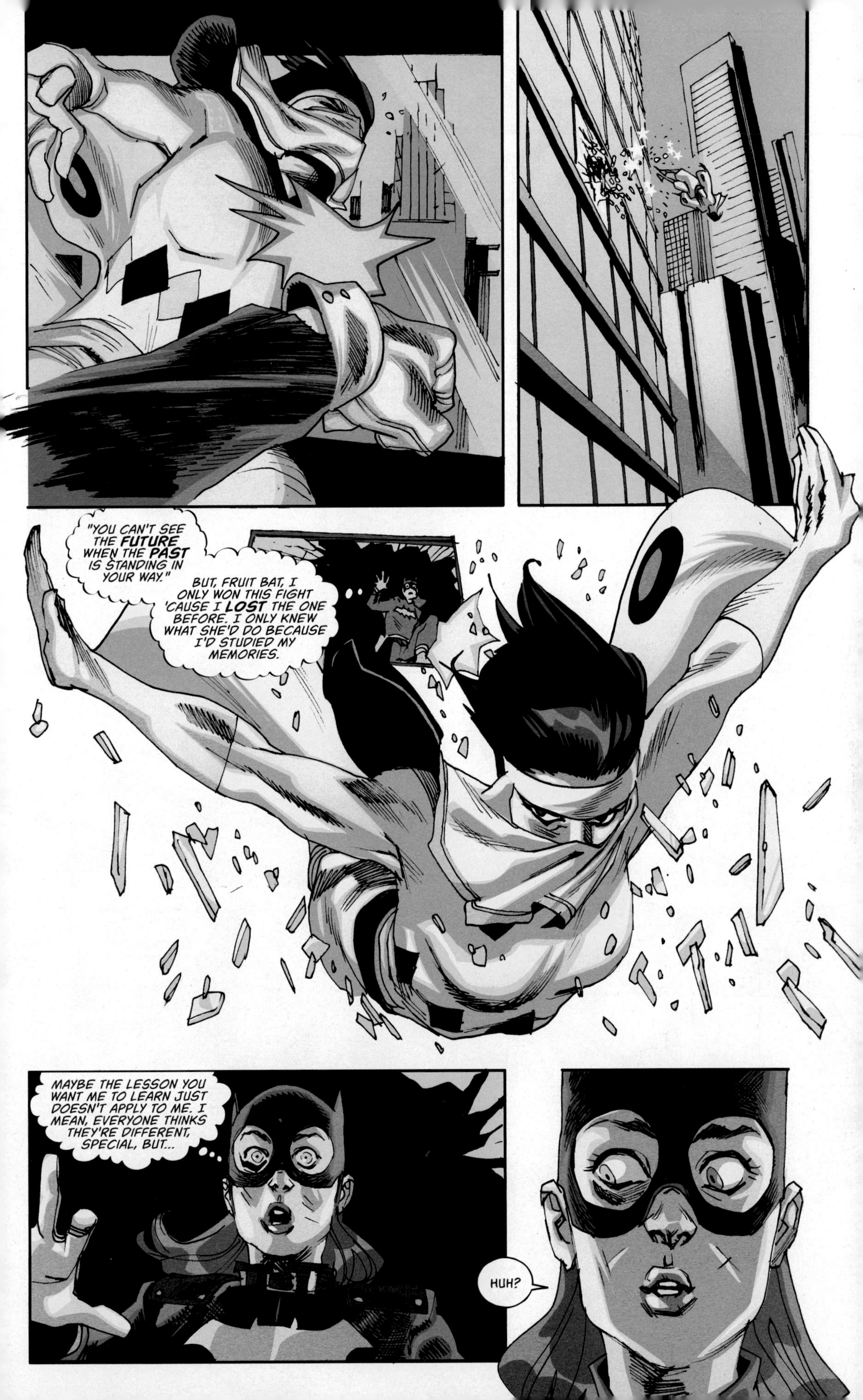
"YOU CAN'T SEE THE FUTURE WHEN THE PAST IS STANDING IN YOUR WAY."
BUT, FRUIT BAT, I ONLY WON THIS FIGHT 'CAUSE I LOST THE ONE BEFORE. I ONLY KNEW WHAT SHE'D DO BECAUSE I'D STUDIED MY MEMORIES.
MAYBE THE LESSON YOU WANT ME TO LEARN JUST DOESN'T APPLY TO ME. I MEAN, EVERYONE THINKS THEY'RE DIFFERENT, SPECIAL, BUT...
HUH?

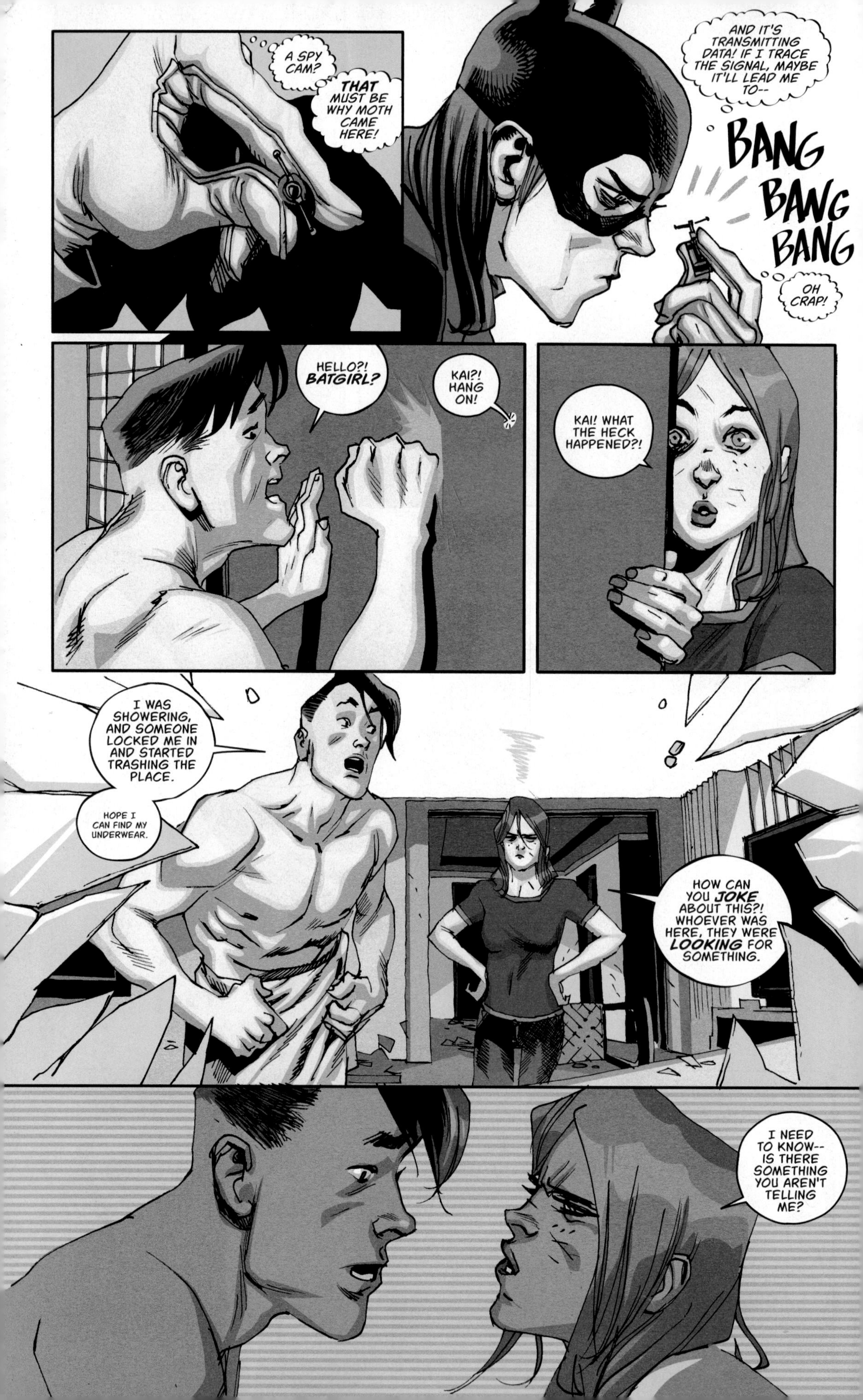
A SPY CAM?
THAT MUST BE WHY MOTH CAME HERE!
AND IT'S TRANSMITTING DATA! IF I TRACE THE SIGNAL, MAYBE IT'LL LEAD ME TO--
BANG BANG BANG
OH CRAP!
HELLO?! BATGIRL?
KAI?! HANG ON!
KAI! WHAT THE HECK HAPPENED?!
I WAS SHOWERING, AND SOMEONE LOCKED ME IN AND STARTED TRASHING THE PLACE.
HOPE I CAN FIND MY UNDERWEAR.
HOW CAN YOU JOKE ABOUT THIS?! WHOEVER WAS HERE, THEY WERE LOOKING FOR SOMETHING.
I NEED TO KNOW-- IS THERE SOMETHING YOU AREN'T TELLING ME?

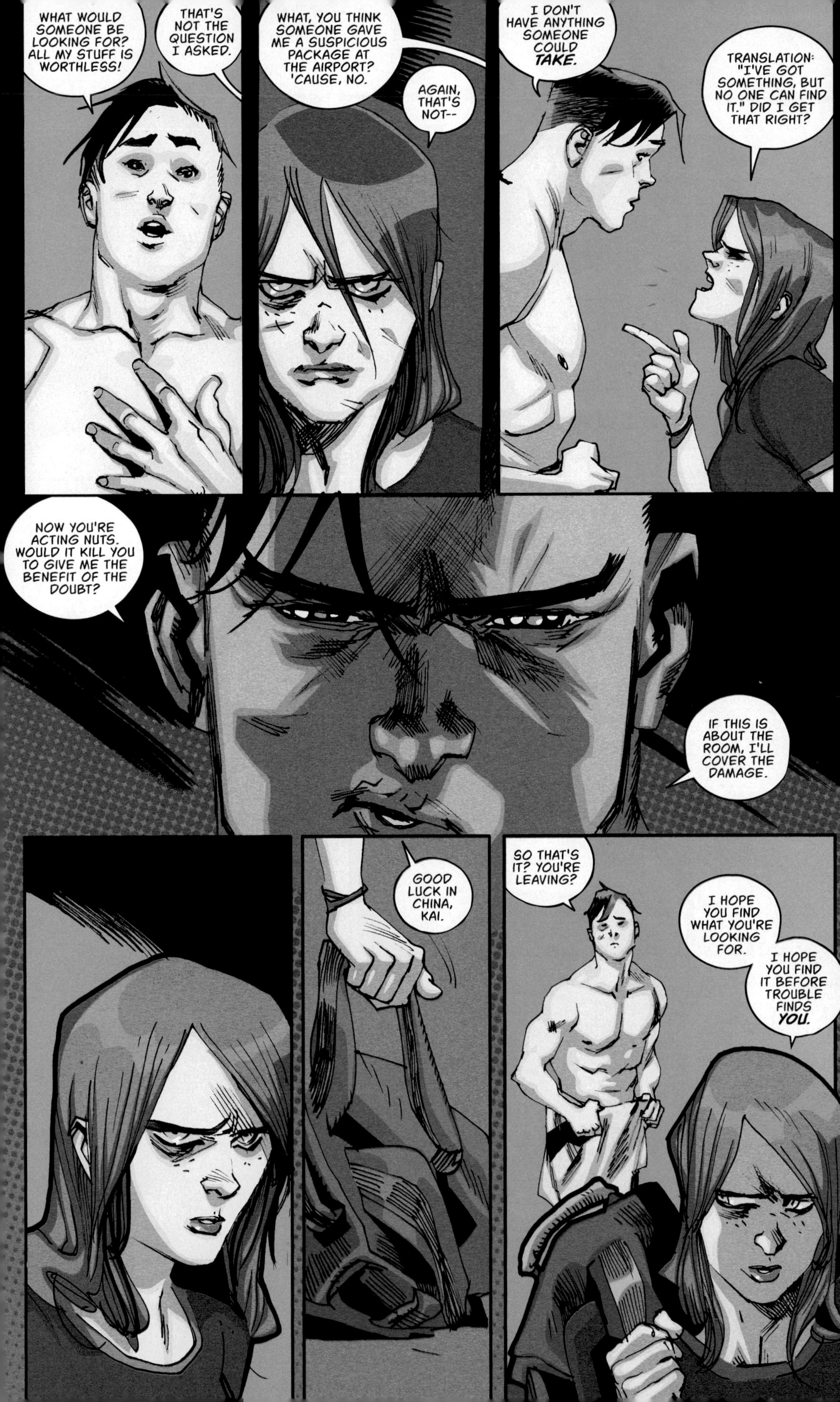
WHAT WOULD SOMEONE BE LOOKING FOR? ALL MY STUFF IS WORTHLESS!
THAT'S NOT THE QUESTION I ASKED.
WHAT, YOU THINK SOMEONE GAVE ME A SUSPICIOUS PACKAGE AT THE AIRPORT? 'CAUSE, NO.
AGAIN, THAT'S NOT--
I DON'T HAVE ANYTHING SOMEONE COULD **TAKE.**
TRANSLATION: "I'VE GOT SOMETHING, BUT NO ONE CAN FIND IT." DID I GET THAT RIGHT?
NOW YOU'RE ACTING NUTS. WOULD IT KILL YOU TO GIVE ME THE BENEFIT OF THE DOUBT?
IF THIS IS ABOUT THE ROOM, I'LL COVER THE DAMAGE.
GOOD LUCK IN CHINA, KAI.
SO THAT'S IT? YOU'RE LEAVING?
I HOPE YOU FIND WHAT YOU'RE LOOKING FOR.
I HOPE YOU FIND IT BEFORE TROUBLE FINDS **YOU.**

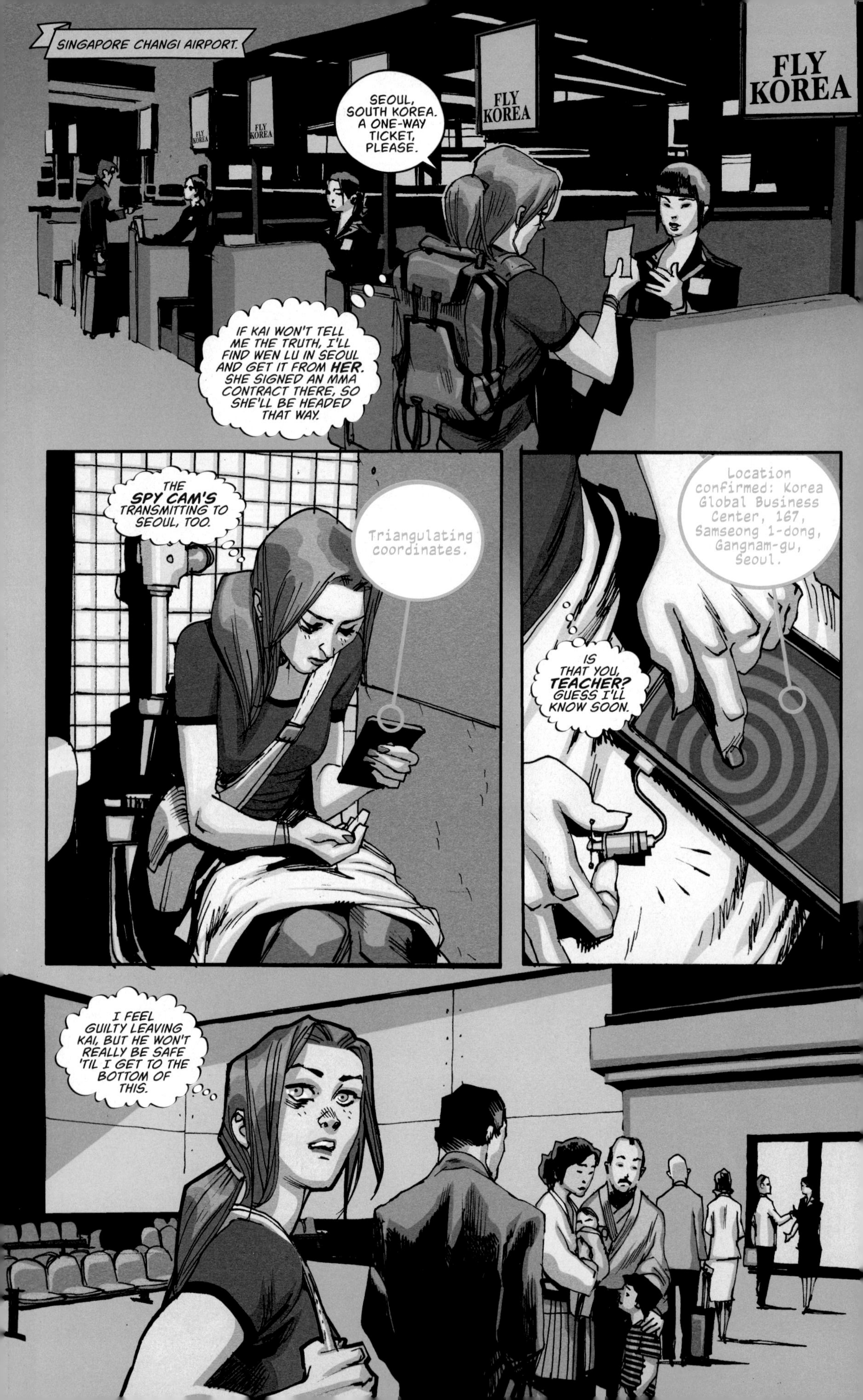
SINGAPORE CHANGI AIRPORT.
FLY KOREA
FLY KOREA
FLY KOREA
FLY KOREA
FLY KOREA
SEOUL, SOUTH KOREA. A ONE-WAY TICKET, PLEASE.
IF KAI WON'T TELL ME THE TRUTH, I'LL FIND WEN LU IN SEOUL AND GET IT FROM HER. SHE SIGNED AN MMA CONTRACT THERE, SO SHE'LL BE HEADED THAT WAY.
THE SPY CAM'S TRANSMITTING TO SEOUL, TOO.
Triangulating coordinates.
Location confirmed: Korea Global Business Center, 167, Samseong 1-dong, Gangnam-gu, Seoul.
IS THAT YOU, TEACHER? GUESS I'LL KNOW SOON.
I FEEL GUILTY LEAVING KAI, BUT HE WON'T REALLY BE SAFE 'TIL I GET TO THE BOTTOM OF THIS.

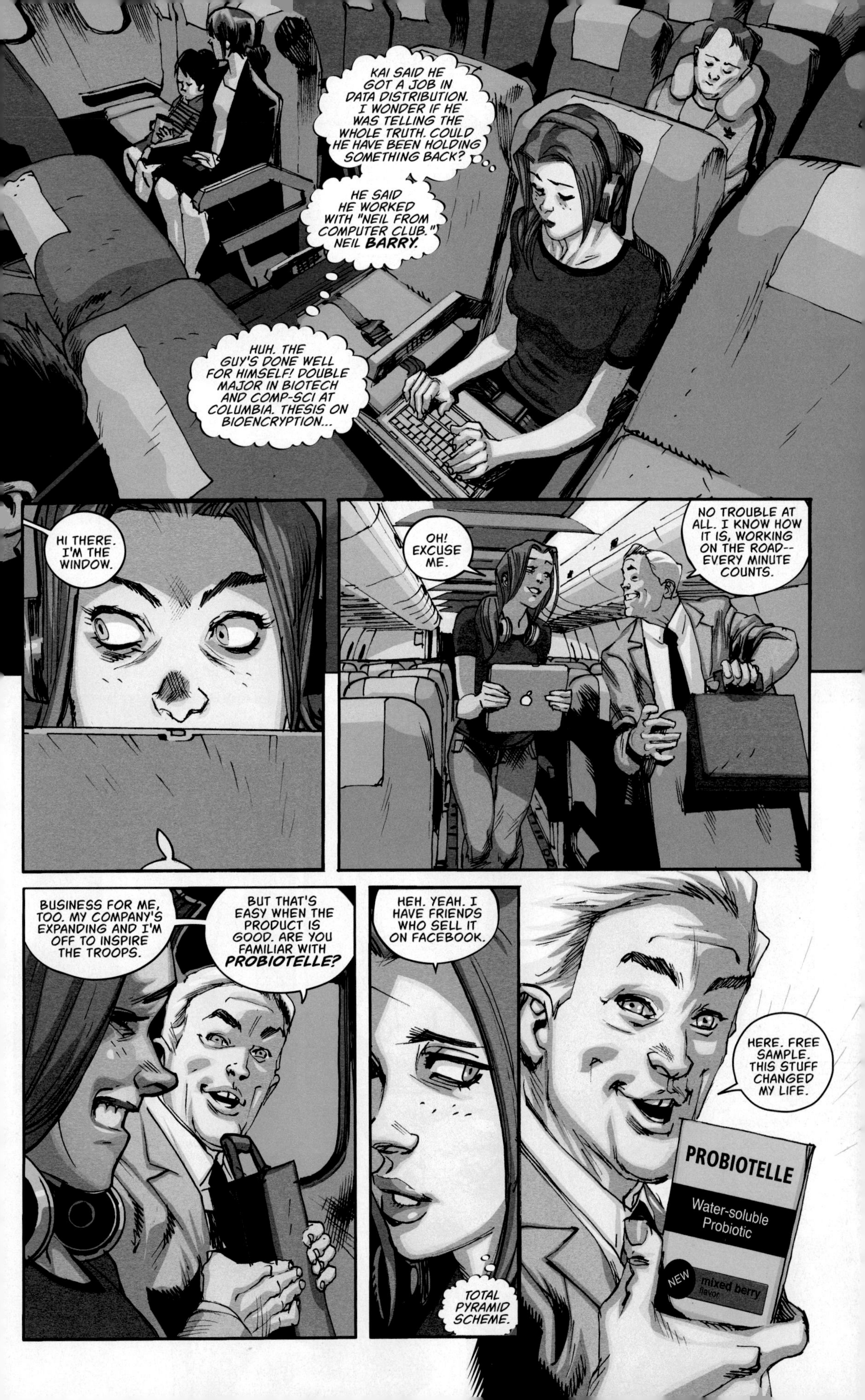
KAI SAID HE GOT A JOB IN DATA DISTRIBUTION. I WONDER IF HE WAS TELLING THE WHOLE TRUTH. COULD HE HAVE BEEN HOLDING SOMETHING BACK?
HE SAID HE WORKED WITH "NEIL FROM COMPUTER CLUB." NEIL BARRY.
HUH. THE GUY'S DONE WELL FOR HIMSELF! DOUBLE MAJOR IN BIOTECH AND COMP-SCI AT COLUMBIA. THESIS ON BIOENCRYPTION...
HI THERE. I'M THE WINDOW.
OH! EXCUSE ME.
NO TROUBLE AT ALL. I KNOW HOW IT IS, WORKING ON THE ROAD-- EVERY MINUTE COUNTS.
BUSINESS FOR ME, TOO. MY COMPANY'S EXPANDING AND I'M OFF TO INSPIRE THE TROOPS.
BUT THAT'S EASY WHEN THE PRODUCT IS GOOD. ARE YOU FAMILIAR WITH PROBIOTELLE?
HEH. YEAH. I HAVE FRIENDS WHO SELL IT ON FACEBOOK.
HERE. FREE SAMPLE. THIS STUFF CHANGED MY LIFE.
PROBIOTELLE
Water-soluble Probiotic
NEW
mixed berry flavor
TOTAL PYRAMID SCHEME.

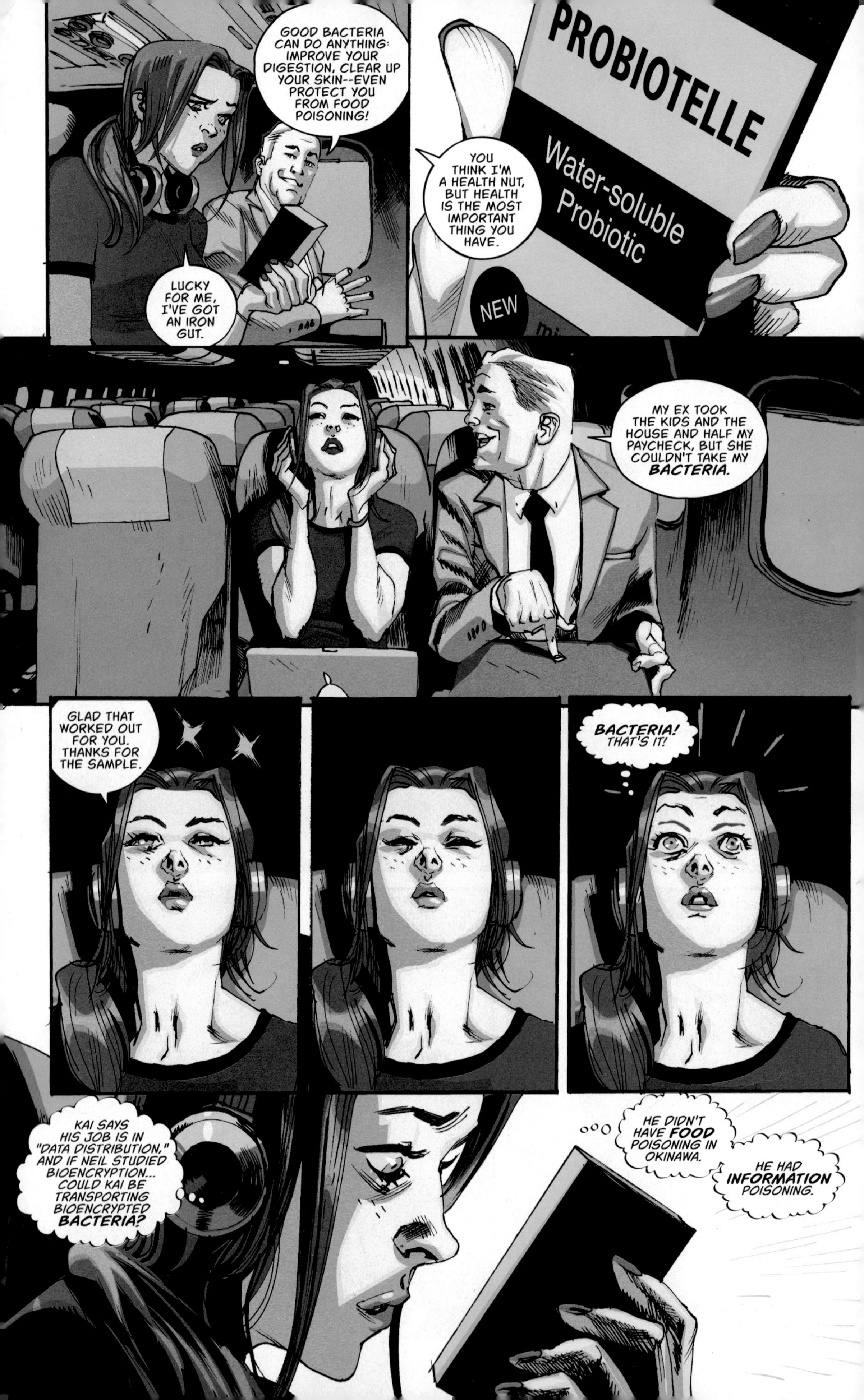
GOOD BACTERIA CAN DO ANYTHING: IMPROVE YOUR DIGESTION, CLEAR UP YOUR SKIN--EVEN PROTECT YOU FROM FOOD POISONING!
LUCKY FOR ME, I'VE GOT AN IRON GUT.
PROBIOTELLE
Water-soluble Probiotic
NEW
YOU THINK I'M A HEALTH NUT, BUT HEALTH IS THE MOST IMPORTANT THING YOU HAVE.
MY EX TOOK THE KIDS AND THE HOUSE AND HALF MY PAYCHECK, BUT SHE COULDN'T TAKE MY **BACTERIA.**
GLAD THAT WORKED OUT FOR YOU. THANKS FOR THE SAMPLE.
**BACTERIA!** THAT'S IT!
KAI SAYS HIS JOB IS IN "DATA DISTRIBUTION," AND IF NEIL STUDIED BIOENCRYPTION... COULD KAI BE TRANSPORTING BIOENCRYPTED **BACTERIA?**
HE DIDN'T HAVE **FOOD** POISONING IN OKINAWA.
HE HAD **INFORMATION** POISONING.

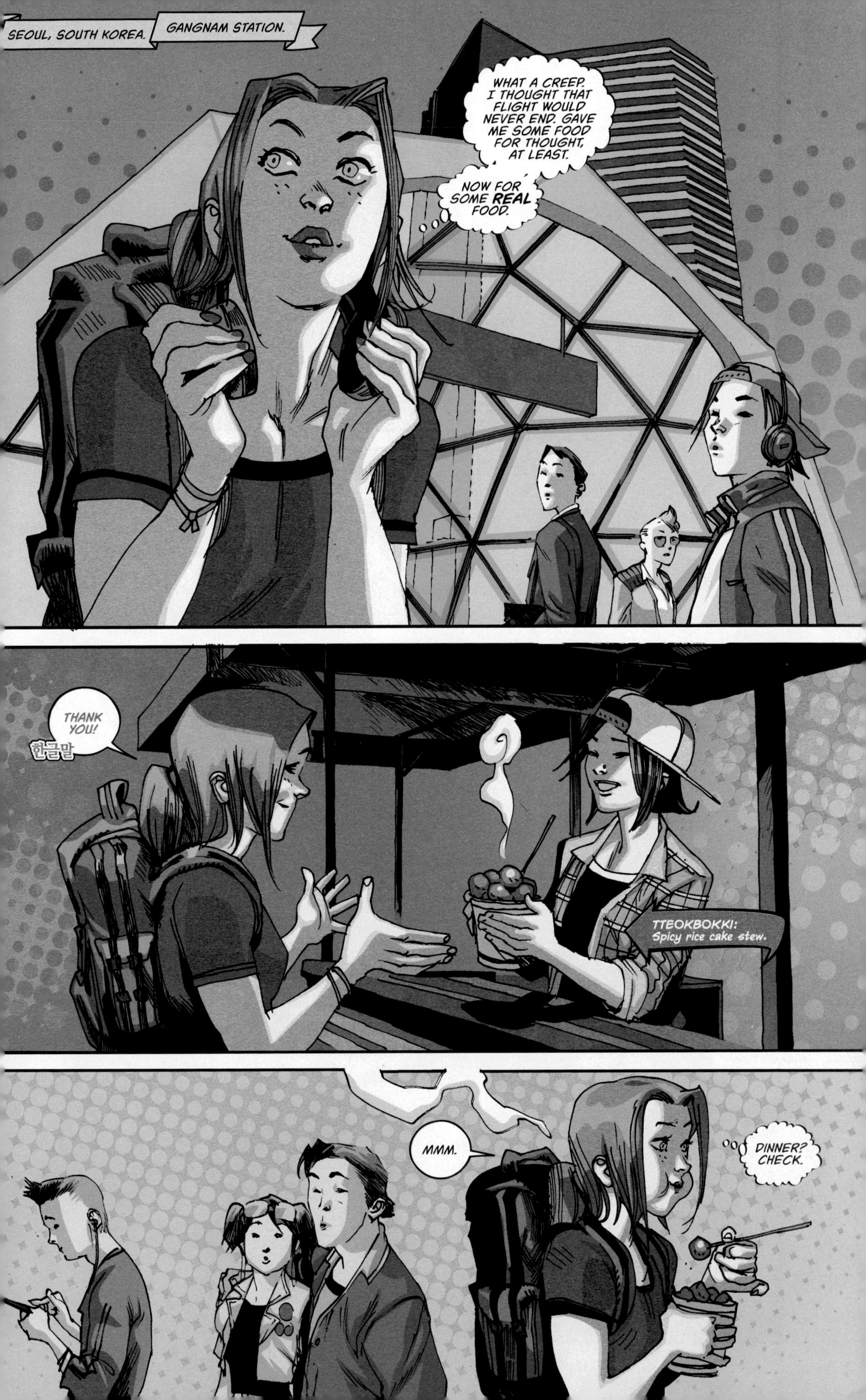
SEOUL, SOUTH KOREA.
GANGNAM STATION.
WHAT A CREEP. I THOUGHT THAT FLIGHT WOULD NEVER END. GAVE ME SOME FOOD FOR THOUGHT, AT LEAST.
NOW FOR SOME **REAL** FOOD.
THANK YOU!
한글말
TTEOKBOKKI: Spicy rice cake stew.
MMM.
DINNER? CHECK.

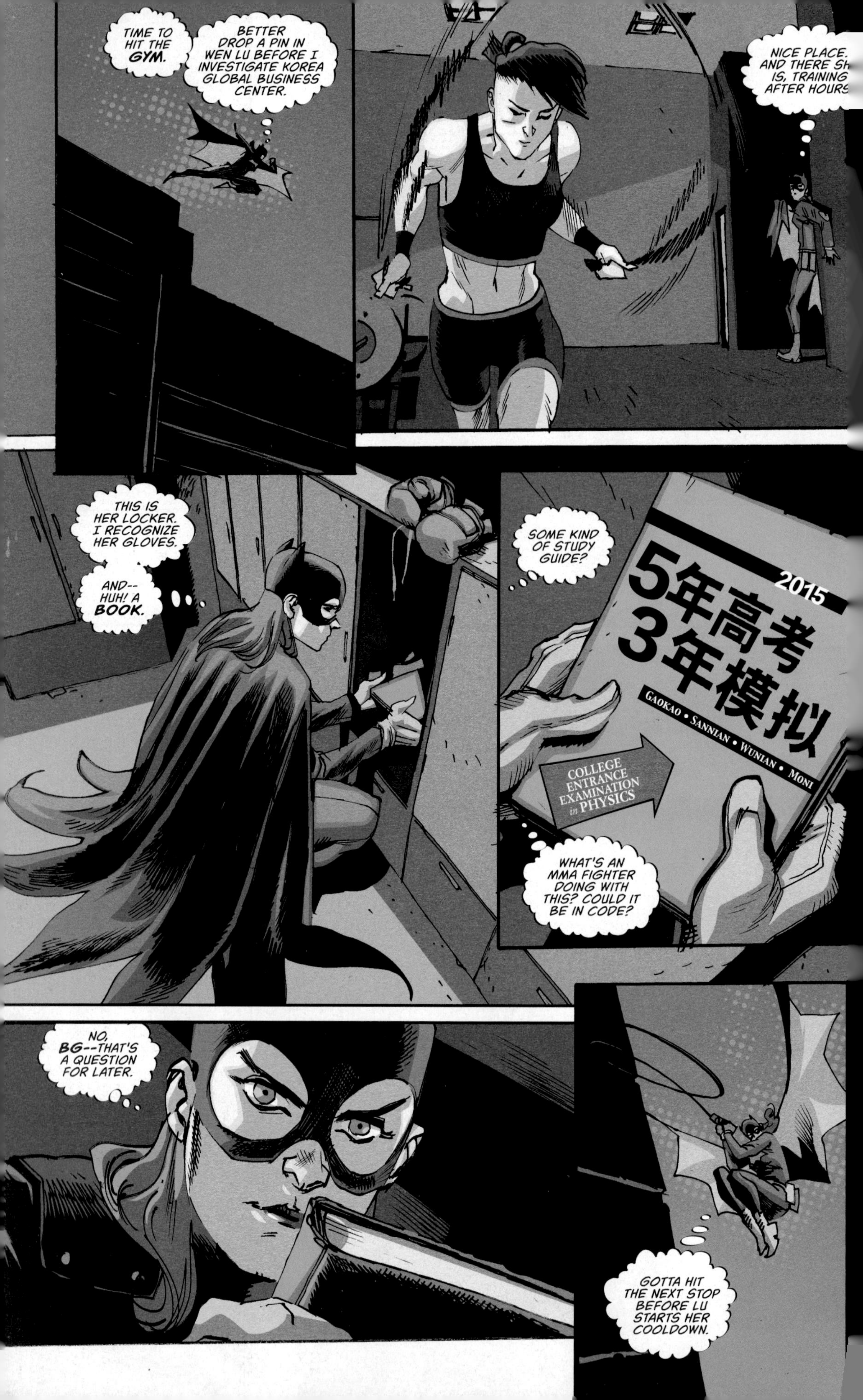

TIME TO HIT THE GYM.
BETTER DROP A PIN IN WEN LU BEFORE I INVESTIGATE KOREA GLOBAL BUSINESS CENTER.
NICE PLACE. AND THERE SH IS, TRAINING AFTER HOURS
THIS IS HER LOCKER. I RECOGNIZE HER GLOVES.
AND-- HUH! A BOOK.
SOME KIND OF STUDY GUIDE?
2015
5年高考
3年模拟
GAOKAO • SANNIAN • WUNIAN • MONI
COLLEGE ENTRANCE EXAMINATION in PHYSICS
WHAT'S AN MMA FIGHTER DOING WITH THIS? COULD IT BE IN CODE?
NO, BG--THAT'S A QUESTION FOR LATER.
GOTTA HIT THE NEXT STOP BEFORE LU STARTS HER COOLDOWN.

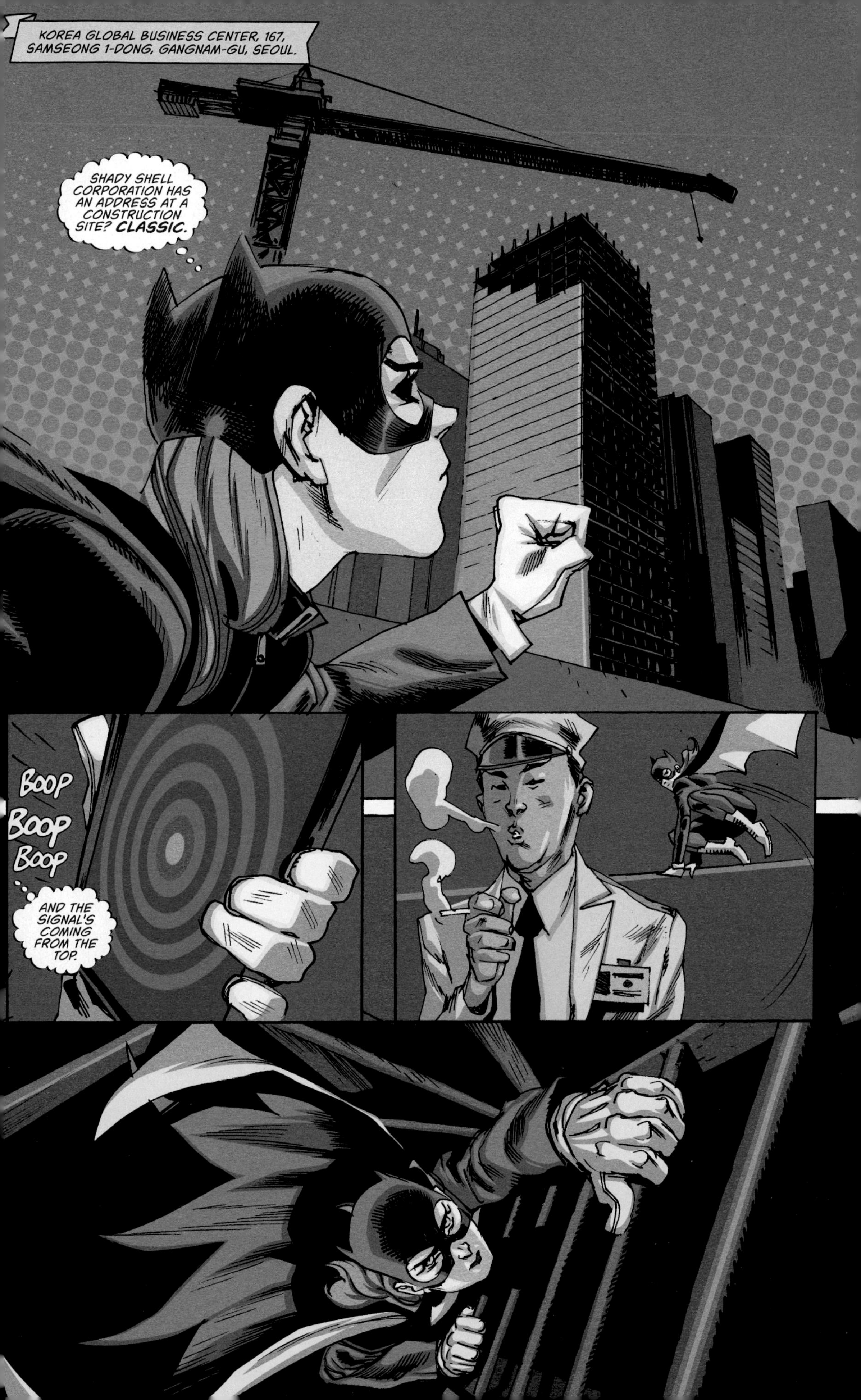
KOREA GLOBAL BUSINESS CENTER, 167, SAMSEONG 1-DONG, GANGNAM-GU, SEOUL.
SHADY SHELL CORPORATION HAS AN ADDRESS AT A CONSTRUCTION SITE? CLASSIC.
BOOP BOOP BOOP
AND THE SIGNAL'S COMING FROM THE TOP.

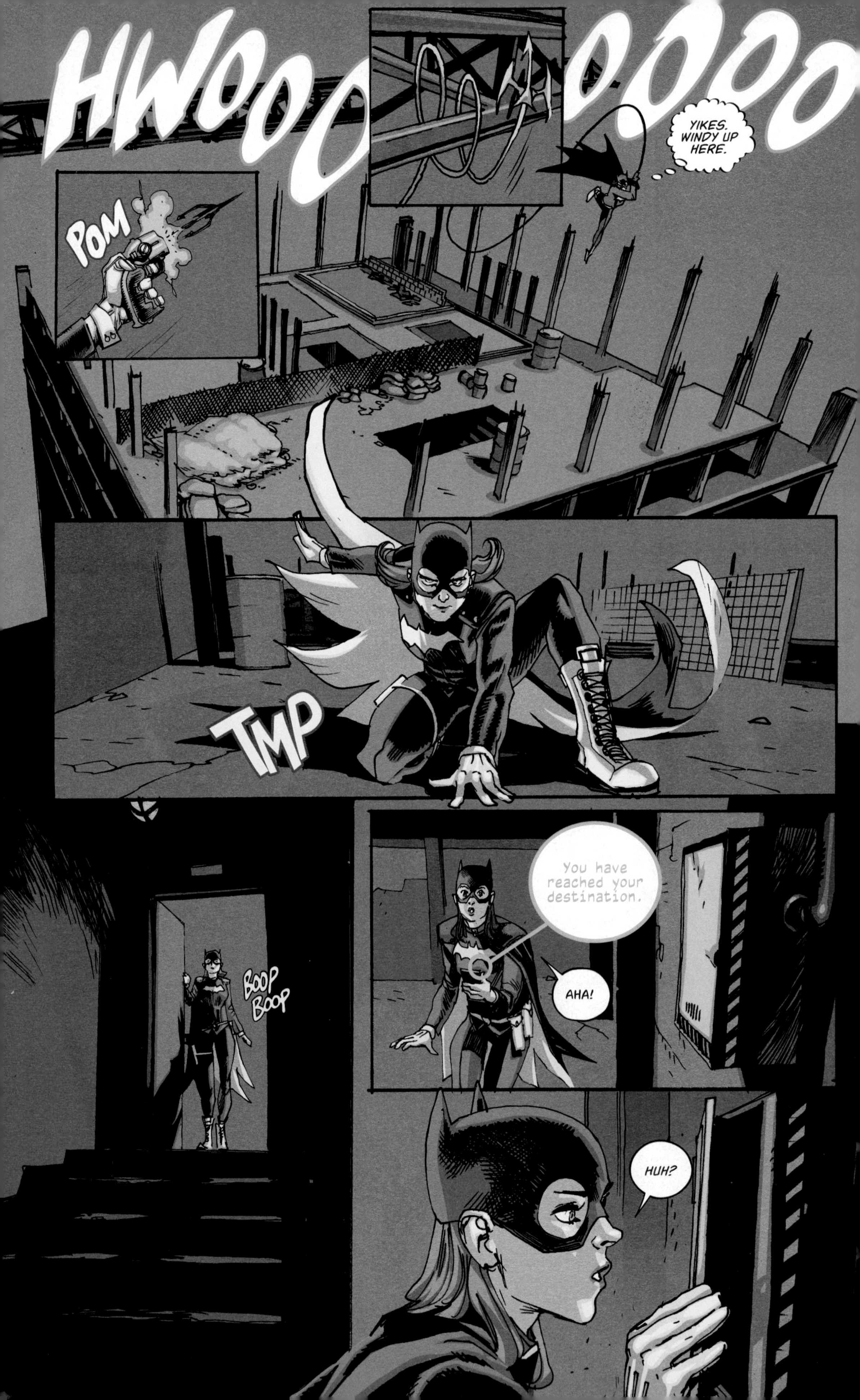
HWOOOOOOOOOO
POM
YIKES. WINDY UP HERE.
TMP
BOOP BOOP
You have reached your destination.
AHA!
HUH?

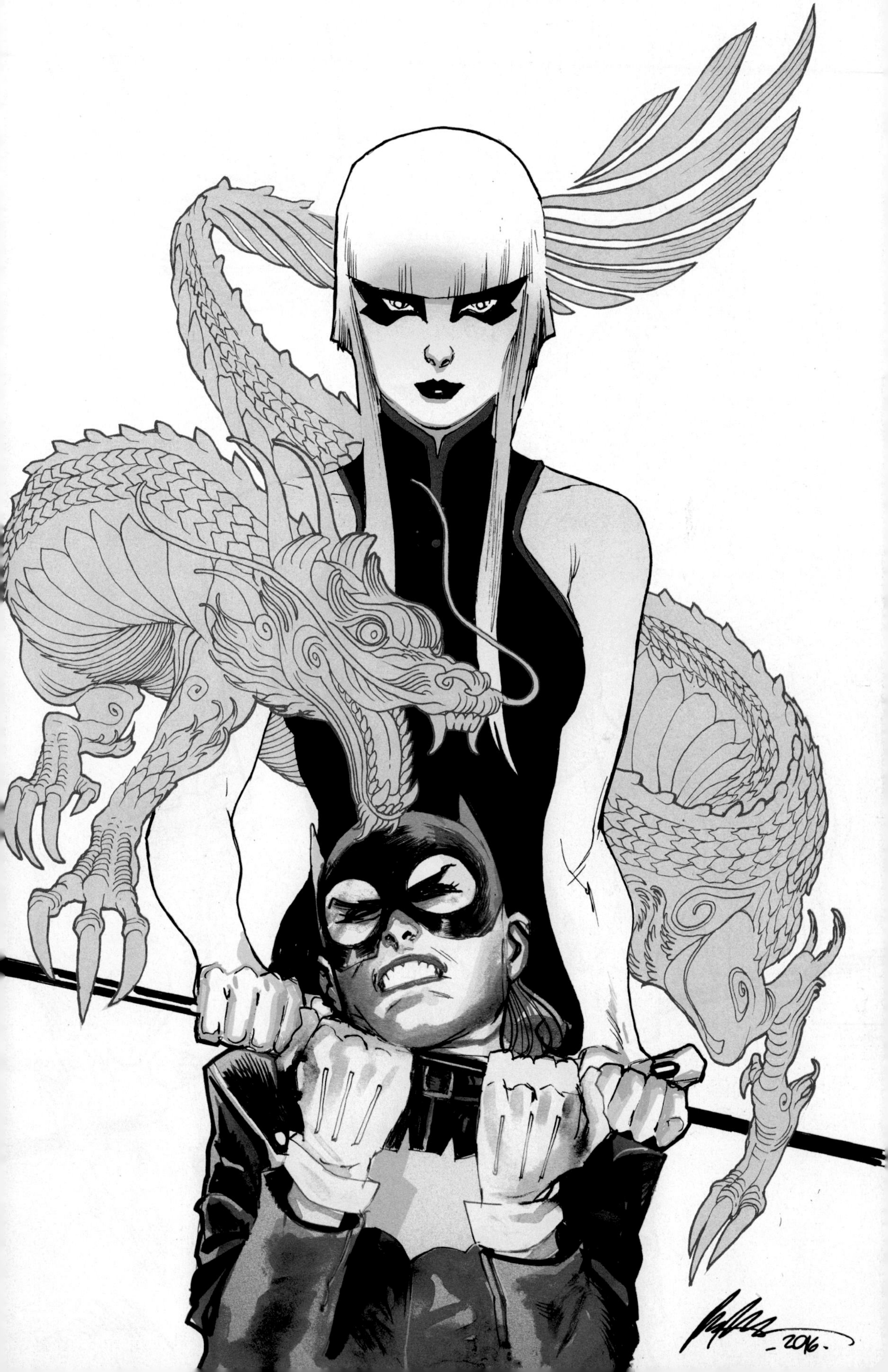
2016

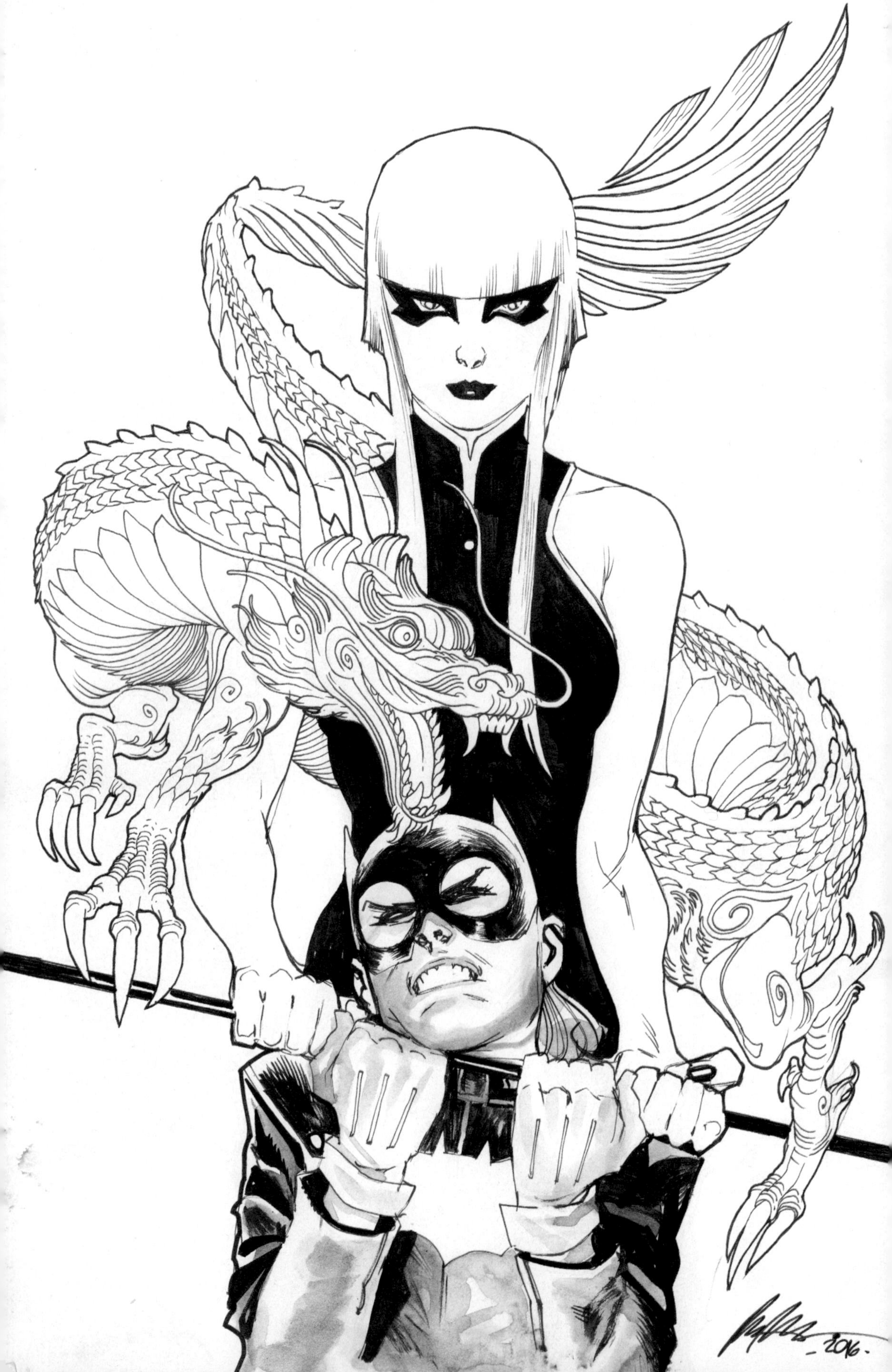
2016

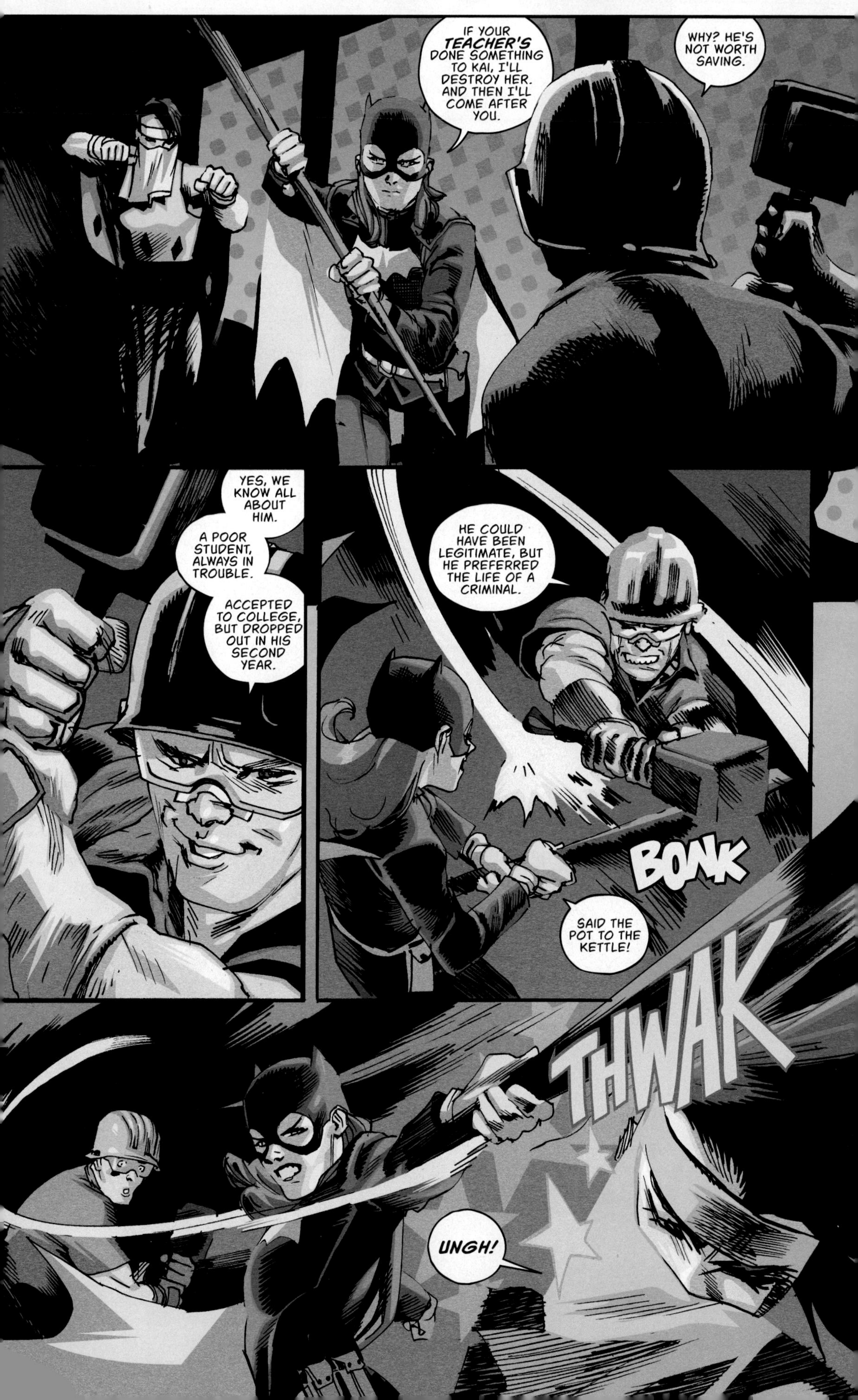
IF YOUR TEACHER'S DONE SOMETHING TO KAI, I'LL DESTROY HER. AND THEN I'LL COME AFTER YOU.
WHY? HE'S NOT WORTH SAVING.
YES, WE KNOW ALL ABOUT HIM.
A POOR STUDENT, ALWAYS IN TROUBLE.
ACCEPTED TO COLLEGE, BUT DROPPED OUT IN HIS SECOND YEAR.
HE COULD HAVE BEEN LEGITIMATE, BUT HE PREFERRED THE LIFE OF A CRIMINAL.
BONK
SAID THE POT TO THE KETTLE!
THWAK
UNGH!

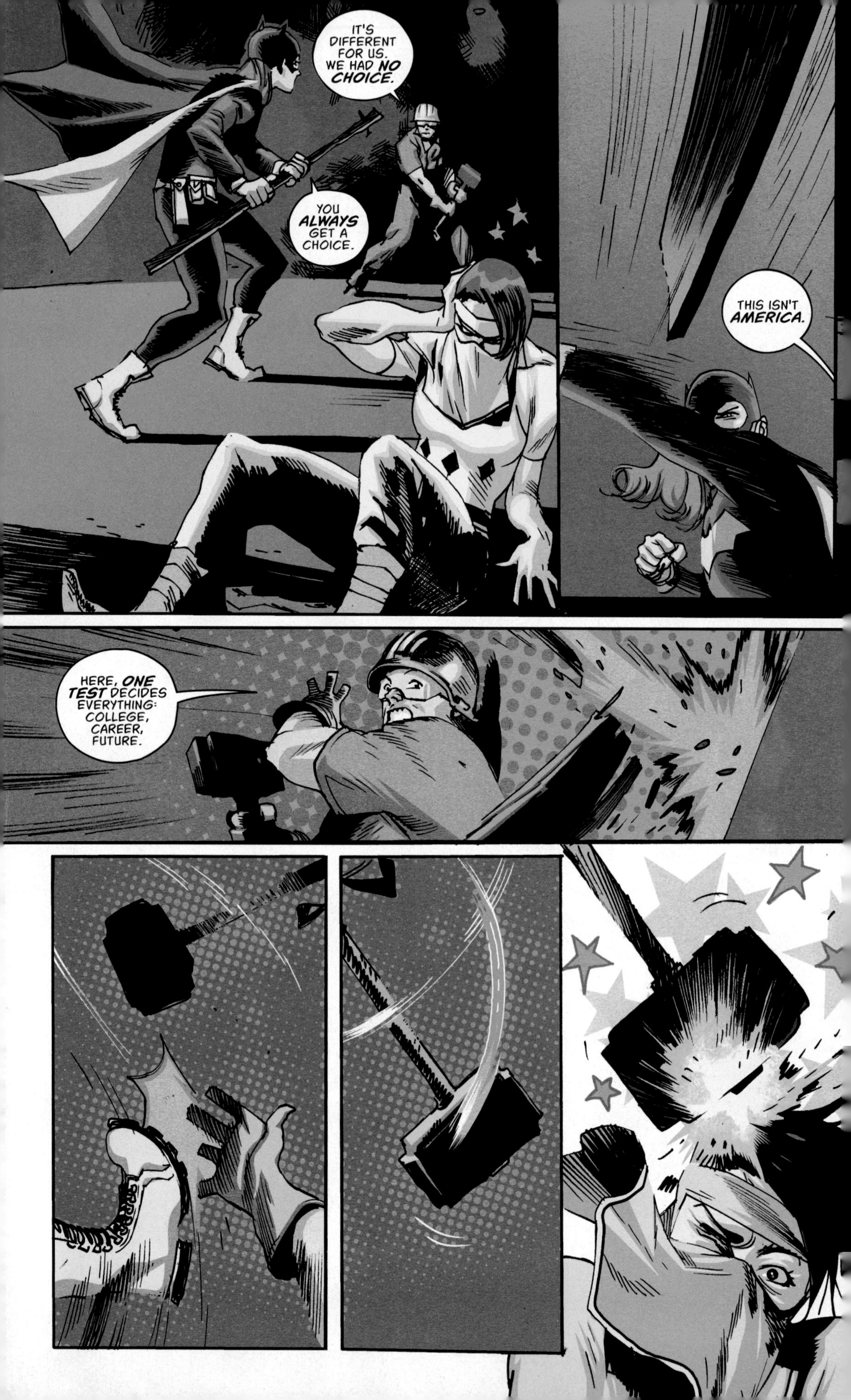
IT'S DIFFERENT FOR US. WE HAD **NO CHOICE.**
YOU **ALWAYS** GET A CHOICE.
THIS ISN'T **AMERICA.**
HERE, **ONE TEST** DECIDES EVERYTHING: COLLEGE, CAREER, FUTURE.

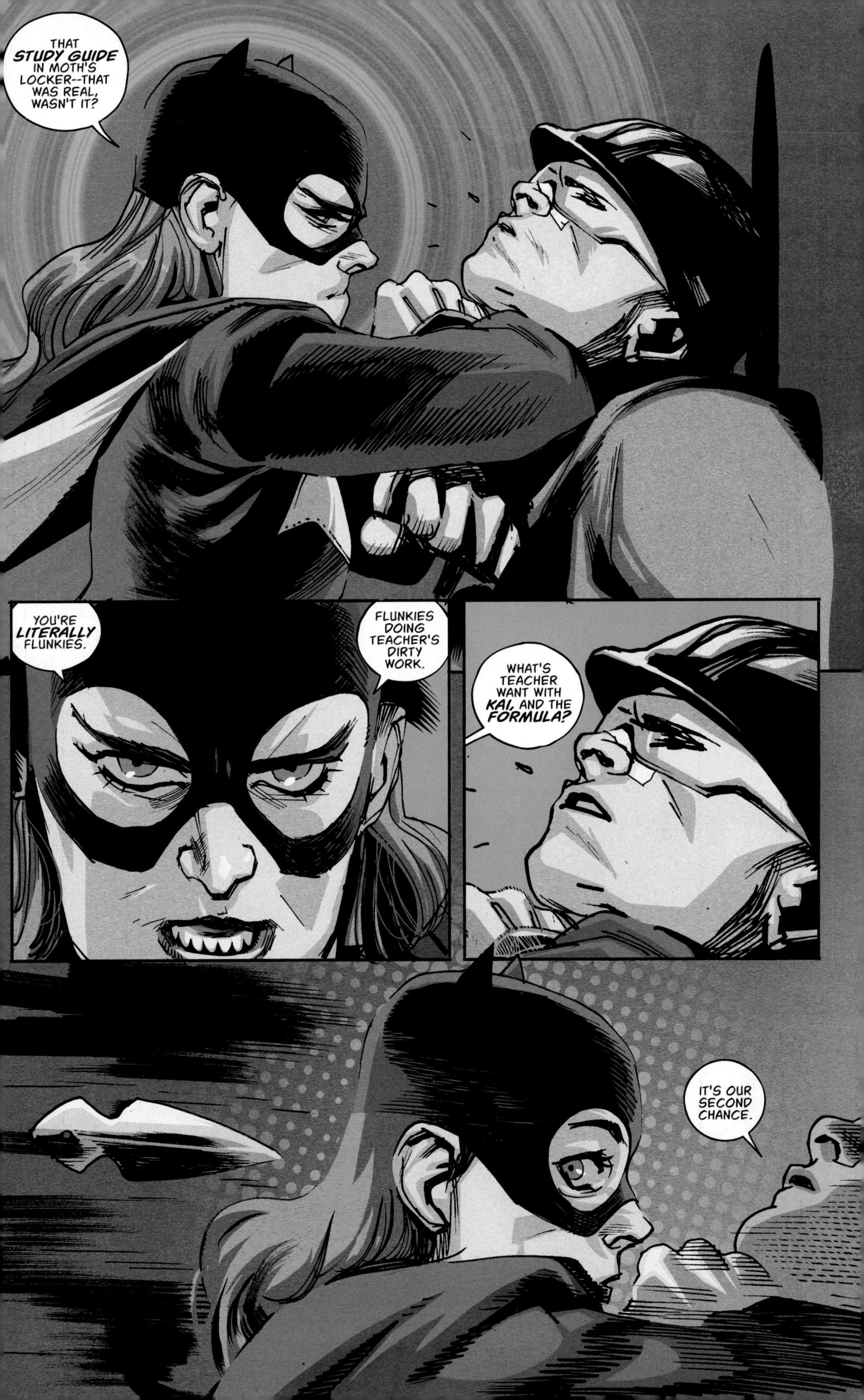
THAT STUDY GUIDE IN MOTH'S LOCKER--THAT WAS REAL, WASN'T IT?
YOU'RE LITERALLY FLUNKIES.
FLUNKIES DOING TEACHER'S DIRTY WORK.
WHAT'S TEACHER WANT WITH KAI, AND THE FORMULA?
IT'S OUR SECOND CHANCE.

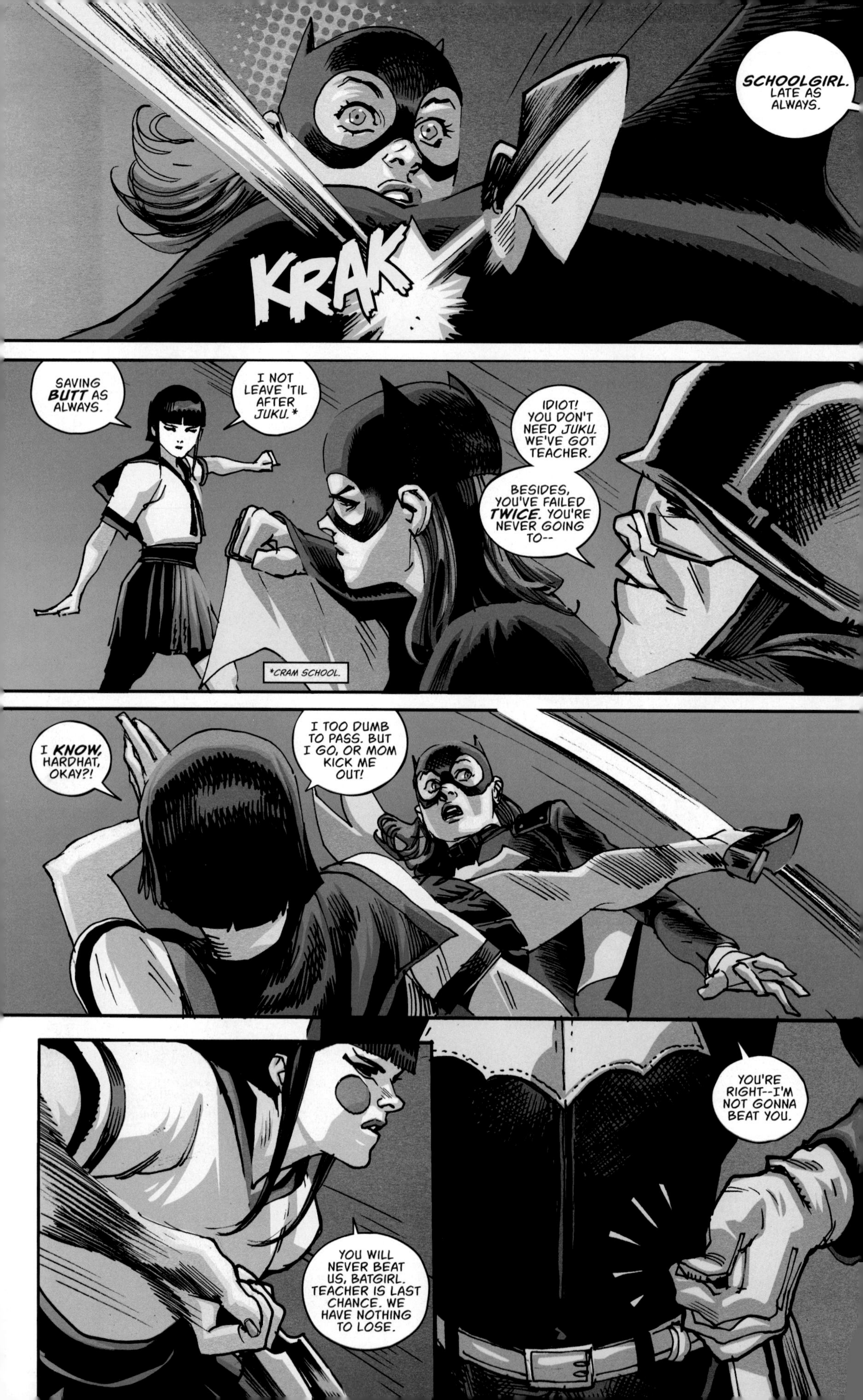

SCHOOLGIRL. LATE AS ALWAYS.
KRAK
SAVING BUTT AS ALWAYS.
I NOT LEAVE 'TIL AFTER JUKU.*
IDIOT! YOU DON'T NEED JUKU. WE'VE GOT TEACHER.
BESIDES, YOU'VE FAILED TWICE. YOU'RE NEVER GOING TO--
*CRAM SCHOOL.
I KNOW, HARDHAT, OKAY?!
I TOO DUMB TO PASS. BUT I GO, OR MOM KICK ME OUT!
YOU WILL NEVER BEAT US, BATGIRL. TEACHER IS LAST CHANCE. WE HAVE NOTHING TO LOSE.
YOU'RE RIGHT--I'M NOT GONNA BEAT YOU.

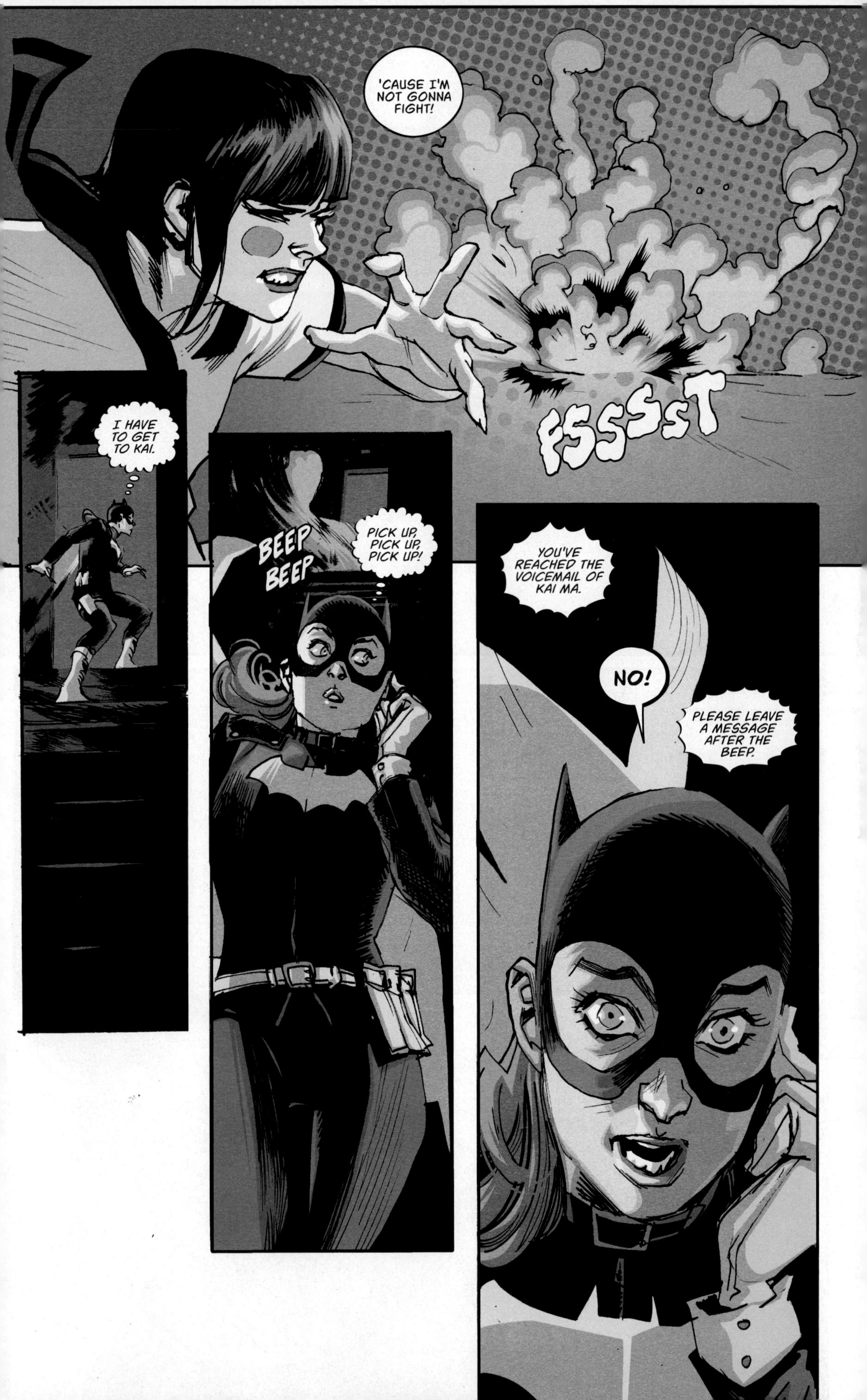
'CAUSE I'M NOT GONNA FIGHT!
FSSSsT
I HAVE TO GET TO KAI.
BEEP BEEP
PICK UP, PICK UP, PICK UP!
YOU'VE REACHED THE VOICEMAIL OF KAI MA.
NO!
PLEASE LEAVE A MESSAGE AFTER THE BEEP.

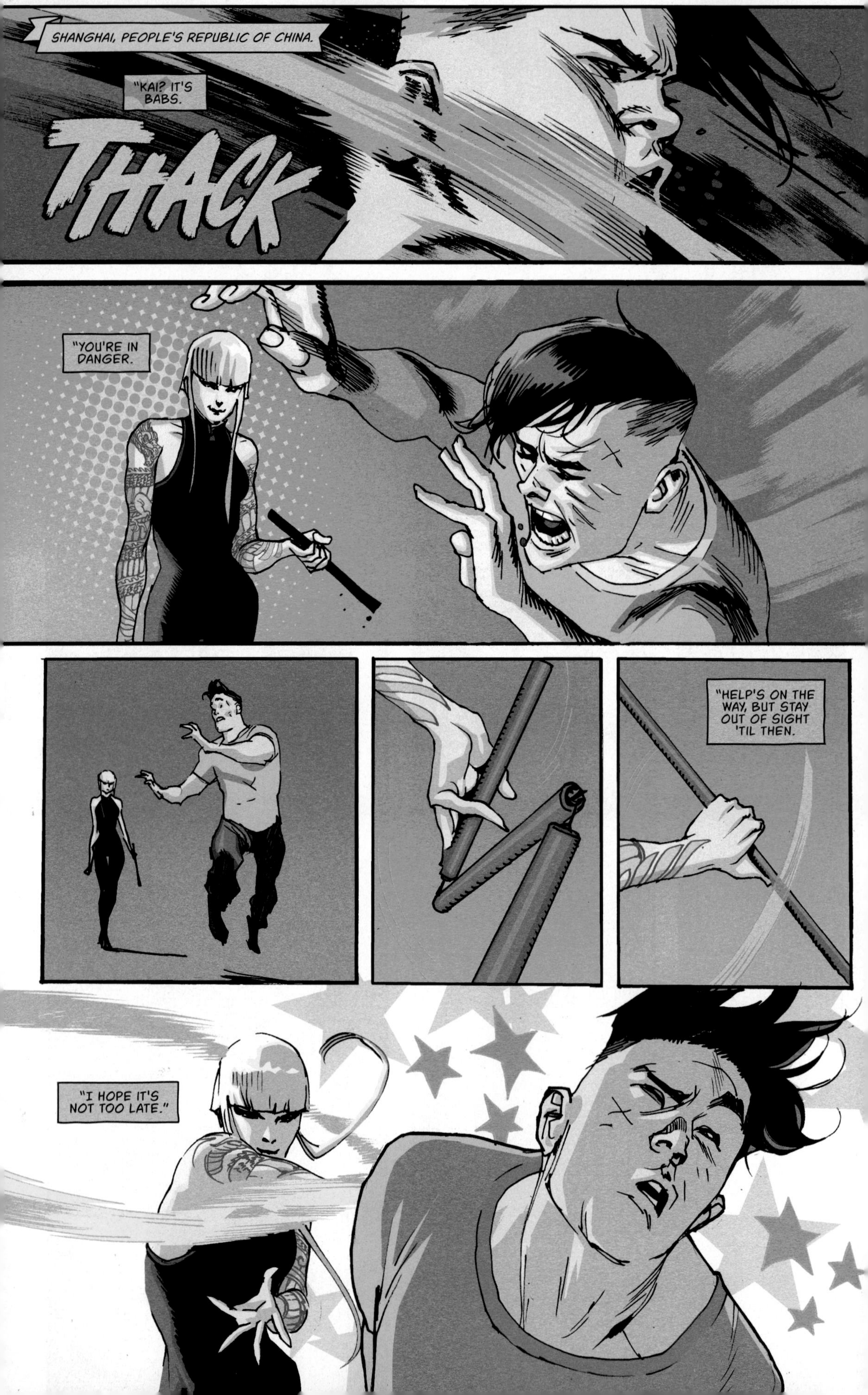
SHANGHAI, PEOPLE'S REPUBLIC OF CHINA.
"KAI? IT'S BABS.
THACK
"YOU'RE IN DANGER.
"HELP'S ON THE WAY, BUT STAY OUT OF SIGHT 'TIL THEN.
"I HOPE IT'S NOT TOO LATE."

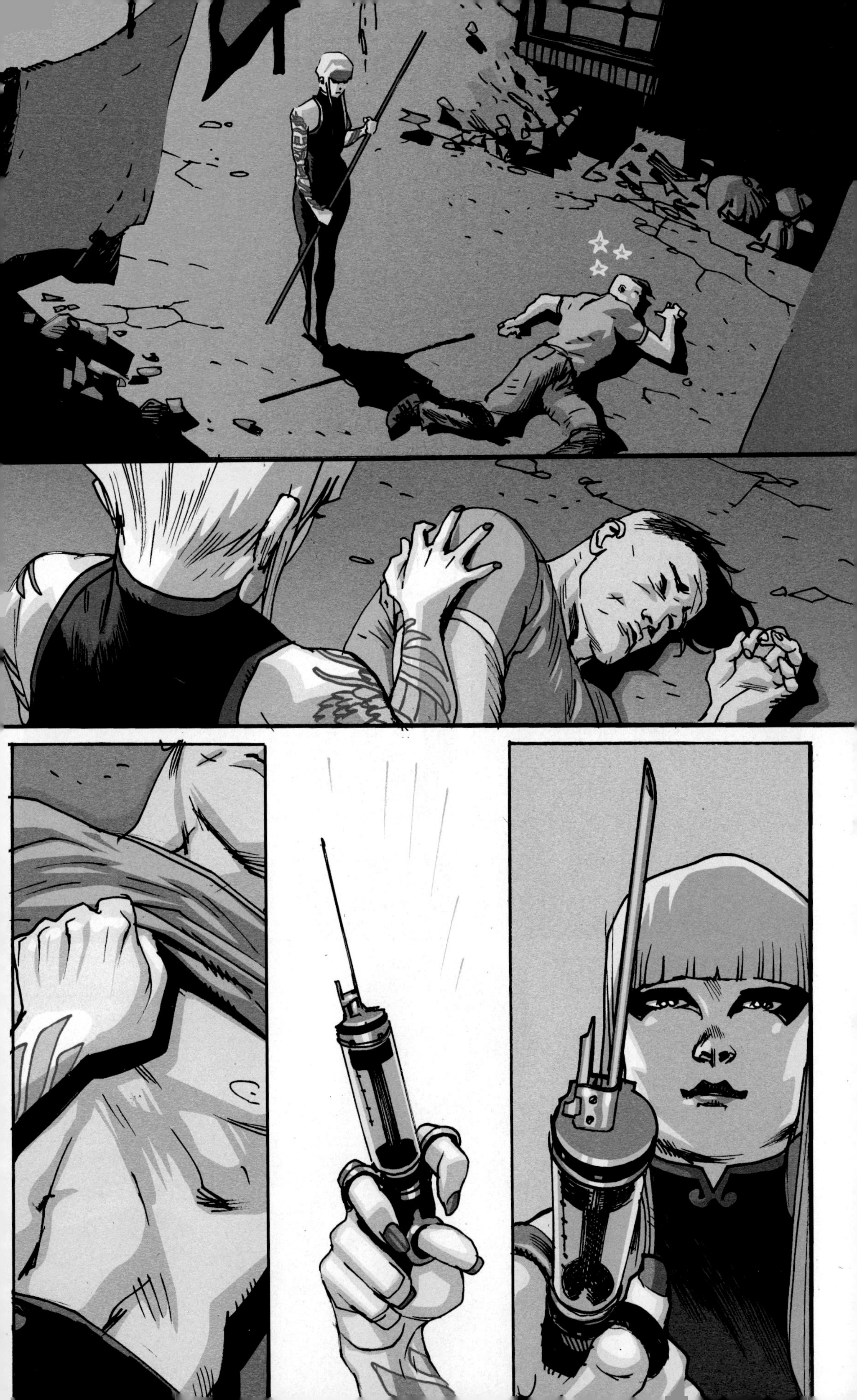

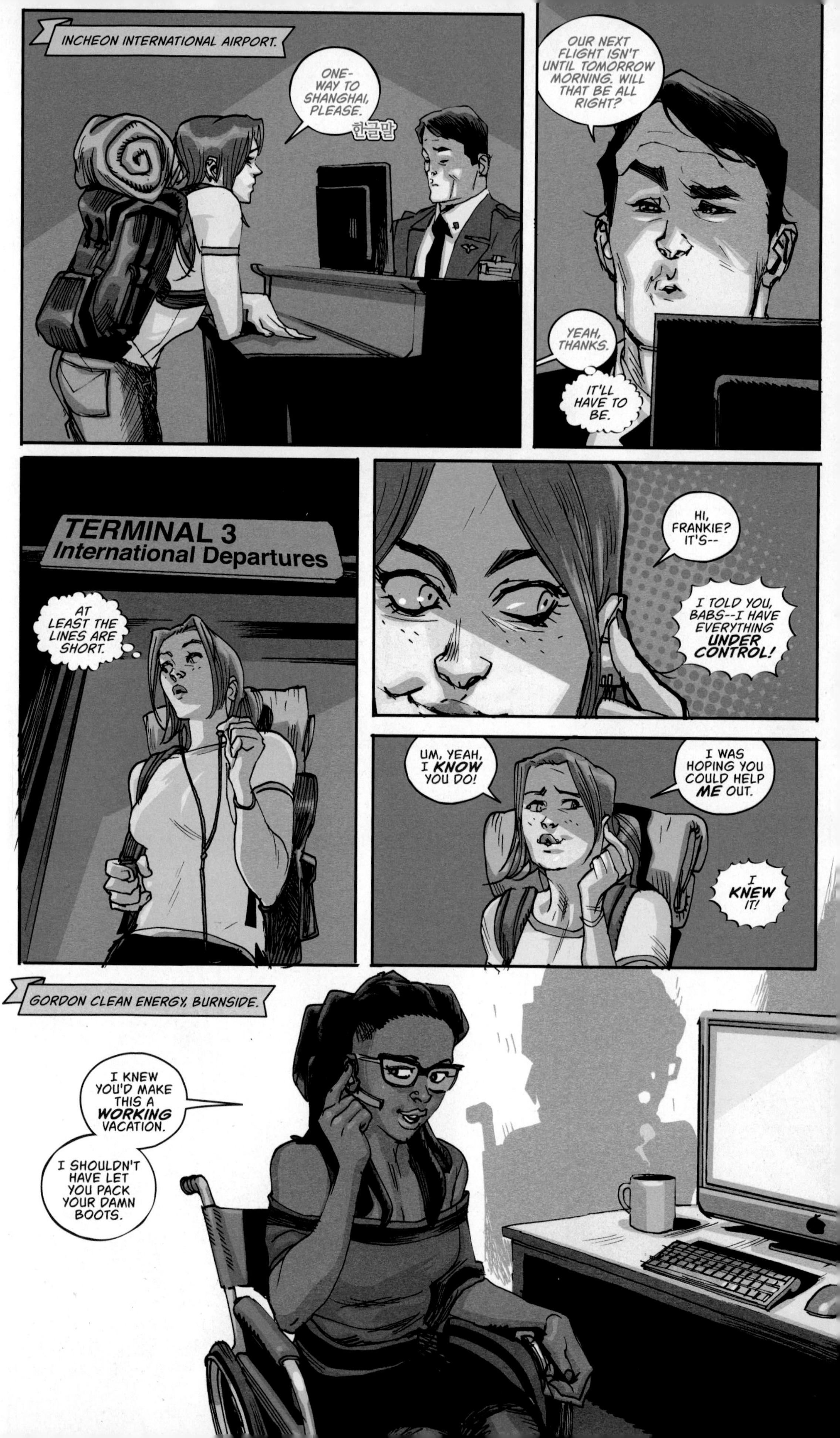
INCHEON INTERNATIONAL AIRPORT.
ONE-WAY TO SHANGHAI, PLEASE. 한글말
OUR NEXT FLIGHT ISN'T UNTIL TOMORROW MORNING. WILL THAT BE ALL RIGHT?
YEAH, THANKS.
IT'LL HAVE TO BE.
TERMINAL 3
International Departures
AT LEAST THE LINES ARE SHORT.
HI, FRANKIE? IT'S--
I TOLD YOU, BABS--I HAVE EVERYTHING UNDER CONTROL!
UM, YEAH, I KNOW YOU DO!
I WAS HOPING YOU COULD HELP ME OUT.
I KNEW IT!
GORDON CLEAN ENERGY, BURNSIDE.
I KNEW YOU'D MAKE THIS A WORKING VACATION.
I SHOULDN'T HAVE LET YOU PACK YOUR DAMN BOOTS.

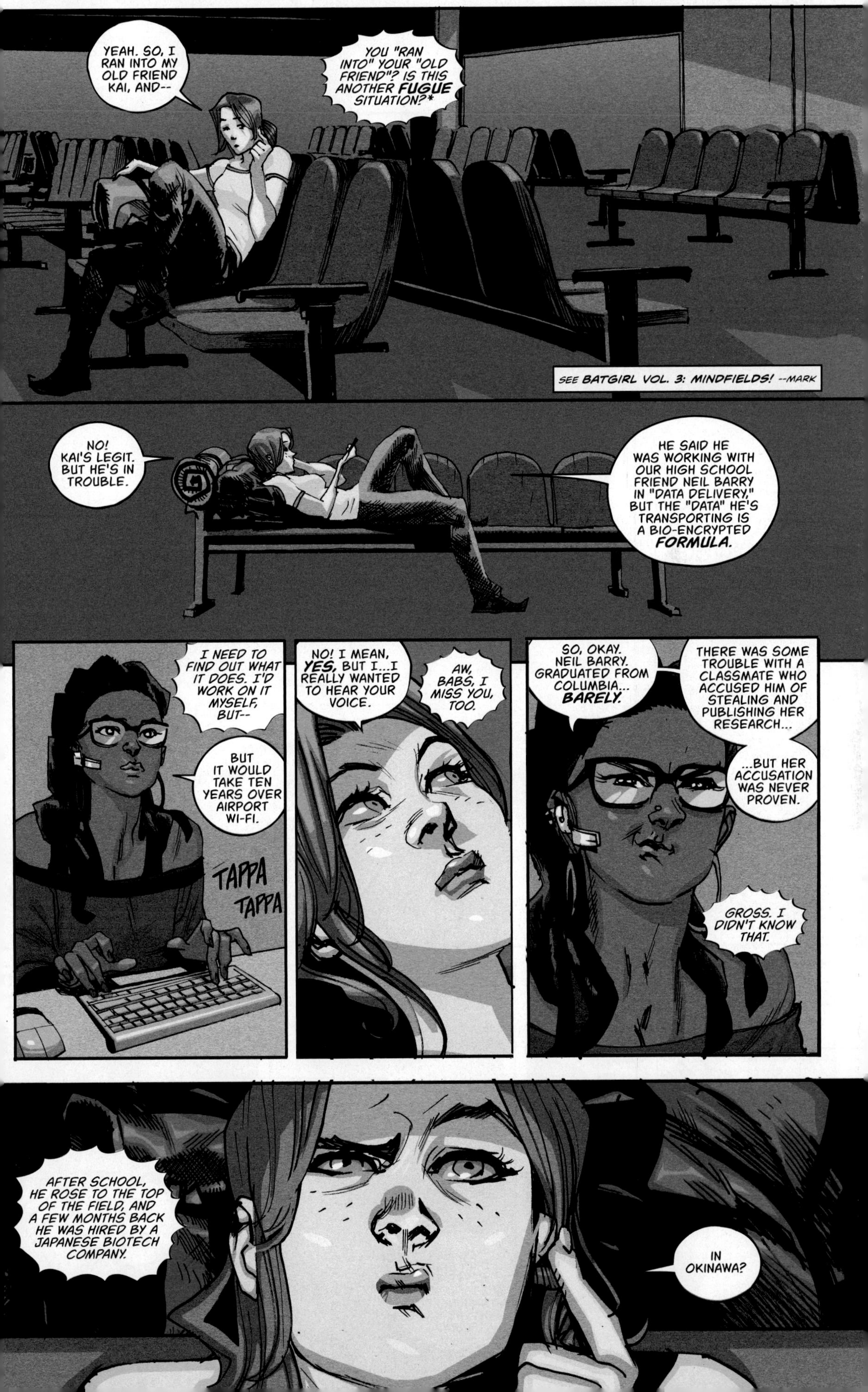
YEAH. SO, I RAN INTO MY OLD FRIEND KAI, AND--
YOU "RAN INTO" YOUR "OLD FRIEND"? IS THIS ANOTHER FUGUE SITUATION?*
SEE BATGIRL VOL. 3: MINDFIELDS! --MARK
NO! KAI'S LEGIT. BUT HE'S IN TROUBLE.
HE SAID HE WAS WORKING WITH OUR HIGH SCHOOL FRIEND NEIL BARRY IN "DATA DELIVERY," BUT THE "DATA" HE'S TRANSPORTING IS A BIO-ENCRYPTED FORMULA.
I NEED TO FIND OUT WHAT IT DOES. I'D WORK ON IT MYSELF, BUT--
BUT IT WOULD TAKE TEN YEARS OVER AIRPORT WI-FI.
TAPPA TAPPA
NO! I MEAN, YES, BUT I...I REALLY WANTED TO HEAR YOUR VOICE.
AW, BABS, I MISS YOU, TOO.
SO, OKAY. NEIL BARRY. GRADUATED FROM COLUMBIA... BARELY.
THERE WAS SOME TROUBLE WITH A CLASSMATE WHO ACCUSED HIM OF STEALING AND PUBLISHING HER RESEARCH...
...BUT HER ACCUSATION WAS NEVER PROVEN.
GROSS. I DIDN'T KNOW THAT.
AFTER SCHOOL, HE ROSE TO THE TOP OF THE FIELD, AND A FEW MONTHS BACK HE WAS HIRED BY A JAPANESE BIOTECH COMPANY.
IN OKINAWA?

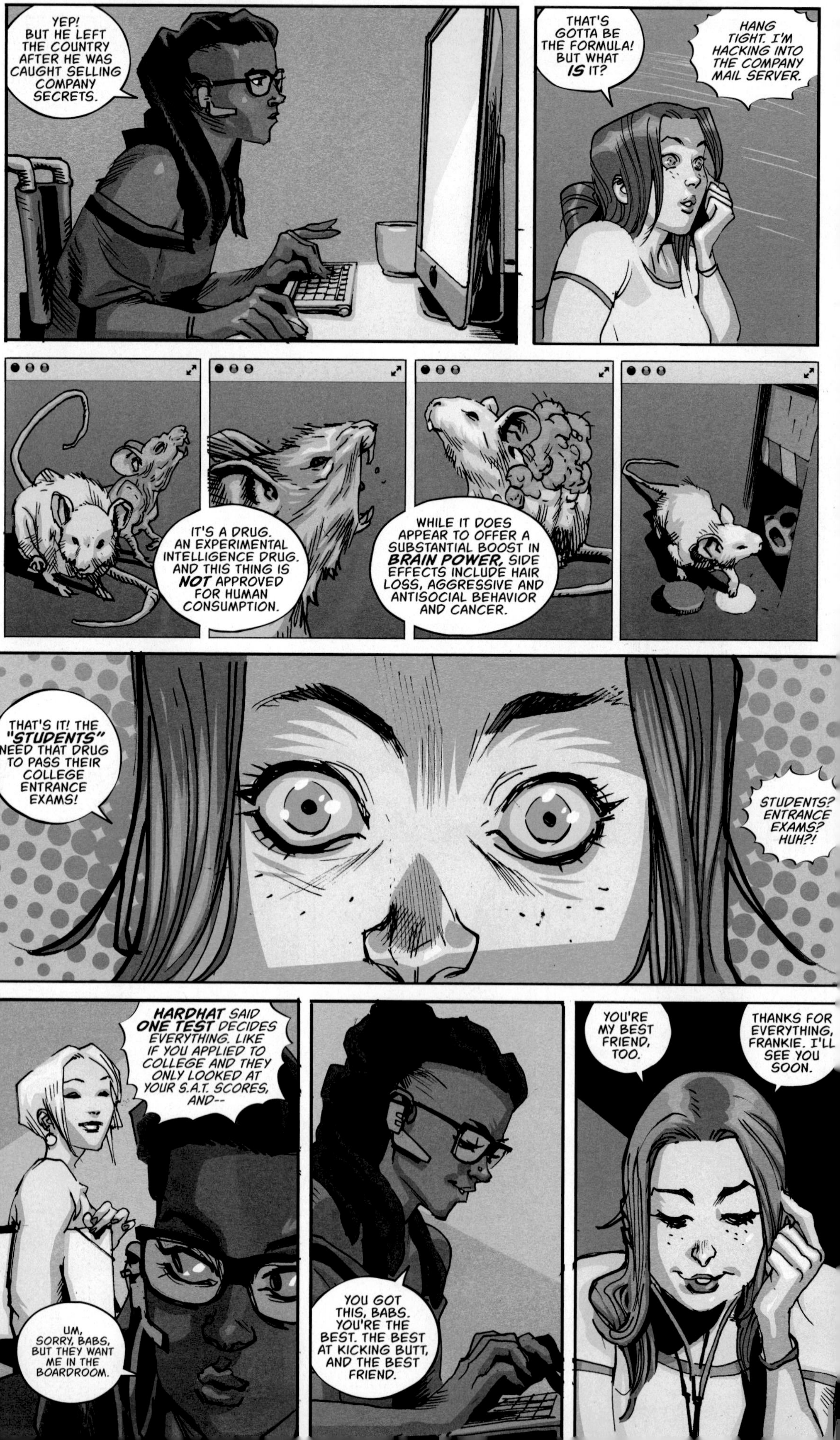

YEP! BUT HE LEFT THE COUNTRY AFTER HE WAS CAUGHT SELLING COMPANY SECRETS.
THAT'S GOTTA BE THE FORMULA! BUT WHAT IS IT?
HANG TIGHT. I'M HACKING INTO THE COMPANY MAIL SERVER.
IT'S A DRUG. AN EXPERIMENTAL INTELLIGENCE DRUG. AND THIS THING IS NOT APPROVED FOR HUMAN CONSUMPTION.
WHILE IT DOES APPEAR TO OFFER A SUBSTANTIAL BOOST IN BRAIN POWER, SIDE EFFECTS INCLUDE HAIR LOSS, AGGRESSIVE AND ANTISOCIAL BEHAVIOR AND CANCER.
THAT'S IT! THE "STUDENTS" NEED THAT DRUG TO PASS THEIR COLLEGE ENTRANCE EXAMS!
STUDENTS? ENTRANCE EXAMS? HUH?!
HARDHAT SAID ONE TEST DECIDES EVERYTHING. LIKE IF YOU APPLIED TO COLLEGE AND THEY ONLY LOOKED AT YOUR S.A.T. SCORES, AND--
UM, SORRY, BABS, BUT THEY WANT ME IN THE BOARDROOM.
YOU GOT THIS, BABS. YOU'RE THE BEST. THE BEST AT KICKING BUTT, AND THE BEST FRIEND.
YOU'RE MY BEST FRIEND, TOO.
THANKS FOR EVERYTHING, FRANKIE. I'LL SEE YOU SOON.

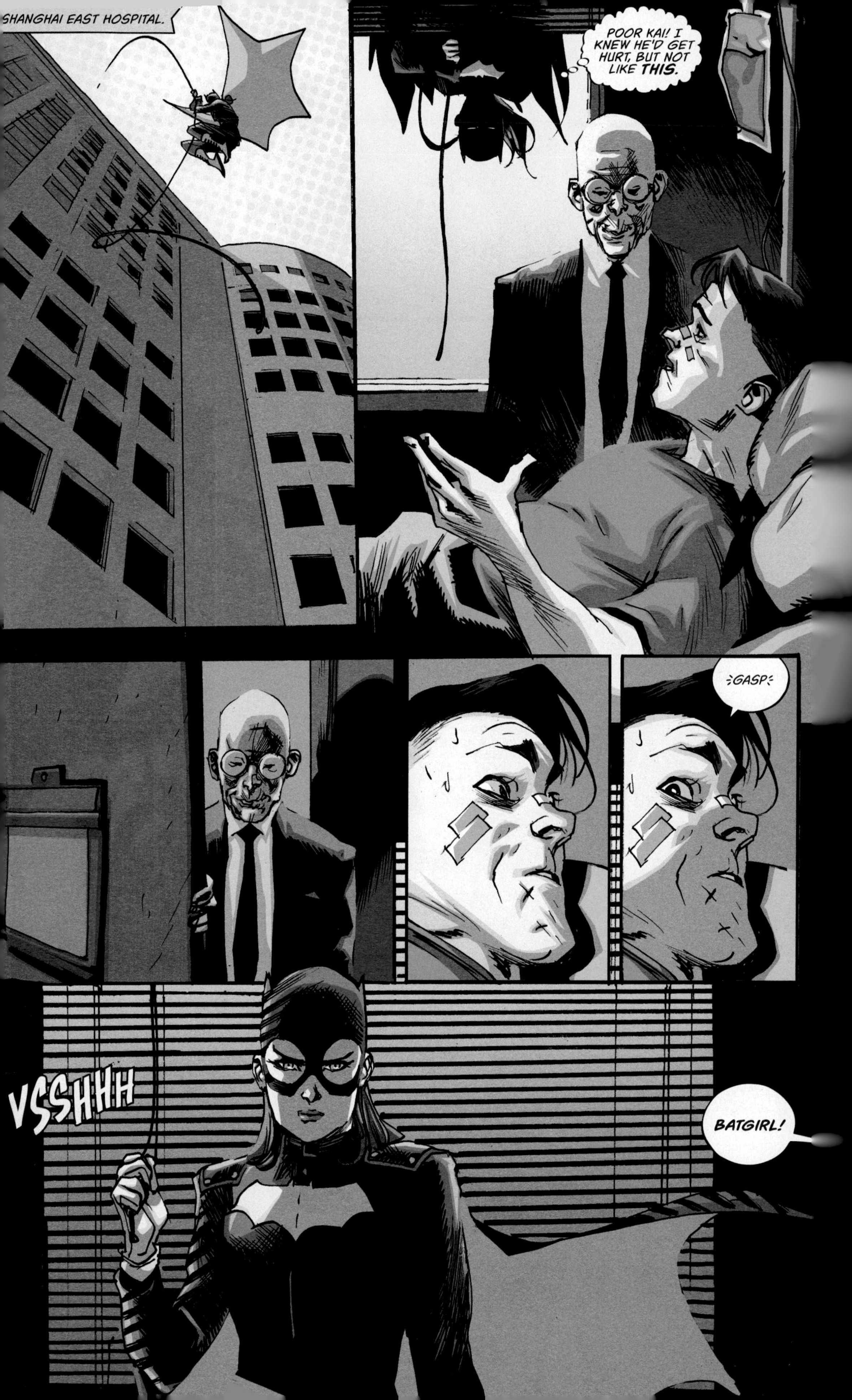
SHANGHAI EAST HOSPITAL.
POOR KAI! I KNEW HE'D GET HURT, BUT NOT LIKE **THIS**.
GASP
VSSHHH
BATGIRL!

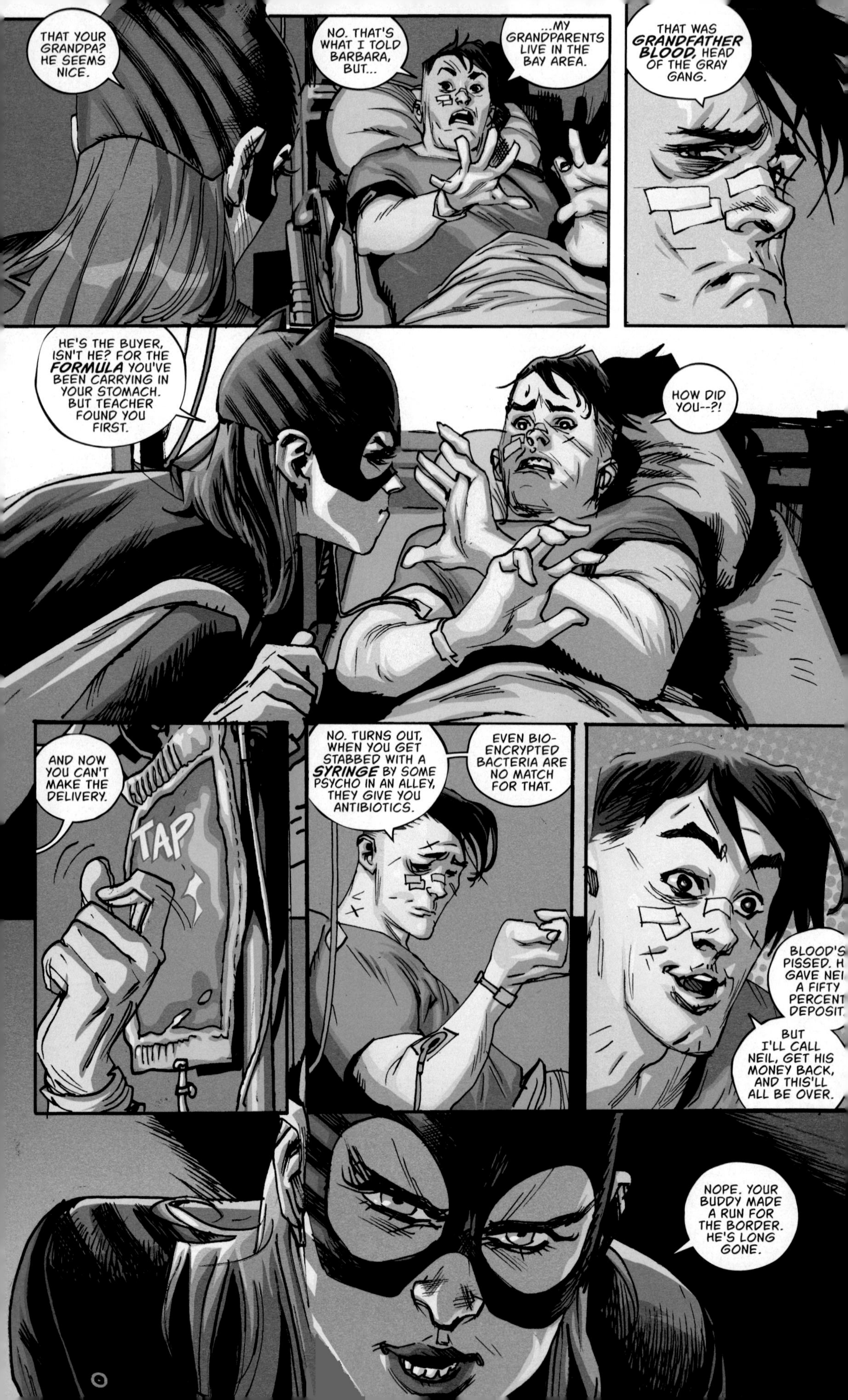
THAT YOUR GRANDPA? HE SEEMS NICE.
NO. THAT'S WHAT I TOLD BARBARA, BUT...
...MY GRANDPARENTS LIVE IN THE BAY AREA.
THAT WAS GRANDFATHER BLOOD, HEAD OF THE GRAY GANG.
HE'S THE BUYER, ISN'T HE? FOR THE FORMULA YOU'VE BEEN CARRYING IN YOUR STOMACH. BUT TEACHER FOUND YOU FIRST.
HOW DID YOU--?!
AND NOW YOU CAN'T MAKE THE DELIVERY.
TAP
NO. TURNS OUT, WHEN YOU GET STABBED WITH A SYRINGE BY SOME PSYCHO IN AN ALLEY, THEY GIVE YOU ANTIBIOTICS.
EVEN BIO-ENCRYPTED BACTERIA ARE NO MATCH FOR THAT.
BUT I'LL CALL NEIL, GET HIS MONEY BACK, AND THIS'LL ALL BE OVER.
NOPE. YOUR BUDDY MADE A RUN FOR THE BORDER. HE'S LONG GONE.

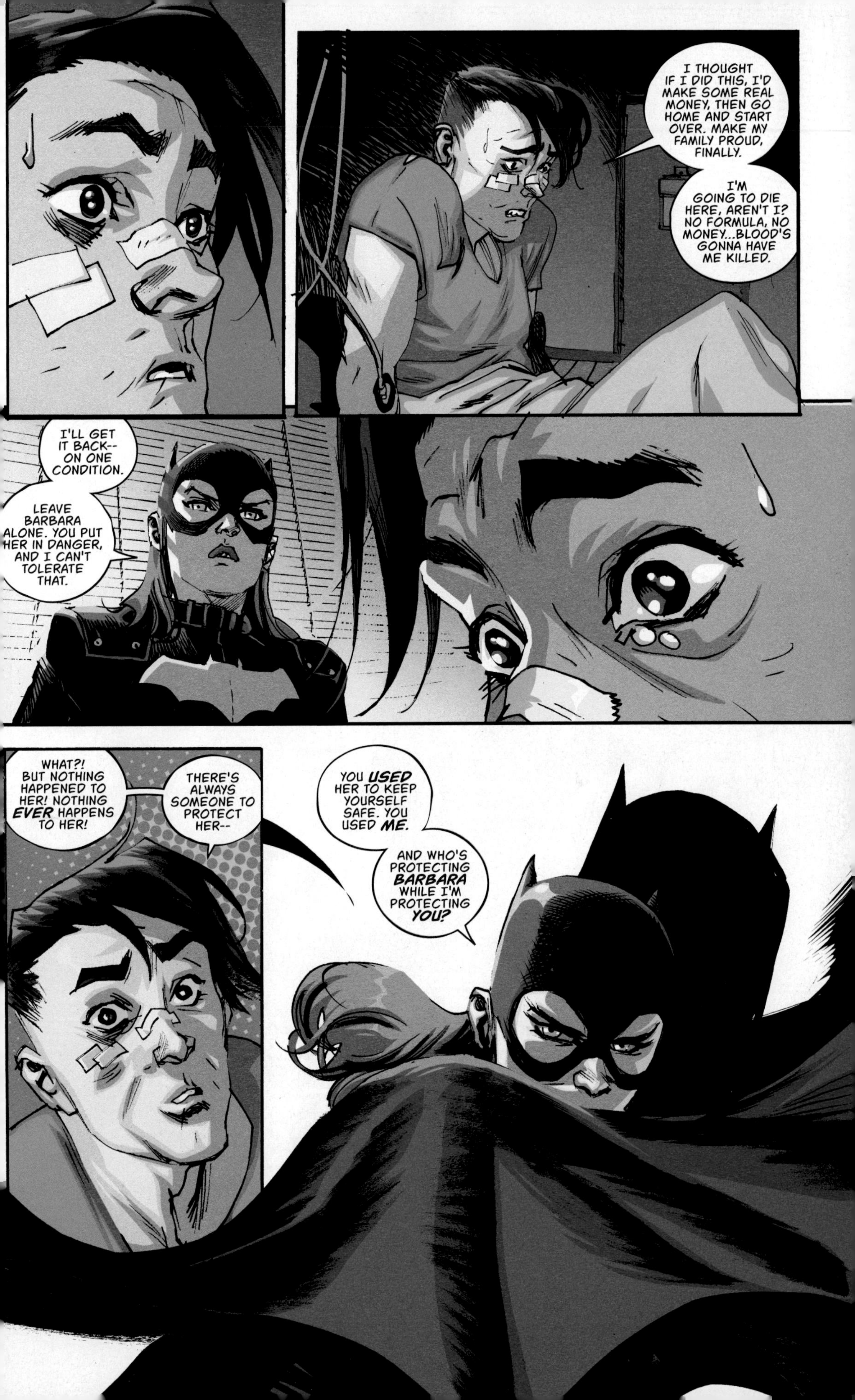
I THOUGHT IF I DID THIS, I'D MAKE SOME REAL MONEY, THEN GO HOME AND START OVER. MAKE MY FAMILY PROUD, FINALLY.
I'M GOING TO DIE HERE, AREN'T I? NO FORMULA, NO MONEY...BLOOD'S GONNA HAVE ME KILLED.
I'LL GET IT BACK--ON ONE CONDITION.
LEAVE BARBARA ALONE. YOU PUT HER IN DANGER, AND I CAN'T TOLERATE THAT.
WHAT?! BUT NOTHING HAPPENED TO HER! NOTHING EVER HAPPENS TO HER!
THERE'S ALWAYS SOMEONE TO PROTECT HER--
YOU USED HER TO KEEP YOURSELF SAFE. YOU USED ME.
AND WHO'S PROTECTING BARBARA WHILE I'M PROTECTING YOU?

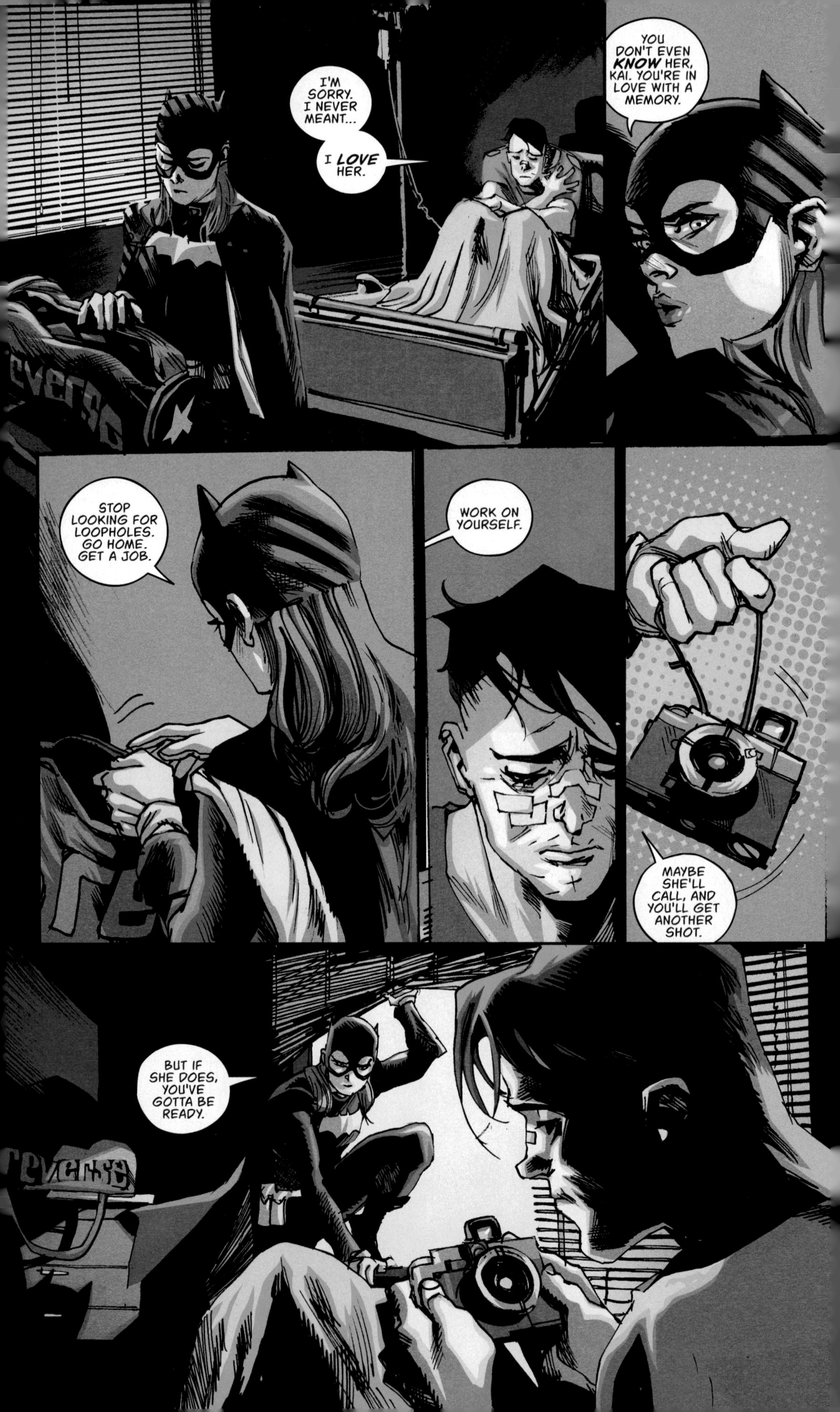
I'M SORRY. I NEVER MEANT...
I **LOVE** HER.
YOU DON'T EVEN **KNOW** HER, KAI. YOU'RE IN LOVE WITH A MEMORY.
STOP LOOKING FOR LOOPHOLES. GO HOME. GET A JOB.
WORK ON YOURSELF.
MAYBE SHE'LL CALL, AND YOU'LL GET ANOTHER SHOT.
BUT IF SHE DOES, YOU'VE GOTTA BE READY.

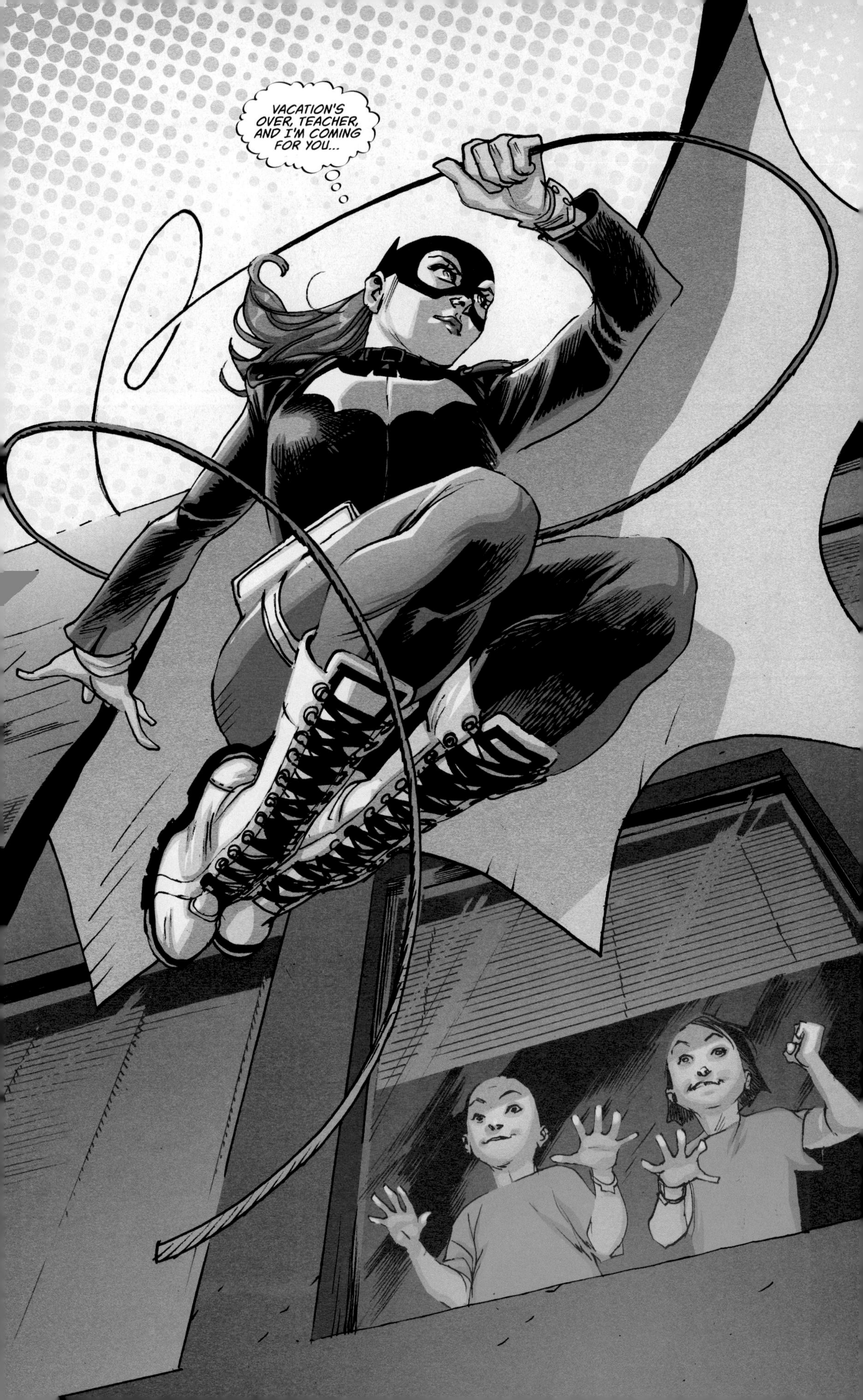
VACATION'S OVER, TEACHER, AND I'M COMING FOR YOU...

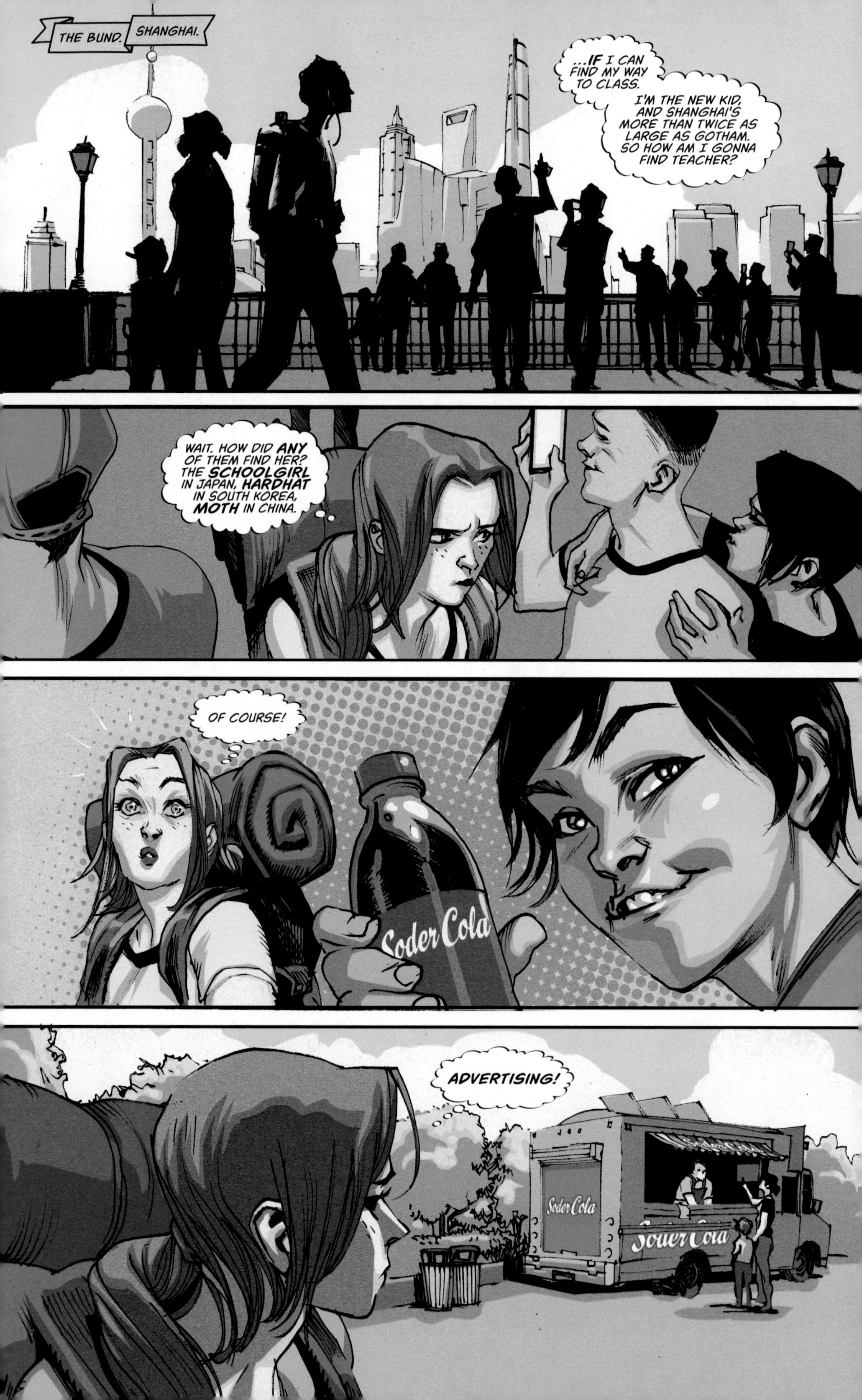
THE BUND. SHANGHAI.
...IF I CAN FIND MY WAY TO CLASS.
I'M THE NEW KID, AND SHANGHAI'S MORE THAN TWICE AS LARGE AS GOTHAM. SO HOW AM I GONNA FIND TEACHER?
WAIT. HOW DID ANY OF THEM FIND HER? THE SCHOOLGIRL IN JAPAN, HARDHAT IN SOUTH KOREA, MOTH IN CHINA.
OF COURSE!
Soder Cola
ADVERTISING!
Soder Cola

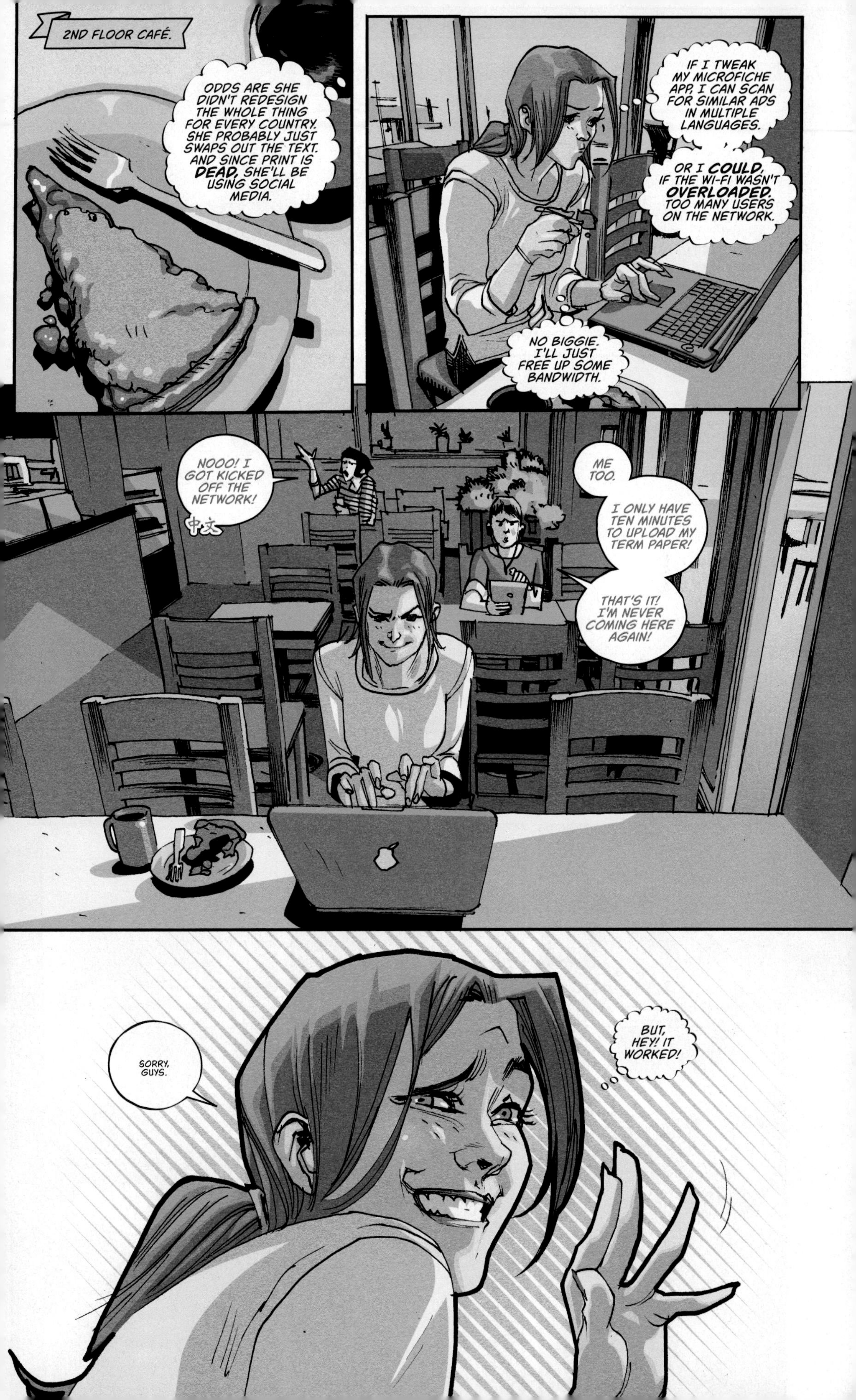
2ND FLOOR CAFÉ.
ODDS ARE SHE DIDN'T REDESIGN THE WHOLE THING FOR EVERY COUNTRY. SHE PROBABLY JUST SWAPS OUT THE TEXT. AND SINCE PRINT IS DEAD, SHE'LL BE USING SOCIAL MEDIA.
IF I TWEAK MY MICROFICHE APP, I CAN SCAN FOR SIMILAR ADS IN MULTIPLE LANGUAGES.
OR I COULD, IF THE WI-FI WASN'T OVERLOADED. TOO MANY USERS ON THE NETWORK.
NO BIGGIE. I'LL JUST FREE UP SOME BANDWIDTH.
NOOO! I GOT KICKED OFF THE NETWORK!
中文
ME TOO.
I ONLY HAVE TEN MINUTES TO UPLOAD MY TERM PAPER!
THAT'S IT! I'M NEVER COMING HERE AGAIN!
SORRY, GUYS.
BUT, HEY! IT WORKED!

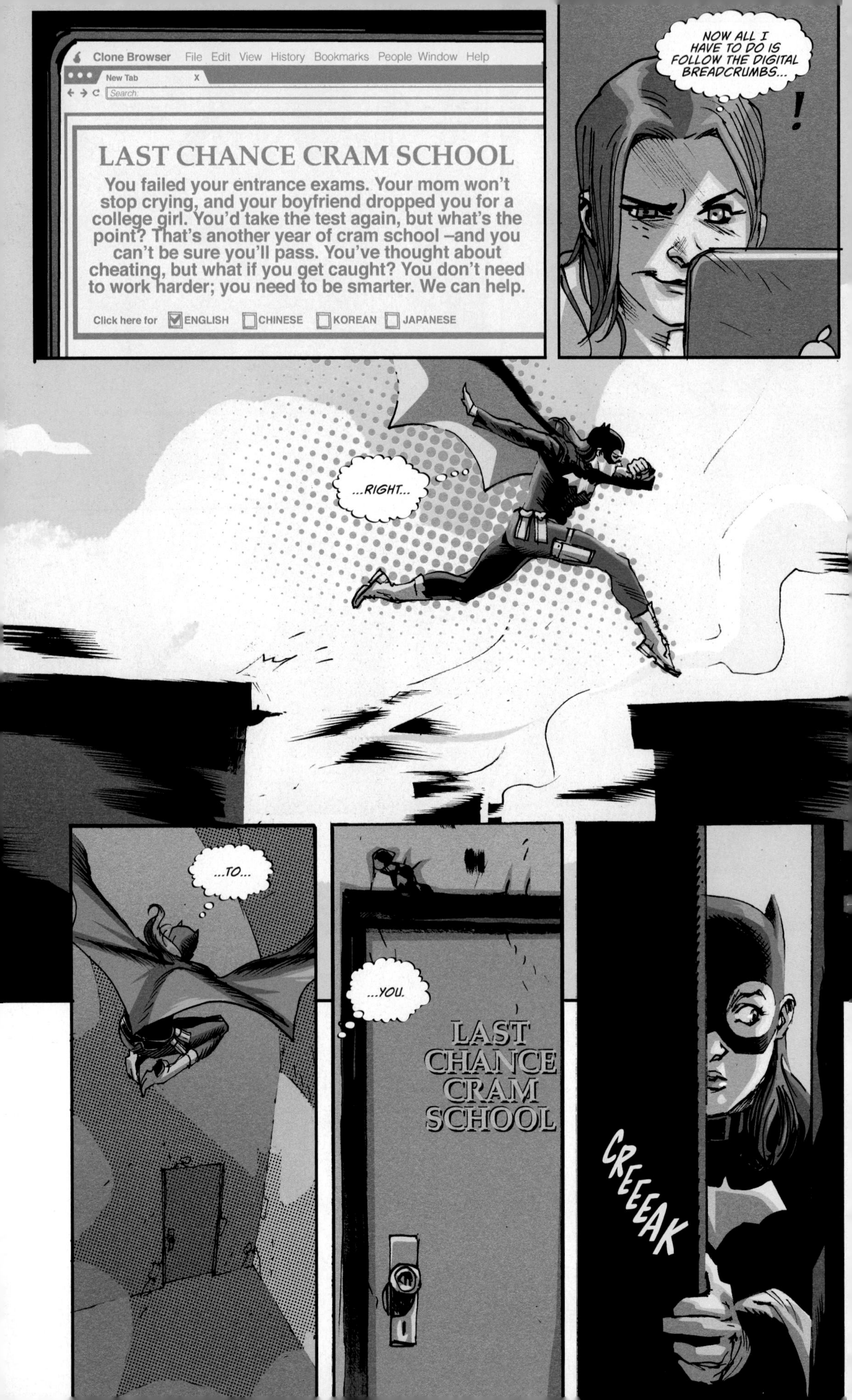
Clone Browser File Edit View History Bookmarks People Window Help
New Tab X
Search:
LAST CHANCE CRAM SCHOOL
You failed your entrance exams. Your mom won't stop crying, and your boyfriend dropped you for a college girl. You'd take the test again, but what's the point? That's another year of cram school –and you can't be sure you'll pass. You've thought about cheating, but what if you get caught? You don't need to work harder; you need to be smarter. We can help.
Click here for ENGLISH CHINESE KOREAN JAPANESE
NOW ALL I HAVE TO DO IS FOLLOW THE DIGITAL BREADCRUMBS...
!
...RIGHT...
...TO...
...YOU.
LAST CHANCE CRAM SCHOOL
CREEEAK

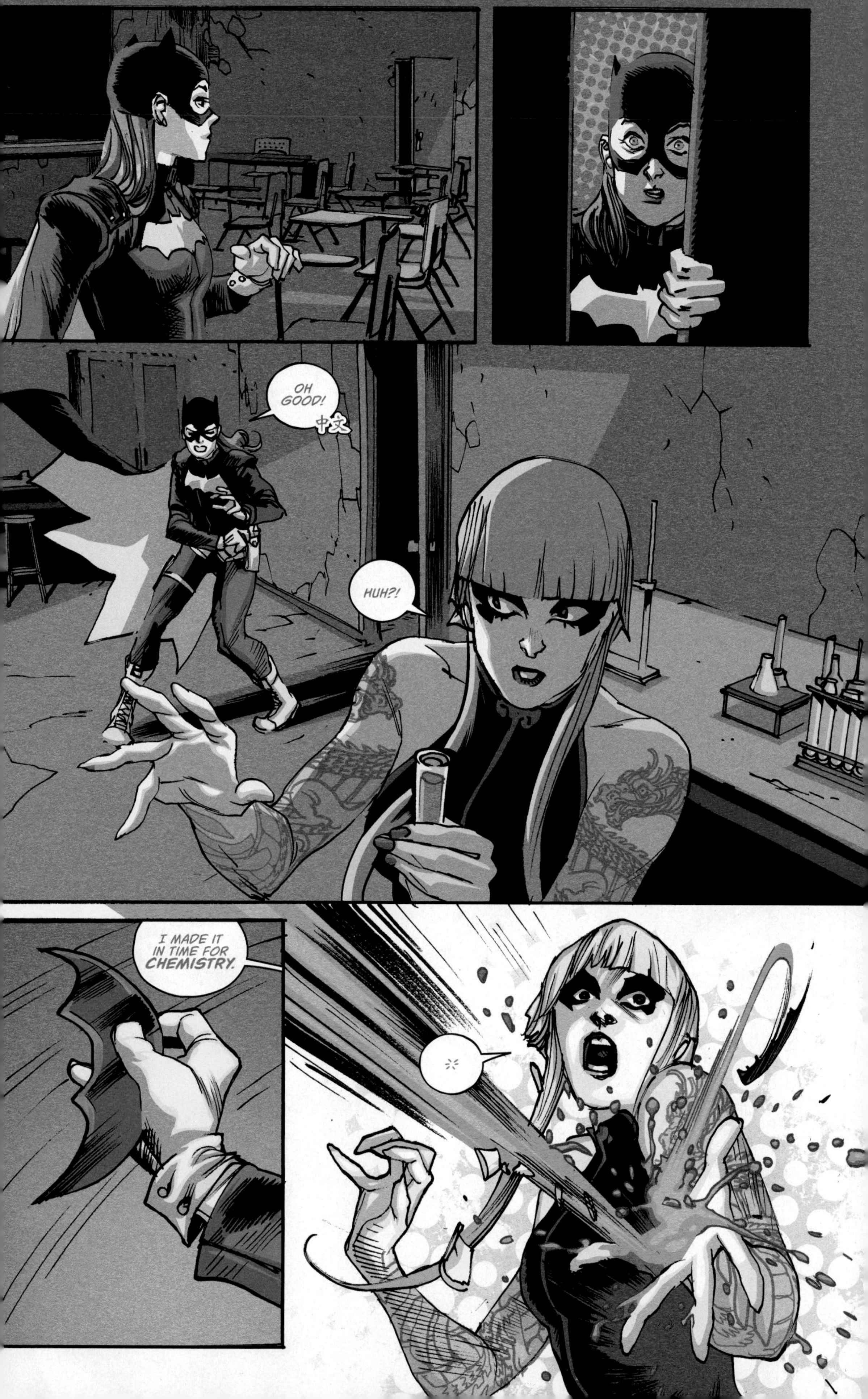
OH GOOD!
中文
HUH?!
I MADE IT IN TIME FOR **CHEMISTRY**.

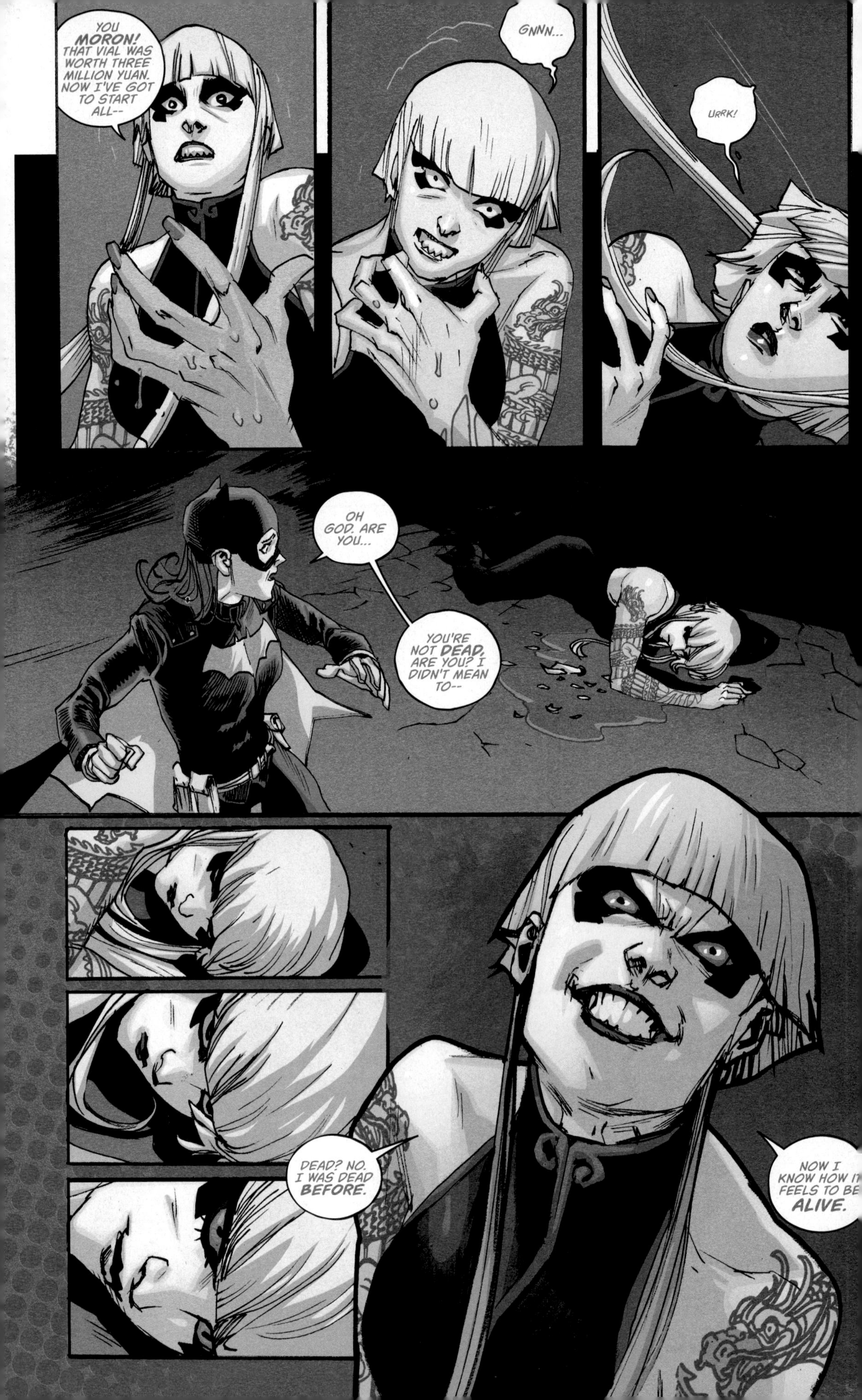
YOU **MORON!** THAT VIAL WAS WORTH THREE MILLION YUAN. NOW I'VE GOT TO START ALL--
GNNN...
URRK!
OH GOD. ARE YOU...
YOU'RE NOT **DEAD,** ARE YOU? I DIDN'T MEAN TO--
DEAD? NO. I WAS DEAD **BEFORE.**
NOW I KNOW HOW IT FEELS TO BE **ALIVE.**

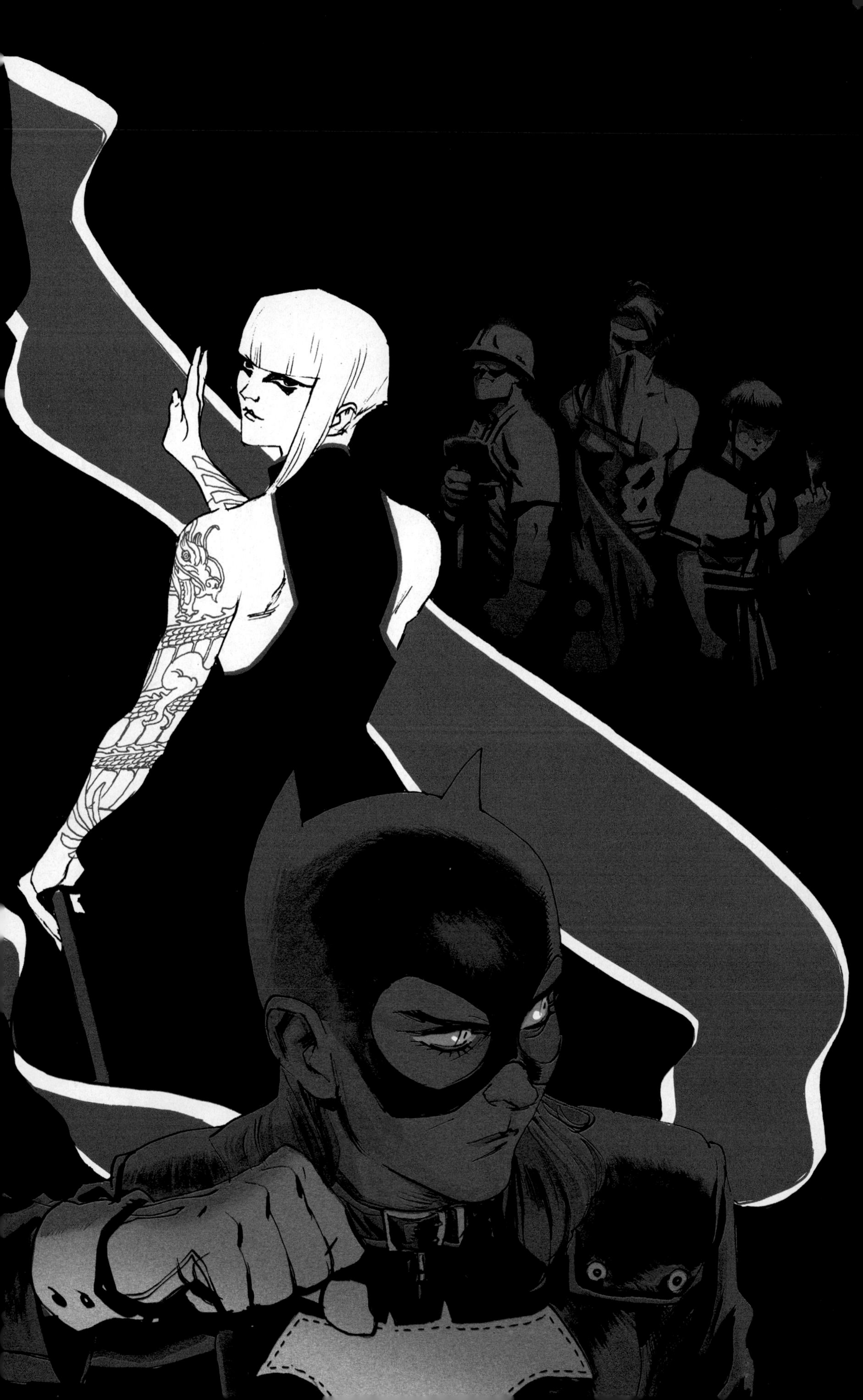

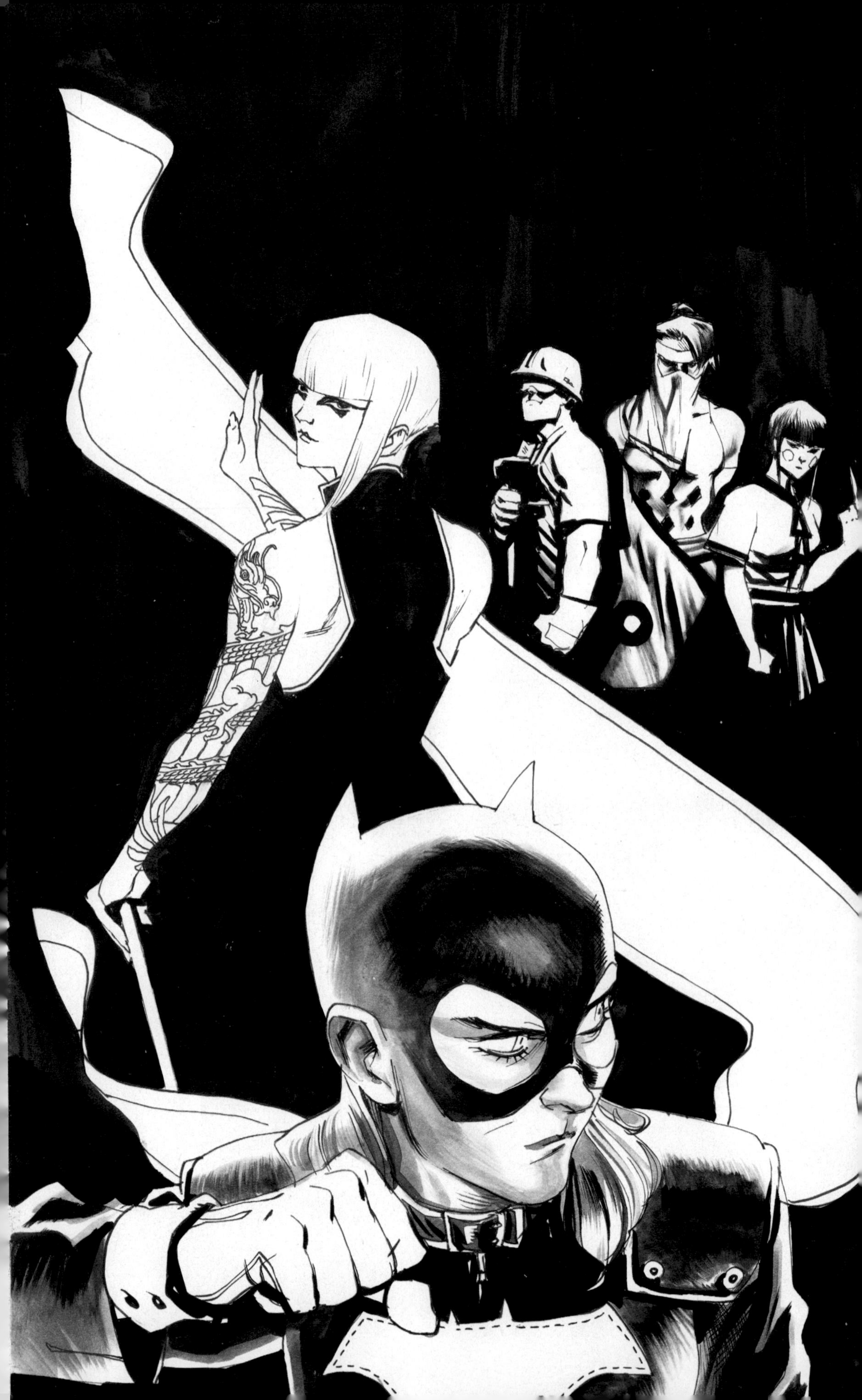

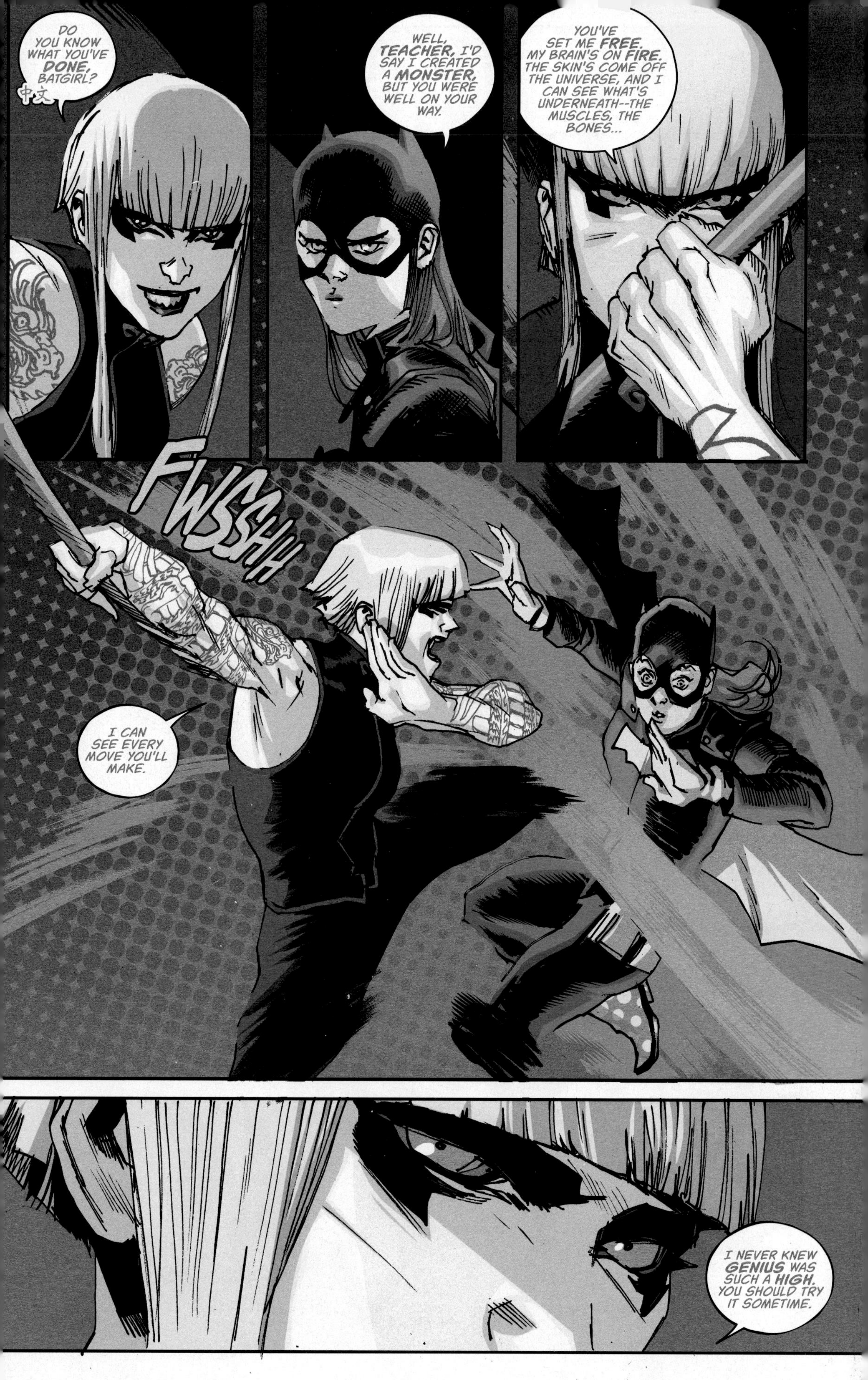
DO YOU KNOW WHAT YOU'VE DONE, BATGIRL?
中文
WELL, TEACHER, I'D SAY I CREATED A MONSTER, BUT YOU WERE WELL ON YOUR WAY.
YOU'VE SET ME FREE. MY BRAIN'S ON FIRE. THE SKIN'S COME OFF THE UNIVERSE, AND I CAN SEE WHAT'S UNDERNEATH--THE MUSCLES, THE BONES...
FWSSHH
I CAN SEE EVERY MOVE YOU'LL MAKE.
I NEVER KNEW GENIUS WAS SUCH A HIGH. YOU SHOULD TRY IT SOMETIME.

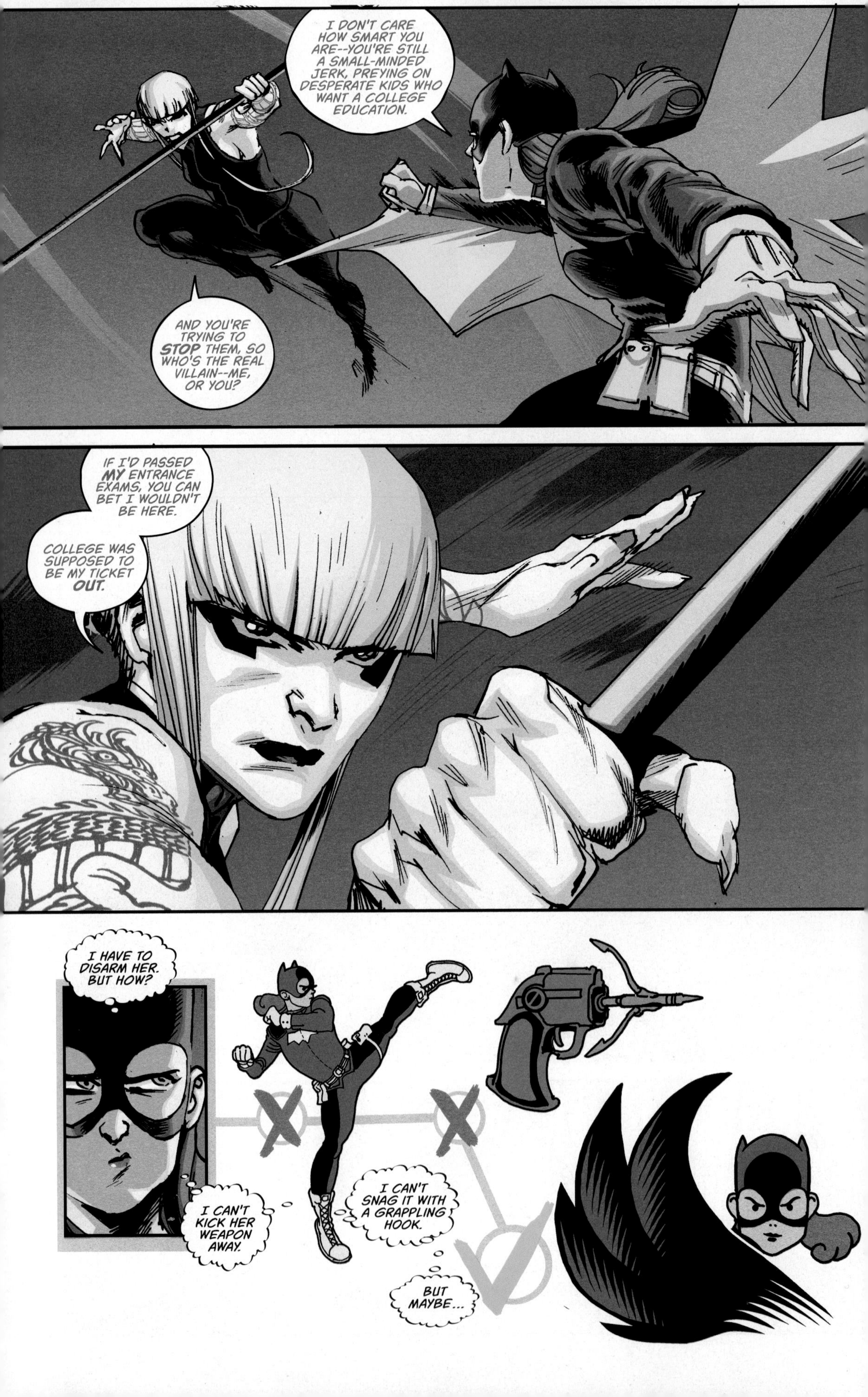
I DON'T CARE HOW SMART YOU ARE--YOU'RE STILL A SMALL-MINDED JERK, PREYING ON DESPERATE KIDS WHO WANT A COLLEGE EDUCATION.
AND YOU'RE TRYING TO STOP THEM, SO WHO'S THE REAL VILLAIN--ME, OR YOU?
IF I'D PASSED MY ENTRANCE EXAMS, YOU CAN BET I WOULDN'T BE HERE.
COLLEGE WAS SUPPOSED TO BE MY TICKET OUT.
I HAVE TO DISARM HER. BUT HOW?
I CAN'T KICK HER WEAPON AWAY.
I CAN'T SNAG IT WITH A GRAPPLING HOOK.
BUT MAYBE...

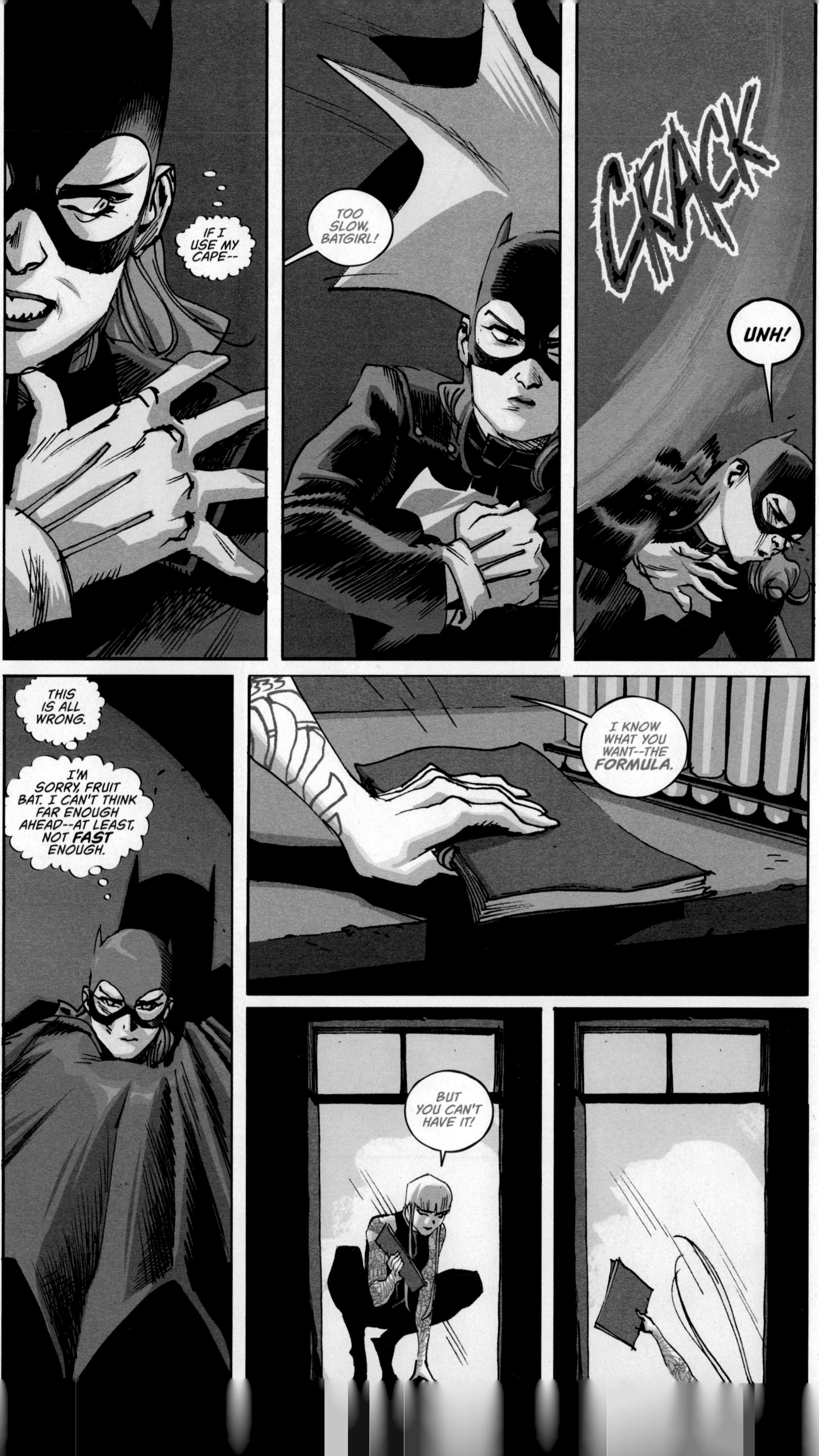
IF I USE MY CAPE--
TOO SLOW, BATGIRL!
CRACK
UNH!
THIS IS ALL WRONG.
I'M SORRY, FRUIT BAT. I CAN'T THINK FAR ENOUGH AHEAD--AT LEAST, NOT FAST ENOUGH.
I KNOW WHAT YOU WANT--THE FORMULA.
BUT YOU CAN'T HAVE IT!

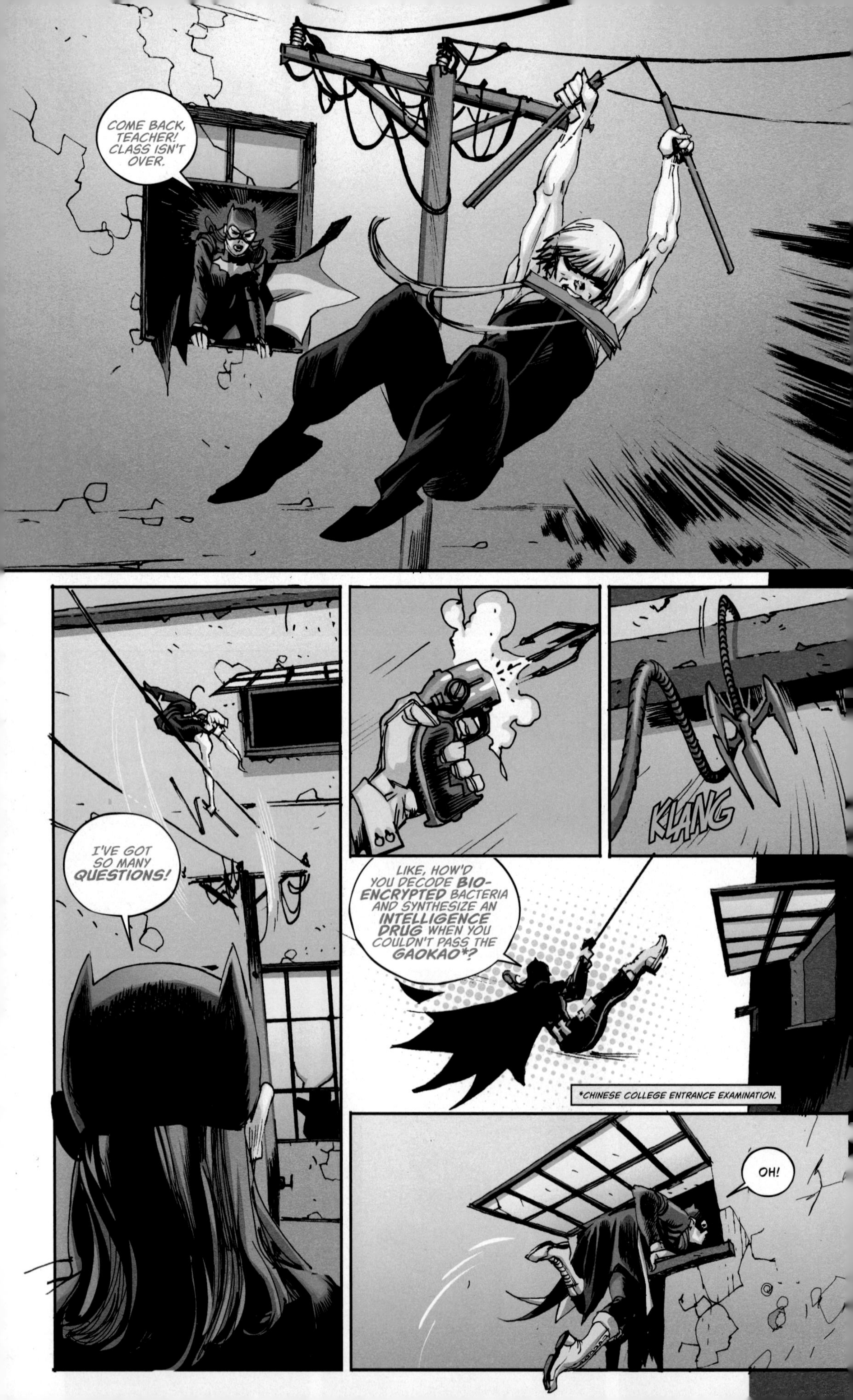
COME BACK, TEACHER! CLASS ISN'T OVER.
I'VE GOT SO MANY QUESTIONS!
KLANG
LIKE, HOW'D YOU DECODE BIO-ENCRYPTED BACTERIA AND SYNTHESIZE AN INTELLIGENCE DRUG WHEN YOU COULDN'T PASS THE GAOKAO*?
*CHINESE COLLEGE ENTRANCE EXAMINATION.
OH!

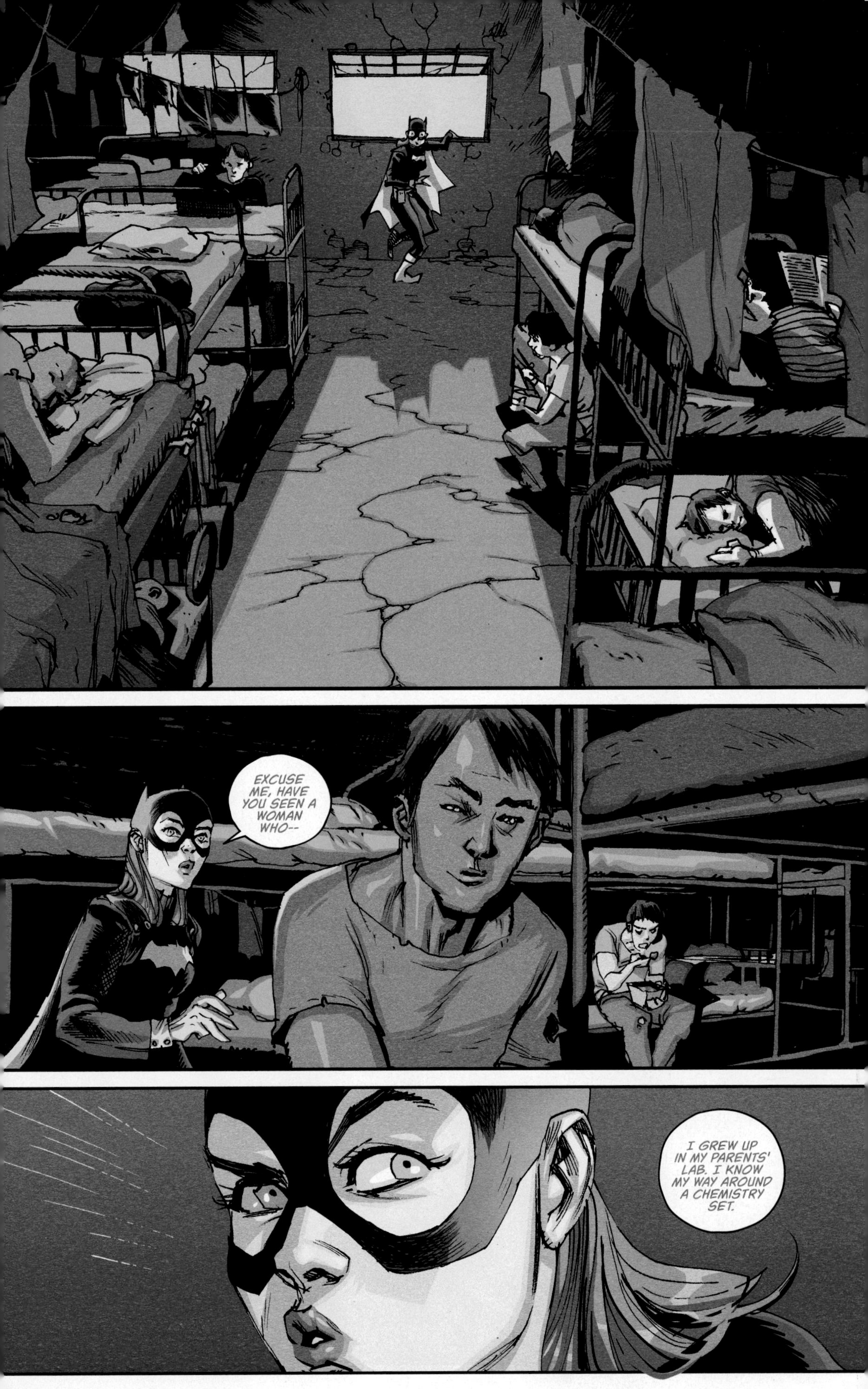
EXCUSE ME, HAVE YOU SEEN A WOMAN WHO--
I GREW UP IN MY PARENTS' LAB. I KNOW MY WAY AROUND A CHEMISTRY SET.

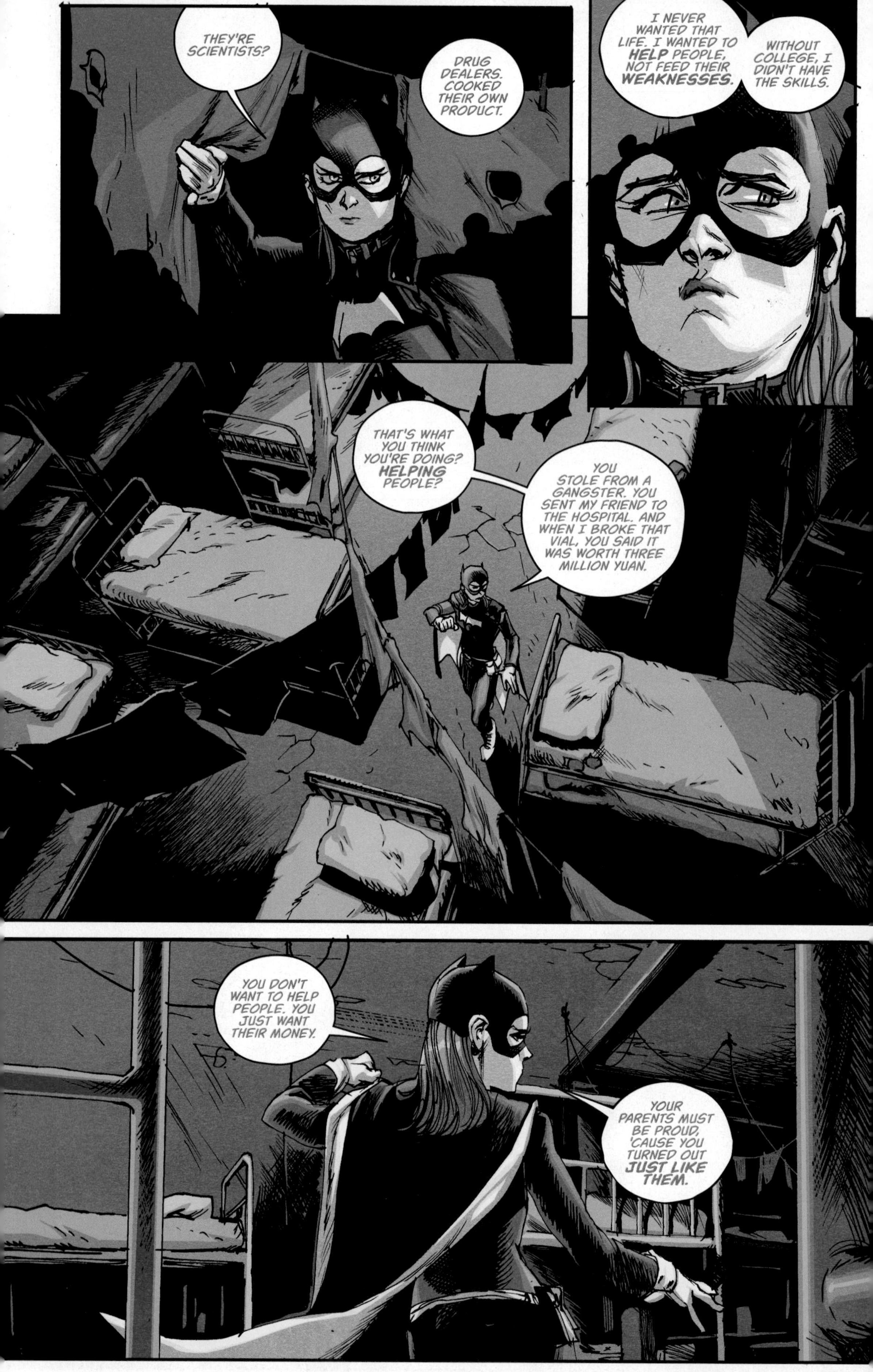
THEY'RE SCIENTISTS?
DRUG DEALERS. COOKED THEIR OWN PRODUCT.
I NEVER WANTED THAT LIFE. I WANTED TO HELP PEOPLE, NOT FEED THEIR WEAKNESSES.
WITHOUT COLLEGE, I DIDN'T HAVE THE SKILLS.
THAT'S WHAT YOU THINK YOU'RE DOING? HELPING PEOPLE?
YOU STOLE FROM A GANGSTER. YOU SENT MY FRIEND TO THE HOSPITAL. AND WHEN I BROKE THAT VIAL, YOU SAID IT WAS WORTH THREE MILLION YUAN.
YOU DON'T WANT TO HELP PEOPLE. YOU JUST WANT THEIR MONEY.
YOUR PARENTS MUST BE PROUD, 'CAUSE YOU TURNED OUT JUST LIKE THEM.

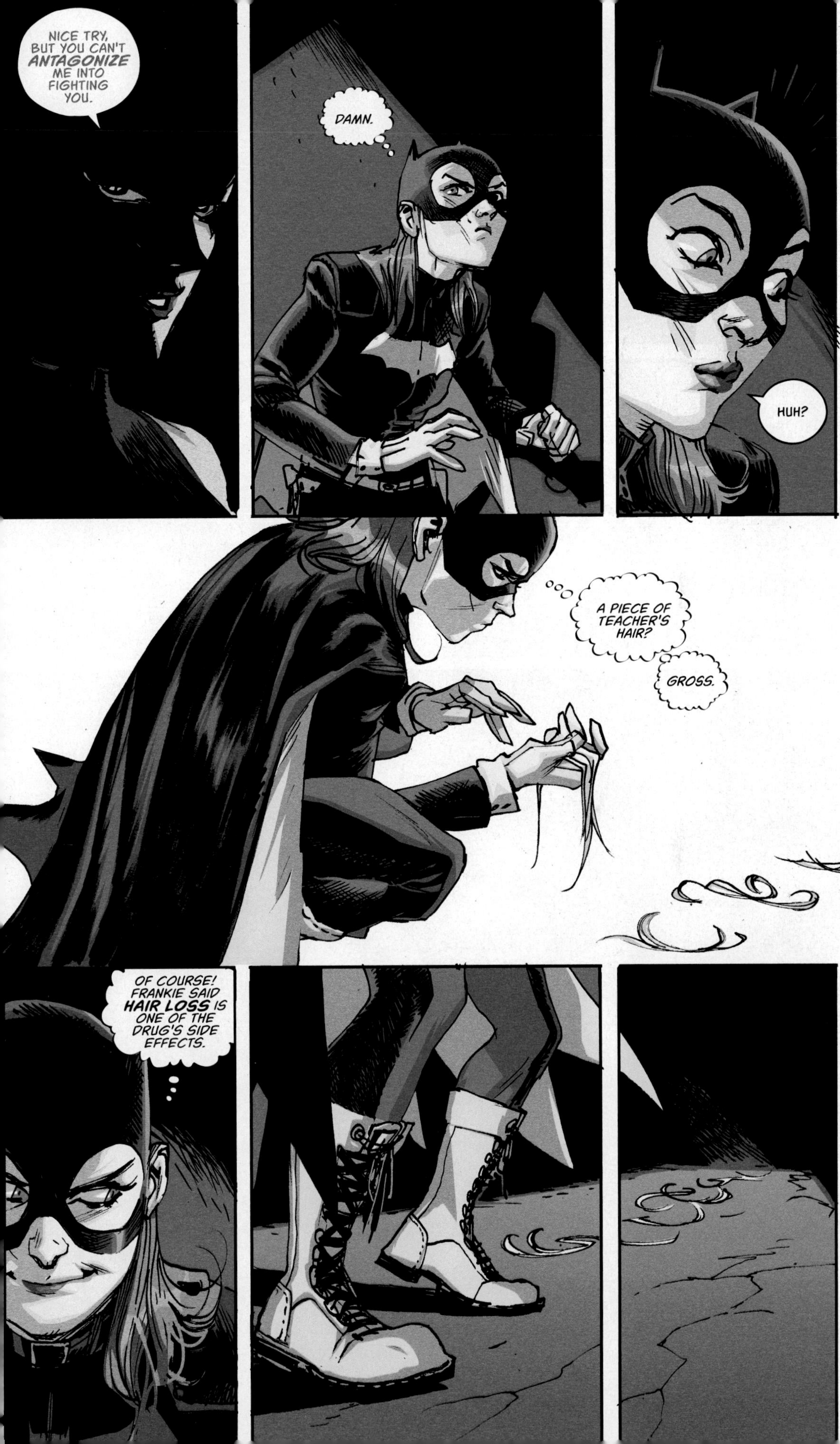
NICE TRY, BUT YOU CAN'T ANTAGONIZE ME INTO FIGHTING YOU.
DAMN.
HUH?
A PIECE OF TEACHER'S HAIR?
GROSS.
OF COURSE! FRANKIE SAID HAIR LOSS IS ONE OF THE DRUG'S SIDE EFFECTS.

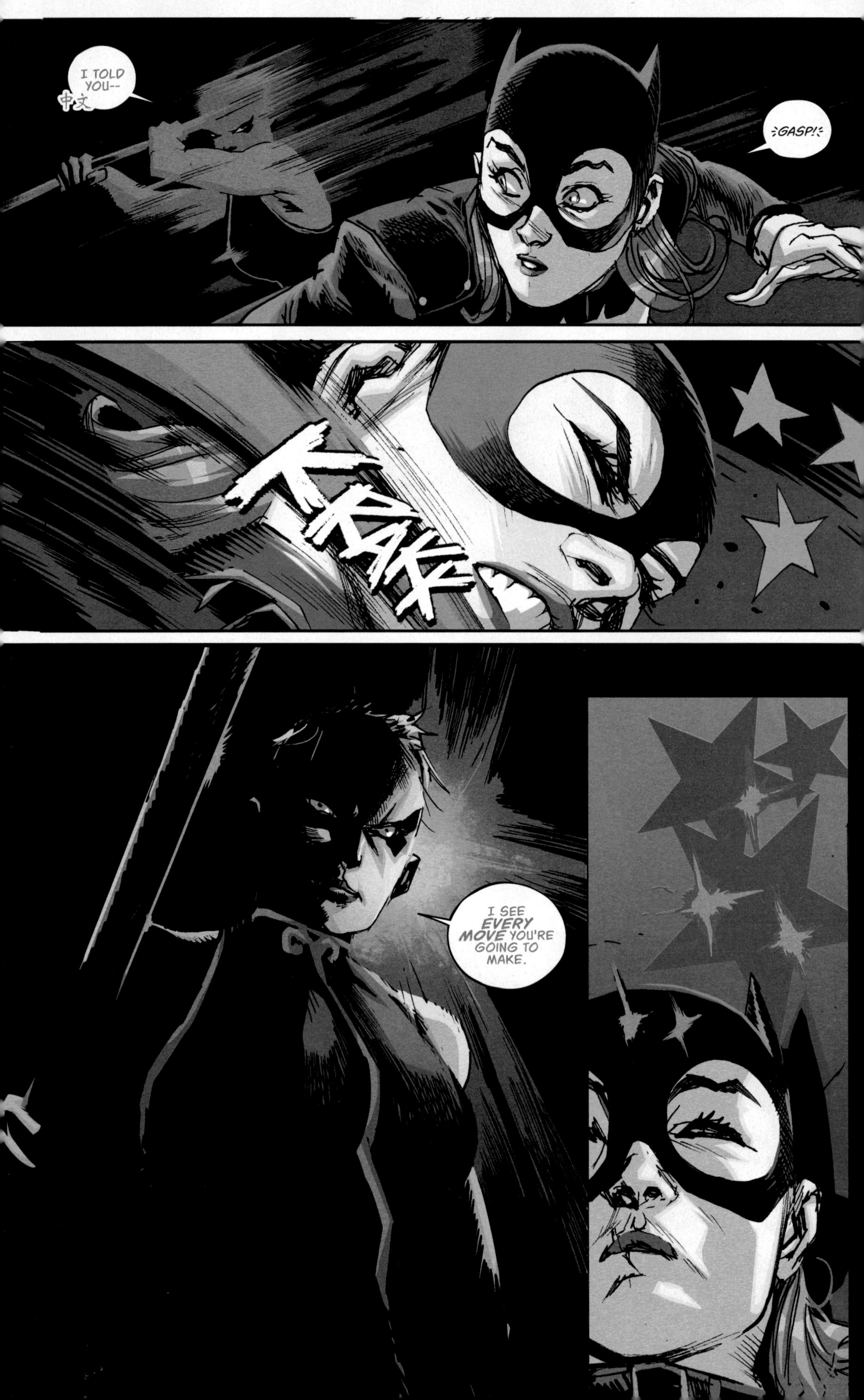
I TOLD YOU--
中文
GASP!
KRAKK
I SEE EVERY MOVE YOU'RE GOING TO MAKE.

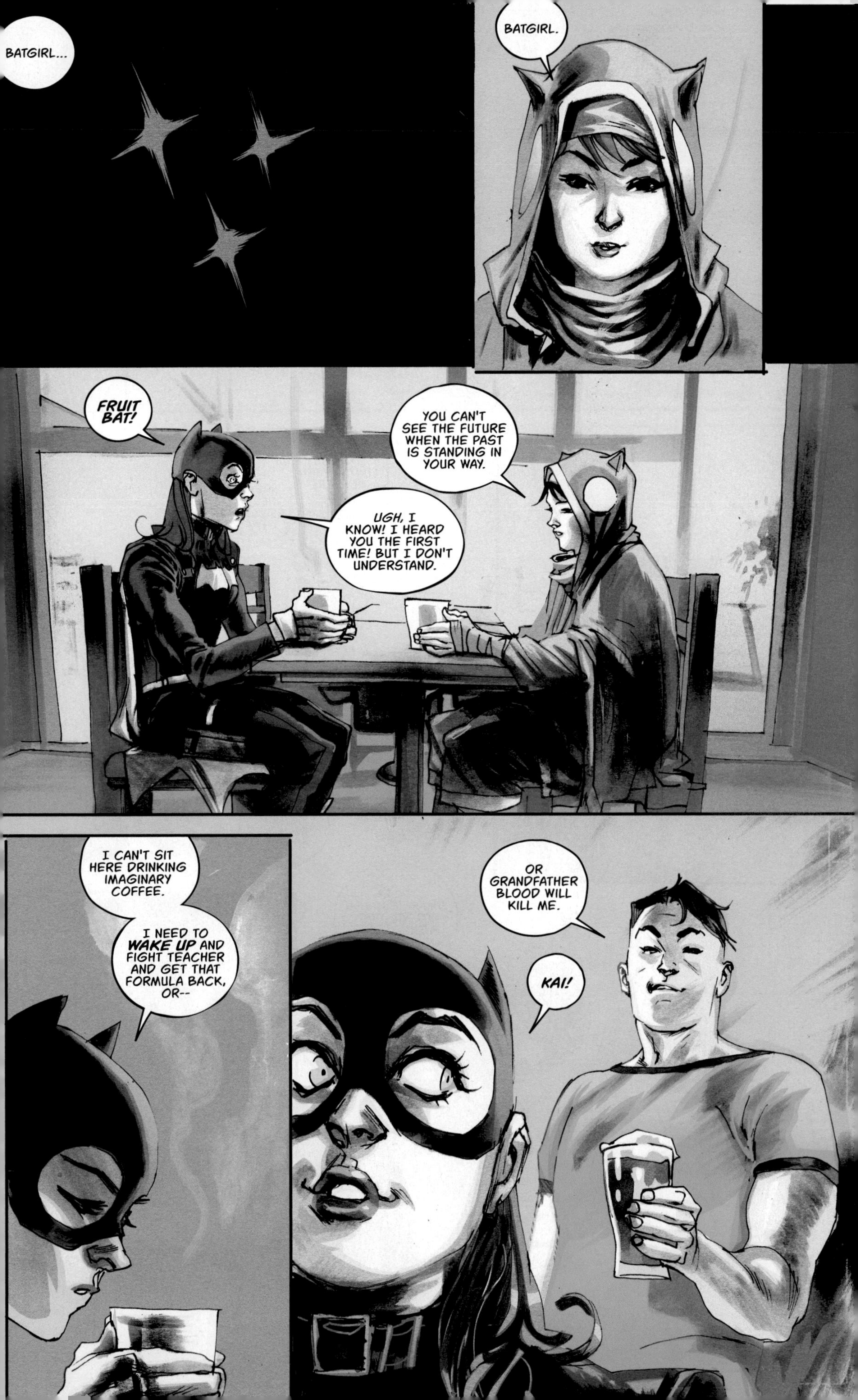
BATGIRL...
BATGIRL.
FRUIT BAT!
YOU CAN'T SEE THE FUTURE WHEN THE PAST IS STANDING IN YOUR WAY.
UGH, I KNOW! I HEARD YOU THE FIRST TIME! BUT I DON'T UNDERSTAND.
I CAN'T SIT HERE DRINKING IMAGINARY COFFEE.
I NEED TO WAKE UP AND FIGHT TEACHER AND GET THAT FORMULA BACK, OR--
OR GRANDFATHER BLOOD WILL KILL ME.
KAI!

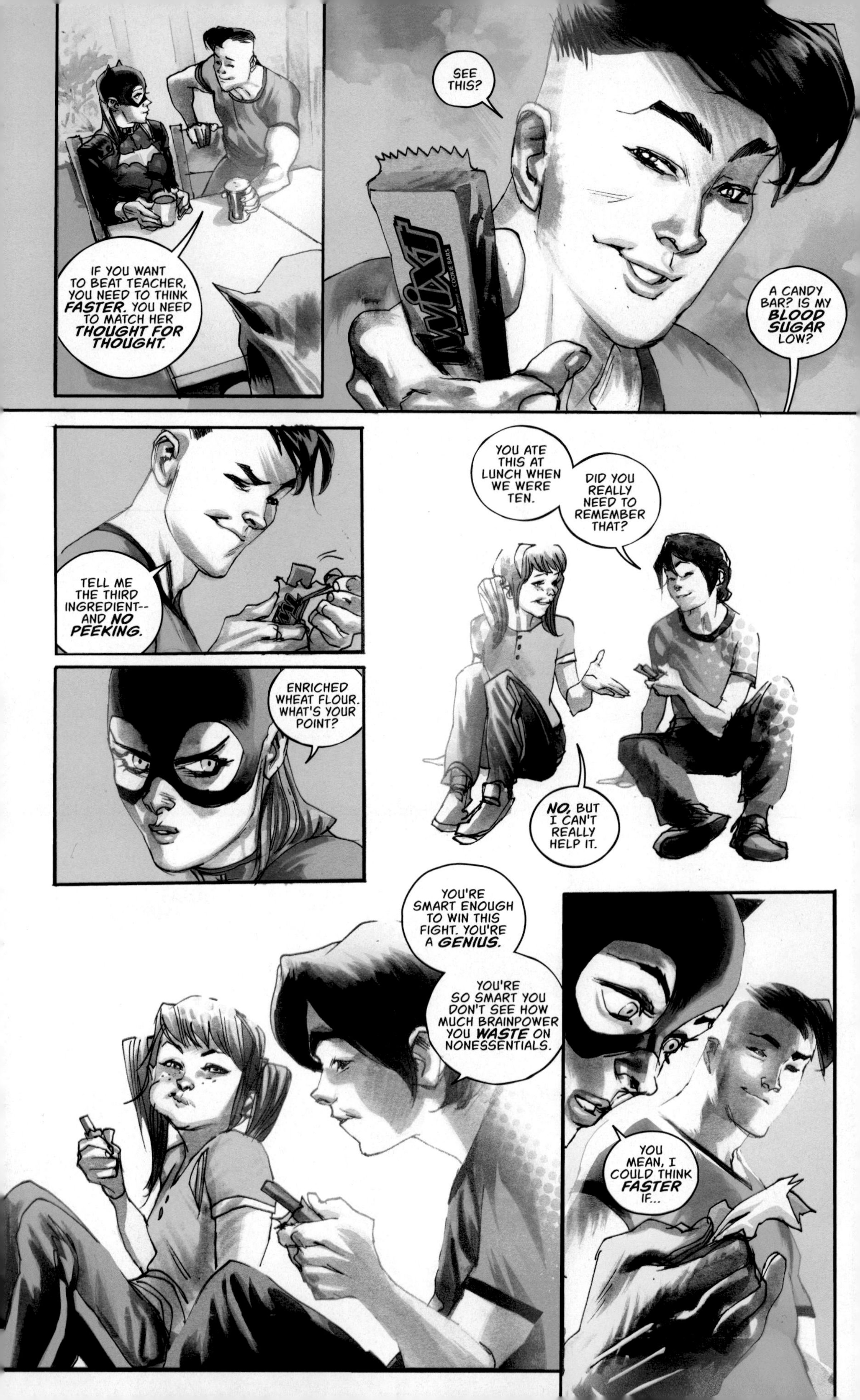
IF YOU WANT TO BEAT TEACHER, YOU NEED TO THINK **FASTER.** YOU NEED TO MATCH HER **THOUGHT FOR THOUGHT.**
SEE THIS?
TWIXT
COOKIE BARS
A CANDY BAR? IS MY **BLOOD SUGAR** LOW?
TELL ME THE THIRD INGREDIENT--AND **NO PEEKING.**
ENRICHED WHEAT FLOUR. WHAT'S YOUR POINT?
YOU ATE THIS AT LUNCH WHEN WE WERE TEN.
DID YOU REALLY NEED TO REMEMBER THAT?
**NO,** BUT I CAN'T REALLY HELP IT.
YOU'RE SMART ENOUGH TO WIN THIS FIGHT. YOU'RE A **GENIUS.**
YOU'RE SO SMART YOU DON'T SEE HOW MUCH BRAINPOWER YOU **WASTE** ON NONESSENTIALS.
YOU MEAN, I COULD THINK **FASTER** IF...

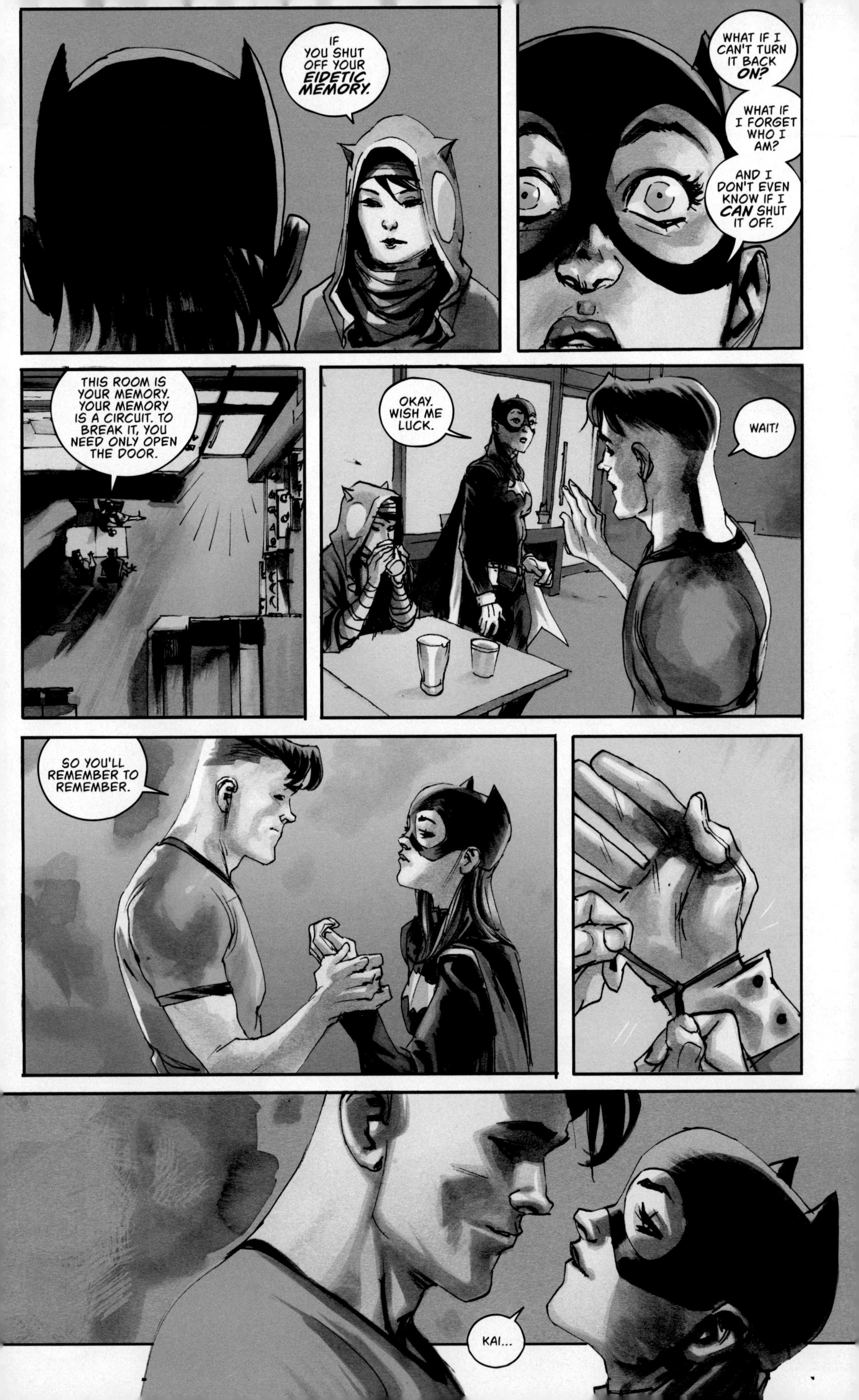
IF YOU SHUT OFF YOUR EIDETIC MEMORY.
WHAT IF I CAN'T TURN IT BACK ON?
WHAT IF I FORGET WHO I AM?
AND I DON'T EVEN KNOW IF I CAN SHUT IT OFF.
THIS ROOM IS YOUR MEMORY. YOUR MEMORY IS A CIRCUIT. TO BREAK IT, YOU NEED ONLY OPEN THE DOOR.
OKAY. WISH ME LUCK.
WAIT!
SO YOU'LL REMEMBER TO REMEMBER.
KAI...

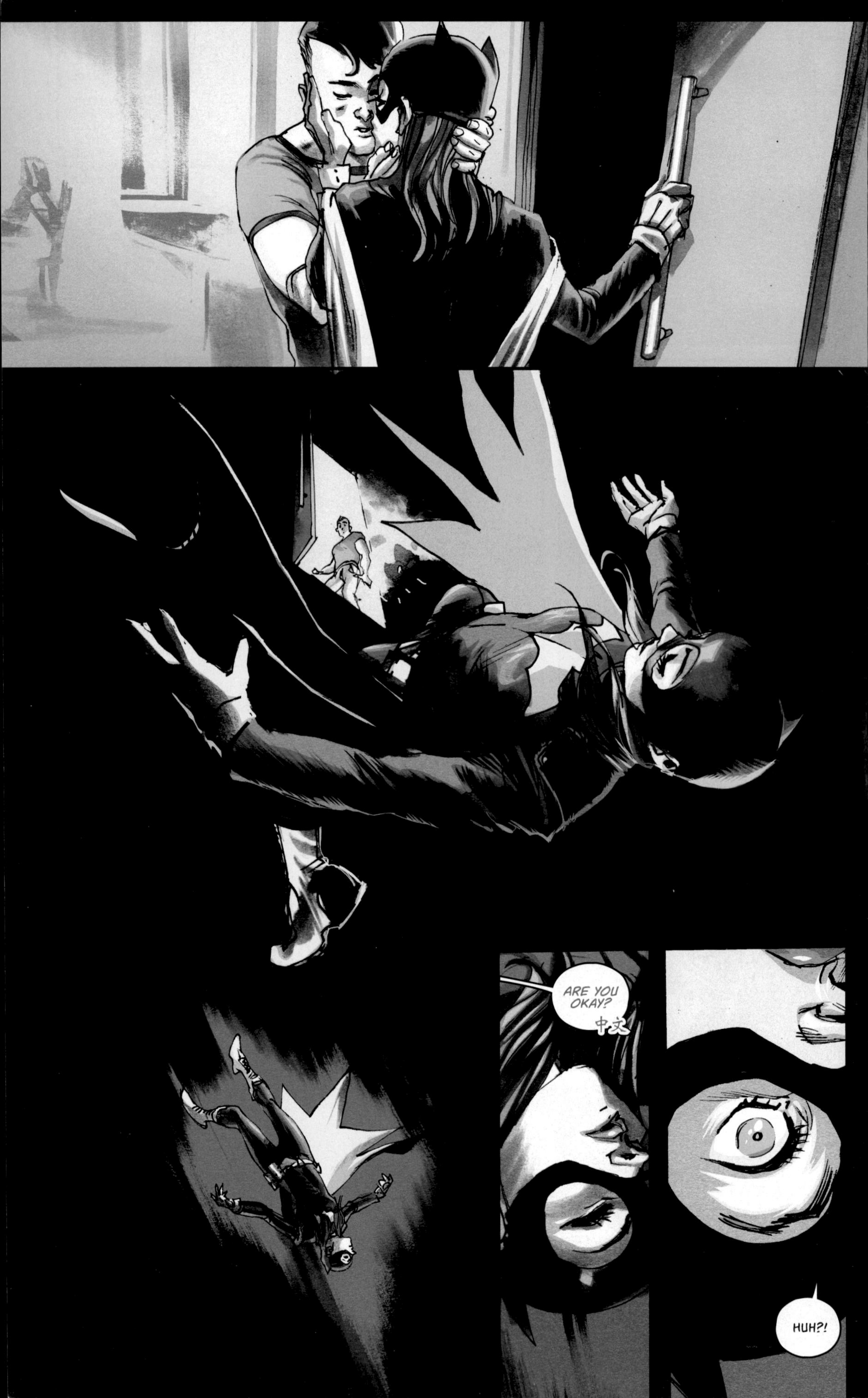
ARE YOU OKAY?
中文
HUH?!

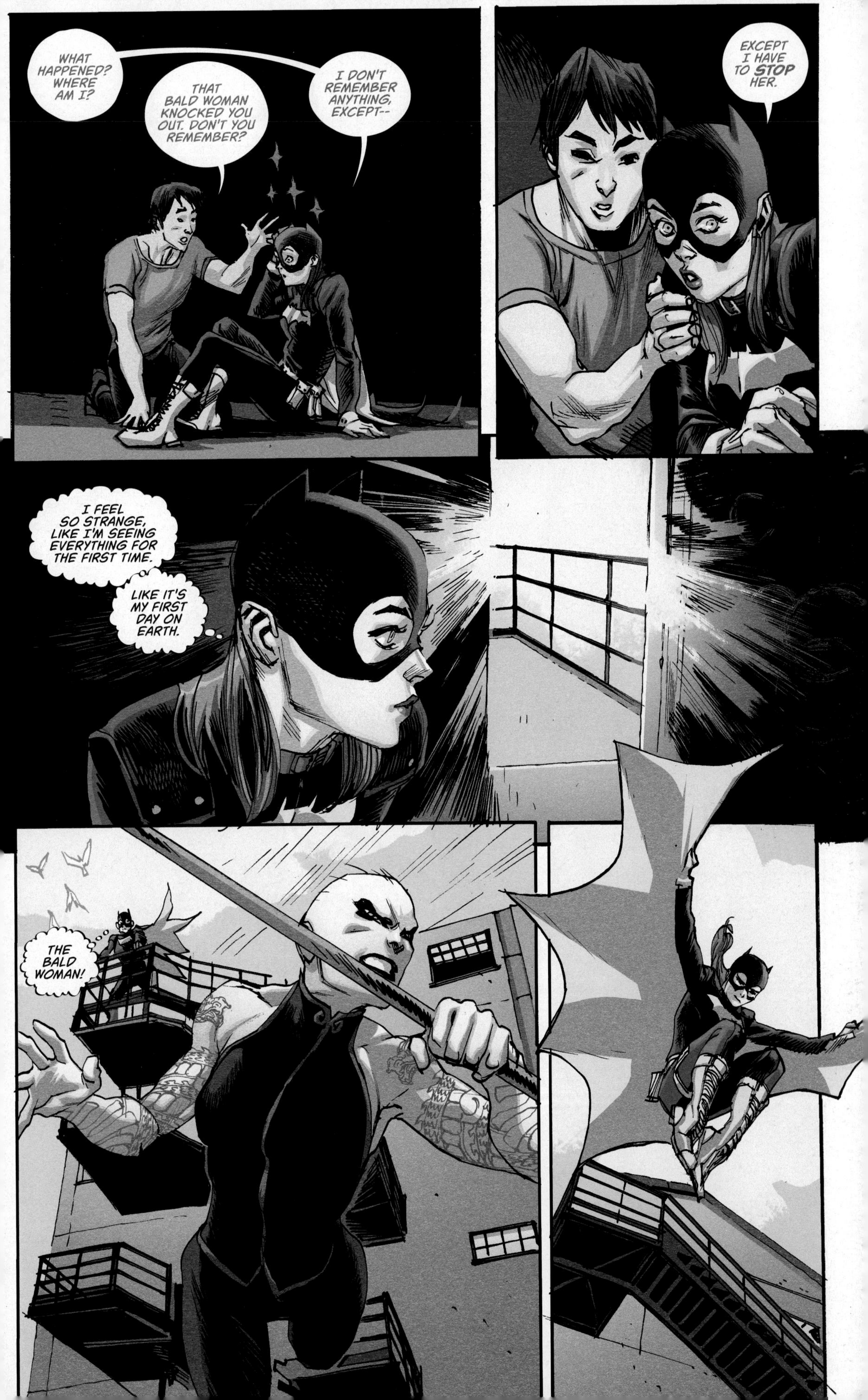
WHAT HAPPENED? WHERE AM I?
THAT BALD WOMAN KNOCKED YOU OUT. DON'T YOU REMEMBER?
I DON'T REMEMBER ANYTHING, EXCEPT--
EXCEPT I HAVE TO STOP HER.
I FEEL SO STRANGE, LIKE I'M SEEING EVERYTHING FOR THE FIRST TIME.
LIKE IT'S MY FIRST DAY ON EARTH.
THE BALD WOMAN!

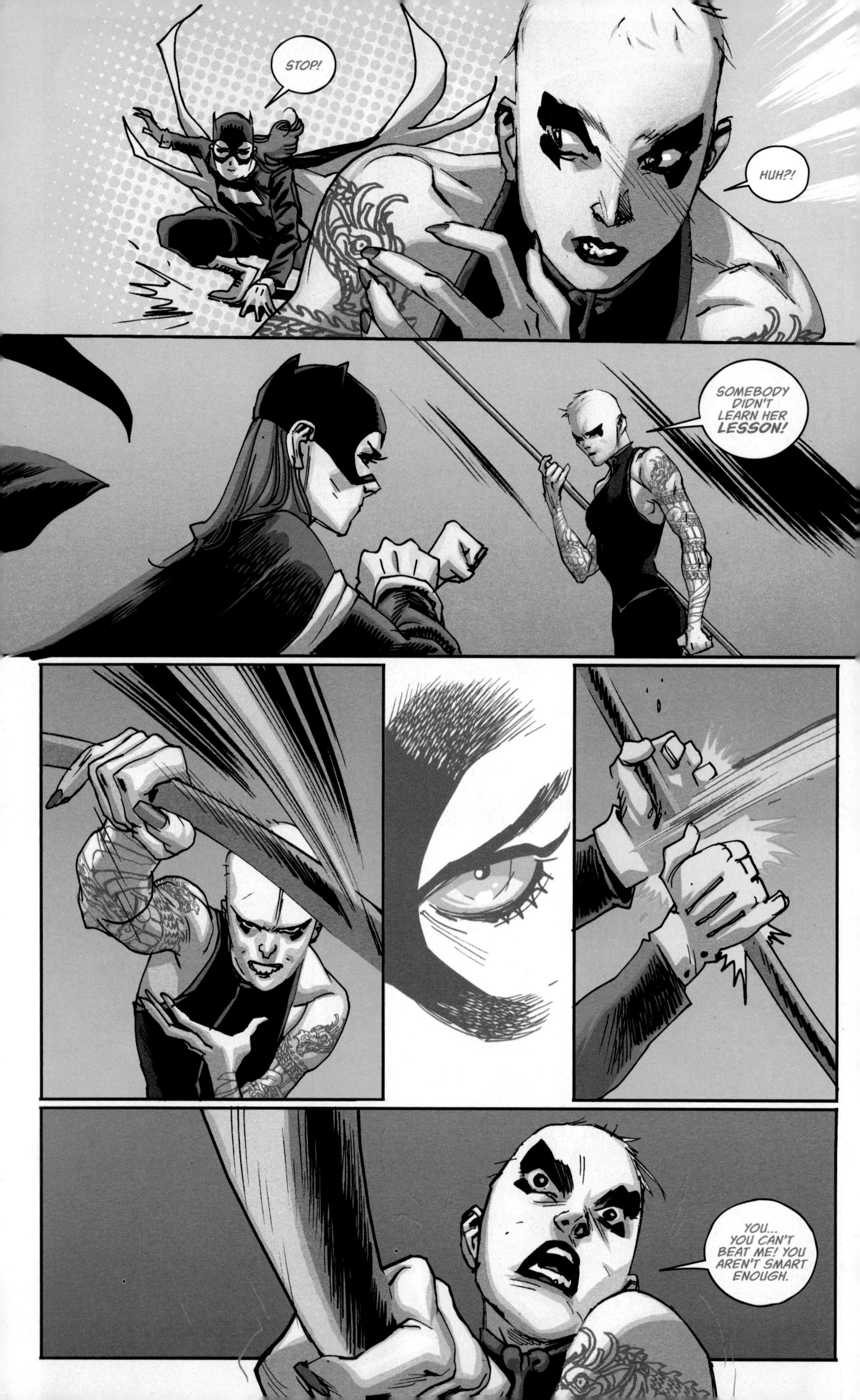
STOP!
HUH?!
SOMEBODY DIDN'T LEARN HER LESSON!
YOU... YOU CAN'T BEAT ME! YOU AREN'T SMART ENOUGH.

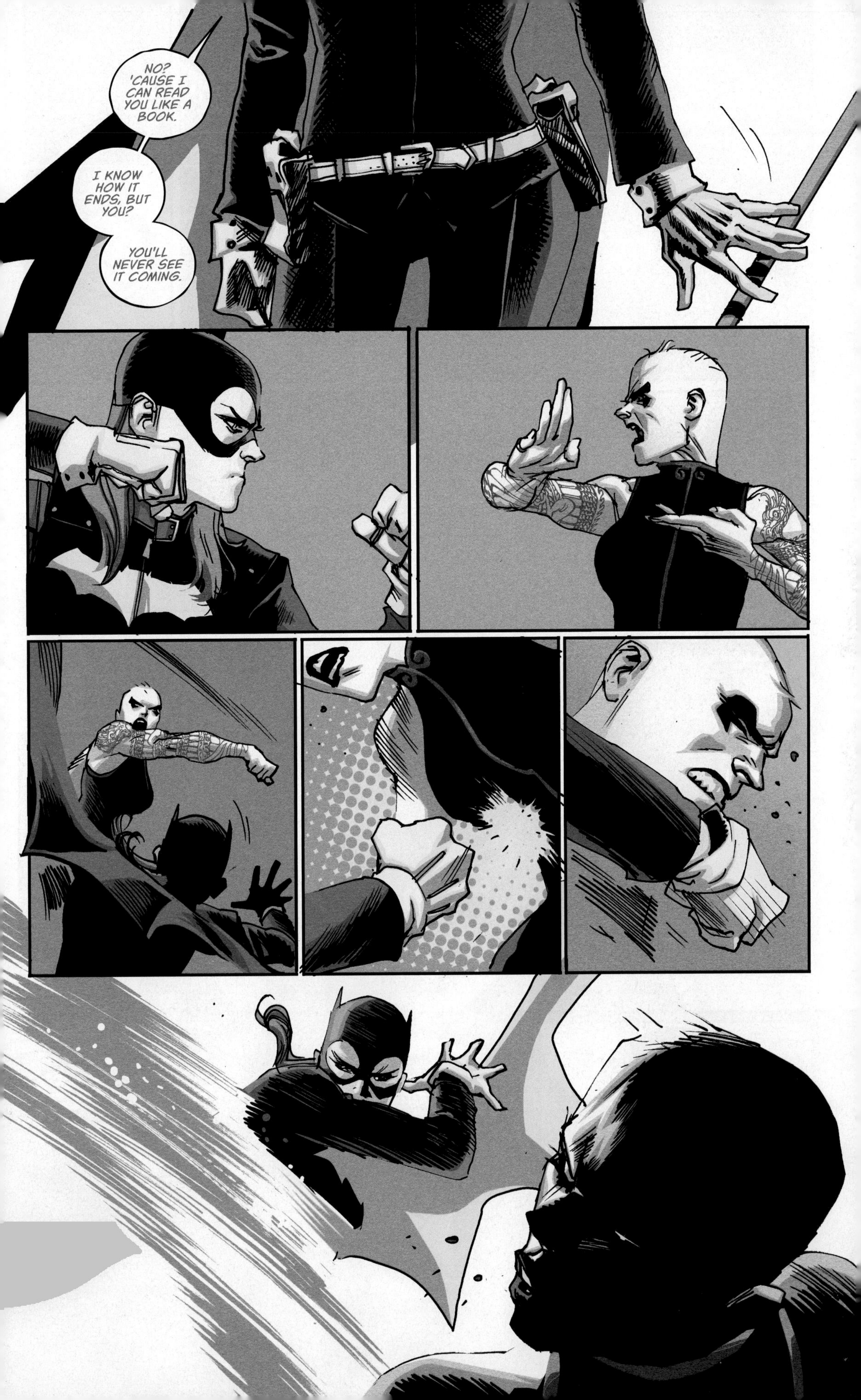
NO? 'CAUSE I CAN READ YOU LIKE A BOOK.
I KNOW HOW IT ENDS, BUT YOU?
YOU'LL NEVER SEE IT COMING.

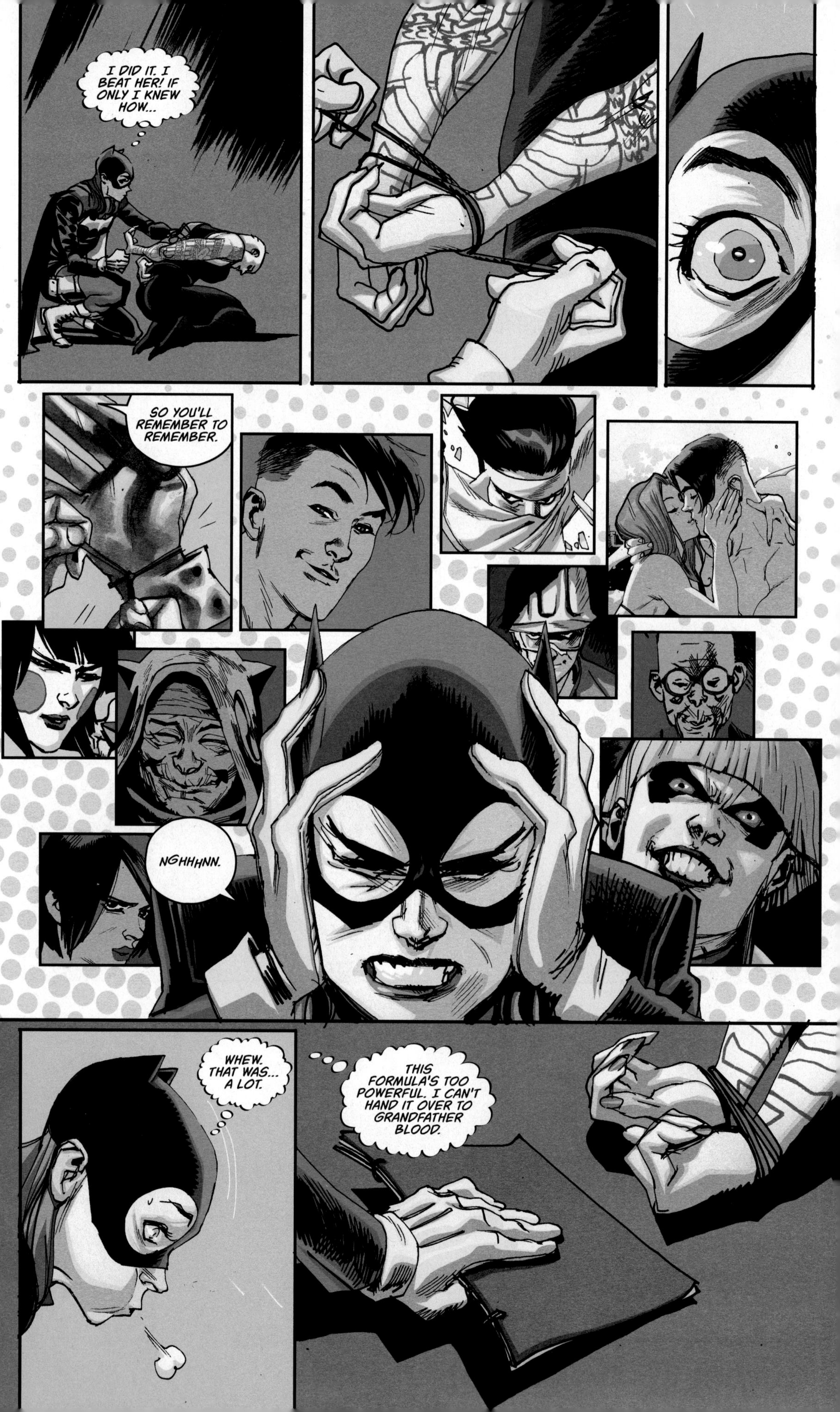
I DID IT. I BEAT HER! IF ONLY I KNEW HOW...
SO YOU'LL REMEMBER TO REMEMBER.
NGHHHNN.
WHEW. THAT WAS... A LOT.
THIS FORMULA'S TOO POWERFUL. I CAN'T HAND IT OVER TO GRANDFATHER BLOOD.

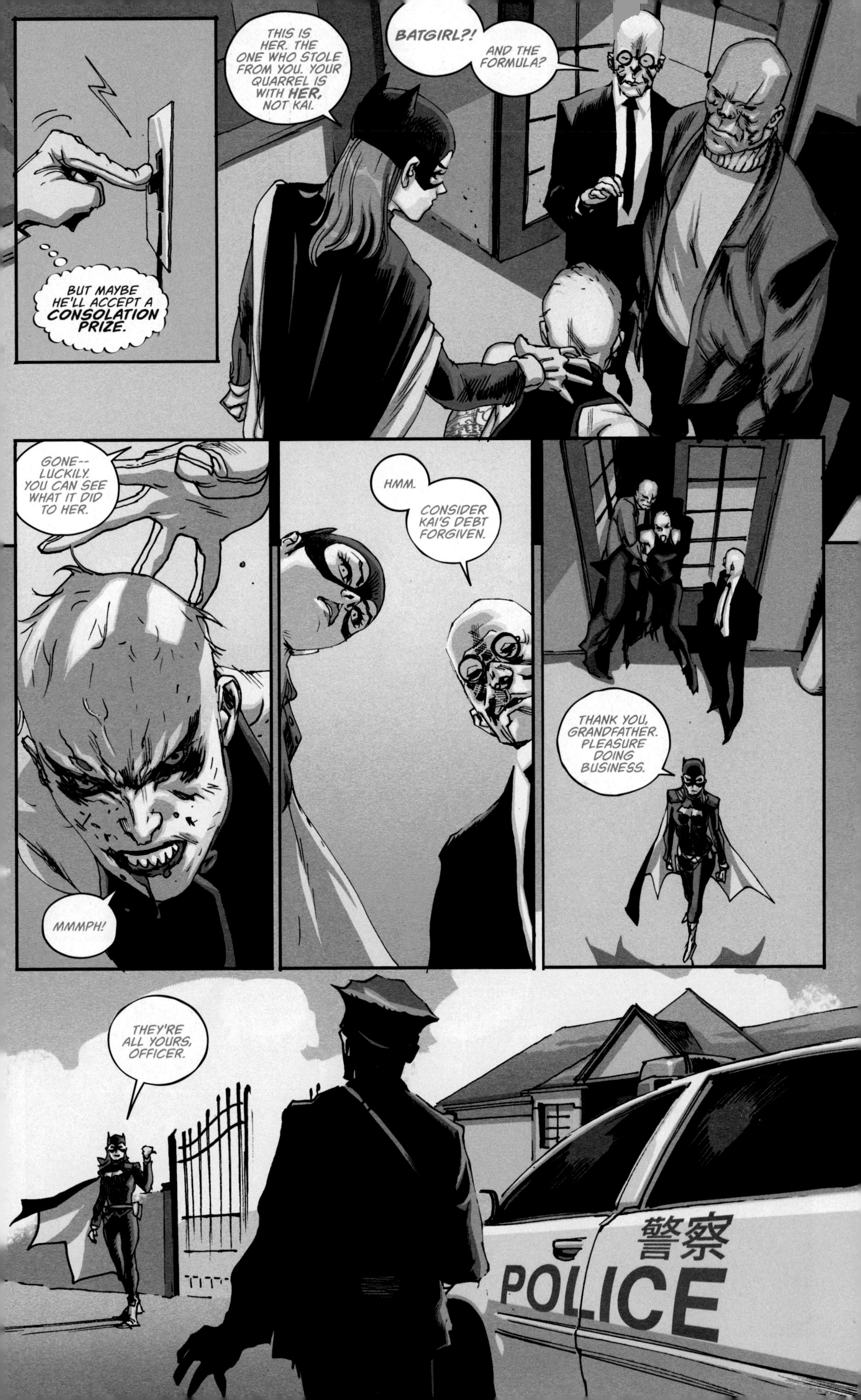
BUT MAYBE HE'LL ACCEPT A CONSOLATION PRIZE.
THIS IS HER. THE ONE WHO STOLE FROM YOU. YOUR QUARREL IS WITH HER, NOT KAI.
BATGIRL?!
AND THE FORMULA?
GONE-- LUCKILY. YOU CAN SEE WHAT IT DID TO HER.
MMMPH!
HMM.
CONSIDER KAI'S DEBT FORGIVEN.
THANK YOU, GRANDFATHER. PLEASURE DOING BUSINESS.
THEY'RE ALL YOURS, OFFICER.
警察
POLICE

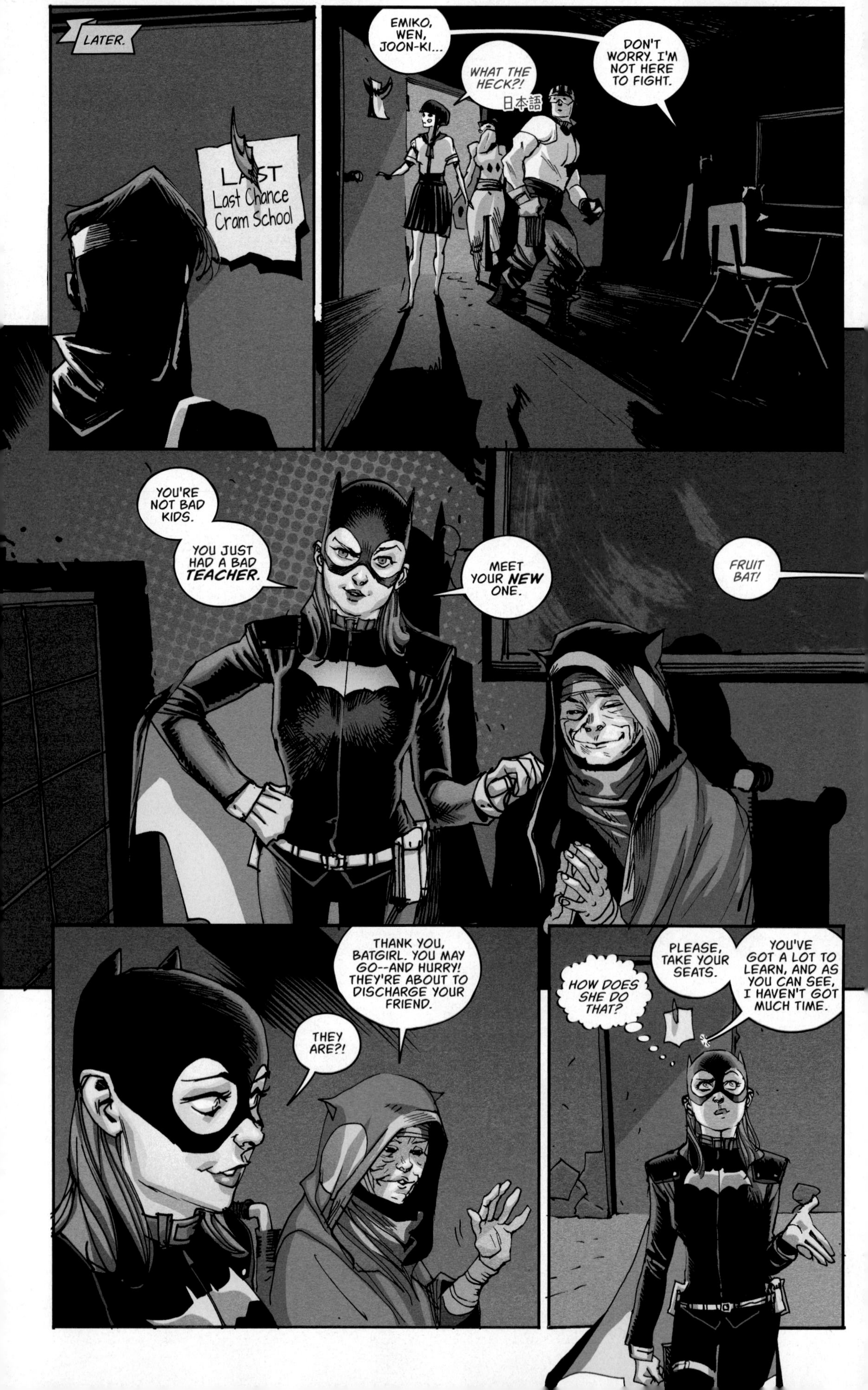

LATER.
LAST
Last Chance
Cram School
EMIKO, WEN, JOON-KI...
WHAT THE HECK?!
日本語
DON'T WORRY. I'M NOT HERE TO FIGHT.
YOU'RE NOT BAD KIDS.
YOU JUST HAD A BAD TEACHER.
MEET YOUR NEW ONE.
FRUIT BAT!
THANK YOU, BATGIRL. YOU MAY GO--AND HURRY! THEY'RE ABOUT TO DISCHARGE YOUR FRIEND.
THEY ARE?!
HOW DOES SHE DO THAT?
PLEASE, TAKE YOUR SEATS.
YOU'VE GOT A LOT TO LEARN, AND AS YOU CAN SEE, I HAVEN'T GOT MUCH TIME.

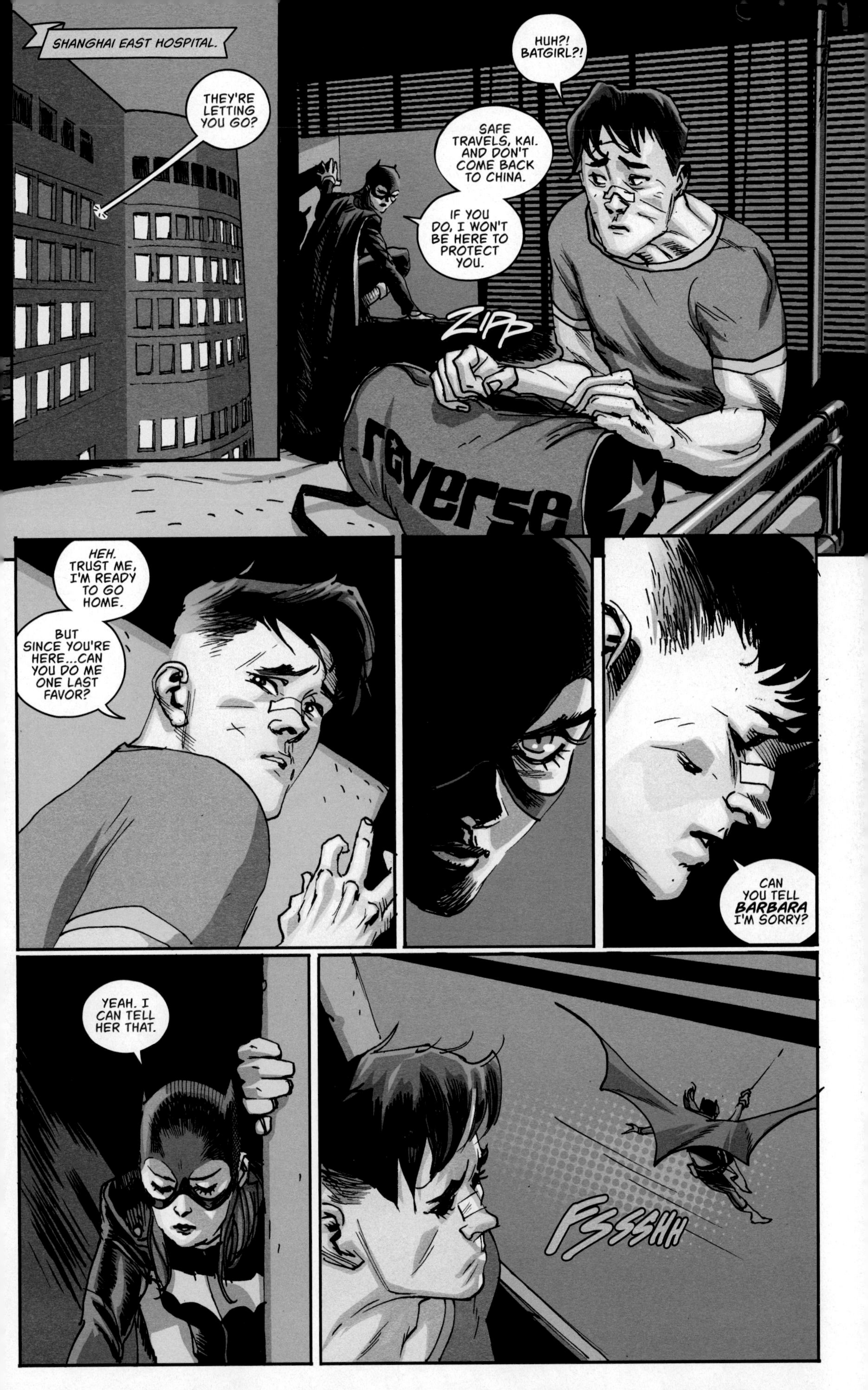
SHANGHAI EAST HOSPITAL.
THEY'RE LETTING YOU GO?
HUH?! BATGIRL?!
SAFE TRAVELS, KAI. AND DON'T COME BACK TO CHINA.
IF YOU DO, I WON'T BE HERE TO PROTECT YOU.
ZIPP
reverse
HEH. TRUST ME, I'M READY TO GO HOME.
BUT SINCE YOU'RE HERE...CAN YOU DO ME ONE LAST FAVOR?
CAN YOU TELL BARBARA I'M SORRY?
YEAH. I CAN TELL HER THAT.
FSSSHH

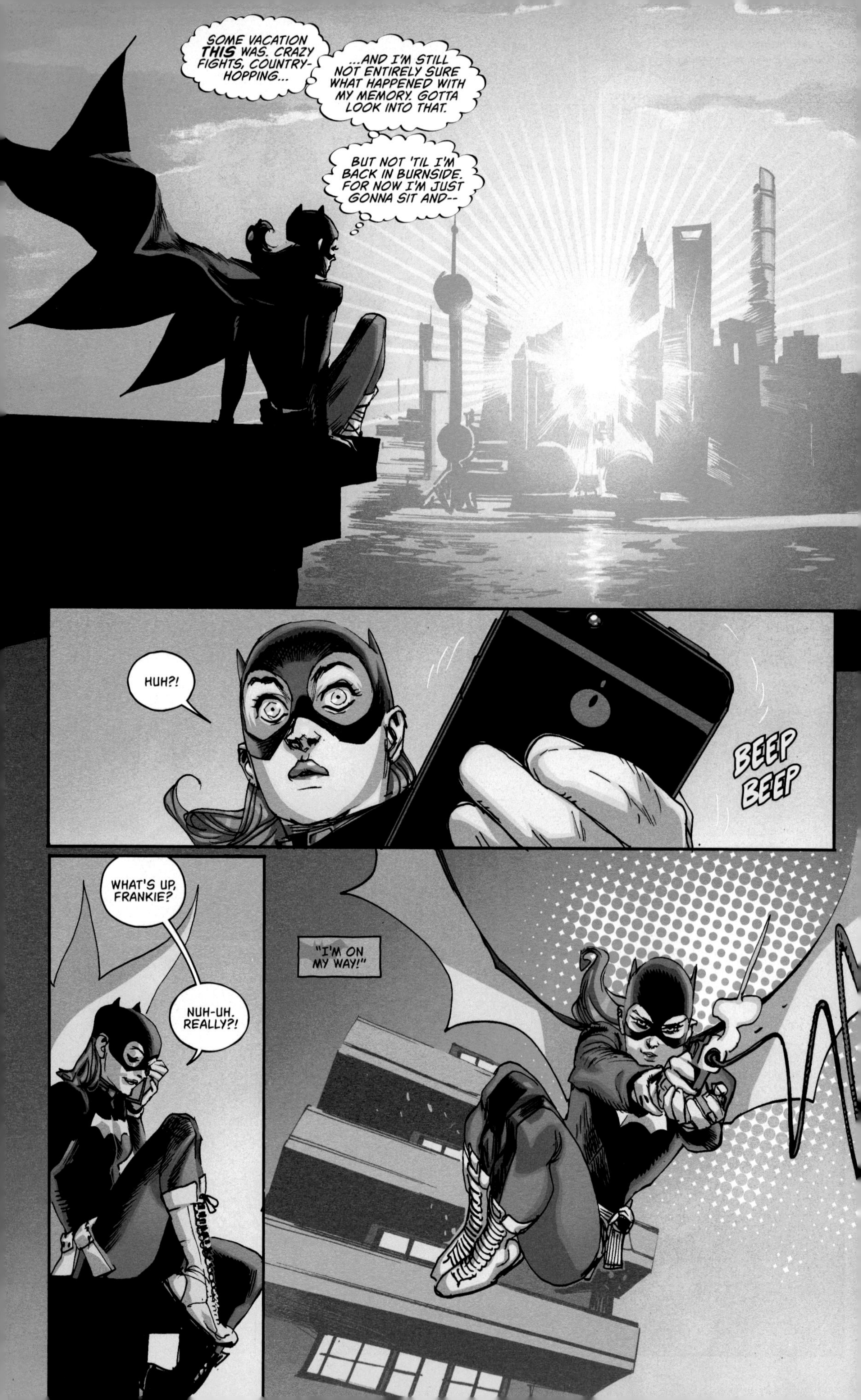
SOME VACATION THIS WAS. CRAZY FIGHTS, COUNTRY-HOPPING...
...AND I'M STILL NOT ENTIRELY SURE WHAT HAPPENED WITH MY MEMORY. GOTTA LOOK INTO THAT.
BUT NOT 'TIL I'M BACK IN BURNSIDE. FOR NOW I'M JUST GONNA SIT AND--
HUH?!
BEEP BEEP
WHAT'S UP, FRANKIE?
NUH-UH. REALLY?!
"I'M ON MY WAY!"

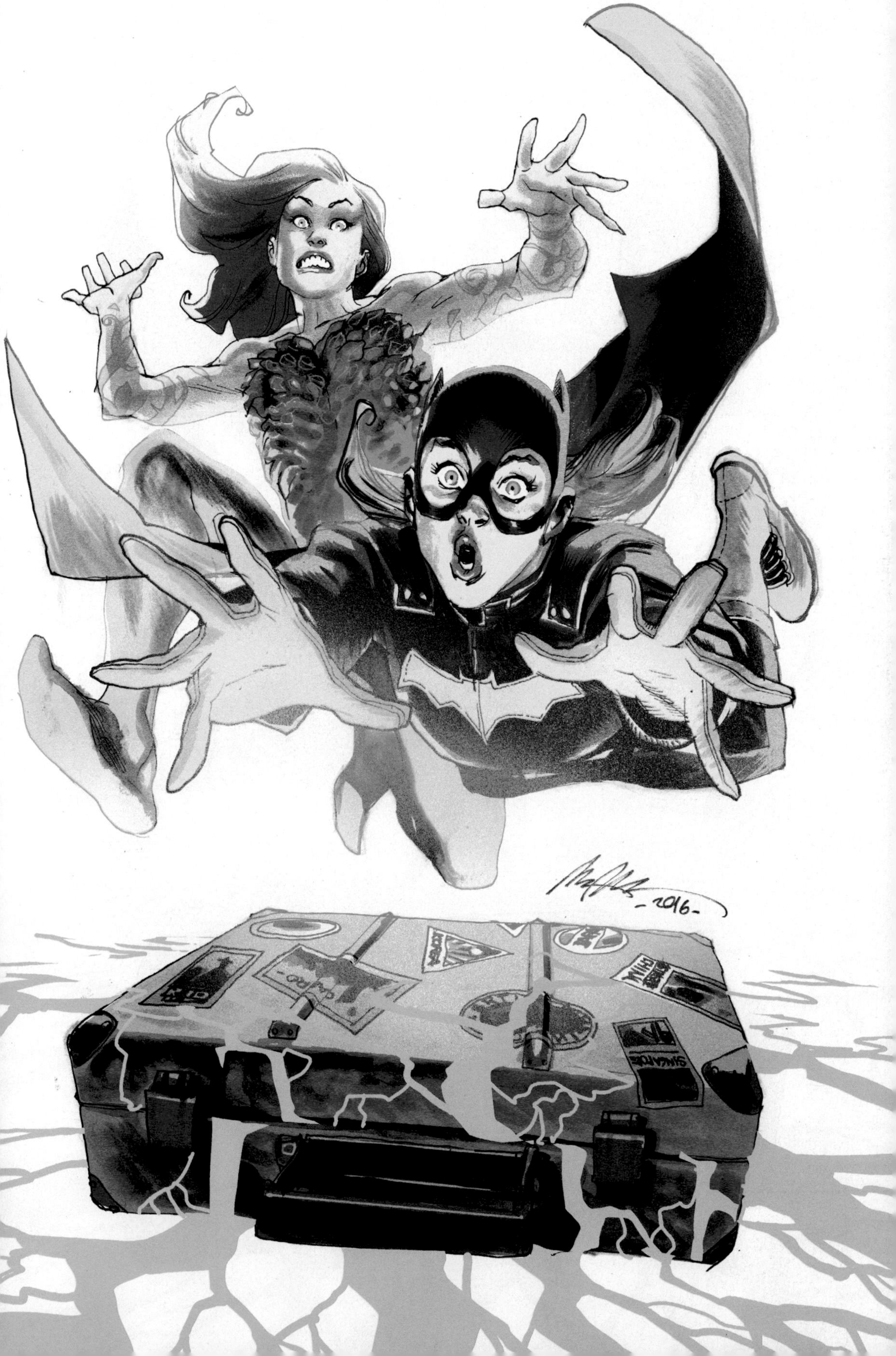
-2016-

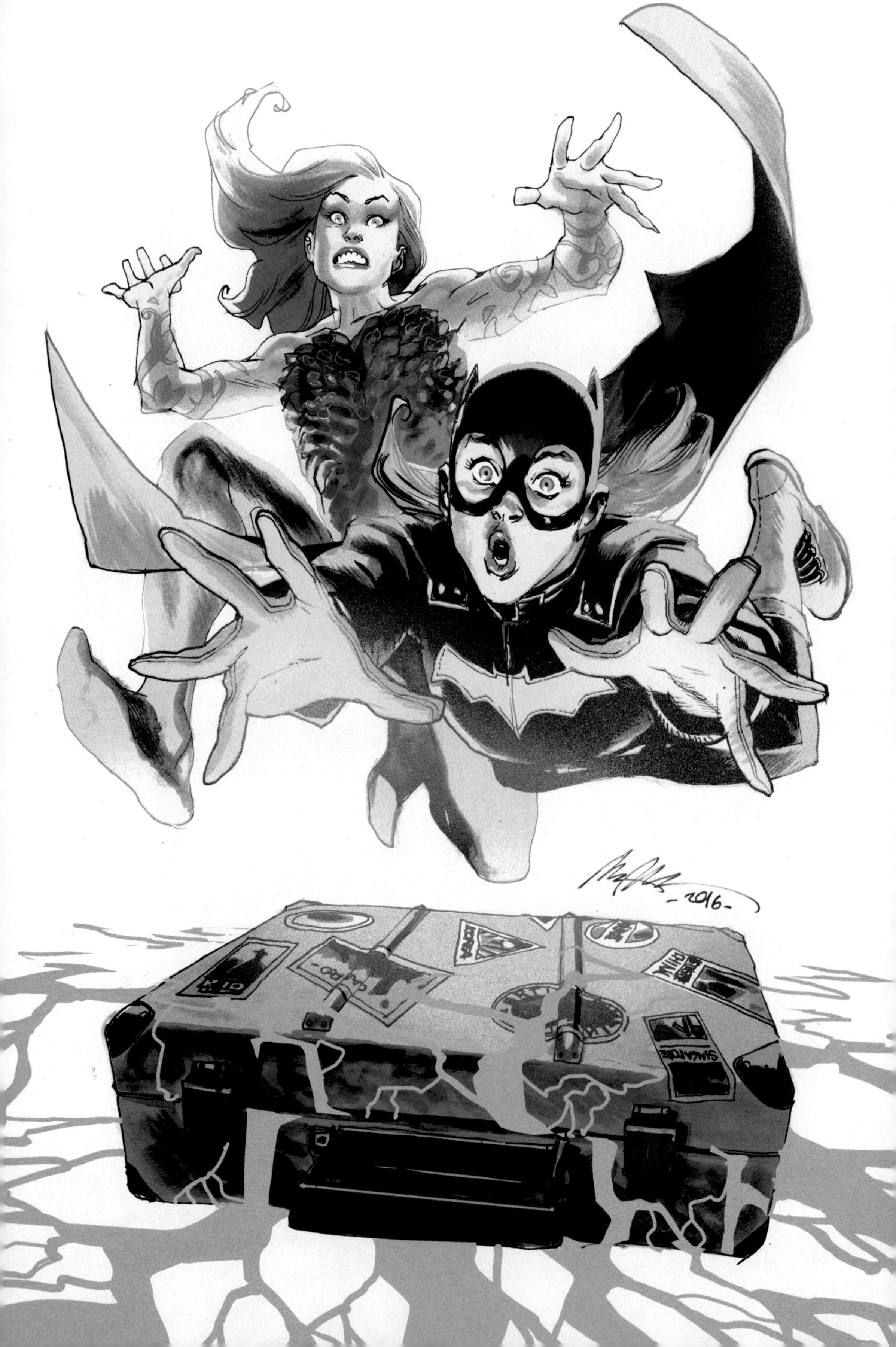
-2016-

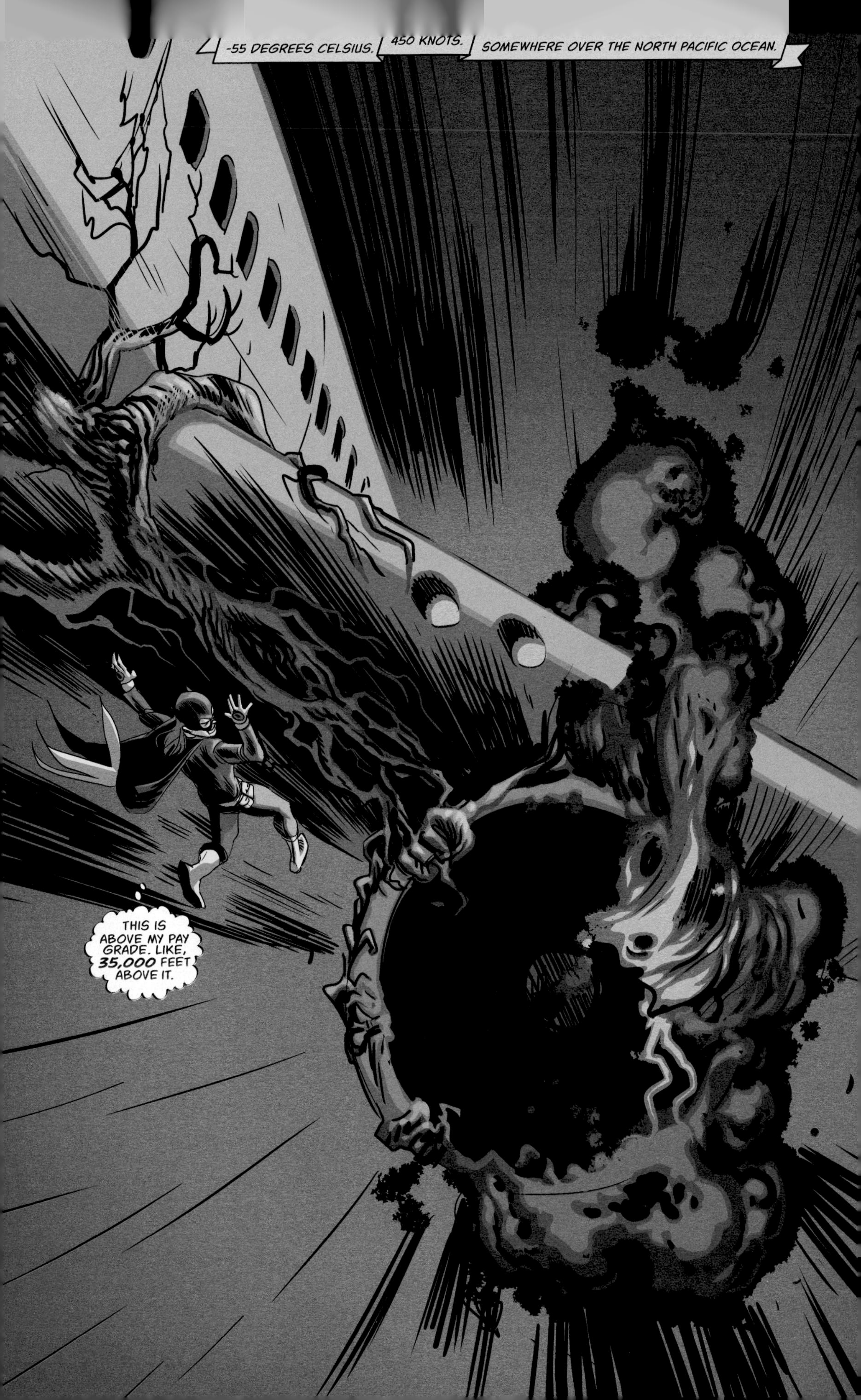

-55 DEGREES CELSIUS.
450 KNOTS.
SOMEWHERE OVER THE NORTH PACIFIC OCEAN.
THIS IS ABOVE MY PAY GRADE. LIKE, 35,000 FEET ABOVE IT.

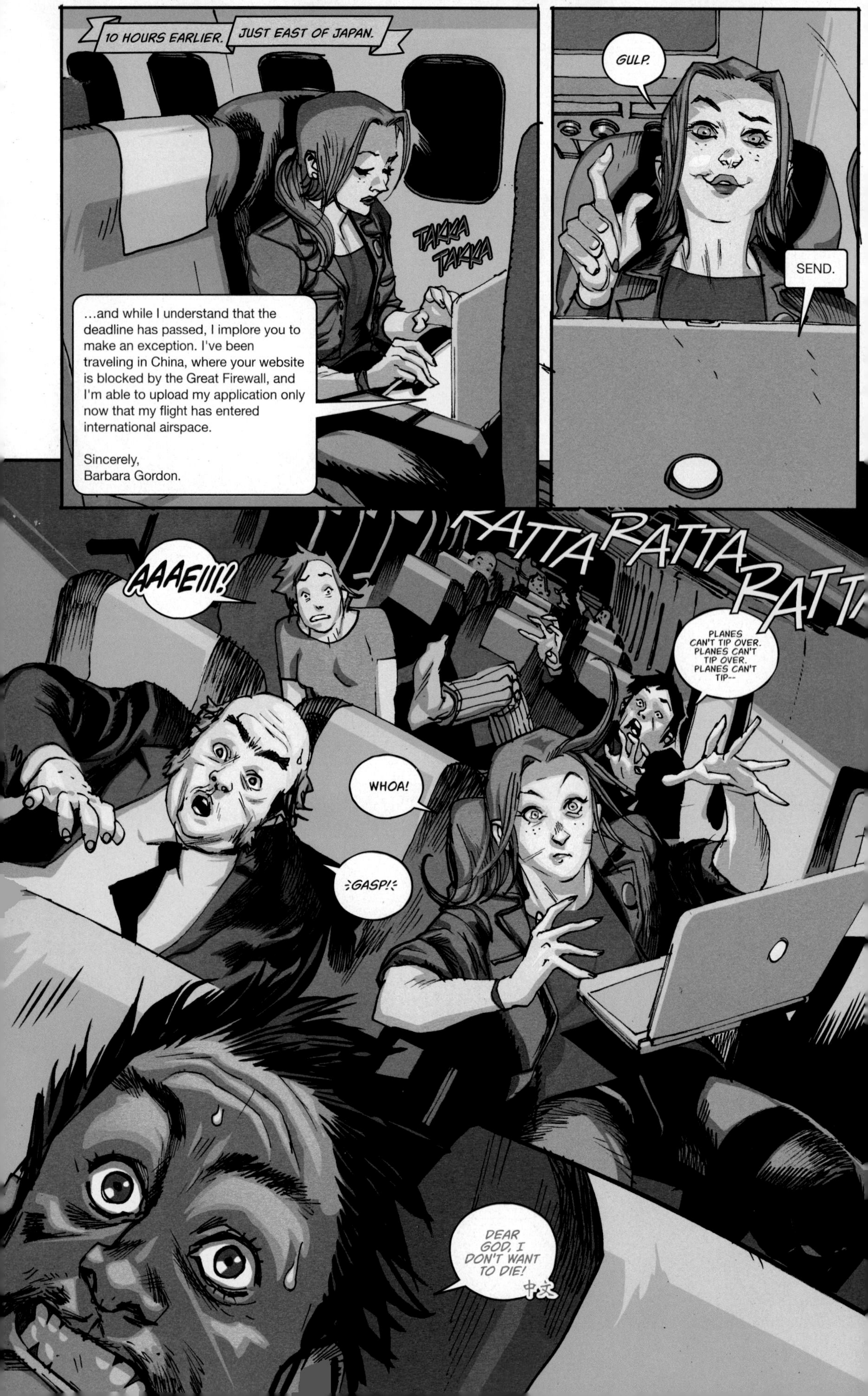
10 HOURS EARLIER.
JUST EAST OF JAPAN.
TAKKA TAKKA
...and while I understand that the deadline has passed, I implore you to make an exception. I've been traveling in China, where your website is blocked by the Great Firewall, and I'm able to upload my application only now that my flight has entered international airspace.
Sincerely,
Barbara Gordon.
GULP.
SEND.
RATTA RATTA RATT
AAAEIII!
PLANES CAN'T TIP OVER. PLANES CAN'T TIP OVER. PLANES CAN'T TIP--
WHOA!
GASP!
DEAR GOD, I DON'T WANT TO DIE! 中文

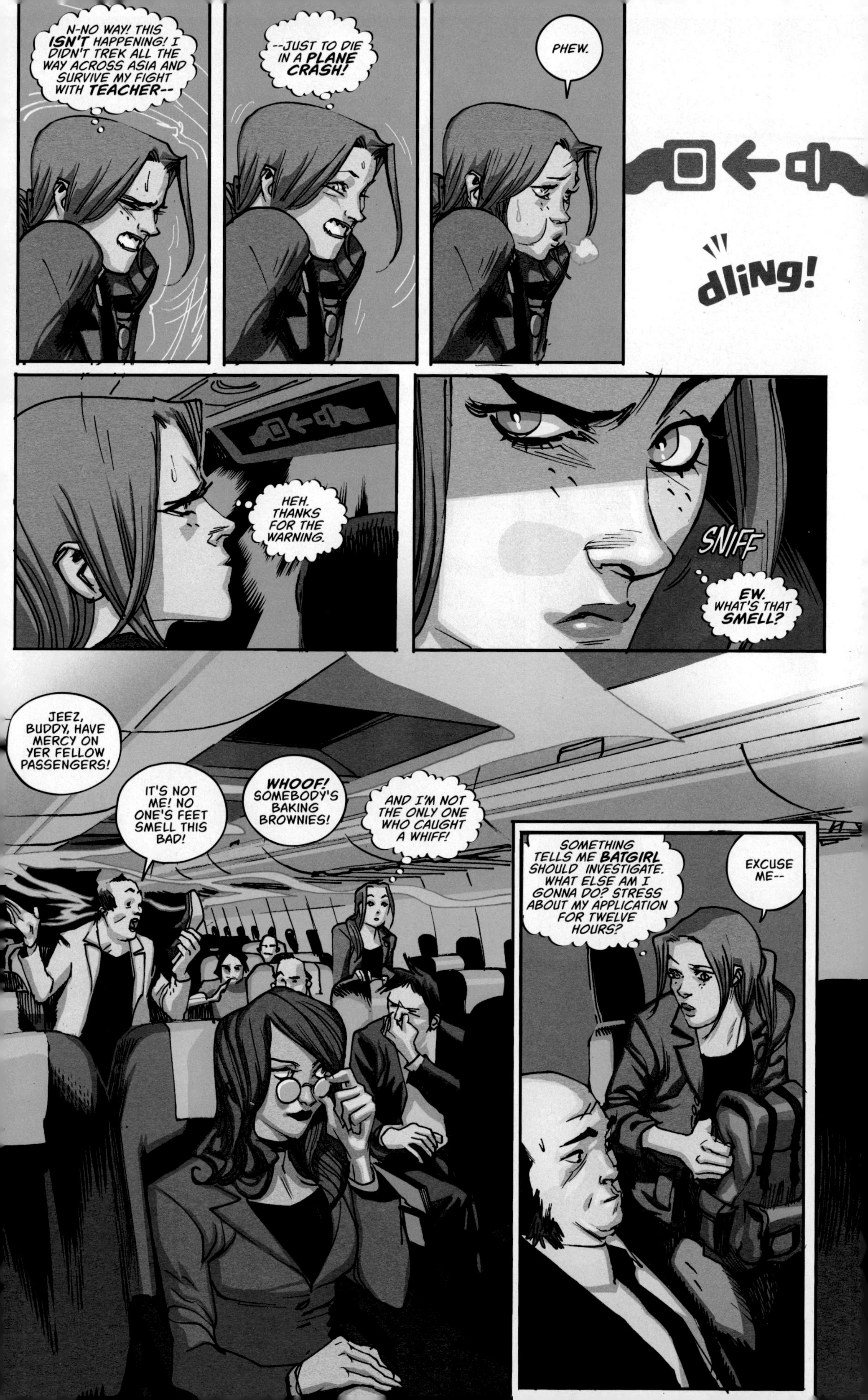
N-NO WAY! THIS ISN'T HAPPENING! I DIDN'T TREK ALL THE WAY ACROSS ASIA AND SURVIVE MY FIGHT WITH TEACHER--
--JUST TO DIE IN A PLANE CRASH!
PHEW.
dling!
HEH. THANKS FOR THE WARNING.
SNIFF
EW. WHAT'S THAT SMELL?
JEEZ, BUDDY, HAVE MERCY ON YER FELLOW PASSENGERS!
IT'S NOT ME! NO ONE'S FEET SMELL THIS BAD!
WHOOF! SOMEBODY'S BAKING BROWNIES!
AND I'M NOT THE ONLY ONE WHO CAUGHT A WHIFF!
SOMETHING TELLS ME BATGIRL SHOULD INVESTIGATE. WHAT ELSE AM I GONNA DO? STRESS ABOUT MY APPLICATION FOR TWELVE HOURS?
EXCUSE ME--

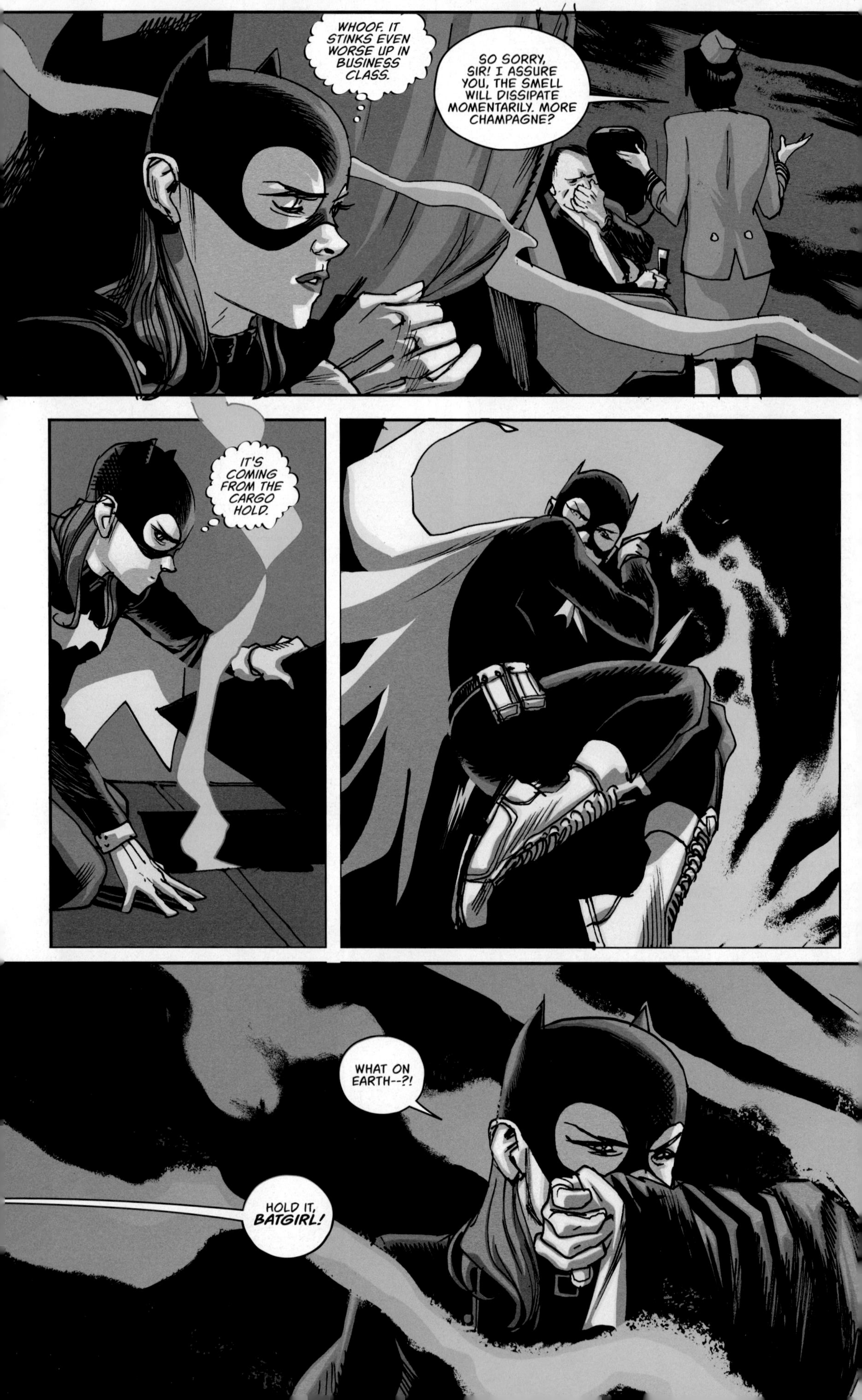
WHOOF. IT STINKS EVEN WORSE UP IN BUSINESS CLASS.
SO SORRY, SIR! I ASSURE YOU, THE SMELL WILL DISSIPATE MOMENTARILY. MORE CHAMPAGNE?
IT'S COMING FROM THE CARGO HOLD.
WHAT ON EARTH--?!
HOLD IT, BATGIRL!

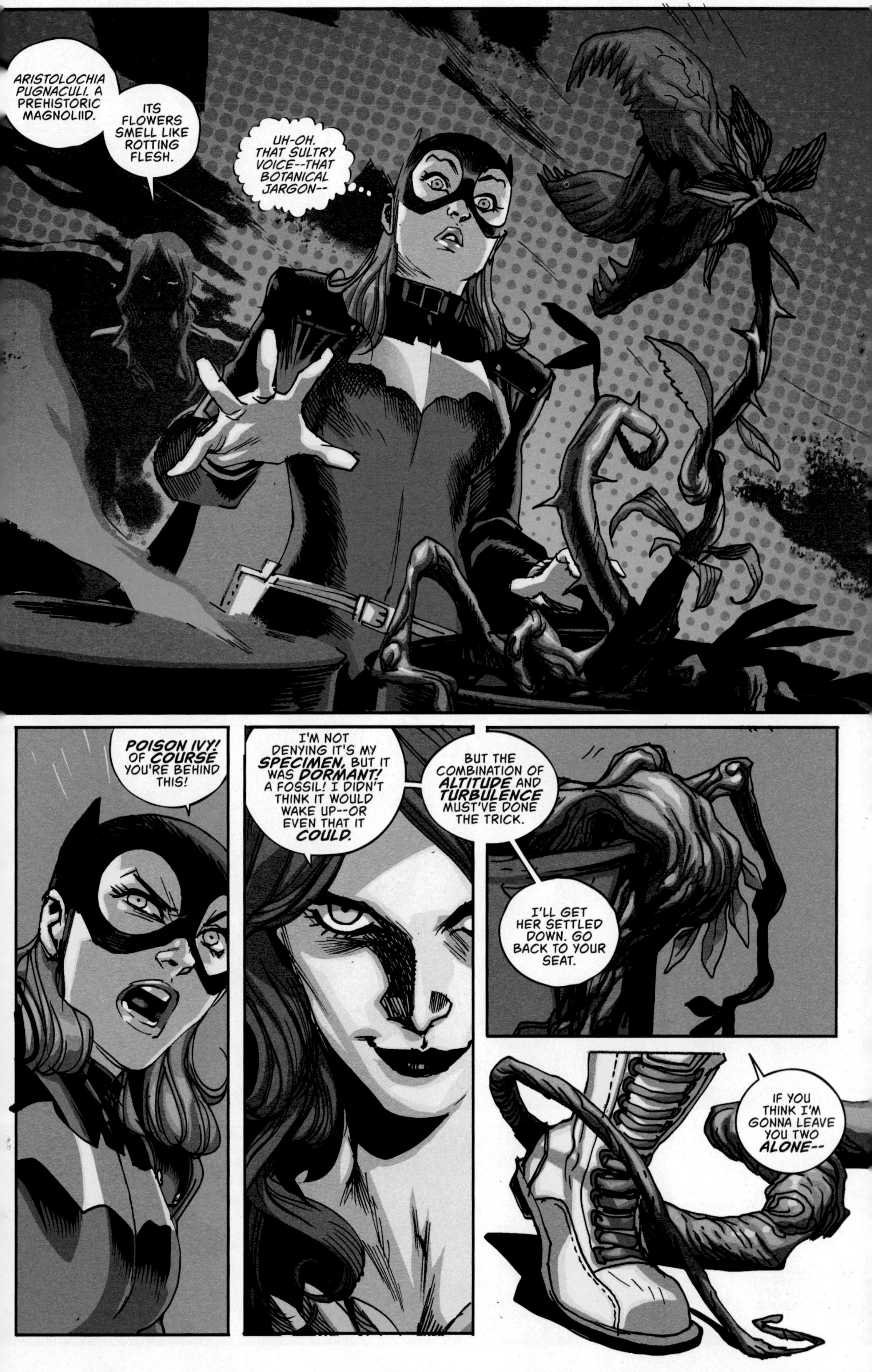
ARISTOLOCHIA PUGNACULI. A PREHISTORIC MAGNOLIID.
ITS FLOWERS SMELL LIKE ROTTING FLESH.
UH-OH. THAT SULTRY VOICE--THAT BOTANICAL JARGON--
POISON IVY! OF COURSE YOU'RE BEHIND THIS!
I'M NOT DENYING IT'S MY SPECIMEN, BUT IT WAS DORMANT! A FOSSIL! I DIDN'T THINK IT WOULD WAKE UP--OR EVEN THAT IT COULD.
BUT THE COMBINATION OF ALTITUDE AND TURBULENCE MUST'VE DONE THE TRICK.
I'LL GET HER SETTLED DOWN. GO BACK TO YOUR SEAT.
IF YOU THINK I'M GONNA LEAVE YOU TWO ALONE--

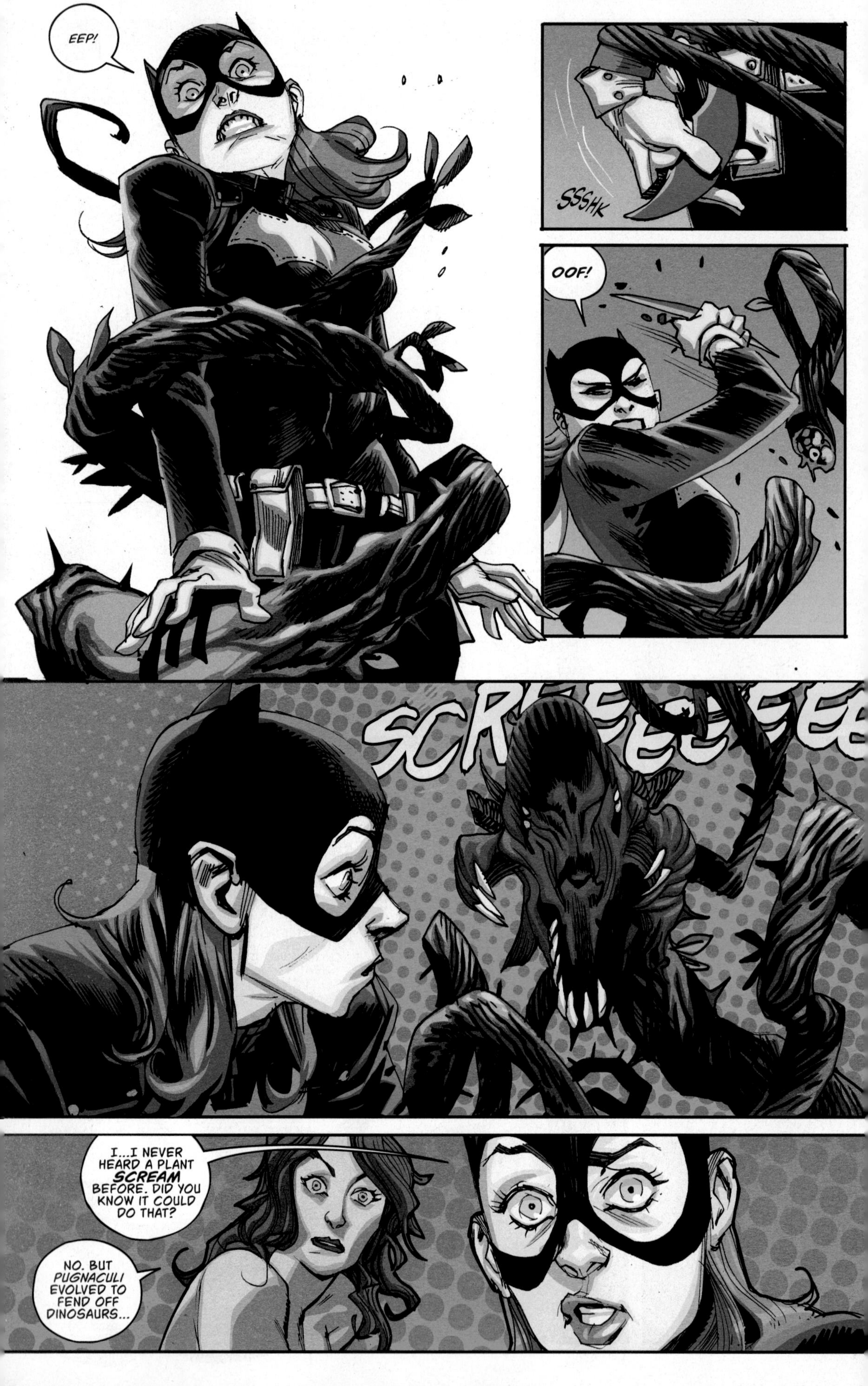

EEP!
SSSHK
OOF!
SCREEEEEEE
I...I NEVER HEARD A PLANT SCREAM BEFORE. DID YOU KNOW IT COULD DO THAT?
NO. BUT PUGNACULI EVOLVED TO FEND OFF DINOSAURS...

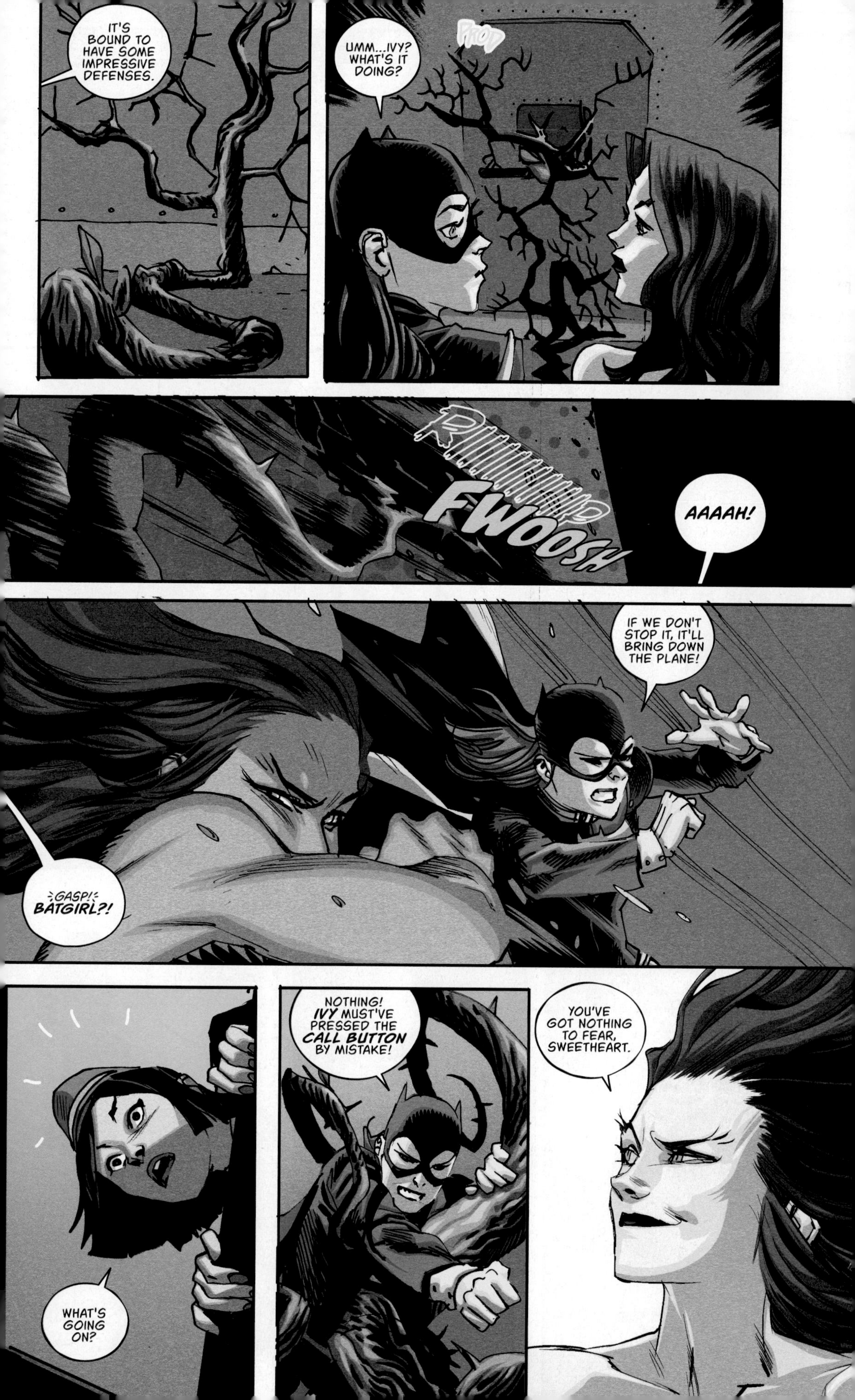
IT'S BOUND TO HAVE SOME IMPRESSIVE DEFENSES.
PROD
UMM...IVY? WHAT'S IT DOING?
FWOOSH
AAAAH!
IF WE DON'T STOP IT, IT'LL BRING DOWN THE PLANE!
GASP! BATGIRL?!
WHAT'S GOING ON?
NOTHING! IVY MUST'VE PRESSED THE CALL BUTTON BY MISTAKE!
YOU'VE GOT NOTHING TO FEAR, SWEETHEART.

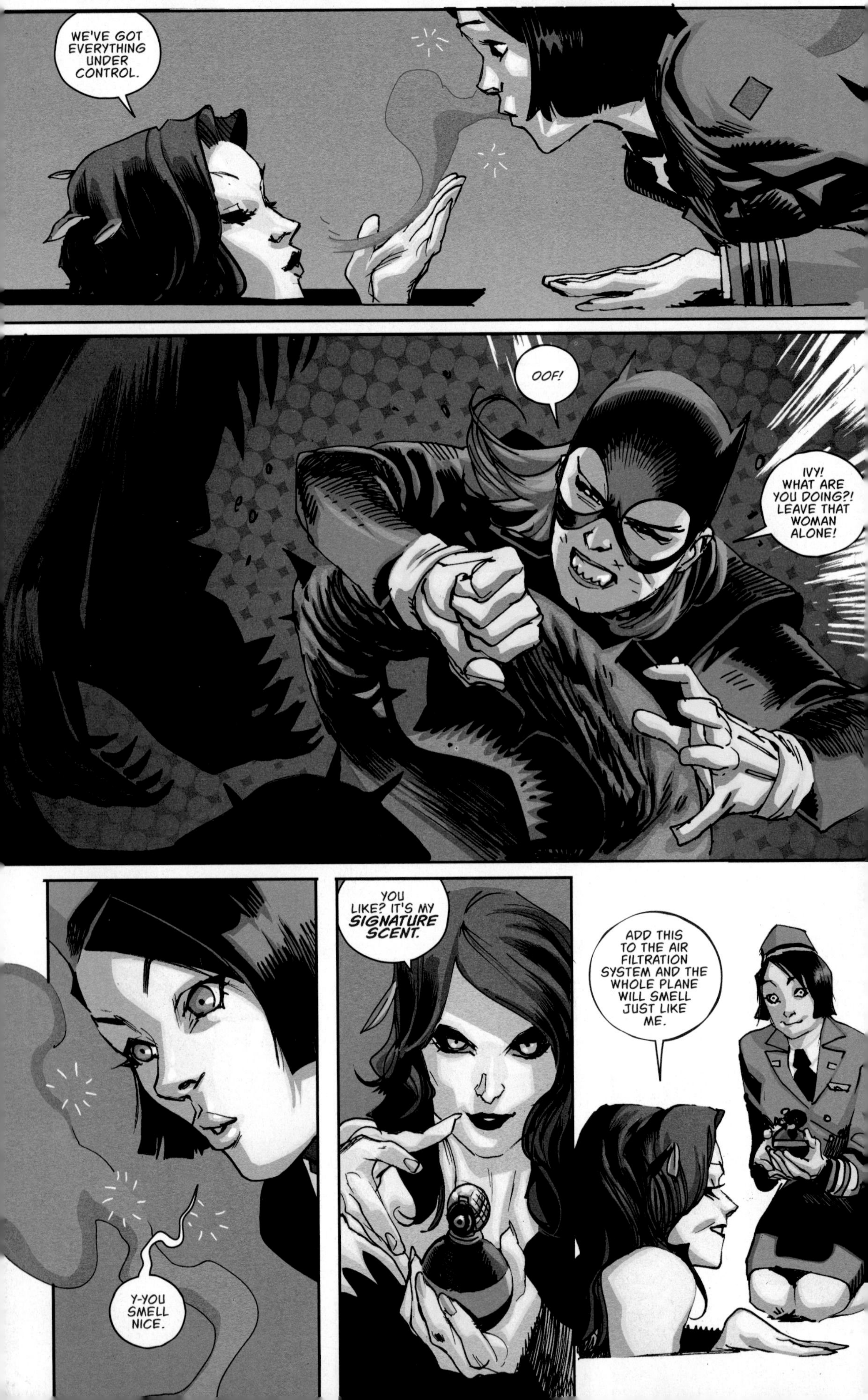
WE'VE GOT EVERYTHING UNDER CONTROL.
OOF!
IVY! WHAT ARE YOU DOING?! LEAVE THAT WOMAN ALONE!
Y-YOU SMELL NICE.
YOU LIKE? IT'S MY *SIGNATURE SCENT.*
ADD THIS TO THE AIR FILTRATION SYSTEM AND THE WHOLE PLANE WILL SMELL JUST LIKE ME.

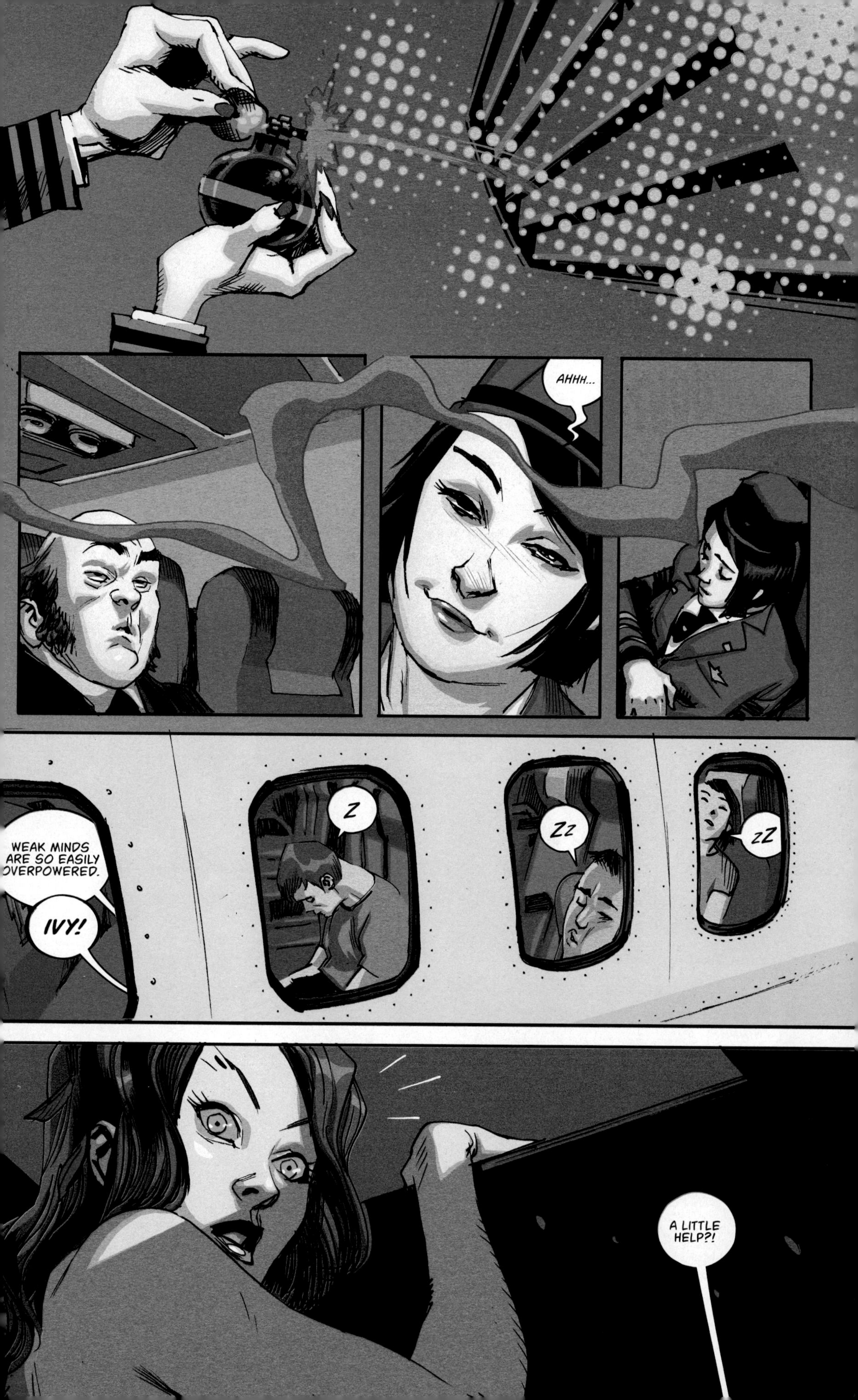
AHHH...
Z
Zz
zZ
WEAK MINDS ARE SO EASILY OVERPOWERED.
IVY!
A LITTLE HELP?!

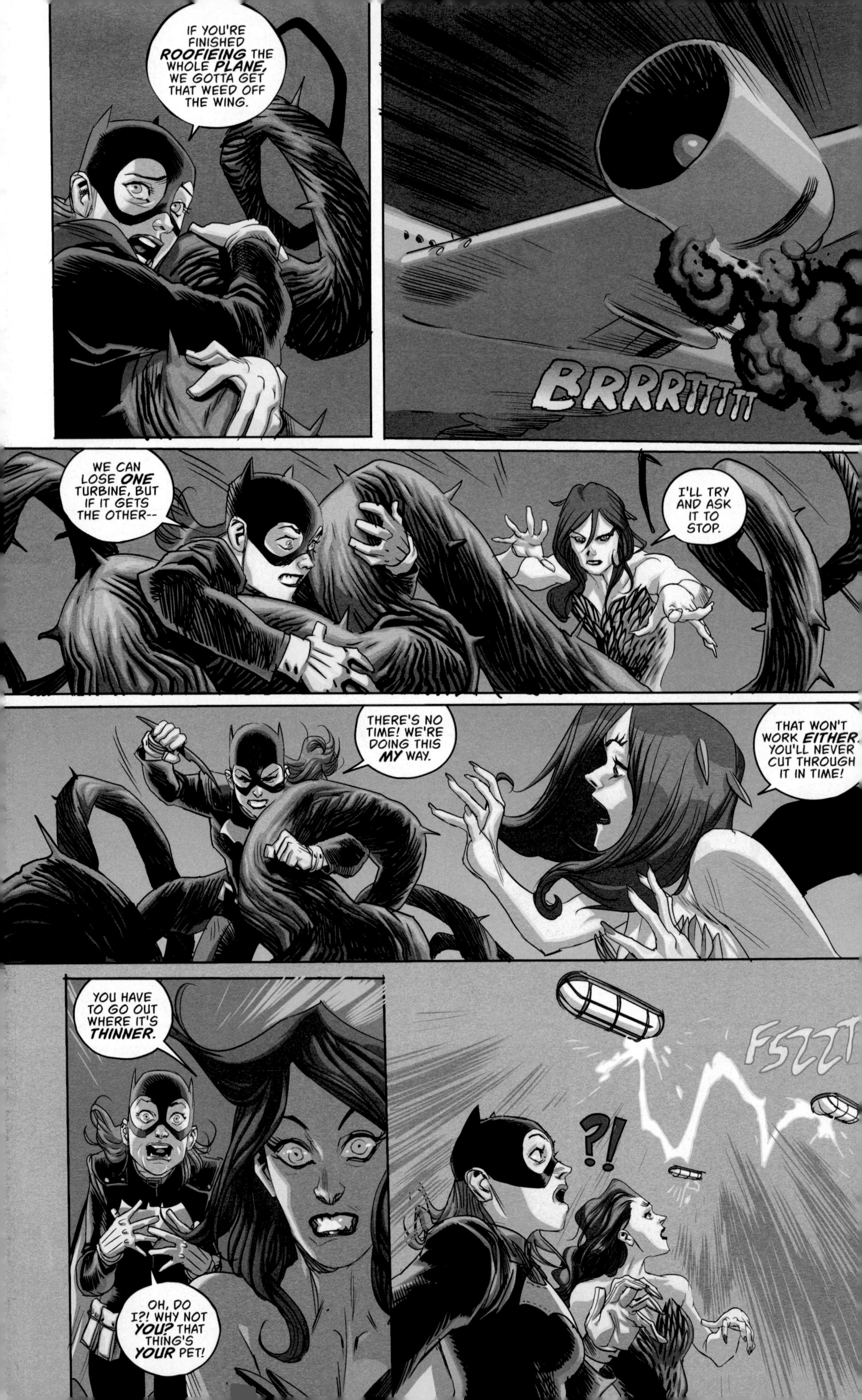

IF YOU'RE FINISHED ROOFIEING THE WHOLE PLANE, WE GOTTA GET THAT WEED OFF THE WING.
BRRRTTTTT
WE CAN LOSE ONE TURBINE, BUT IF IT GETS THE OTHER--
I'LL TRY AND ASK IT TO STOP.
THERE'S NO TIME! WE'RE DOING THIS MY WAY.
THAT WON'T WORK EITHER. YOU'LL NEVER CUT THROUGH IT IN TIME!
YOU HAVE TO GO OUT WHERE IT'S THINNER.
OH, DO I?! WHY NOT YOU? THAT THING'S YOUR PET!
FSZZT
?!

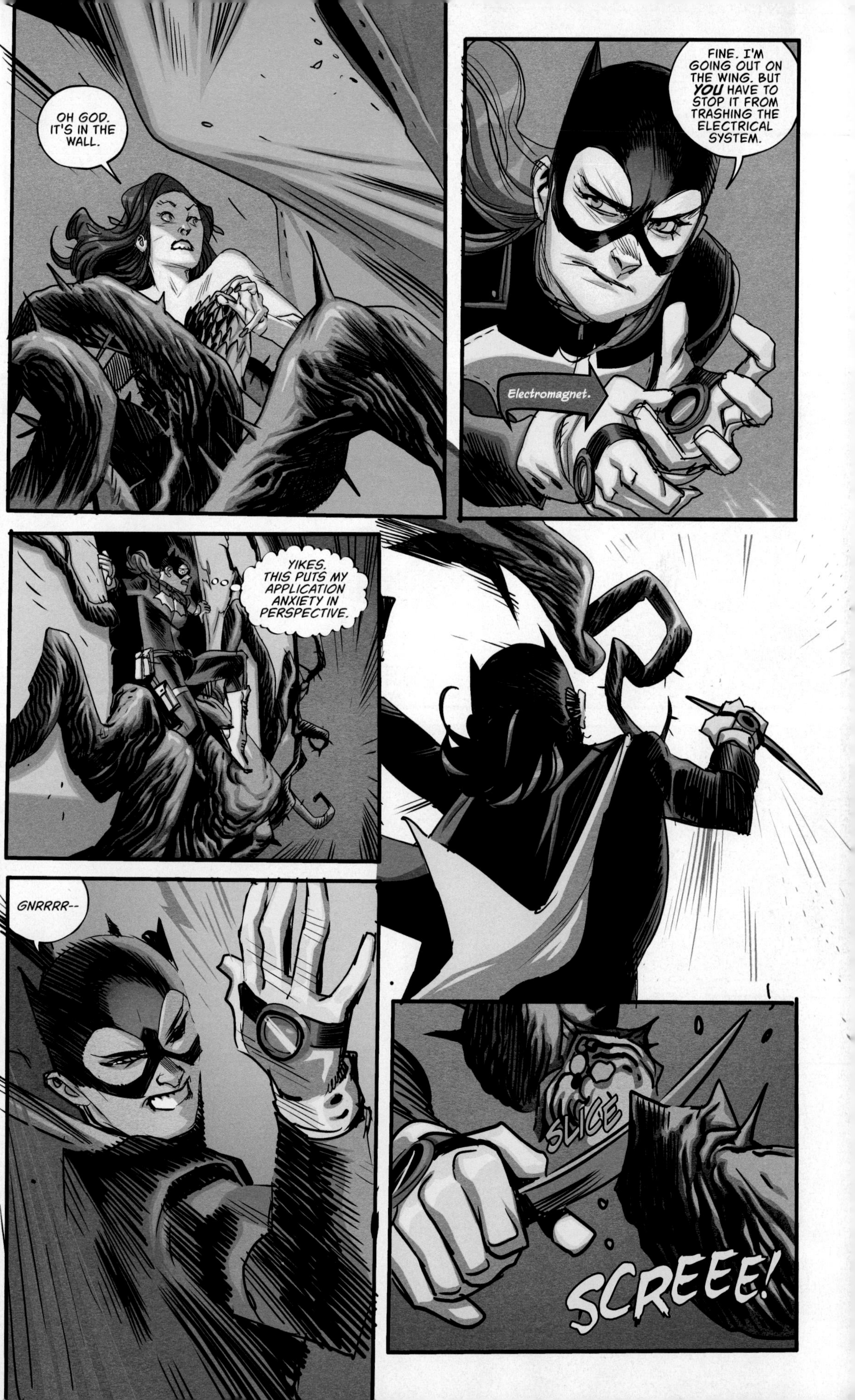

OH GOD. IT'S IN THE WALL.
FINE. I'M GOING OUT ON THE WING. BUT YOU HAVE TO STOP IT FROM TRASHING THE ELECTRICAL SYSTEM.
Electromagnet.
YIKES. THIS PUTS MY APPLICATION ANXIETY IN PERSPECTIVE.
GNRRRR--
SLICE
SCREEE!

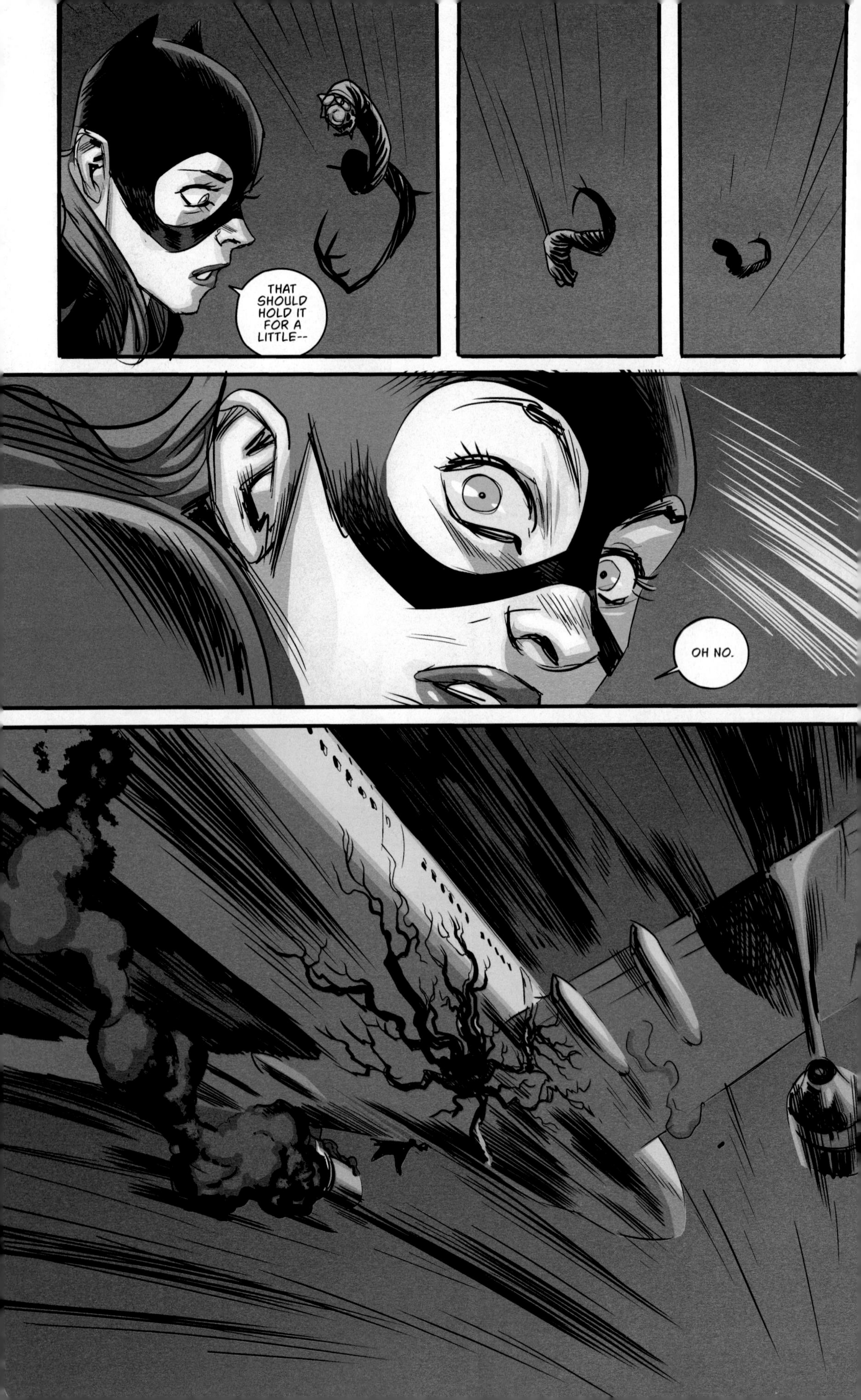
THAT SHOULD HOLD IT FOR A LITTLE--
OH NO.

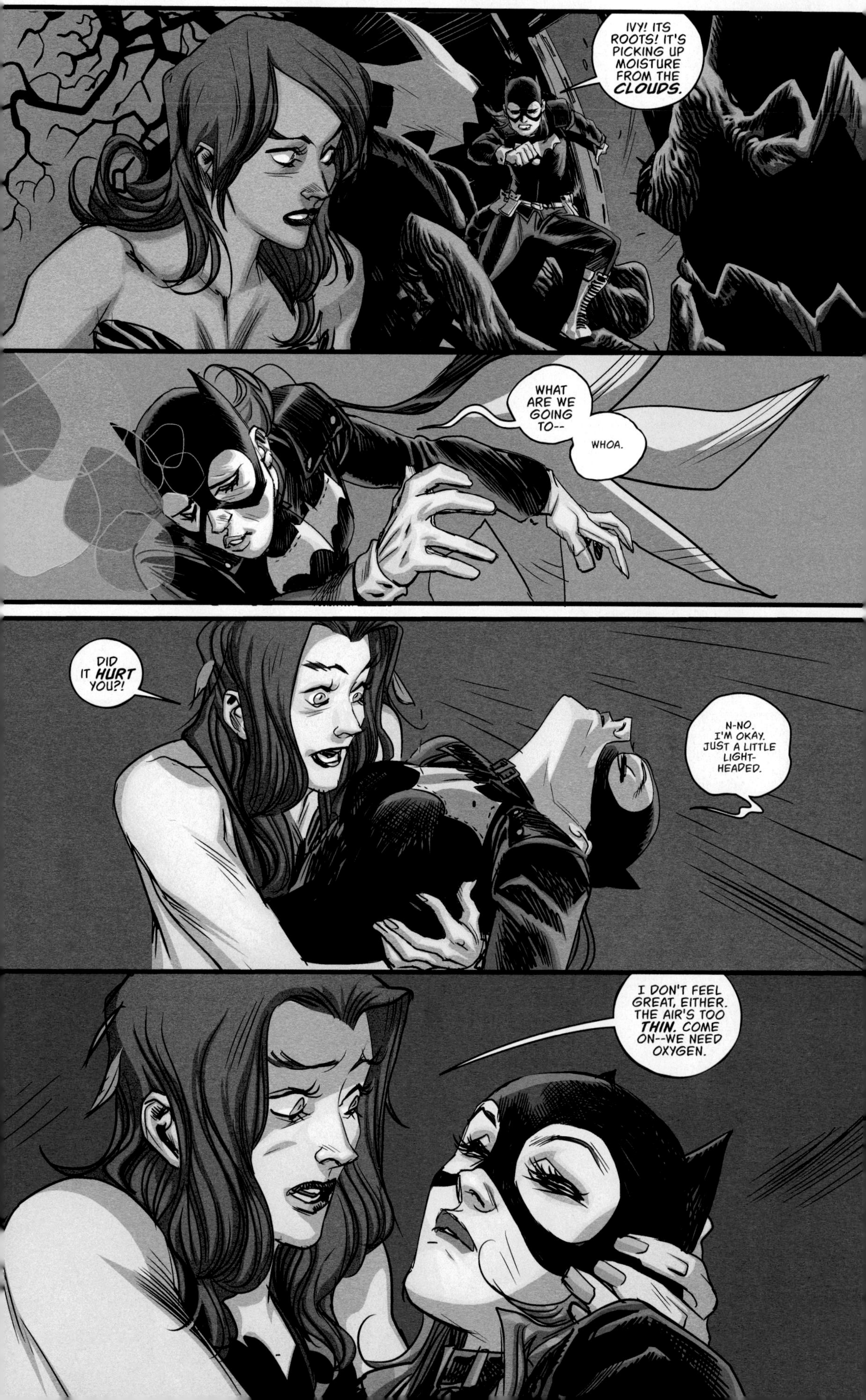
IVY! ITS ROOTS! IT'S PICKING UP MOISTURE FROM THE CLOUDS.
WHAT ARE WE GOING TO--
WHOA.
DID IT HURT YOU?!
N-NO. I'M OKAY. JUST A LITTLE LIGHT-HEADED.
I DON'T FEEL GREAT, EITHER. THE AIR'S TOO THIN. COME ON--WE NEED OXYGEN.

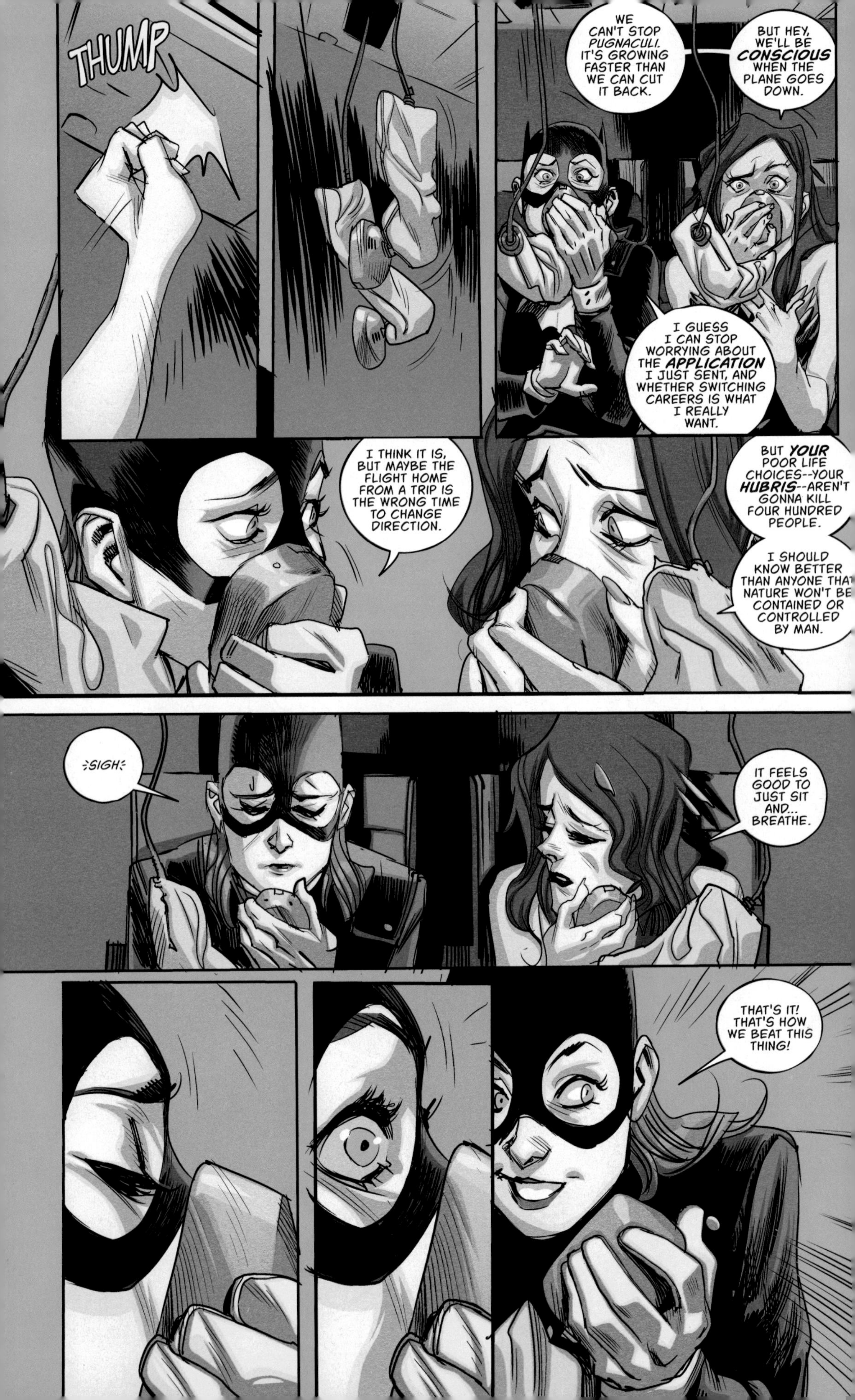
THUMP
WE CAN'T STOP PUGNACULI. IT'S GROWING FASTER THAN WE CAN CUT IT BACK.
BUT HEY, WE'LL BE CONSCIOUS WHEN THE PLANE GOES DOWN.
I GUESS I CAN STOP WORRYING ABOUT THE APPLICATION I JUST SENT, AND WHETHER SWITCHING CAREERS IS WHAT I REALLY WANT.
I THINK IT IS, BUT MAYBE THE FLIGHT HOME FROM A TRIP IS THE WRONG TIME TO CHANGE DIRECTION.
BUT YOUR POOR LIFE CHOICES--YOUR HUBRIS--AREN'T GONNA KILL FOUR HUNDRED PEOPLE.
I SHOULD KNOW BETTER THAN ANYONE THAT NATURE WON'T BE CONTAINED OR CONTROLLED BY MAN.
SIGH
IT FEELS GOOD TO JUST SIT AND... BREATHE.
THAT'S IT! THAT'S HOW WE BEAT THIS THING!

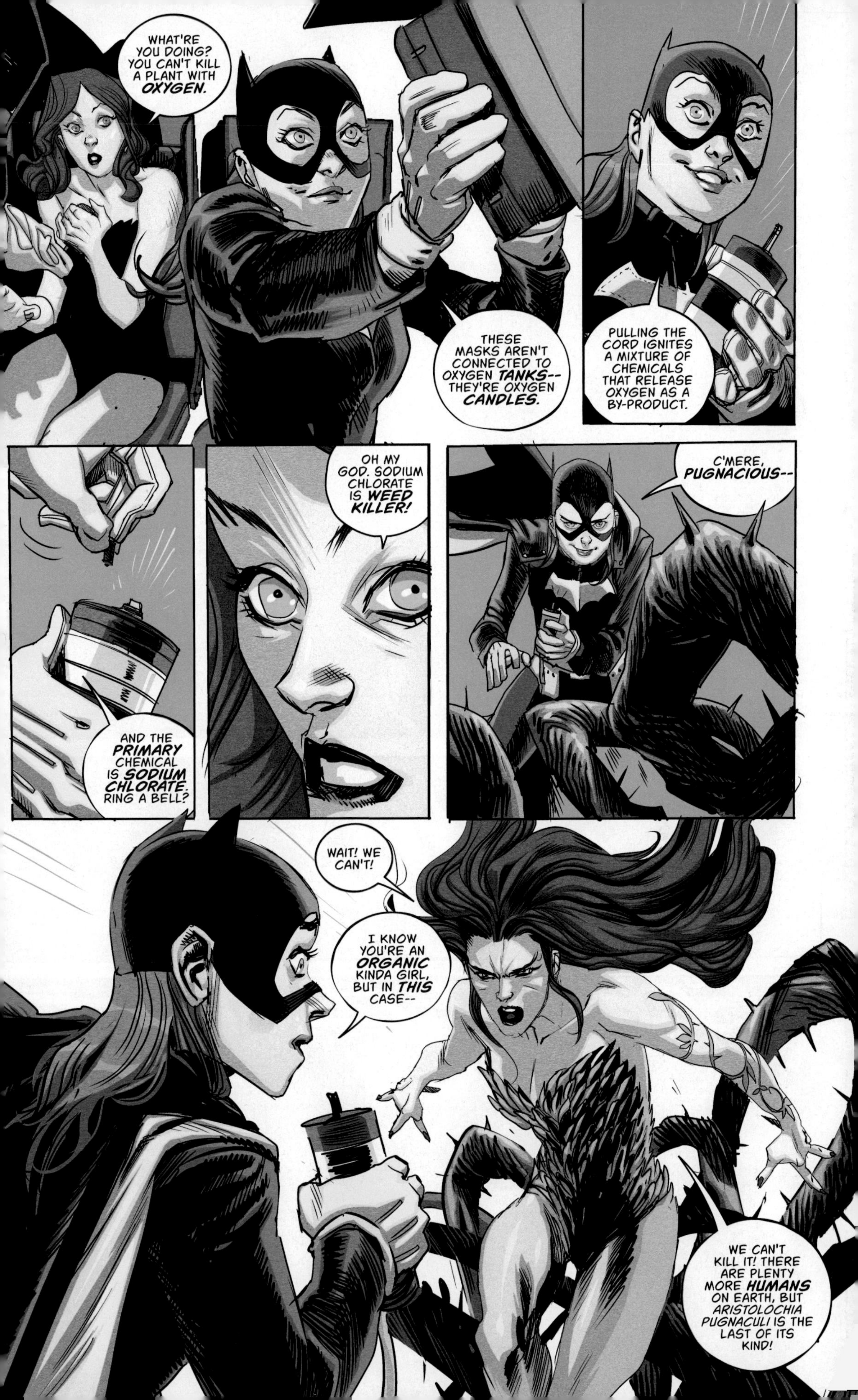
WHAT'RE YOU DOING? YOU CAN'T KILL A PLANT WITH OXYGEN.
THESE MASKS AREN'T CONNECTED TO OXYGEN TANKS-- THEY'RE OXYGEN CANDLES.
PULLING THE CORD IGNITES A MIXTURE OF CHEMICALS THAT RELEASE OXYGEN AS A BY-PRODUCT.
AND THE PRIMARY CHEMICAL IS SODIUM CHLORATE. RING A BELL?
OH MY GOD. SODIUM CHLORATE IS WEED KILLER!
C'MERE, PUGNACIOUS--
WAIT! WE CAN'T!
I KNOW YOU'RE AN ORGANIC KINDA GIRL, BUT IN THIS CASE--
WE CAN'T KILL IT! THERE ARE PLENTY MORE HUMANS ON EARTH, BUT ARISTOLOCHIA PUGNACULI IS THE LAST OF ITS KIND!

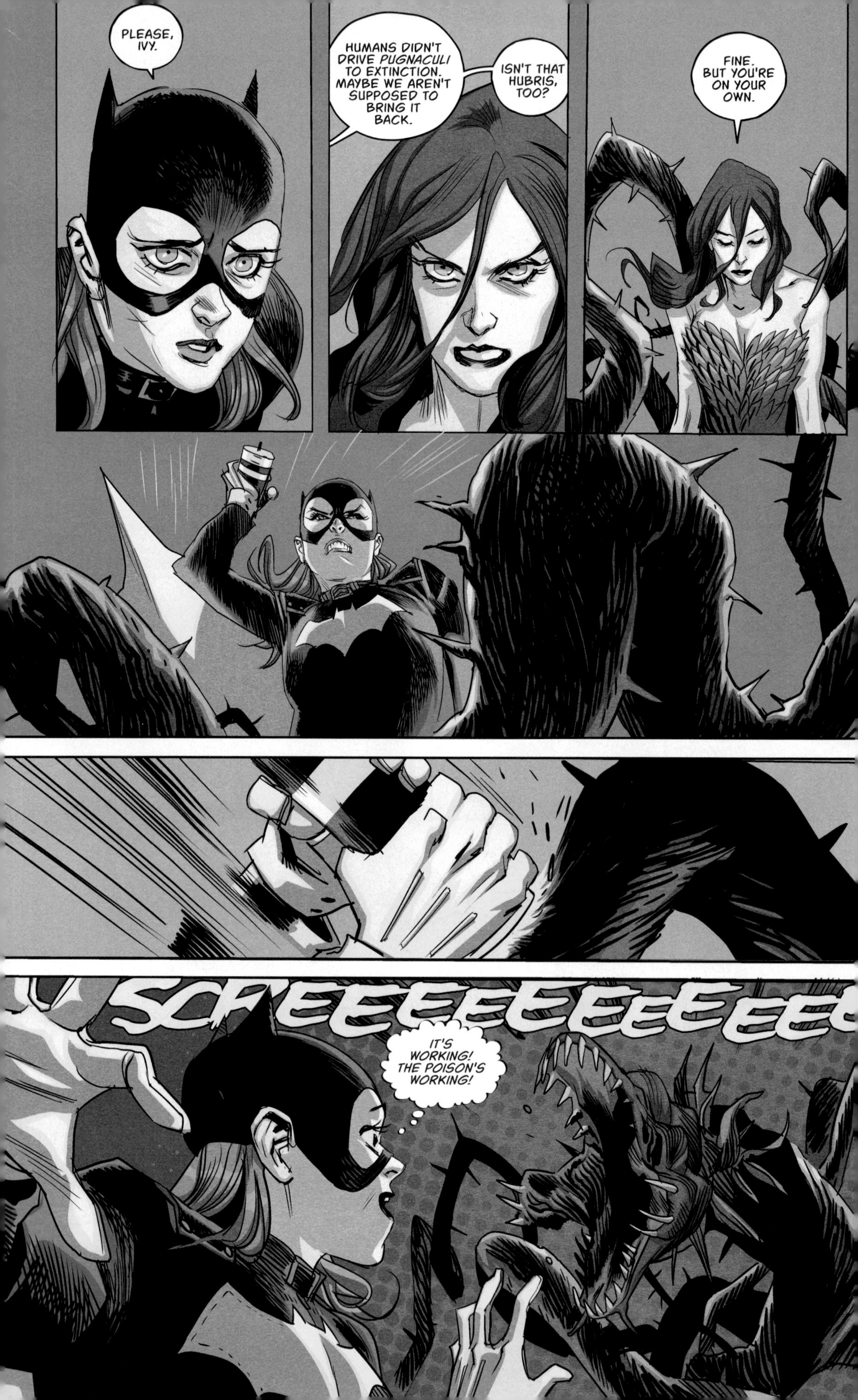
PLEASE, IVY.
HUMANS DIDN'T DRIVE PUGNACULI TO EXTINCTION. MAYBE WE AREN'T SUPPOSED TO BRING IT BACK.
ISN'T THAT HUBRIS, TOO?
FINE. BUT YOU'RE ON YOUR OWN.
SCREEEEEEEEEEEEE
IT'S WORKING! THE POISON'S WORKING!

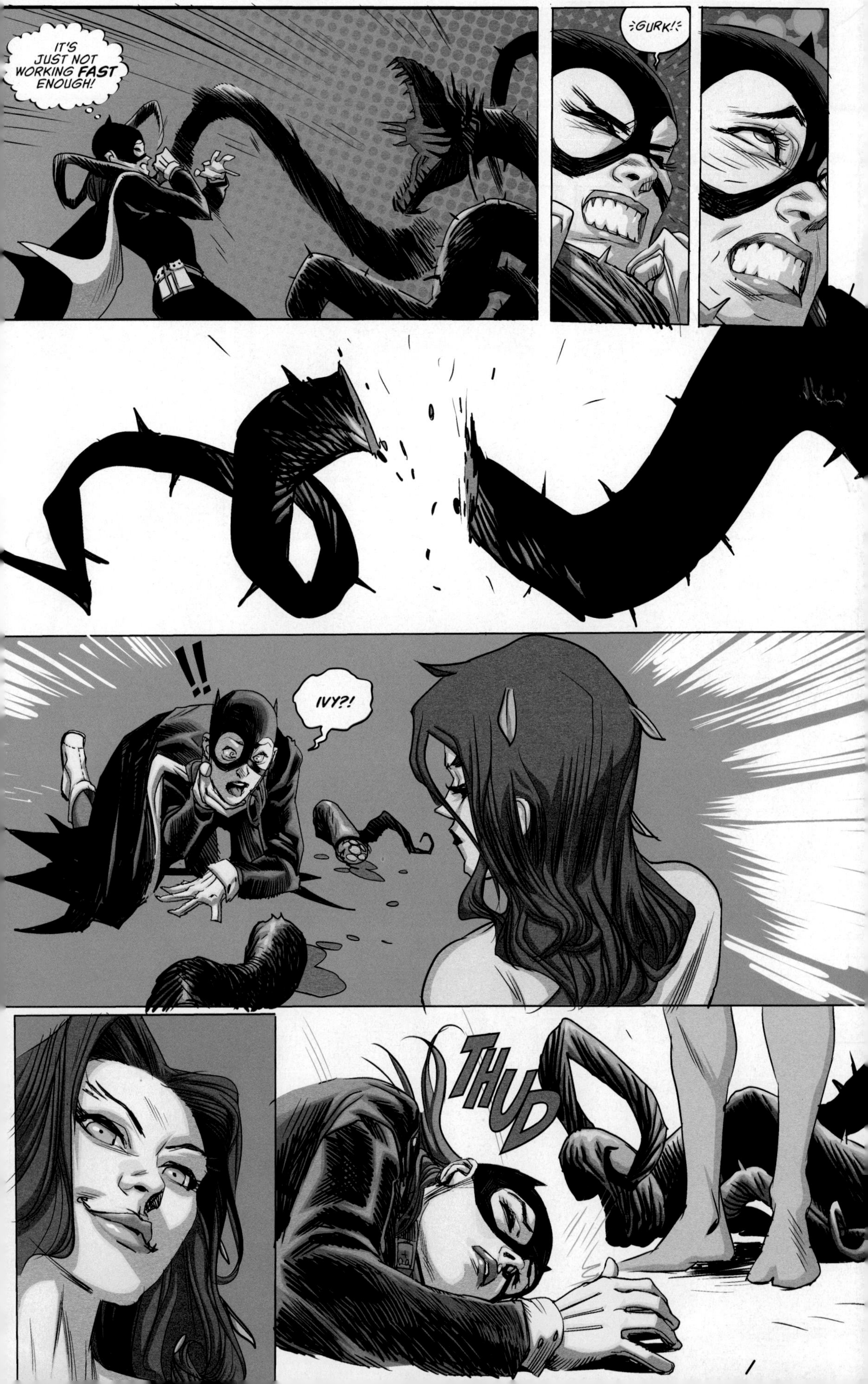
IT'S JUST NOT WORKING FAST ENOUGH!
GURK!
!!
IVY?!
THUD

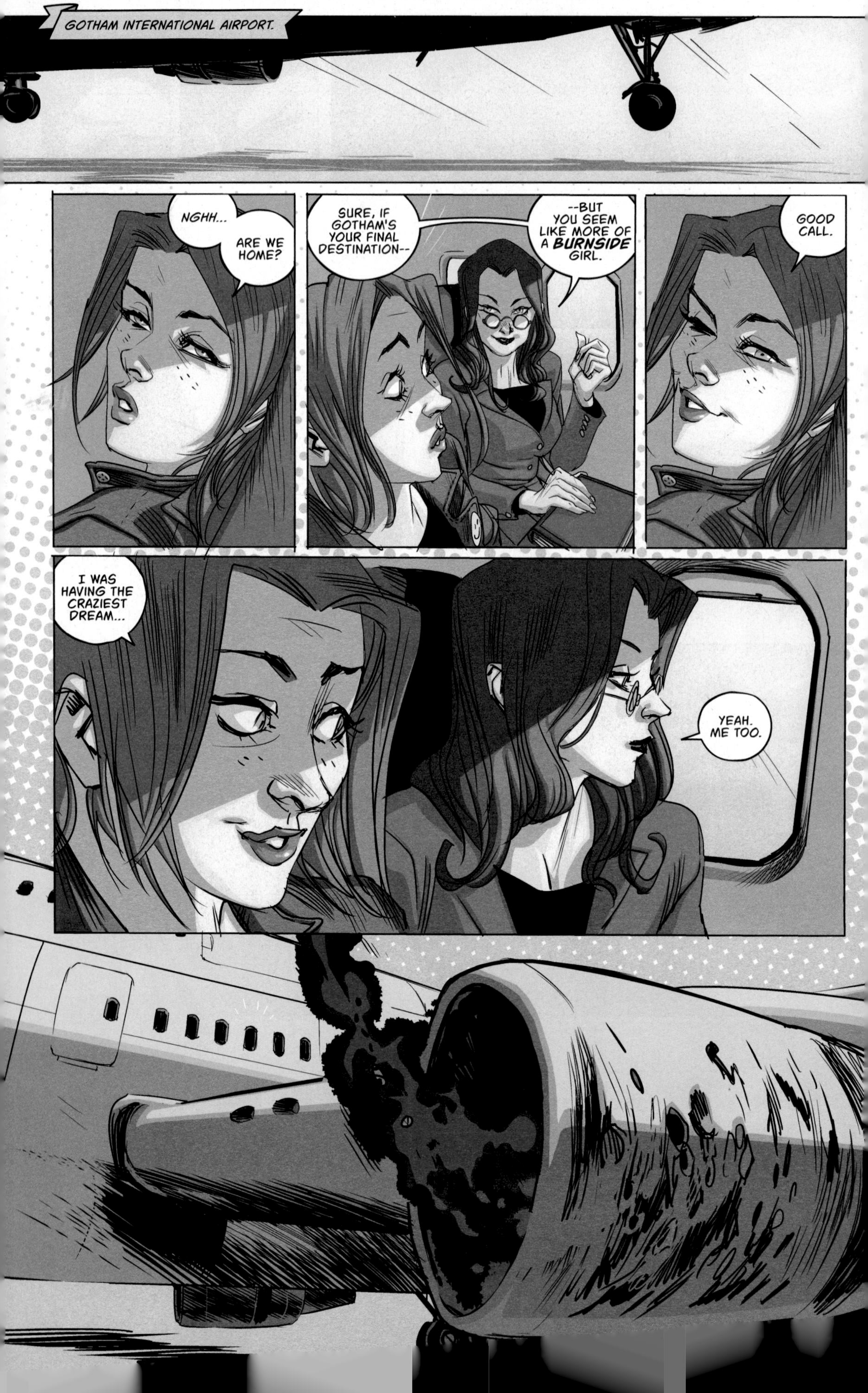
GOTHAM INTERNATIONAL AIRPORT.
NGHH...
ARE WE HOME?
SURE, IF GOTHAM'S YOUR FINAL DESTINATION--
--BUT YOU SEEM LIKE MORE OF A BURNSIDE GIRL.
GOOD CALL.
I WAS HAVING THE CRAZIEST DREAM...
YEAH. ME TOO.

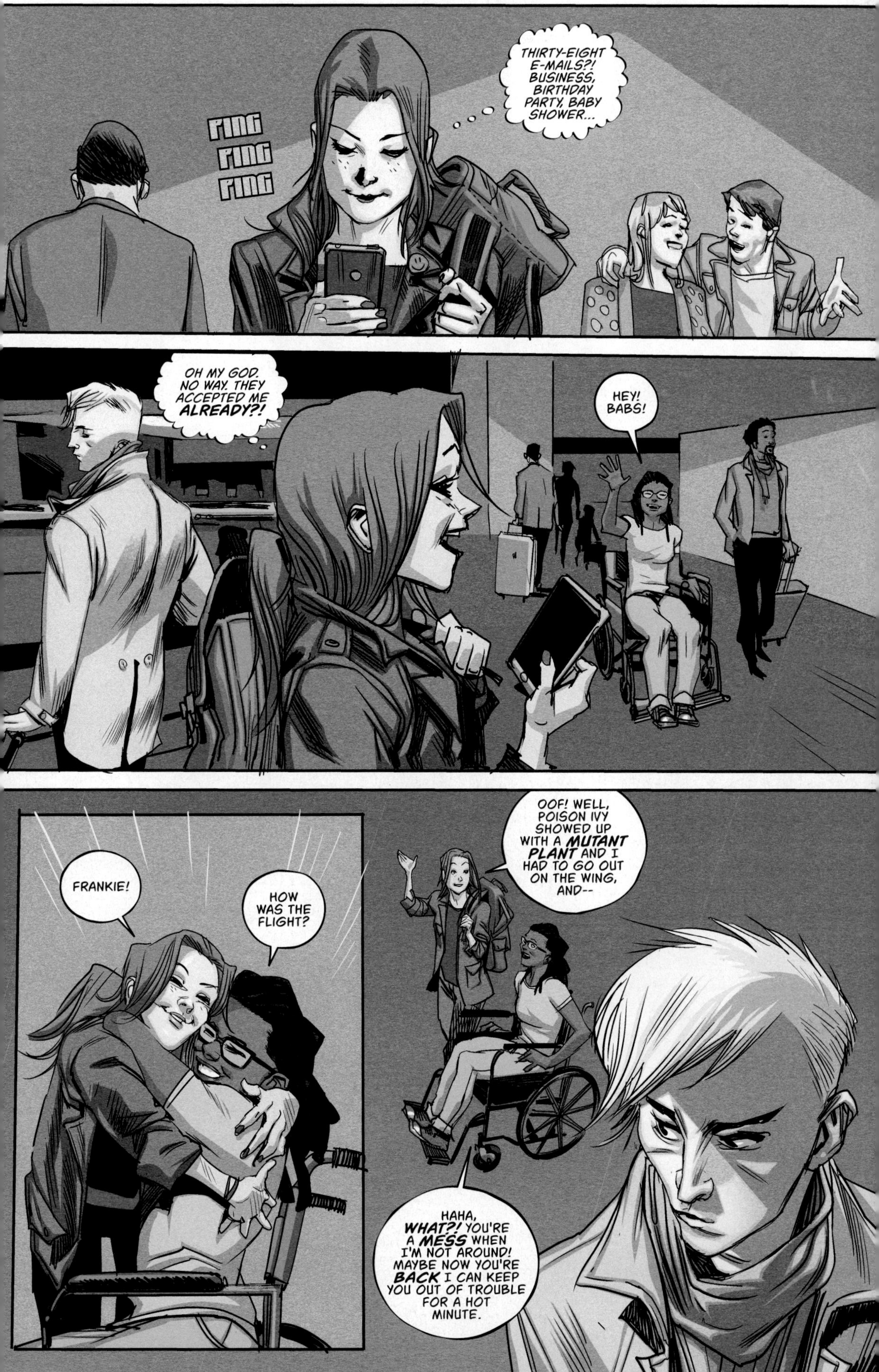
PING
PING
PING
THIRTY-EIGHT E-MAILS?! BUSINESS, BIRTHDAY PARTY, BABY SHOWER...
OH MY GOD. NO WAY. THEY ACCEPTED ME ALREADY?!
HEY! BABS!
FRANKIE!
HOW WAS THE FLIGHT?
OOF! WELL, POISON IVY SHOWED UP WITH A MUTANT PLANT AND I HAD TO GO OUT ON THE WING, AND--
HAHA, WHAT?! YOU'RE A MESS WHEN I'M NOT AROUND! MAYBE NOW YOU'RE BACK I CAN KEEP YOU OUT OF TROUBLE FOR A HOT MINUTE.

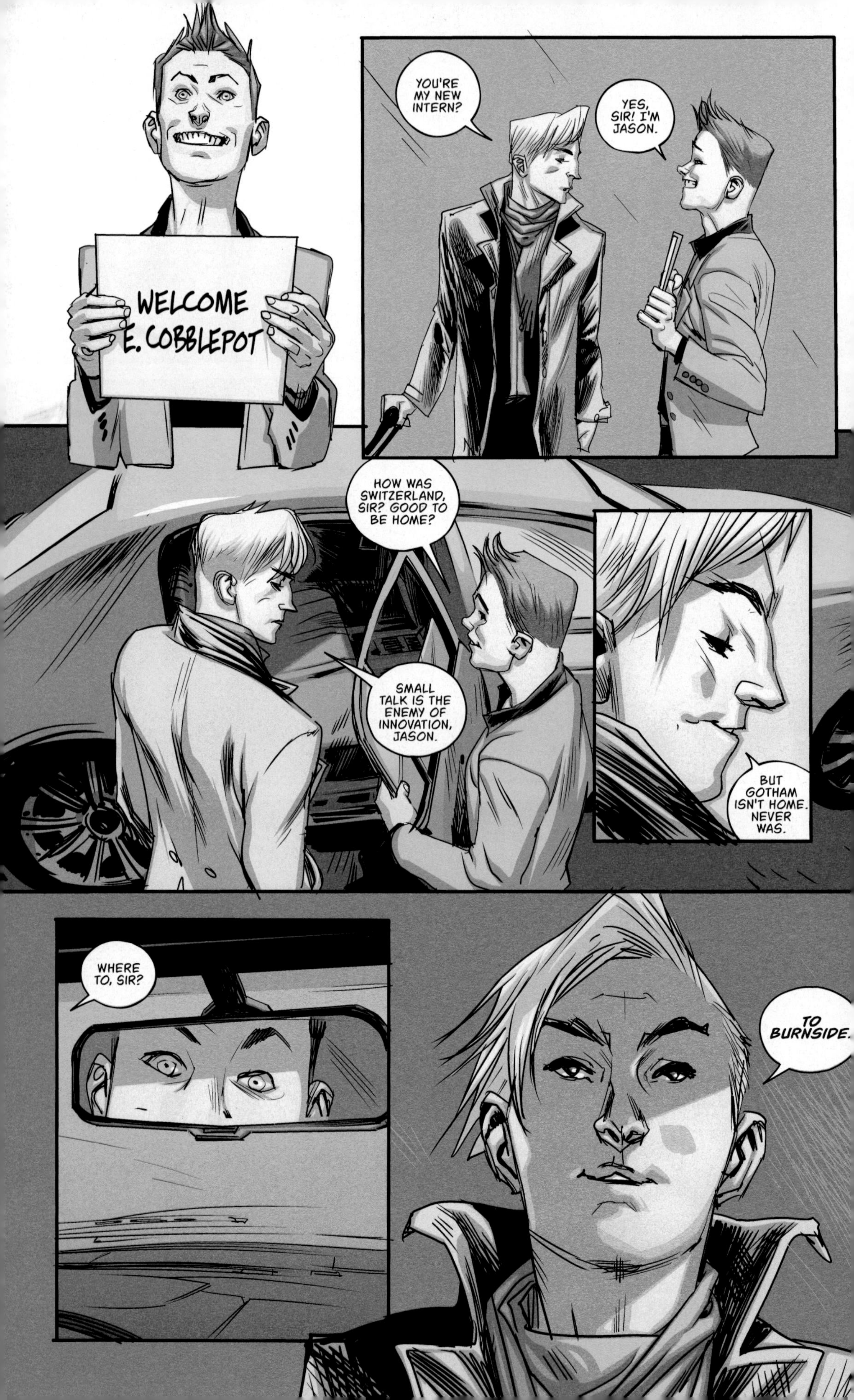
WELCOME
E. COBBLEPOT
YOU'RE MY NEW INTERN?
YES, SIR! I'M JASON.
HOW WAS SWITZERLAND, SIR? GOOD TO BE HOME?
SMALL TALK IS THE ENEMY OF INNOVATION, JASON.
BUT GOTHAM ISN'T HOME. NEVER WAS.
WHERE TO, SIR?
TO BURNSIDE.

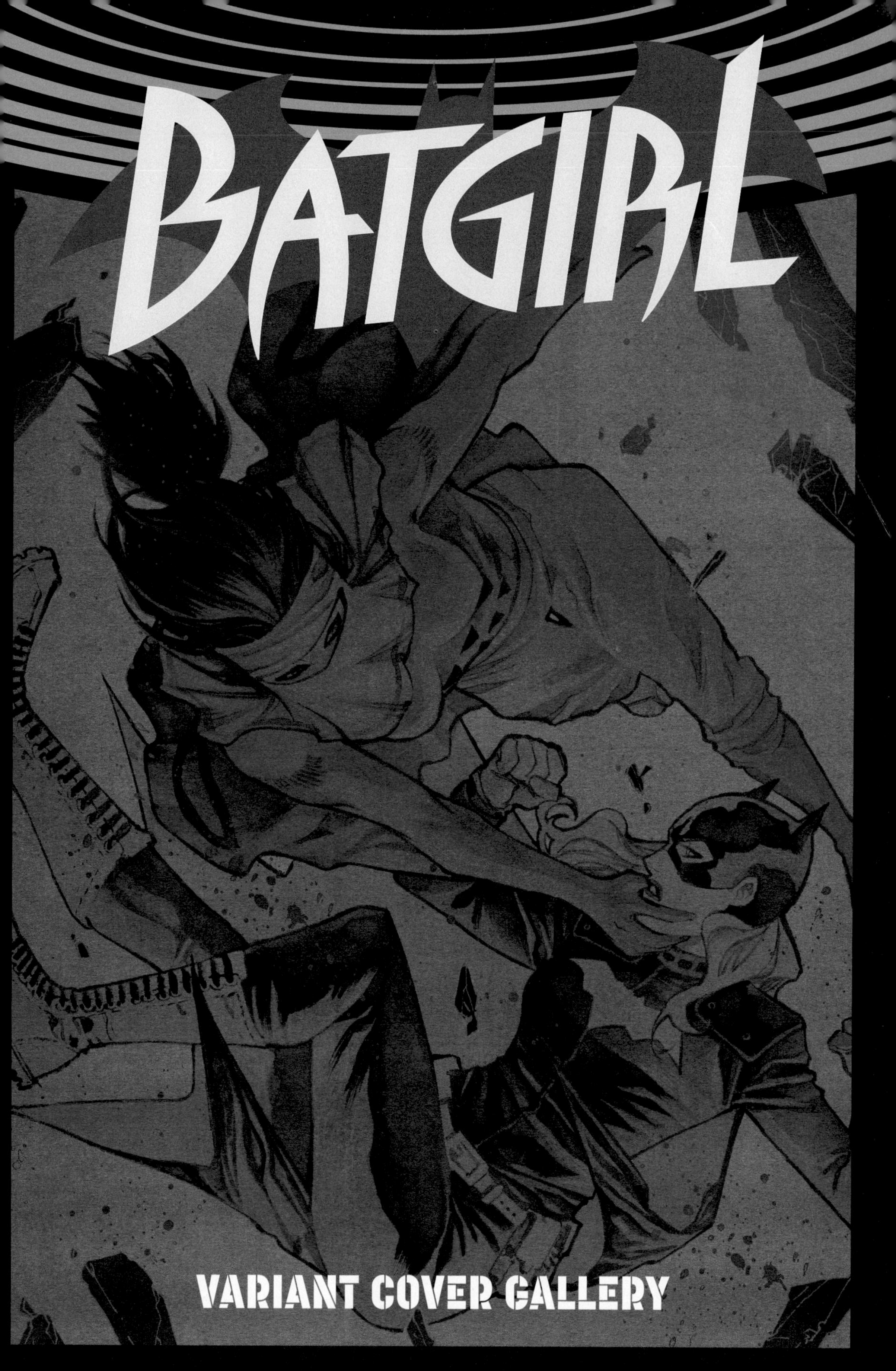
BATGIRL
VARIANT COVER GALLERY

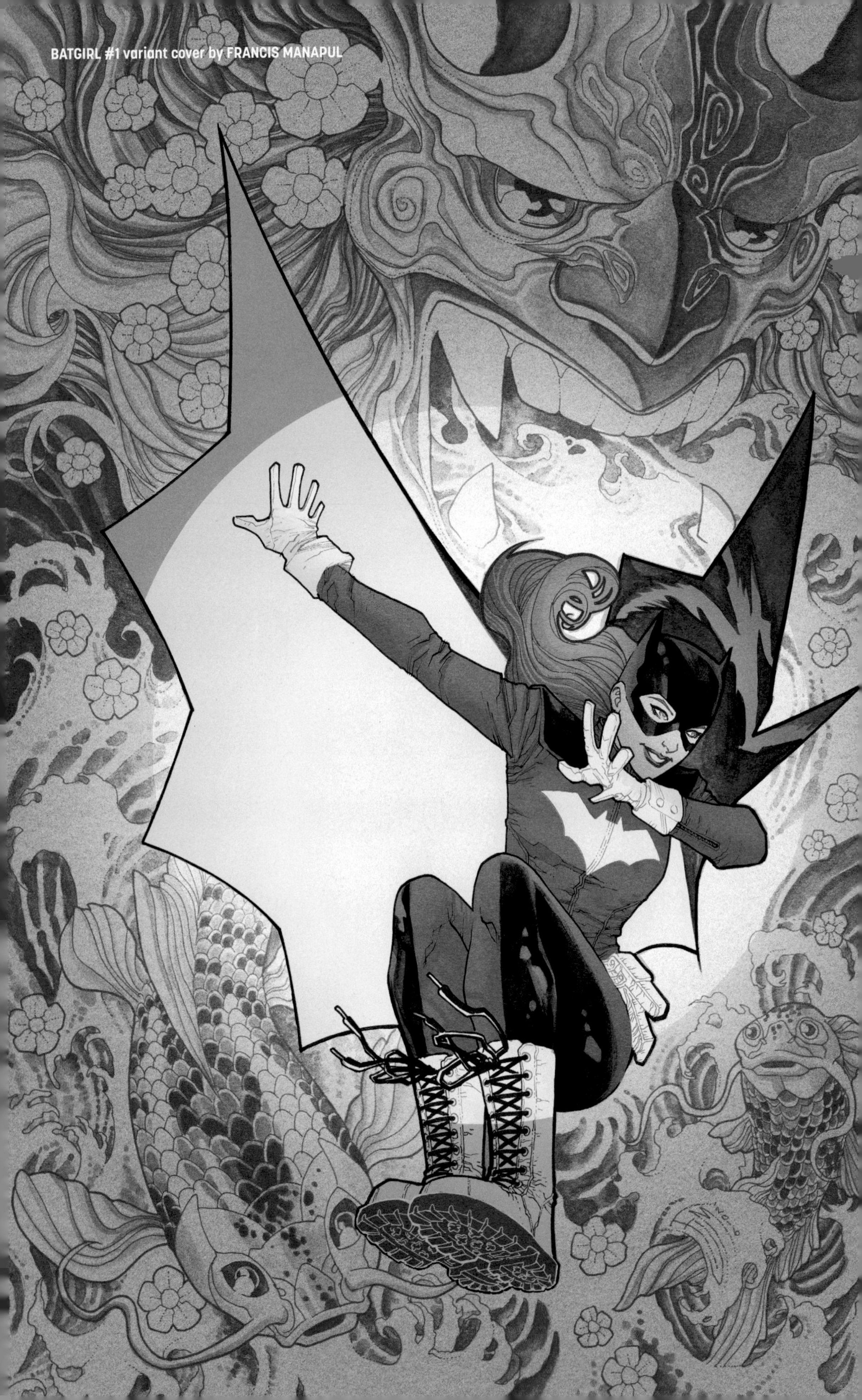

BATGIRL #1 variant cover by FRANCIS MANAPUL

**BATGIRL #2 variant cover by FRANCIS MANAPUL**

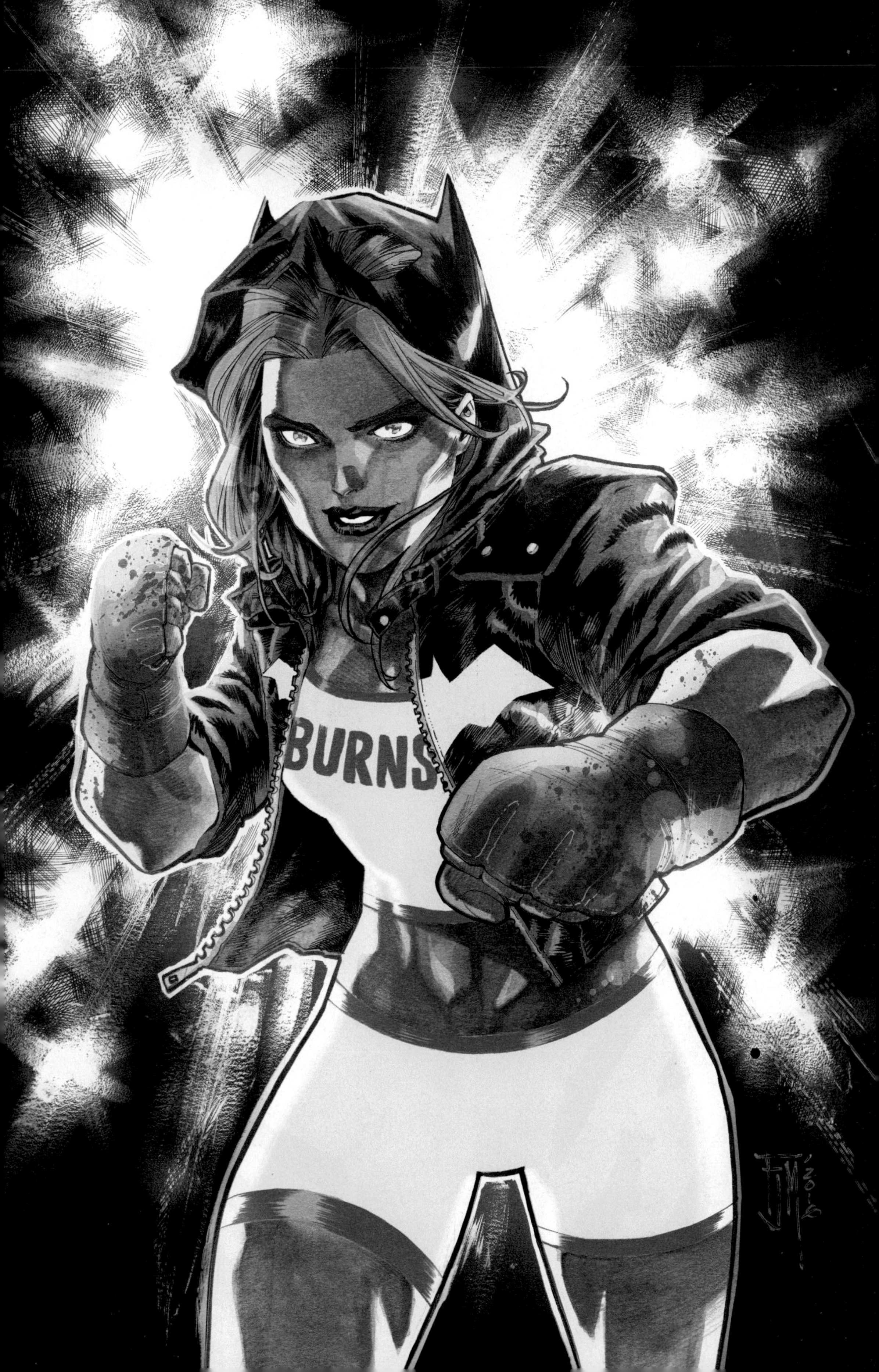
BURNS

BATGIRL #3 variant cover by FRANCIS MANAPUL

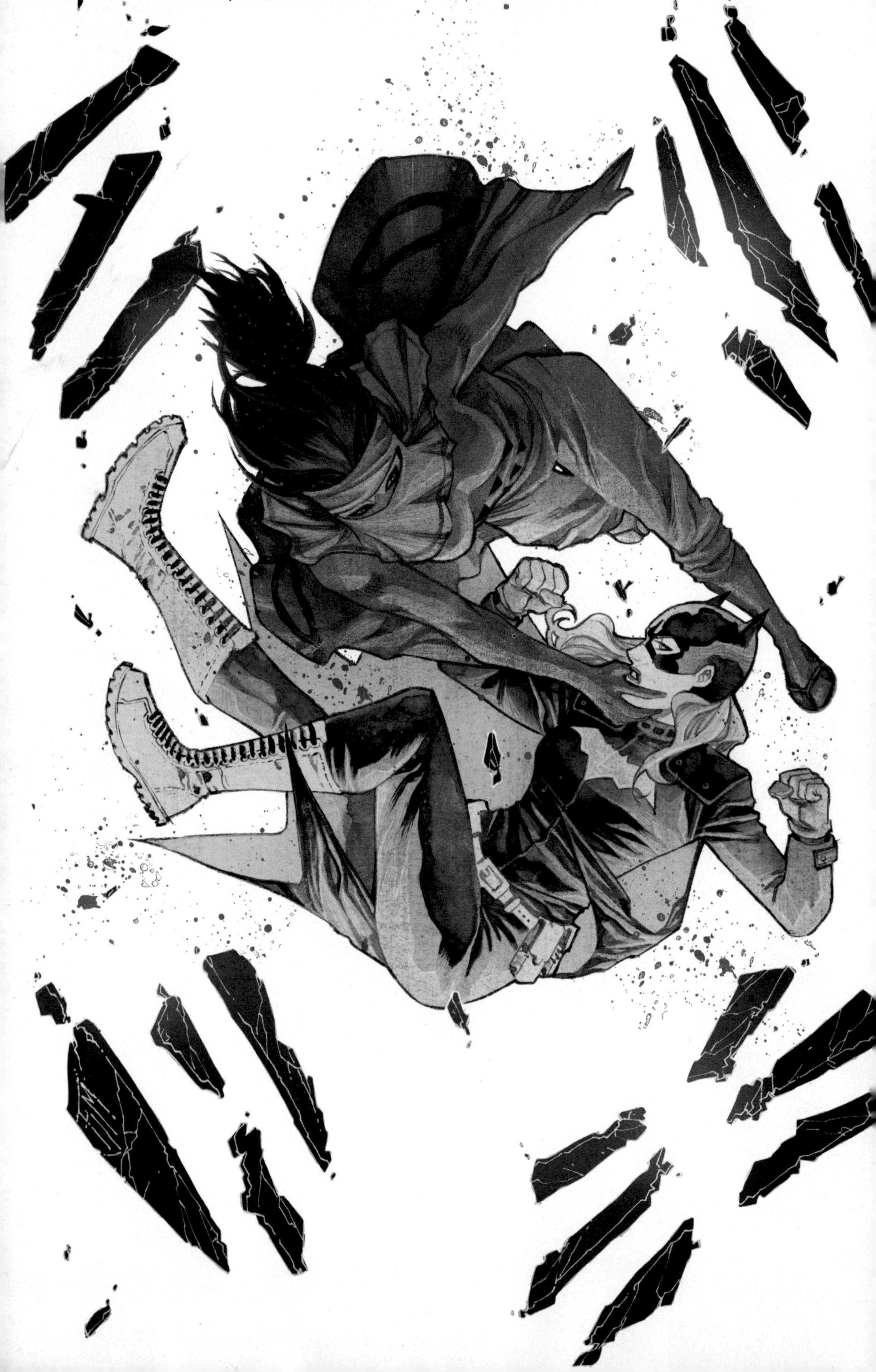

BATGIRL #4 variant cover by FRANCIS MANAPUL

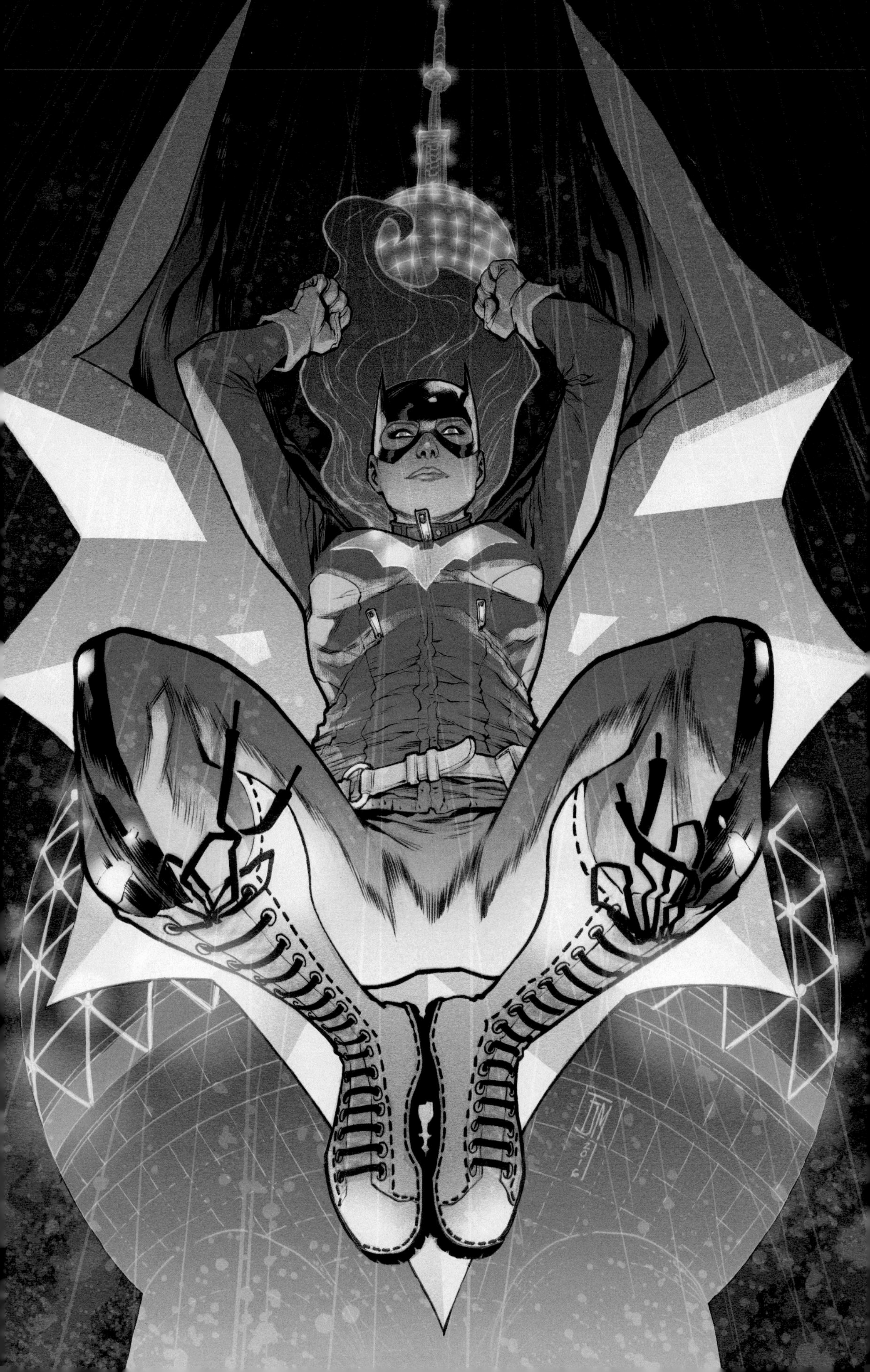

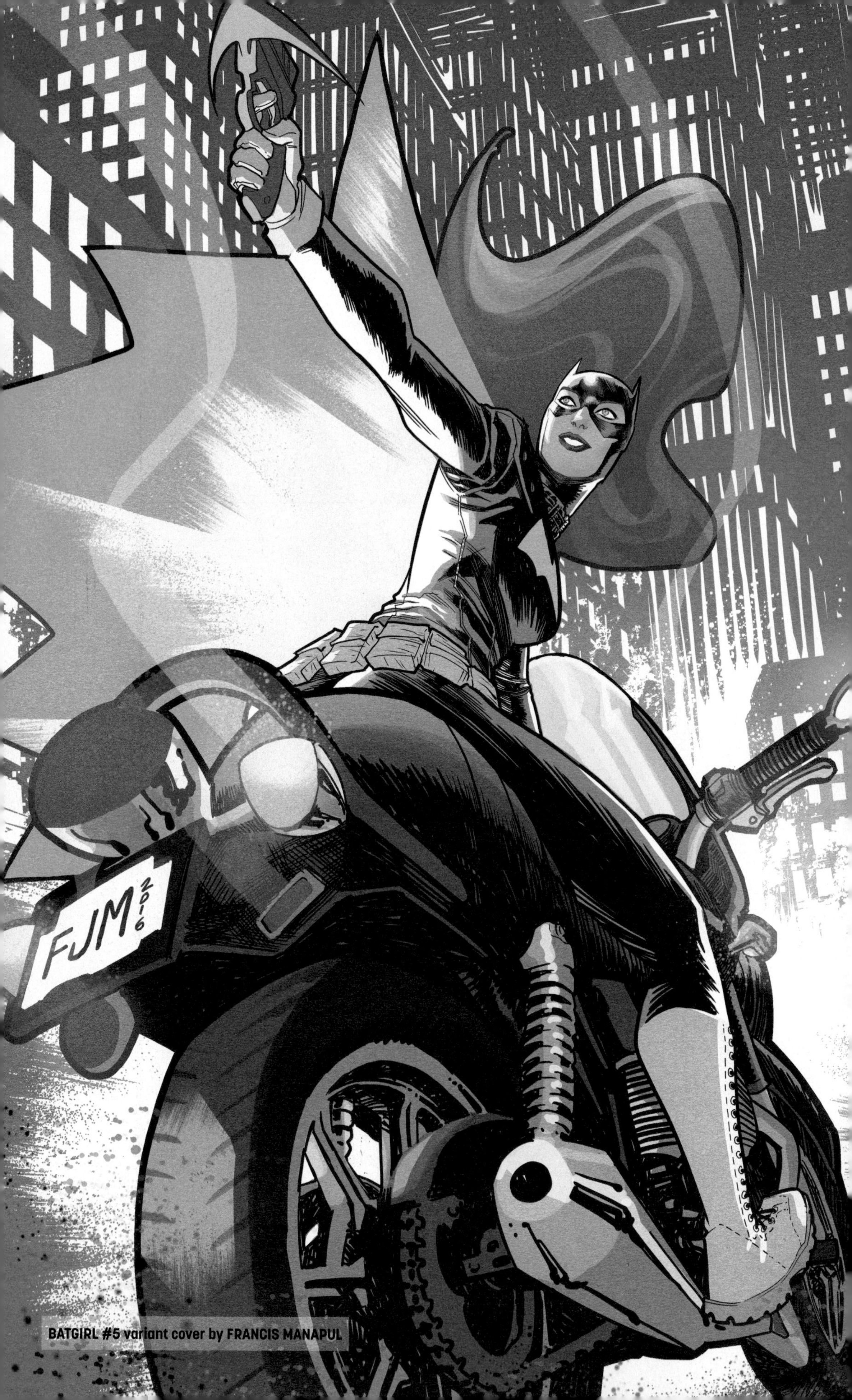
FJM 2016

BATGIRL #5 variant cover by FRANCIS MANAPUL

BATGIRL #6 variant cover by FRANCIS MANAPUL

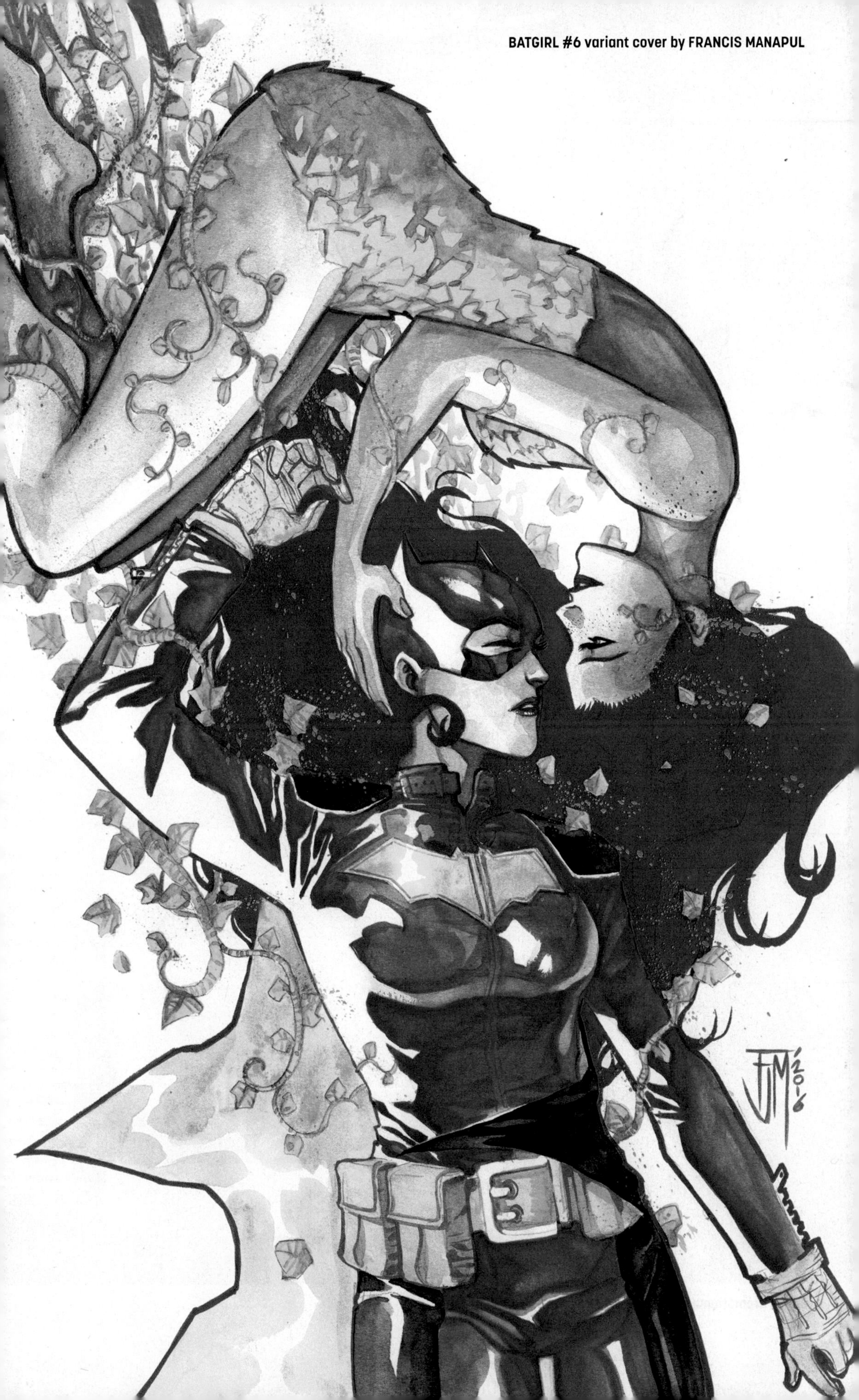

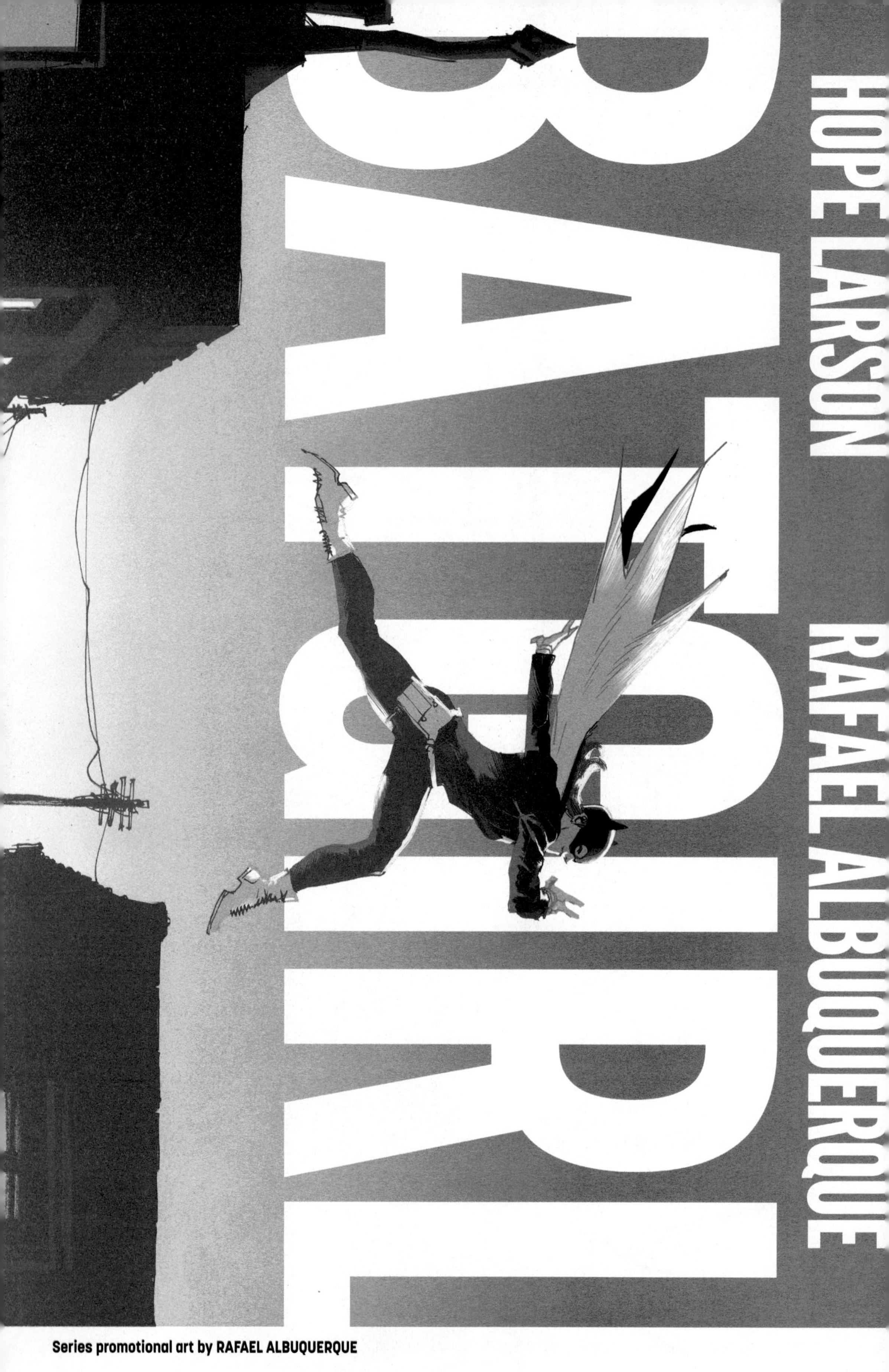
BATGIRL
HOPE LARSON
RAFAEL ALBUQUERQUE

Series promotional art by RAFAEL ALBUQUERQUE

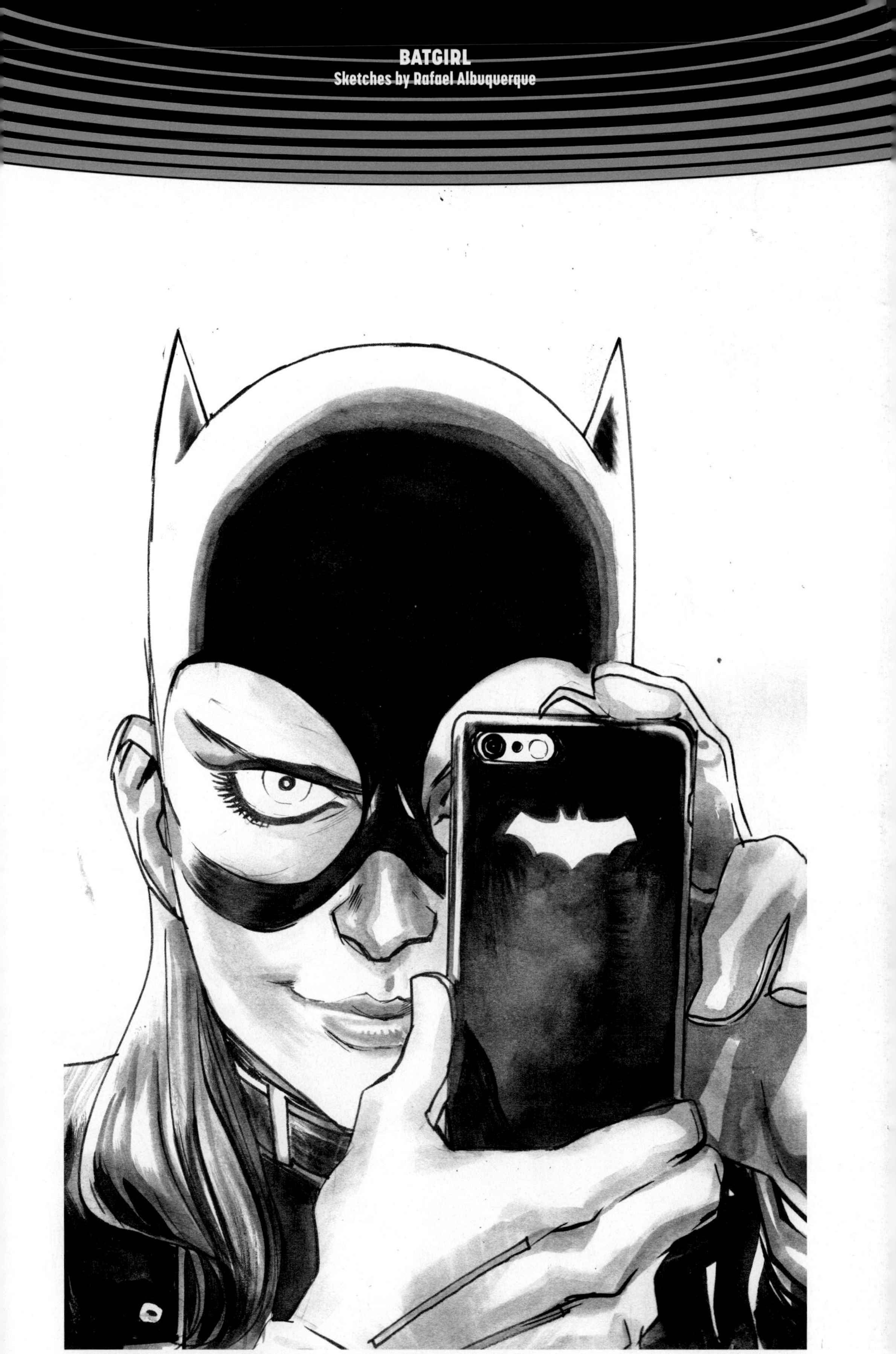

Unused cover concept for BATGIRL VOL. 1: BEYOND BURNSIDE paperback

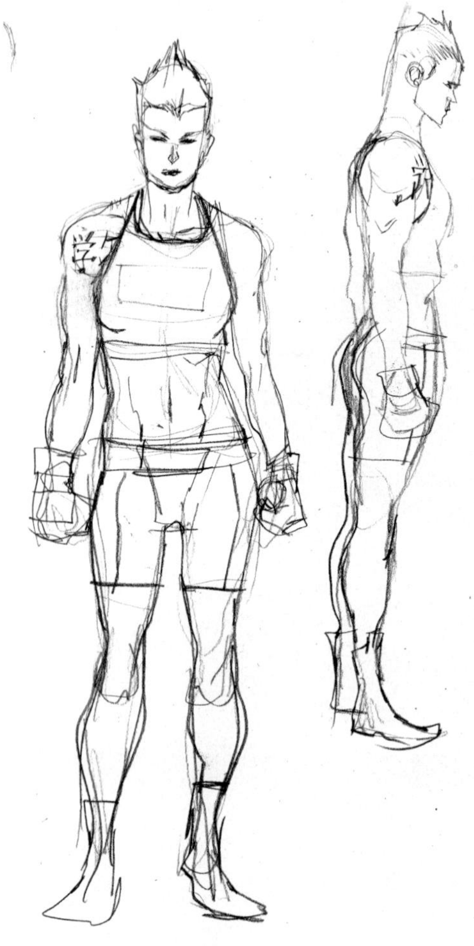

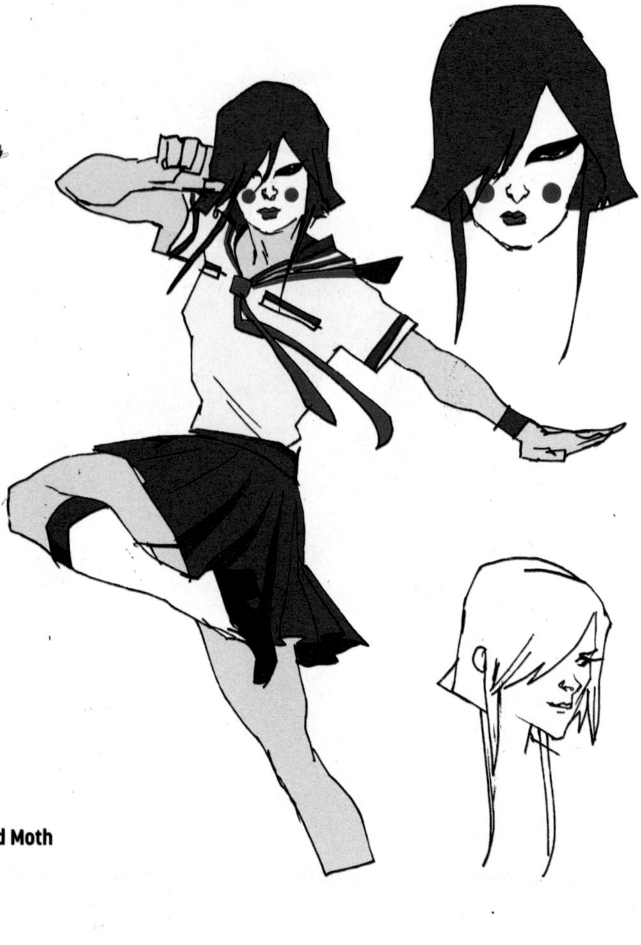

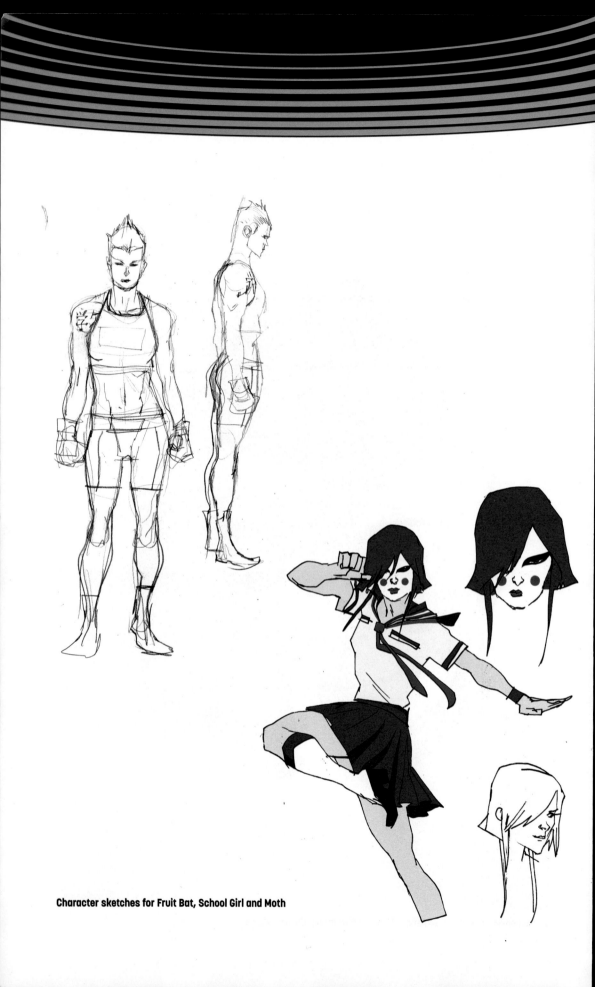

Character sketches for Fruit Bat, School Girl and Moth

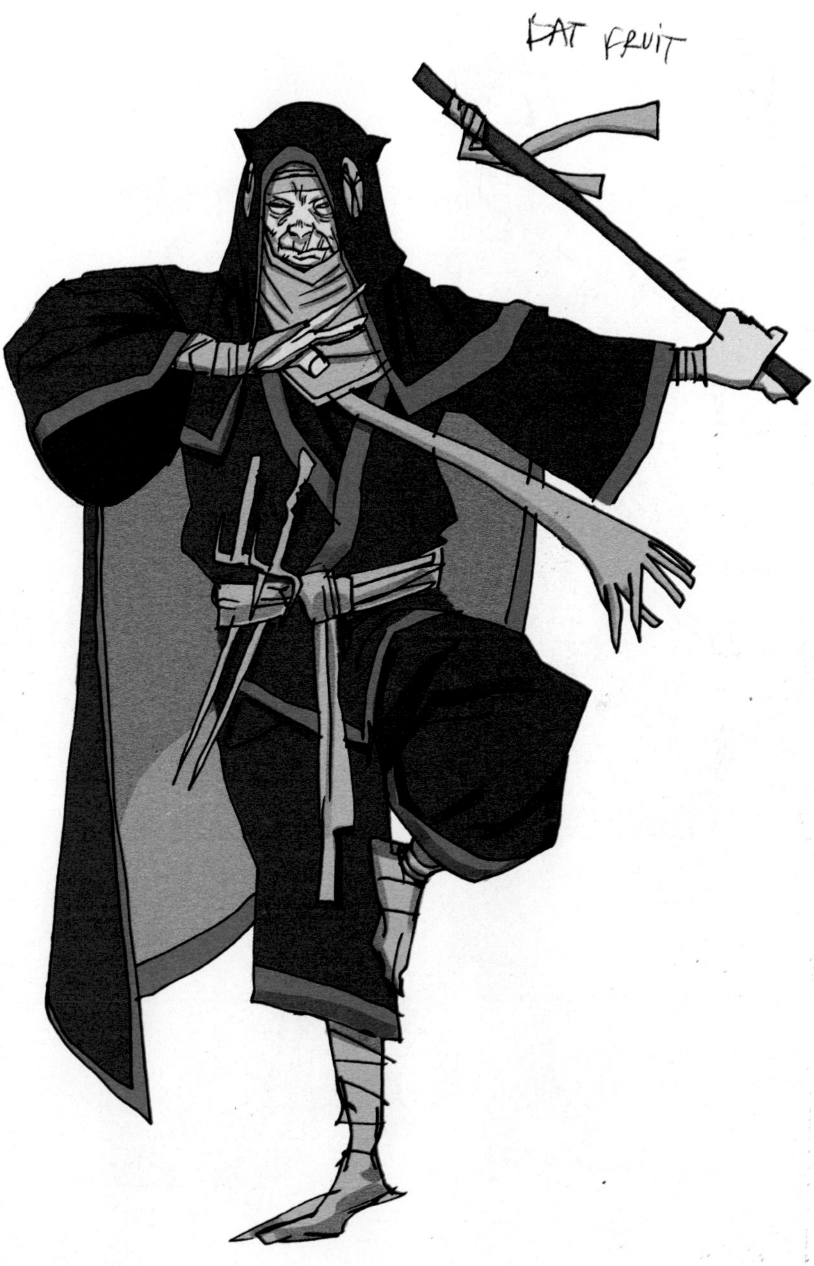
FAT FRUIT

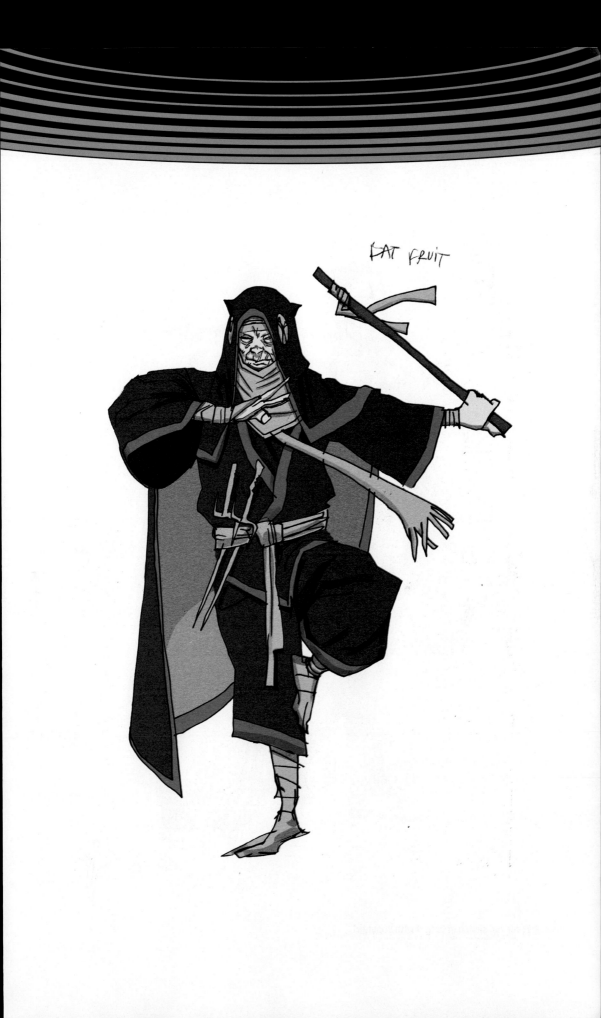

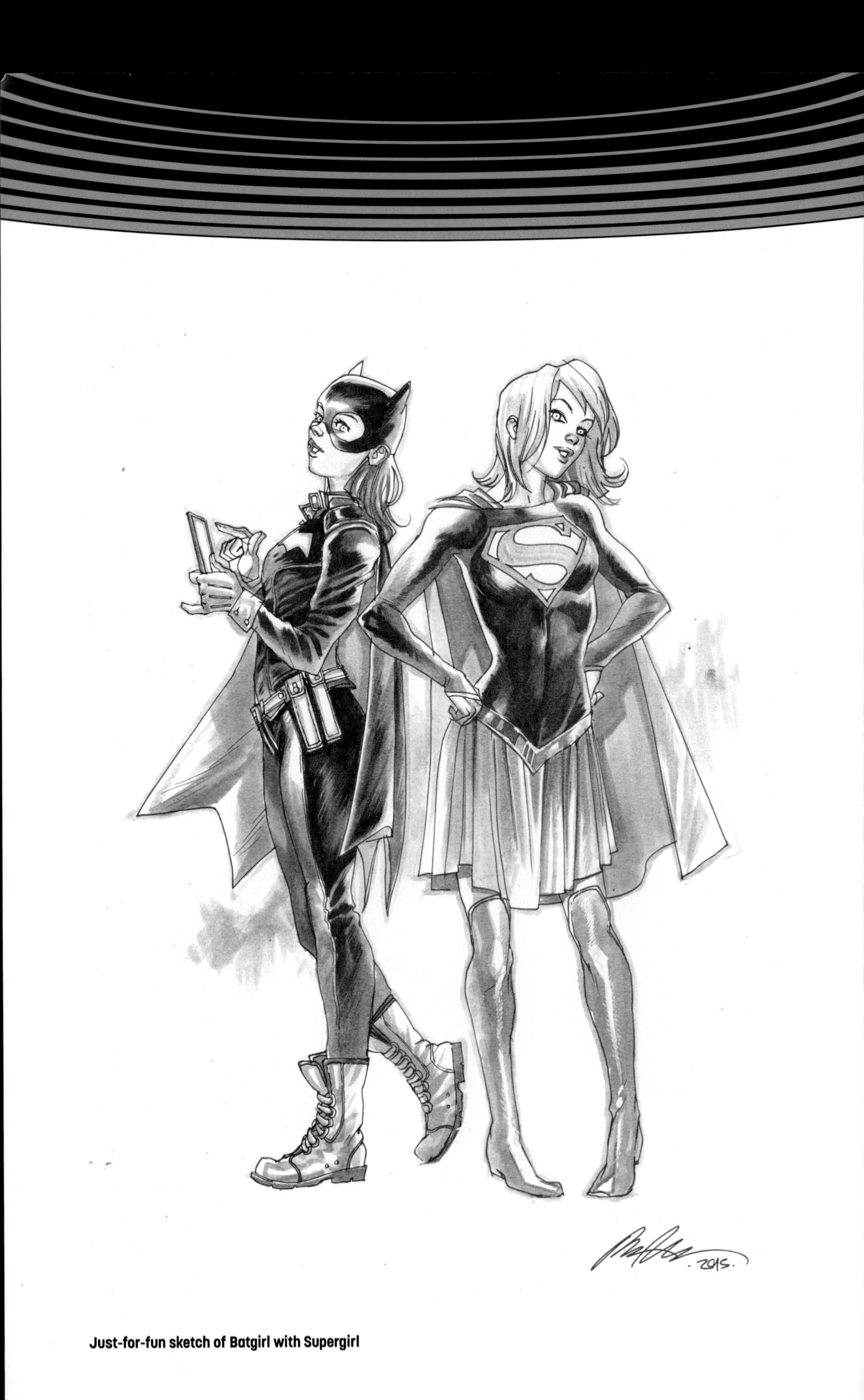

**Just-for-fun sketch of Batgirl with Supergirl**

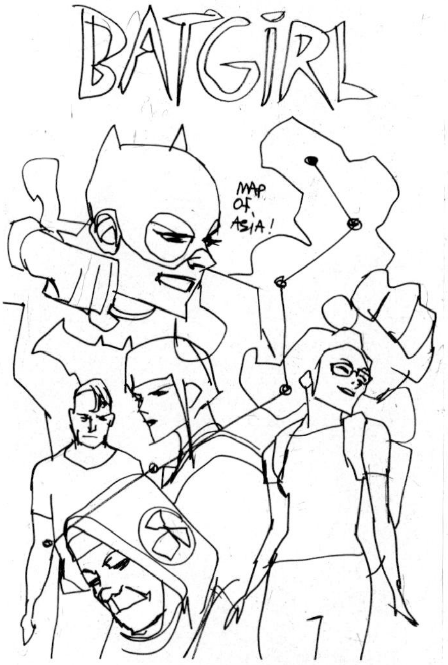
BATGIRL
MAP OF ASIA!

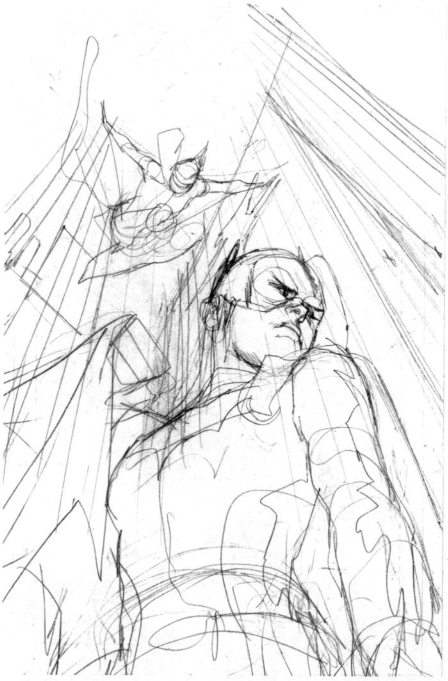

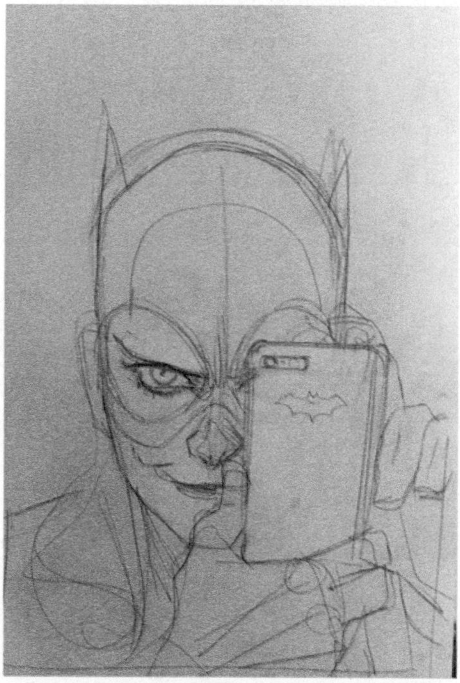

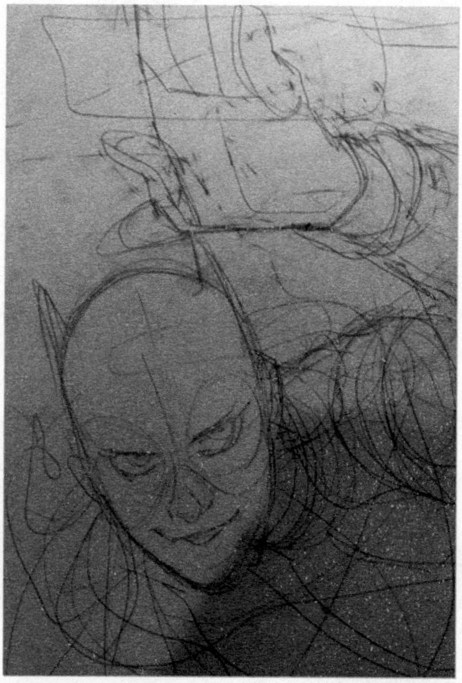

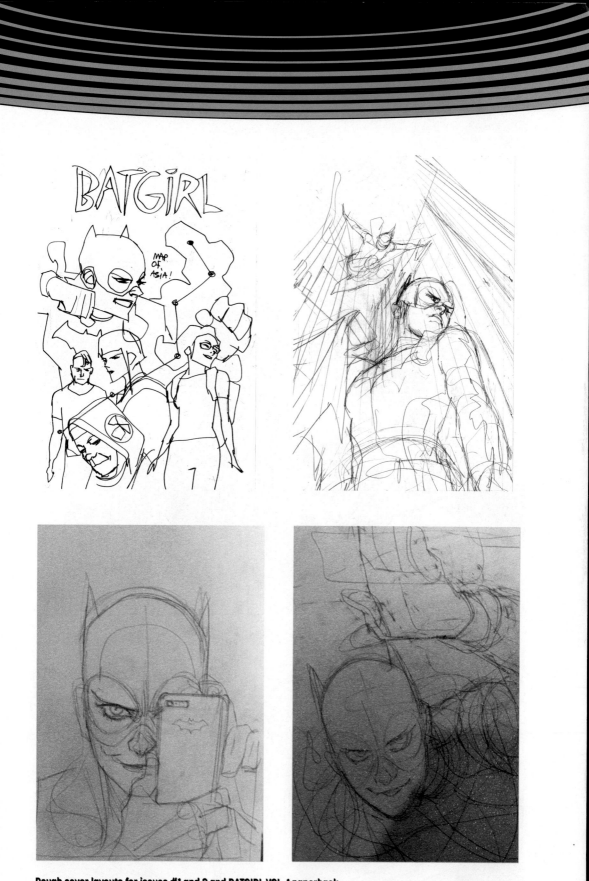

**Rough cover layouts for issues #1 and 3 and BATGIRL VOL. 1 paperback**

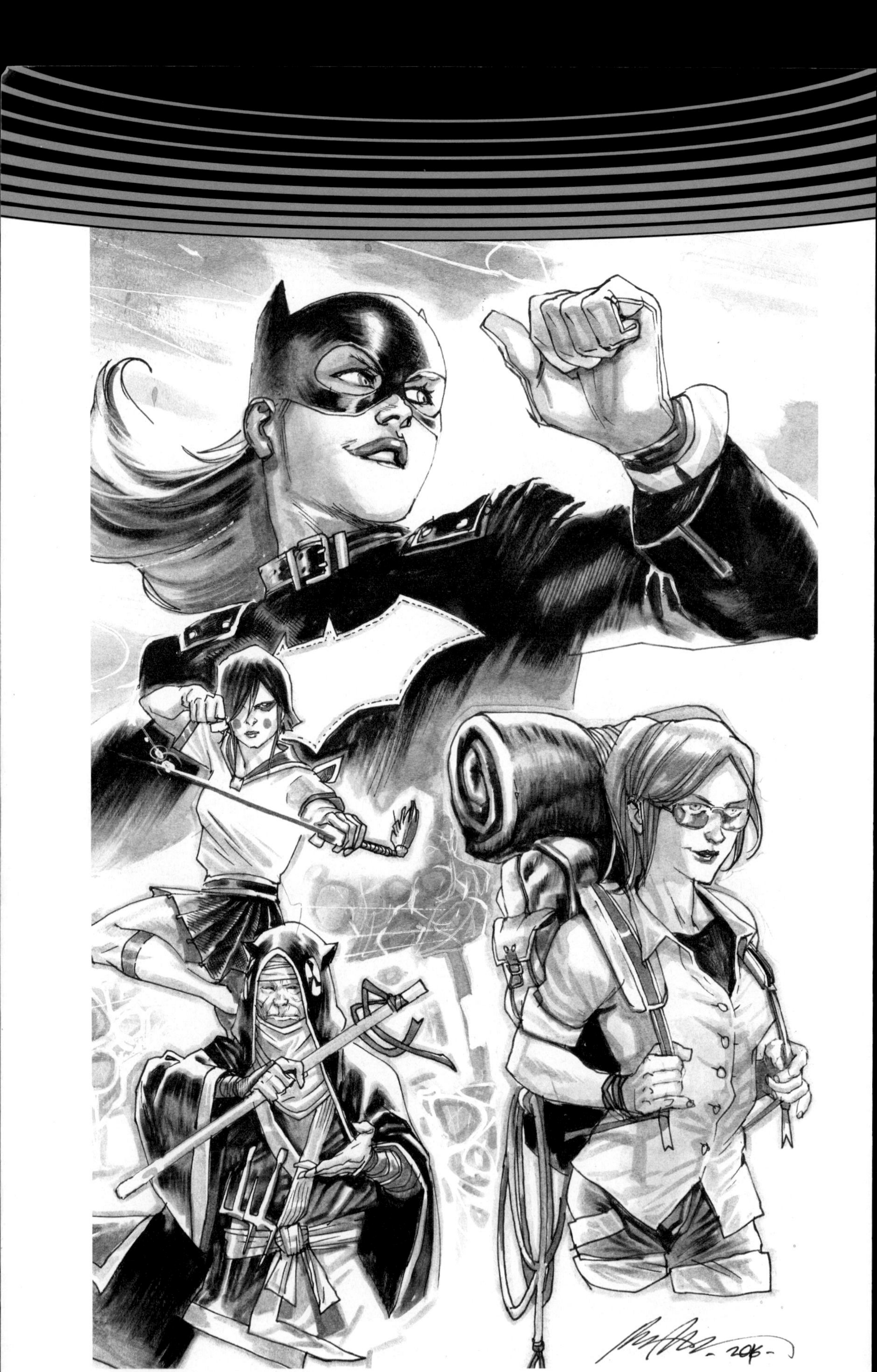

**Art for BATGIRL #1 cover before color**

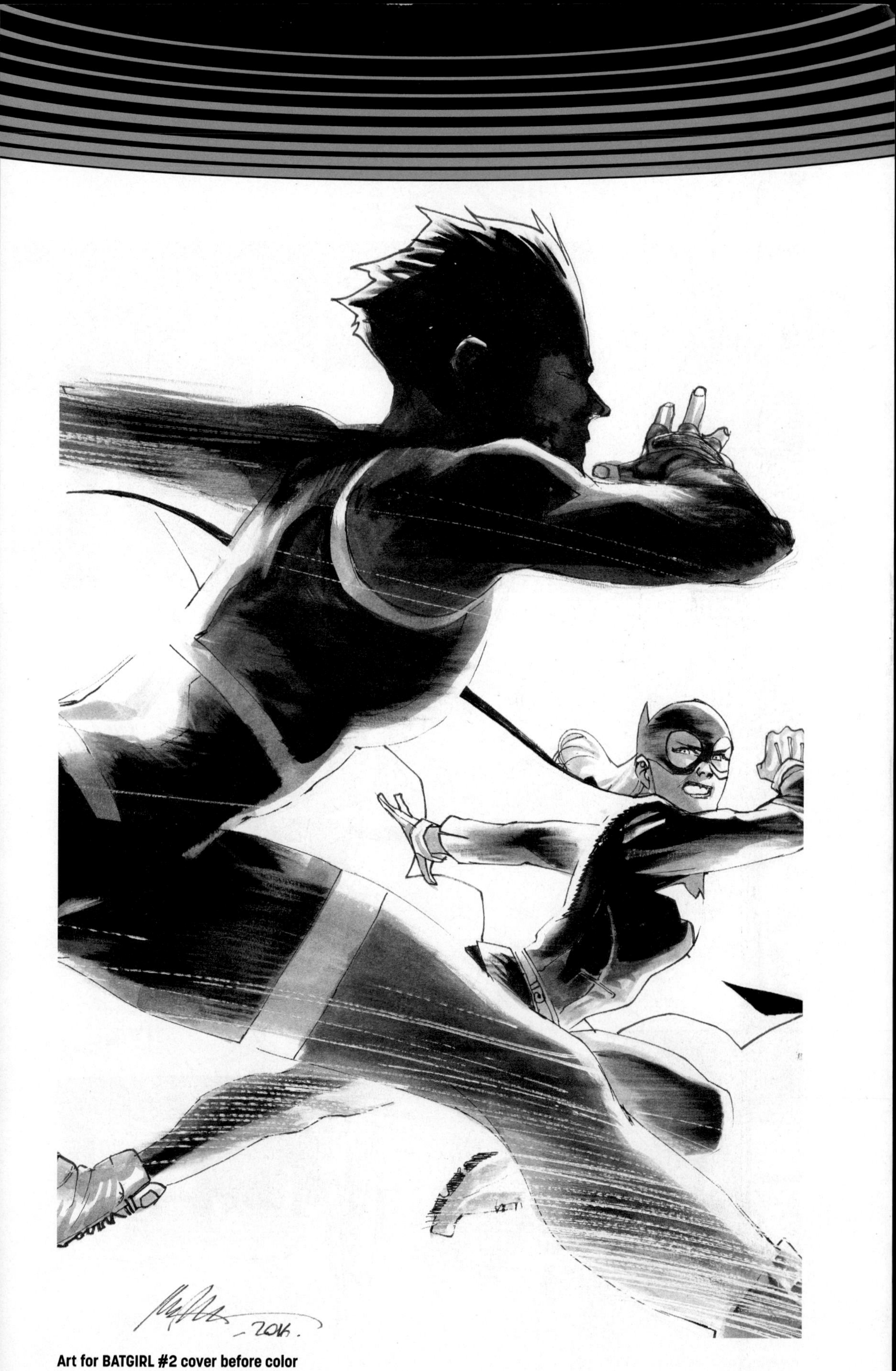

Art for BATGIRL #2 cover before color

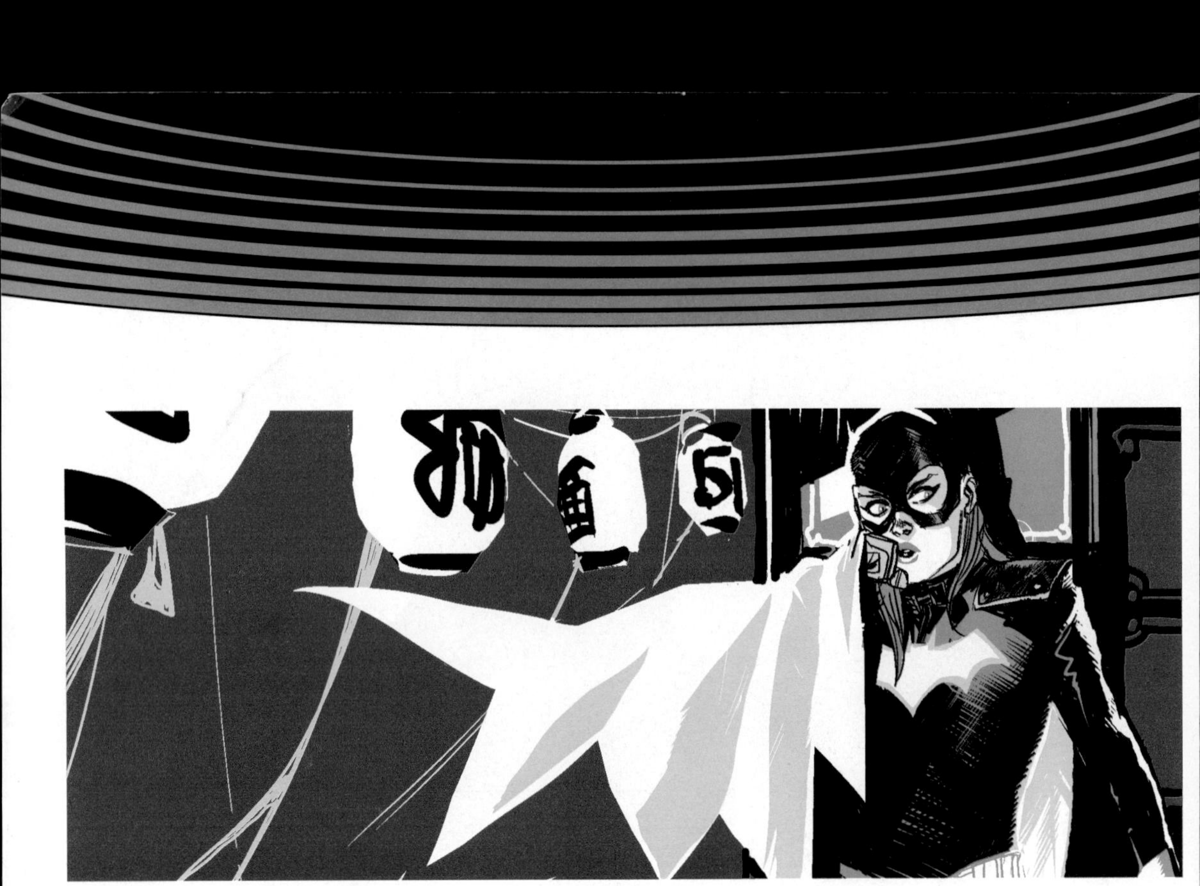

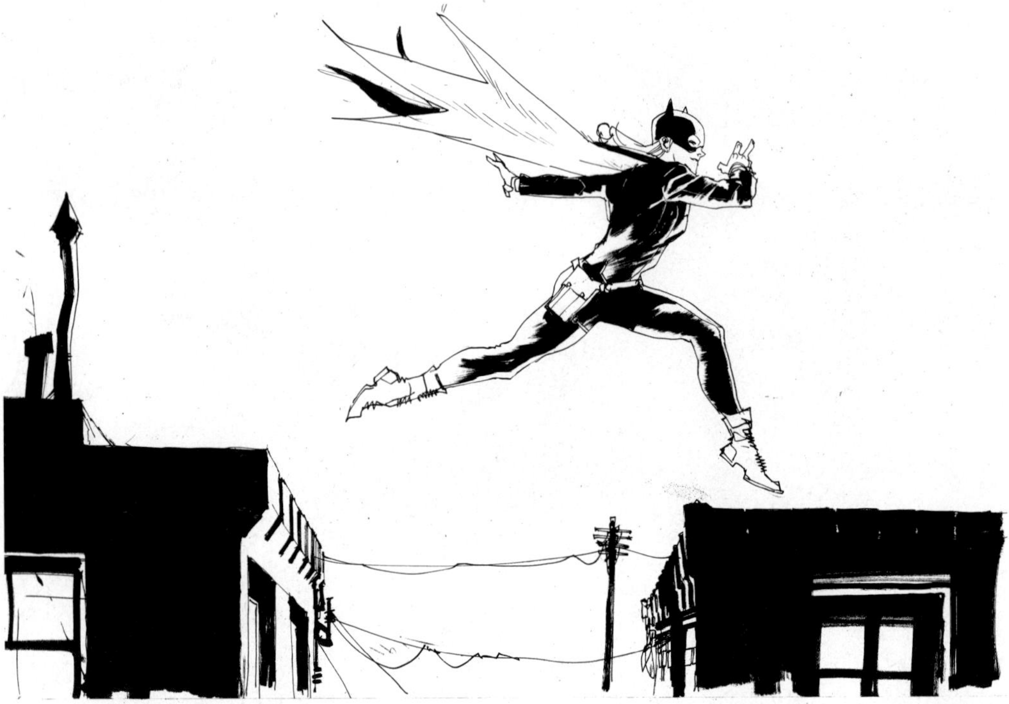

**Additional Batgirl series promotional art**

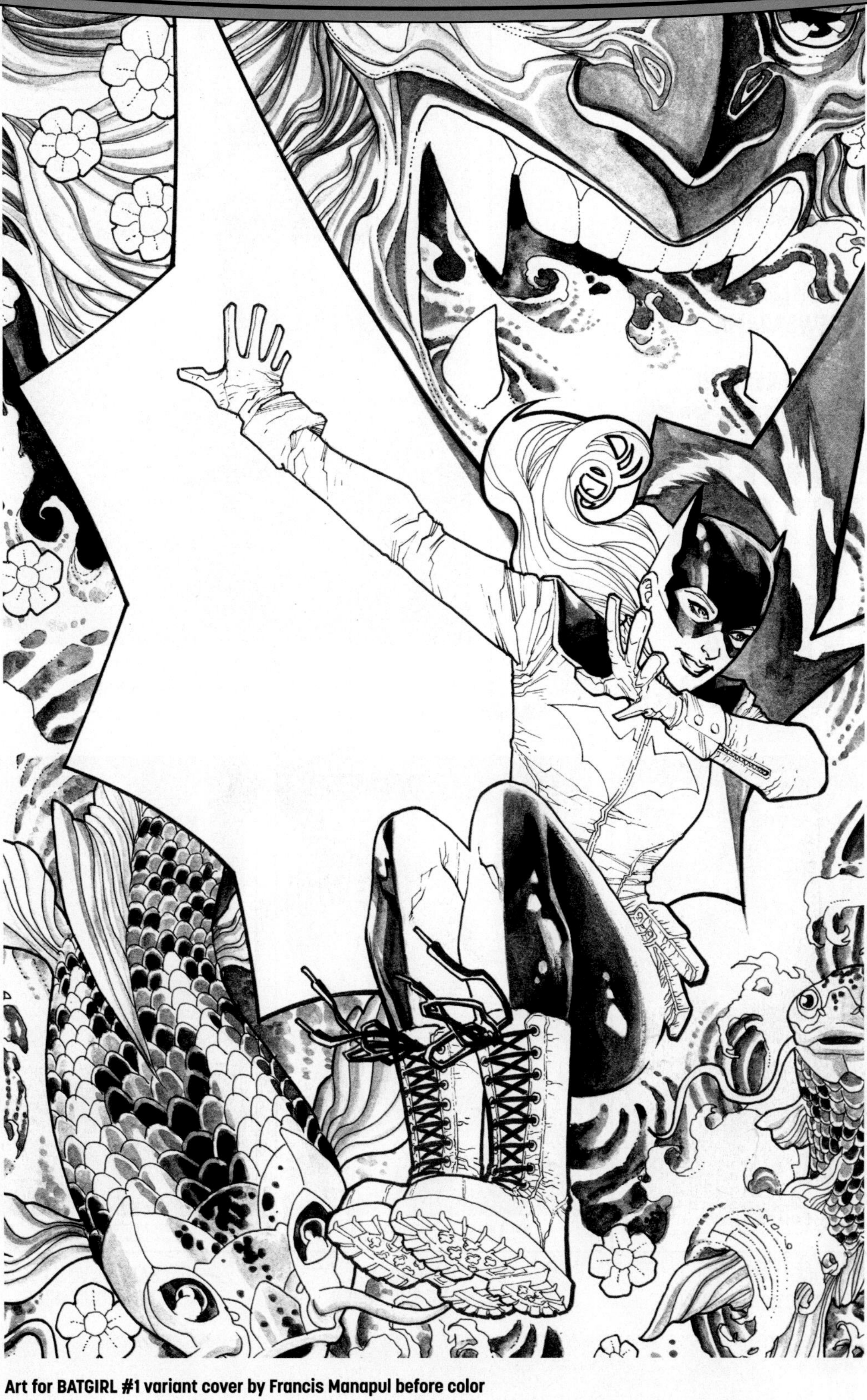

Art for BATGIRL #1 variant cover by Francis Manapul before color

"Greg Rucka and company have created a compelling narrative for fans of the Amazing Amazon." **– NERDIST**

"(A) heartfelt and genuine take on Diana's origin." **– NEWSARAMA**

DC UNIVERSE REBIRTH

# WONDER WOMAN

## VOL. 1: THE LIES
### GREG RUCKA
### with LIAM SHARP

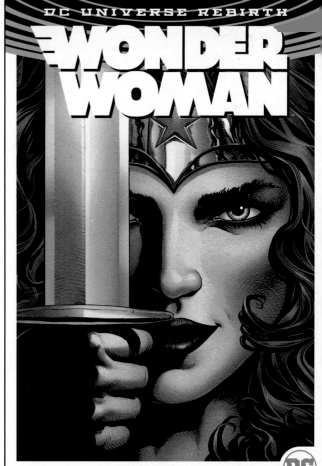

**VOL.1 THE LIES**
GREG RUCKA ∗ LIAM SHARP ∗ LAURA MARTIN

**JUSTICE LEAGUE VOL. 1:**
**THE EXTINCTION MACHINES**

**SUPERGIRL VOL. 1:**
**REIGN OF THE SUPERMEN**

**BATGIRL VOL. 1:**
**BEYOND BURNSIDE**

 Get more DC graphic novels wherever comics and books are sold!